THE GREAT TREATISE
ON THE STAGES OF THE PATH
TO ENLIGHTENMENT

The Lamrim Chenmo Translation Committee

José Ignacio Cabezón
Daniel Cozort
Joshua W. C. Cutler
Natalie Hauptman
Roger R. Jackson
Karen Lang
Donald S. Lopez, Jr.
John Makransky
Elizabeth S. Napper
Guy Newland
John Newman
Gareth Sparham
B. Alan Wallace
Joe B. Wilson

THE GREAT TREATISE
ON THE STAGES OF THE PATH
TO ENLIGHTENMENT

by
Tsong-kha-pa

Volume Three

Translated by
The Lamrim Chenmo Translation Committee

Joshua W. C. Cutler, Editor-in-Chief
Guy Newland, Editor

Snow Lion Publications
Ithaca, New York
Boulder, Colorado

Snow Lion Publications
605 West State Street
P. O. Box 6483
Ithaca, NY 14851
(607) 273-8519
www.snowlionpub.com

First edition USA 2002

Printed in Canada on acid-free, recycled paper.

ISBN 1-55939-166-9

Library of Congress Cataloging-in-Publication Data

Tsoṅ-kha-pa Blo-bzaṅ-grags-pa, 1357-1419.
  [sKyes bu gsum gyi rnyams su blaṅ ba'i rim pa thams cad tshaṅ bar ston pa'i
    byaṅ chub lam gyi rim pa/ Lam rim chen mo. English]
  The great treatise on the stages of the path to enlightenment / by Tsong-kha-pa;
    translated by the Lamrim Chenmo Translation Committee ; Joshua W. C. Cutler,
    editor-in-chief ; Guy Newland, editor.
      p.   cm.
  Includes bibliographical references and index.
  Volume 1 ISBN 1-55939-152-9 (alk. paper)
  Volume 2 ISBN 1-55939-168-5 (alk. paper)
  Volume 3 ISBN 1-55939-166-9 (alk. paper)
  1. Lam-rim—Early works to 1800. I. Title.

BQ7950.T754.L34413 2000
294.3'444—dc21

00-044664

TABLE OF CONTENTS

DEDICATION

*We dedicate this translation to
His Holiness the Fourteenth Dalai Lama
and the people of Tibet.*

EDITOR'S PREFACE

In 1992 the Tibetan Buddhist Learning Center (TBLC) began its three-volume translation of the *Great Treatise on the Stages of the Path to Enlightenment (Byang chub lam rim che ba)*. Volume one was published by Snow Lion Publications in 2000. We have decided to publish volume three now because there is a great interest in its subject matter, meditative serenity (*śamatha; zhi gnas*) and insight (*vipaśyanā; lhag mthong*). The second volume will be published subsequently.

The Lamrim Chenmo Translation Committee has followed the same procedure and format that was used for the first volume. The committee members who worked on this volume were Roger Jackson, B. Alan Wallace, Elizabeth S. Napper, José Cabezón, Guy Newland, and Donald Lopez. These translators again referred to the commentary *Four Interwoven Annotations (Lam rim mchan bzhi sbrags ma)* and used it consistently to interpret citations. With respect to the serenity section the editors had the invaluable assistance of the eminent contemporary Tibetan Buddhist scholars Denma Lochö Rimbochay and Loling Geshe Yeshe Tapkay to read through the text and discuss difficult passages. For the insight section they also had the very capable help of Dr. Thupten Jinpa, whose great skill at translation served this project well.

There are many people to whom I am very grateful for their help and support in bringing this volume to completion. First and foremost is His Holiness the Dalai Lama, who is a constant beacon of light and inspiration for this project. I am also very mindful of the kindness of my guru, the late Geshe Ngawang Wangyal, an unending source of strength. Then I am most thankful to the above-mentioned translators and Tibetan scholars, without whom this project would not have been possible. Guy Newland's contribution stands out amongst these because he also took full responsibility for editing the insight section with great care and skill. I also very much appreciate the editing suggestions of Gray Tuttle and the careful work of Snow Lion editor Susan Kyser. I also thank Gareth Sparham, Ladakhi Geshe Lozang Jamspal, and Geshe Yeshe Tapkay.

Cooperative undertakings of this kind entail much help in areas other than scholarship. It is with great pleasure that I express my deep gratitude to all the family, friends, students, and kind supporters of the TBLC who have given so much of their invaluable assistance to facilitate the completion of this volume of translation: to my parents, Nancy and Eric Cutler, whose abiding love and faith in me bring great encouragement; to Thupten T. Taikang for his wise counsel and good example; to Buff and Johnnie Chace, Randall and Jane Imai, Joel McCleary, Stuart and Lillie Scudder, Jim and Bonnie Onembo, Frank and Khady Lusby, Chot and Armen Elliott, Nick and Shelley Guarriello, Thao and Gai Nguyen, Mike and Debbie Joye, and Frank and Raksha Weber, all of whose great friendship and support far exceed mere interest in the work of the TBLC; to Jeffrey Hopkins and Douglas Crichton, both writers who kindly share their deep knowledge of the trade with one in great need; to Valerie Stephens for her constant help to her husband Guy Newland; to the TBLC doctors, Peter Beskyd, James Goodwin, Jerry Cohen, Rajinder Sharma, Deedee Eisenberg, David and Ming Ming Molony, Phil Lecso, and Frank Viverette, all of whose excellent advice and support help me through difficult times; to John and Margaret Brzostoski, David and Victoria Urubshurow, Sam and Lisa Badushow, and Ray McAdam, all loyal friends of the TBLC; and to my dear students and their spouses, Amy and John Miller, Brady and Tasha Whitton, and Davis Smith and Kendra Lawrence, all of whom are constant sources of support, affection, and inspiration. There are many other people whom I have not mentioned. Please know that you all are always in my thoughts with gratitude.

All of this would not have been possible without the loving support and great perseverance of my wife, Diana, to whom I am deeply grateful.

Joshua W.C. Cutler
Tibetan Buddhist Learning Center
Washington, New Jersey

PART ONE: MEDITATIVE SERENITY

1

SERENITY AND INSIGHT

2″ In particular, how to train in the last two perfections
  (a) The benefits of cultivating serenity and insight
  (b) How serenity and insight include all states of meditative concentration
  (c) The nature of serenity and insight
  (d) Why it is necessary to cultivate both
  (e) How to be certain about their order

The most venerable teachers have great compassion; I bow with respect at their feet. [468]

2″ In particular, how to train in the last two perfections[1]

Training in the last two perfections, in particular, is the way to cultivate meditative serenity and insight because serenity and insight are included under the perfections of meditative stabilization and wisdom respectively. This section has six parts:

1. The benefits of cultivating serenity and insight
2. Showing that these two include all states of meditative concentration
3. The nature of serenity and insight
4. Why it is necessary to cultivate both
5. How to be certain about their order
6. How to train in each (Chapters 2-26)

(a) The benefits of cultivating serenity and insight

All of the mundane and supramundane good qualities of the Mahāyāna and Hīnayāna are the result of serenity and insight. The

Sūtra Unravelling the Intended Meaning (Saṃdhi-nirmocana-sūtra) says:[2]

> Maitreya, you should know that all mundane and supramundane virtuous qualities, whether of *śrāvakas*, bodhisattvas, or *tathāgatas*, are the result of meditative serenity and insight.

Qualm: Are not serenity and insight good qualities in the mind-stream of someone who has reached them through meditation? [469] How is it possible for all good qualities to result from those two?

Reply: As will be explained, actual serenity and insight are good qualities in the mind-stream of someone who has attained them through meditation, so all the good qualities of the Mahāyāna and Hīnayāna do not result from them. However, concentrations which at least involve one-pointedness on a virtuous object are classified with serenity; virtuous cognitions that distinguish an ultimate or conventional object are classified with insight. This is what the sūtra means in stating that all of the virtuous qualities of the three vehicles result from serenity and insight, so there is no contradiction.

With that same purport, the *Sūtra of Cultivating Faith in the Mahāyāna (Mahāyāna-prasāda-prabhāvanā-sūtra)* states:[3]

> Child of good lineage, this list should inform you that faith in the Mahāyāna of the bodhisattvas—and indeed, everything resulting from the Mahāyāna—comes from accurately reflecting on facts and meanings with an undistracted mind.

An undistracted mind is mental one-pointedness, the serenity aspect, while accurate reflection on facts and meanings refers to discerning wisdom, the insight aspect. Thus, you must achieve all good qualities of the two vehicles through both (1) sustained analysis with discerning wisdom and (2) one-pointed focus on the object of meditation. You do not achieve them through one-sided practice of either analytical meditation or stabilizing meditation.

Also, the *Sūtra Unravelling the Intended Meaning* states:[4]

> Once people have cultivated insight
> And serenity, they are free
> From the bondage of dysfunctional tendencies
> And from the bondage of signs.

Here, "dysfunctional tendencies" refers to latent propensities in your mind-stream which can produce increasing degrees of misconceptions; "signs" refers to ongoing attachments to erroneous objects, which foster those propensities. [470] Ratnākaraśānti's

Instructions for the Perfection of Wisdom (Prajñāpāramitopadeśa) says that insight eliminates the former, while serenity eliminates the latter.[5]

These are the benefits attributed to "serenity" and "insight," but even when the terms serenity and insight are not used, there are similar statements about the benefits of meditative stabilization and wisdom. Realize that such statements describe the benefits of serenity and insight.

(b) **How serenity and insight include all states of meditative concentration**

The branches, leaves, flowers, and fruits of a tree are limitless, yet the core point at which they all come together is the root. As in this example, serenity and insight are the sublime core at which gathers all that the Buddha says about the limitless states of meditative concentration in Mahāyāna and Hīnayāna. The *Sūtra Unravelling the Intended Meaning* states:[6]

> Know that serenity and insight include all of the many aspects of the states of meditative concentration which I have taught for śrāvakas, bodhisattvas and tathāgatas.

Therefore, since those who are intent on attaining meditative concentration cannot comprehend a limitless number of distinct forms, they should know well and always rely on the techniques for sustaining serenity and insight, the synthesis of all concentrations. Kamalaśīla's third *Stages of Meditation (Bhāvanā-krama)* says:[7]

> Although the Bhagavan therein presented distinct bodhisattva concentrations beyond number or measure, serenity and insight cover all of them. Therefore, we will discuss just that path which unites serenity and insight.

And, as stated in Kamalaśīla's second *Stages of Meditation*:[8]

> Since those two include all states of meditative concentration, all yogis should at all times definitely rely upon serenity and insight.
> [471]

(c) **The nature of serenity and insight**

As to the nature of serenity, it is as stated in the *Sūtra Unravelling the Intended Meaning*:[9]

> While you dwell in solitude and properly direct your attention inward, you attend to just those topics upon which you have carefully reflected. Your attention is mentally engaged by continuously attending inwardly. The state of mind wherein you do this, and

stay this way often, and in which both physical and mental pliancy arise, is called "serenity."

This means that you take as an object of meditation any appropriate object, such as the five aggregates, having determined that it is a topic in the twelve branches of scripture.[10] With undistracted mindfulness and vigilance, you focus your attention on this object and fix it to the object continuously, so that your mind stabilizes of its own accord on the object of meditation. When you produce the delight and bliss of physical and mental pliancy, then your state of meditative concentration becomes serenity. This comes about through just sustaining your attention inwardly, without distraction from the object of meditation; it is not contingent upon understanding the reality of the thing.

As to the nature of insight, the same sūtra says:[11]

> After you have attained mental pliancy and physical pliancy, you stay therein and eliminate other mental aspects. You then regard inwardly and with discernment the mental image which is the domain of the meditative concentration on the topics upon which you have reflected. With relation to the images that are the domain of such concentration, any differentiation of the meaning of these topics, or full differentiation, thorough examination, thorough analysis, forbearance, wish, differentiation of particulars, view, or thought is called "insight." Thus is a bodhisattva skilled in insight. [472]

It is said that the Chinese master Ha-shang (Hva-shang), having seen this sūtra's very clear and undeniable explanation that insight is discerning wisdom, exclaimed, "I don't know how this can be a sūtra!" and kicked it. He did this because the sūtra's statement did not agree with his claim that since all conceptualization of any sort involves an apprehension of signs, you should dispense with discerning wisdom and meditate on the profound meaning by not bringing anything to mind. This approach has a great number of adherents.[12]

In that sūtra passage, "differentiation" means distinguishing the diversity of conventional phenomena; "full differentiation" means distinguishing their real [ultimate] nature. The noble Asaṅga explains that "thorough examination" is when conceptual attention possessed of wisdom apprehends a sign; "thorough analysis" means proper examination. "Examination" means rough examination; "analysis" means detailed analysis. The apprehension of a sign does not here refer to a conception of true existence, but rather to distinguishing the exact particulars of an object. Accordingly, there is both examination and analysis of both the real nature and the diversity of phenomena.

In accord with the *Sūtra Unravelling the Intended Meaning*, the *Cloud of Jewels Sūtra* (*Ratna-megha-sūtra*) also clearly states:[13]

> Serenity is one-pointed attention; insight is proper discernment.

Also, the venerable Maitreya says in the *Ornament for the Mahāyāna Sūtras* (*Mahāyāna-sūtrālaṃkāra-kārikā*):[14]

> Know as the path of serenity
> Abbreviating the name of a phenomenon;[15]
> Understand the path of insight
> To be analysis of its meanings.

And,[16]

> Based on a genuine stability,
> Through directing your attention to your mind
> And through differentiating phenomena,
> There is meditative serenity and insight.

This states that stabilization of your mind on the basis of genuine concentration is serenity and the wisdom that differentiates phenomena is insight. [473] Since this comments to the same effect on what those sūtras say, it is inappropriate to construe those sūtra passages in some other sense.

Also, Asaṅga's *Bodhisattva Levels* (*Bodhisattva-bhūmi*) says:[17]

> With your mind definitely directed at an object of meditation which is simply some inexpressible thing or its meaning, an attentive perception free from all elaboration and free from all mental distraction takes up any object of meditation. Then, "meditative serenity" exists from the point at which internal concentration stabilizes and focuses your attention on a sign, and for as long as it maintains a single, extended flow and maintains concentration. What is insight? You bring to mind the signs of those very phenomena upon which you have reflected, using the same attention with which you cultivated serenity. "Insight" is anything from the point of either differentiation, full differentiation, or full differentiation of phenomena, and for as long as skill and wisdom are operating extensively.

This statement accords with those cited above. It gives commentary to the same effect as the sūtra and the text of the Venerable One, so it confirms the certainty of the foregoing identification of serenity and insight. Also, the second *Stages of Meditation* says:[18]

After you have quelled the distraction of external objects, you rest in a delighted and pliant mind which naturally and continuously engages an internal object of meditation. This is called meditative serenity. While you remain in serenity, any analysis of that very object is called insight.

Also, Ratnākaraśānti's *Instructions for the Perfection of Wisdom* says:[19]

With regard to that, serenity's object of meditation is a non-discursive image of something.which is either a case of the diversity of phenomena or which represents the real nature. [474] Insight's object of meditation is a discursive image of something which is a case of the diversity of phenomena or which represents the real nature.

This states that meditative serenity is non-discursive stabilization on something among either the diversity or the real nature of phenomena, and that insight is analysis of either of those two objects. This is also the intended meaning of a passage in the *Sūtra Unravelling the Intended Meaning*:[20]

"O Bhagavan, how many objects does serenity have?"
The Buddha replied, "One, namely, a non-discursive image."
"How many objects does insight have?"
"Just one, a discursive image."
"How many objects of both are there?"
"Two, namely, the limits of existence and achievement of your
    purpose."

Asaṅga's *Compendium of Knowledge* (*Abhidharma-samuccaya*) states that "the limits of existence" refers to both the diversity and real nature of phenomena,[21] so serenity and insight each take both ultimates and conventionalities as objects of meditation, just as Ratnākaraśānti explained above. Thus, meditative serenity and insight are not differentiated in terms of their respective objects of meditation, for there is meditative serenity that knows emptiness and there is insight which does not know emptiness. Also, meditative serenity (*zhi gnas*) is your mind quieting (*zhi*) movement toward external objects, and then abiding (*gnas*) on an internal object of meditation; insight (*lhag mthong*) is superior (*lhag pa*), i.e., special, seeing (*mthong*).

Some claim that a mind resting in a non-discursive state without vivid intensity is serenity, while such a mind with vivid intensity is insight. This is not correct because it contradicts the definitions of serenity and insight that are established at length in sources such as the words of the Conqueror, the treatises of the Regent,[22] the texts of Asaṅga, and Kamalaśīla's *Stages of Meditation*. These texts say that meditative serenity is attention concentrated one-pointedly on an object of meditation, while insight is wisdom that properly distinguishes the meaning of an object of knowledge. [475] In particular, the presence or absence of vivid intensity of mind in a non-conceptual consciousness indicates whether the concentration is lax; it is utterly incorrect to claim that it indicates the difference between serenity and insight. This is because in all concentrations of meditative serenity you definitely must clear away laxity, and because all concentrations free from laxity are invariably limpid states of mind.[23]

Thus, identify concentration and wisdom that focus on the real nature according to whether your mind knows as its object either of the two selflessnesses.[24] Do not identify them according to whether your mind rests in a non-discursive, clear, and blissful state, because there are countless states of concentration which are blissful, clear, and non-discursive, yet which do not orient your mind toward the reality of objects, their lack of self. Even without finding the view that knows the way things are, any totally non-discursive mind can be adequate to induce bliss and clarity. Even without understanding emptiness by establishing it in perception, nothing at all prevents you from developing non-discursive concentration. If you keep your mind that way for a long time, you cause the wind-energies to become serviceable. Once this occurs, nothing precludes the arising of bliss, as it is the nature of such serviceability to create mental and physical delight and bliss. Once bliss has arisen, then there will be mental clarity by virtue of the quality of clarity in the feelings of delight and bliss. For this reason, there is not a single authentic source to prove that all blissful, clear, non-discursive concentrations know reality. Therefore, since bliss, clarity, and non-discursiveness are present in concentrations that know emptiness, yet very often occur in concentrations that are not directed toward emptiness, you have to differentiate these two.

(d) Why it is necessary to cultivate both

Why is it insufficient to cultivate either serenity or insight alone? Why is it necessary to cultivate both? I will explain. [476]

If you light an oil-lamp for the purpose of viewing a picture in the middle of the night, you will see the depictions very clearly if the lamp is both very bright and undisturbed by wind. If the lamp is not bright, or is bright but flickering in the wind, then you will not see the images clearly. Likewise, when looking for the profound meaning, you will clearly see reality if you have both the wisdom that unerringly discerns the meaning of reality and an unmoving attention that stays as you wish on the object of meditation. However, if you do not have wisdom that knows how things are—even if you have a non-discursive concentration in which your mind is stable and does not scatter to other objects—then you lack the eyes which see reality. Hence, it will be impossible to know how things are no matter how much you develop your concentration. And even with a perspective that understands reality—selflessness—if you lack a firm concentration that stays one-pointedly on its object, then it will be impossible to clearly see the meaning of the way things are because you will be disturbed by the winds of uncontrollably fluctuating discursive thought. This is why you need both serenity and insight. Kamalaśīla's second *Stages of Meditation* says:[25]

> With bare insight that lacks serenity, the yogi's mind is distracted by objects; like an oil-lamp in the wind, it will not be stable. For this reason, what sublime wisdom sees will not be very clear. As this is so, rely equally on both. Therefore, the *Great Final Nirvāṇa Sūtra (Mahā-parinirvāṇa-sūtra)* says:
>
>> *Śrāvakas* do not see the lineage of the *tathāgatas* because their concentration is greater than their wisdom; bodhisattvas see it, but unclearly, because their wisdom is greater than their concentration. The *tathāgatas* see everything because they have serenity and insight in equal measure. [477]
>
> With the power of serenity, your mind—like a lamp placed where there is no wind—will be unmoved by the winds of discursive thought. With insight, others cannot divert you since you have abandoned the infinite entanglements of bad views. As the *Moon Lamp Sūtra (Candra-pradīpa-sūtra)* says:
>
>> The power of meditative serenity makes your mind steady;
>> insight makes it like a mountain.

So, the mark of meditative serenity is that your attention stays right where it is placed without distraction from the object of meditation. The mark of insight is that you know the reality of selflessness and eliminate bad views such as the view of self; your mind is like a mountain in that it cannot be shaken by opponents. Therefore, you should distinguish these two marks.

Before you achieve meditative serenity, you may use discerning wisdom to analyze the meaning of selflessness, but your mind is extremely unsteady, like a lamp in the wind, so your concept of selflessness is unclear. On the other hand, if you analyze when you have achieved serenity, you avoid the fault of extreme unsteadiness, so your concept of selflessness will be clear. Thus, the mental state of insight has a quality of steadiness which derives from non-discursive meditative serenity and a quality of knowing how things exist which does not derive from meditative serenity. For example, a lamp's ability to illumine forms derives from the wick and the preceding moments of flame; it does not derive from such things as the screen that protects it from the wind. However, the stability of the steady flame of the lamp does derive from this screen. Thus, if you engage in analysis with a wisdom possessed of the meditative equipoise of serenity—a state undisturbed by laxity or excitement— then you will understand the meaning of reality. With this in mind, the *Compendium of the Teachings Sūtra* (*Dharma-saṃgīti-sūtra*) states:[26]

> When your mind is in meditative equipoise, you will understand reality just as it is.

Kamalaśila's first *Stages of Meditation* says:[27] **[478]**

> Because your mind moves like a river, it does not rest without the foundation of meditative serenity; a mind that is not in meditative equipoise cannot understand reality just as it is. Also, the Bhagavan says, "With meditative equipoise, you know reality just as it is."

When you achieve serenity, you not only stop the fault of movement in the wisdom consciousness that properly analyzes selflessness, you also stop the fault of distraction from the object of meditation whenever you use discerning wisdom to conduct analytical meditation on topics such as impermanence, karma and its effects, the faults of cyclic existence, love, compassion, or the practice of the spirit of enlightenment. No matter what your object of meditation, you engage it without distraction, so that any virtue you cultivate is much more powerful. On the other hand, before you reach serenity, you weaken all of your virtuous deeds by frequent distraction to other objects. As Śāntideva's *Engaging in the Bodhisattva Deeds* (*Bodhisattva-caryāvatāra*) says:[28]

> The person whose mind is distracted
> Lives between the fangs of the afflictions.

And:[29]

> The One Who Knows Reality has said that
> Prayers, austerities, and such—

> Even if practiced for a long time—
> Are pointless if done with a distracted mind.

Thus, the aim of attaining a concentration in which your mind is non-discursively stabilized on a single object without distraction is to have mental serviceability—the ability to willfully direct your attention to virtuous objects of meditation. If you fix your attention on a single object of meditation, you can keep it there, but if you release it, it will proceed as you wish to limitless virtuous objects, just like water drawn into smoothly flowing irrigation ditches. [479] Therefore, after you have achieved meditative serenity, you must sustain in meditation objects and attitudes that stop limitless faults and bring together limitless virtues, such as wisdom consciousnesses focusing on the real nature and the diversity of phenomena, generosity, the attitude of restraint, patience, joyous perseverance, faith, and disenchantment with cyclic existence. Realize that continuously stabilizing your mind by fixing it on a single object of meditation yields no great advantages in the practice of virtue, for those who do this fail to appreciate the purpose of achieving serenity.

Thus, if you reject analytical meditation with discerning wisdom both in the deeds section of the perfections and in the view section of the perfections, your cultivation of one-pointed concentration will be very weak. The technique for producing forceful and long-lasting certainty about the meaning of selflessness is sustained analysis with discerning wisdom. Without such insight into the real nature, no matter how long you cultivate serenity, you can only suppress manifest afflictions; you cannot eradicate their seeds. Therefore, do not cultivate only serenity; you need to cultivate insight as well because, as Kamalaśila's second *Stages of Meditation* says:[30]

> Cultivating just serenity alone does not get rid of a practitioner's obscurations; it only suppresses the afflictions for a while. Unless you have the light of wisdom, you do not destroy dormant tendencies. For this reason the *Sūtra Unravelling the Intended Meaning* says:[31]
>
>> Meditative stabilization suppresses afflictions; wisdom destroys dormant tendencies.

Also, the *King of Concentrations Sūtra (Samādhi-rāja-sūtra)* says:[32]

> Although worldly persons cultivate concentration
> They do not destroy the notion of self.
> Their afflictions return and disturb them,
> As they did Udraka, who cultivated concentration in this way.[33]

If you analytically discern the lack of self in phenomena
And if you cultivate that analysis in meditation,
This will cause the result, attainment of nirvāṇa; [480]
There is no peace through any other means.

Also, the *Scriptural Collection of the Bodhisattvas* (*Bodhisattva-piṭaka*) says:[34]

Those who are unlearned in the contents of the *Scriptural Collection of the Bodhisattvas*, unlearned in the discipline of the noble teaching, and who derive a sense of sufficiency from mere concentration fall by virtue of their pride into an inflated sense of themselves. They will not escape from birth, aging, sickness, death, sorrow, lamentation, suffering, unhappiness, or perturbation; they will not escape from the six realms of cyclic existence; they will not escape from the aggregation of suffering. With that in mind, the Tathāgata said, "Learning from others what is appropriate, you will escape aging and death."

As this is so, those who seek completely pure sublime wisdom from which every obscuration has been eliminated should cultivate wisdom while they remain in serenity. On this point, the *Ratna-kūṭa Collection* (*Ratna-kuṭa-grantha*) says:[35]

Keeping ethical discipline, you will attain concentration;
Attaining concentration, you cultivate wisdom;
With wisdom you attain pure, sublime wisdom;
As your sublime wisdom is pure, your ethical discipline is
    perfect.

And the *Sūtra of Cultivating Faith in the Mahāyāna* says:[36]

Child of good lineage, if you did not have wisdom, I would not say that you had faith in the Mahāyāna of bodhisattvas, nor would I say you knew the real nature in the Mahāyāna.

(e) How to be certain about their order

Śāntideva's *Engaging in the Bodhisattva Deeds* says:[37]

Insight possessed of serenity
Destroys the afflictions. Knowing this,
Seek serenity at the outset.

According to this statement, you first achieve meditative serenity and then cultivate insight on that basis. [481]

Qualm: Kamalaśīla's first *Stages of Meditation* says,[38] "Its object of meditation is indeterminate," meaning that the object of meditation of meditative serenity is indeterminate. As explained above, the object of meditation of serenity may be either reality itself or a conventional phenomenon possessed of reality. If you first understand the meaning of selflessness, and then meditate while focusing on this, it should be enough to simultaneously produce both the serenity of an undistracted mind and insight focused on emptiness. Why, then, is it said that you first seek serenity and then cultivate insight?

Reply: The way in which serenity precedes insight is as follows. You do not need to have serenity already in order to develop an understanding of the view that knows that there is no self, for we see that even those who lack serenity develop this view. Nor do you need to have serenity already in order to experience mental transformation in regard to the view, for nothing precludes mental transformation being brought on by the practice of repeated analysis with discerning wisdom, even in the absence of serenity. If you claim that the absence of serenity precludes mental transformation in regard to the view, then the very same reasoning forces you to the extremely absurd conclusion that serenity is required even to experience mental transformation when meditating on impermanence, the faults of cyclic existence, or the spirit of enlightenment.

So, why is serenity required for insight? According to the *Sūtra Unravelling the Intended Meaning*,[39] as long as the practice of discrimination and special discrimination with discerning wisdom cannot generate physical and mental pliancy, it constitutes a type of attention which approximates insight; when it generates pliancy, then it is insight. Thus, if you have not attained serenity, then no matter how much analytical meditation you do with discerning wisdom, in the end you will not be able generate the delight and bliss of physical and mental pliancy. Once you have attained meditative serenity, then even the analytical meditation of discerning wisdom will culminate in pliancy. [482] Hence, insight requires meditative serenity as a cause. This will be explained below.

Discerning wisdom becomes insight when, without focusing on a single object, it can generate pliancy through the power of analysis. So generating pliancy by setting your attention on a single object of meditation—even if the object is emptiness—is nothing more than a way to achieve serenity; that alone does not count as attaining insight. Why? If you thus first seek an understanding of selflessness, analyzing its meaning again and again, it will be impossible to achieve serenity on the basis of this analysis since you have not previously achieved serenity. If you do stabilizing meditation without analysis, you will achieve serenity on that basis. However, as there is no way to sustain insight except by sustaining serenity, you have to seek insight later. Hence, this does not fall outside the pattern in which, having previously sought serenity, you cultivate insight based on it.

Accordingly, the way insight develops is that discerning analytical meditation generates pliancy. If this were not so, there would not be the slightest good reason to seek serenity first and then cultivate insight based on it. Failing to do these meditations in this order is quite inappropriate because the *Sūtra Unravelling the Intended Meaning*[40] states in a passage cited above that you cultivate insight on the basis of having attained serenity. Also, the order of meditative stabilization and wisdom among the six perfections—of which it is said that "the latter develop based on the former"—as well as the sequence in which training in higher wisdom is based on training in higher concentration are in agreement with the sequence in which, having previously cultivated serenity, you later cultivate insight. Asaṅga's *Bodhisattva Levels* (cited earlier)[41] and his *Śrāvaka Levels* (*Śrāvaka-bhūmi*) indicate that insight is cultivated on the basis of meditative serenity. [483] Also, Bhāvaviveka's *Heart of the Middle Way* (*Madhyamaka-hṛdaya*), Śāntideva's *Engaging in the Bodhisattva Deeds*, Kamalaśīla's three *Stages of Meditation*, Jñānakīrti,[42] and Ratnakaraśānti all state that you cultivate insight after previously seeking serenity. Some Indian masters claim that, without seeking serenity separately, you generate insight from the outset through analysis by discerning wisdom. Since this view contradicts the texts of the great trailblazers, the wise deem it to be untrustworthy.

This is the sequence in which you newly develop serenity and insight for the first time; later the sequence is indefinite, as you may cultivate serenity after previously cultivating insight.

Qualm: Asaṅga's *Compendium of Knowledge* states,[43] "Some attain insight, but do not attain serenity; they strive for serenity on the basis of insight." How do you account for this?

Reply: This means that they have not attained the serenity of the actual first meditative stabilization, or beyond; it does not preclude their having attained the serenity which is included in the access to the first meditative stabilization.[44] Also, once you have perceptual knowledge of the four truths, you can establish on that basis the serenity of the actual first meditative stabilization and the higher meditative stabilizations. For Asaṅga's *Levels of Yogic Deeds* (*Yogacaryā-bhūmi*) says:[45]

Moreover, you can accurately know the reality of the truths from suffering to path, without having attained the first meditative stabilization, etc. As soon as this knowledge of the truths occurs, you stabilize your mind and do not analyze phenomena. Based on this higher wisdom, you pursue the practice of higher states of consciousness.

In general, for the sake of comprehensive terminology, the nine mental states[46] are called meditative serenity and the fourfold analysis[47] is called insight. However, you must apply the terms "actual serenity" and "actual insight"—as will be explained—after the generation of pliancy.

2

PREPARING FOR MEDITATIVE SERENITY

(f) How to train in each
    (i) How to train in meditative serenity
        (a') Relying on the preconditions for meditative serenity
            (1') Dwelling in an appropriate area
            (2') Having little desire
            (3') Being content
            (4') Completely giving up many activities
            (5') Pure ethical discipline
            (6') Completely getting rid of thoughts of desire, etc.
        (b') How to cultivate serenity on that basis
            (1') Preparation
            (2') Actual practice
                (a") Meditative posture
                (b") The meditative process
                    (1") How to develop flawless concentration
                        (a)) What to do prior to focusing the attention on an object of meditation
                        (b)) What to do while focusing on an object of meditation
                            (1)) Identifying the object of meditation upon which your attention is set
                              (a')) A general presentation of objects of meditation
                                (1')) The objects of meditation themselves
                                  (a")) Universal objects of meditation
                                    (1")) Discursive images
                                    (2")) Non-discursive images
                                    (3")) The limits of existence
                                    (4")) Achievement of your purpose
                                (b")) Objects of meditation for purifying your behavior
                                  (1")) Ugliness

    (2″)) Love
    (3″)) Dependent-arising
    (4″)) Differentiation of constituents
    (5″)) Inhalation and exhalation
   (c″)) Objects of meditation for expertise
    (1″)) The aggregates
    (2″)) The constituents
    (3″)) The sources
    (4″)) Dependent-arising
    (5″)) What is and is not possible
   (d″)) Objects of meditation for purifying
    afflictions
  (2′)) Who should meditate on which objects
  (3′)) Synonyms of the object of meditation
 (b′)) Identifying objects of meditation for this context

——————— ✸ ———————

(f) How to train in each

This has three sections:

1. How to train in meditative serenity (Chapters 2-6)
2. How to train in insight (Chapters 7-26) **[484]**
3. How to unite them (Chapter 26)

(i) How to train in meditative serenity

This section has three parts:

1. Relying on the preconditions for meditative serenity
2. How to cultivate serenity on that basis (Chapters 2-5)
3. The measure of successful cultivation of serenity (Chapters 5-6)

(a′) Relying on the preconditions for meditative serenity

At the outset, the yogi should rely on the preconditions for serenity, which make it possible to achieve serenity quickly and comfortably. There are six:

(1′) Dwelling in an appropriate area

The area should have five attributes: (a) easy access, so that necessities such as food and clothing may be readily obtained; (b) being a good place to live, where there are no wild beasts such as predators, no enemies, etc.; (c) being on a good piece of ground, in that it does not breed sickness; (d) offering good companionship insofar as your companions are ethically disciplined and like-minded; and (e) being well-situated inasmuch as there are not many people about in the day and little noise at night. Maitreya's *Ornament for the Mahāyāna Sūtras* states:[48]

> The intelligent practice in a place
> Which is accessible, is a good place to live,
> Offers good ground and good companions,
> And has the requisites for comfortable yogic practice.

(2') Having little desire

You do not strongly crave more or better robes, etc.

(3') Being content

You are always content to have even the poorest robes, etc.

(4') Completely giving up many activities

You give up base activities such as buying and selling; you also abandon excessive socializing with householders and renunciates, as well as pursuits such as medicine and astrology.

(5') Pure ethical discipline

You do not violate precepts, doing deeds that are wrong by nature or wrong by prohibition, either in the case of vows of individual liberation or in the case of bodhisattva vows. If you do violate them through carelessness, you restore them promptly with regret in accordance with the teaching.

(6') Completely getting rid of thoughts of desire, etc.

In the case of desires, contemplate their disadvantages in this life-time, such as their leading to being killed or imprisoned, as well their disadvantages for the future, such as their leading to rebirth in miserable realms. [485] Alternatively, eliminate all thoughts of desire and such by meditating with the thought that "Everything in cyclic existence, pleasant or unpleasant, is ephemeral and im-permanent. Since it is certain that I will shortly be separated from all of these things, why should I crave them?"

I have explained these points according to the purport of Kamalaśila's second *Stages of Meditation*; you should learn more about them from Asaṅga's *Śrāvaka Levels*. These six topics cover the key causes and conditions for newly developing good concentration, for maintaining an existing concentration without deterioration, and for heightening your concentration. In particular, the most important ones are good ethical discipline, seeing desires as disadvantageous, and dwelling in an appropriate area. Geshe Drom-dön-ba (dGe-bshes 'Brom-ston-pa-rgyal-ba'i-'byung-gnas) said:

> We think that the fault lies only in our personal instructions. As we then seek only personal instructions, we are unable to attain concentration. This is the result of not abiding under its conditions.

The term "conditions" refers to the six explained above.

Moreover, the first four perfections serve as preconditions for the fifth, meditative stabilization. Kamalaśīla's first *Stages of Meditation* states:[49]

> You quickly accomplish serenity when you disregard the desire for possessions and such, keep good ethical discipline, have a disposition to readily tolerate suffering, and joyously persevere. That being the case, sources such as the *Sūtra Unravelling the Intended Meaning* teach that generosity and the other perfections are causes of the successively higher perfections.

Atiśha's *Lamp for the Path to Enlightenment* (*Bodhi-patha-pradīpa*) states:[50]

> When you lack the elements of serenity,
> Even if you meditate assiduously,
> You will not achieve concentration
> Even in thousands of years.

[486] Therefore, it is very important for those who sincerely wish to achieve the concentrations of serenity and insight to work on the elements or preconditions for serenity, such as the thirteen which are set forth in Asaṅga's *Śrāvaka Levels*.[51]

(b') How to cultivate serenity on that basis

This has two parts: (1) preparation and (2) actual practice.

(1') Preparation

Practice the six preparatory teachings explained above and especially cultivate the spirit of enlightenment for a long time; also, in support of that you should do the meditative practices that are shared with persons of small and medium capacities.[52]

(2') **Actual practice**

This has two parts: (1) meditative posture and (2) the meditative process itself.

(a") **Meditative posture**

Kamalaśila's second and third *Stages of Meditation* say[53] that you should take up an eight-point posture on a very soft and comfortable seat: (1) Cross your legs in the manner of the venerable Vairocana, using either the full-lotus posture or the half-lotus posture as appropriate. (2) Your eyes should be neither wide open nor too far closed, and they should be fixed on the tip of your nose. (3) Sit with your awareness directed inward, keeping your body straight without leaning too far back or being bent too far forward. (4) Keep your shoulders straight and even. (5) Do not raise or lower your head nor turn it to one side; set it so that your nose and navel are aligned. (6) Set your teeth and lips in their usual, natural positions. (7) Draw your tongue up close to your upper teeth. (8) Your inhalation and exhalation should not be noisy, forced, or uneven; let it flow effortlessly, ever so gently, without any sense that you are moving it here or there.

Asaṅga's *Śrāvaka Levels* gives five reasons for sitting as the Buddha taught, cross-legged on a seat, stool, or grass mat:[54] (1) This posture in which the body is pulled together well is conducive to the arising of pliancy, so you will develop pliancy very quickly. [487] (2) Sitting in this way makes it possible to maintain the posture for a long time; the posture does not lead to physical exhaustion. (3) This posture is not common to non-Buddhists and our opponents. (4) When others see you sitting in this posture, they are inspired. (5) The Buddha and his disciples used this posture and bestowed it upon us. Asaṅga's *Śrāvaka Levels* says that, in light of these reasons, you should sit cross-legged. It also says that you keep your body straight so that lethargy and sleepiness will not occur.

Thus, at the outset you have to meet these eight points of physical conduct, particularly the calming of breathing just as I have described above.

(b") **The meditative process**

Broadly speaking, the "stages of the path" tradition indicates that you achieve serenity by means of the eight antidotes which eliminate the five faults listed in Maitreya's *Separation of the Middle from the Extremes* (*Madhyānta-vibhāga*).[55] Personal instructions passed down from Geshe Lak-sor-wa (dGe-bshes Lag-sor-ba) explain that in addition to that you have to achieve serenity through the six powers, the four types of attention, and the nine mental states which Asaṅga's *Śrāvaka Levels* explains. The scholar Yön-den-drak (Yon-tan-grags) says:[56]

> The methods of the nine mental states are included in the four attentions, and the six faults and the eight applications which are their antidotes are the method [for achieving] all concentrations. This is agreed upon in all teachings about the techniques for meditative stabilization—including those in most sūtras, Maitreya's *Ornament for the Mahāyāna Sūtras* and *Separation of the Middle from the Extremes*, Asaṅga's texts on the levels,[57] and Kamalaśīla's three *Stages of Meditation*. Those who first have the preconditions for concentration will definitely attain concentration if they use these methods to work at it. Nowadays, supposedly profound oral traditions on meditative stabilization lack even the names of these techniques. [488] These texts do not indicate that you will achieve concentration without the preconditions for concentration and these techniques, even if you work at it for a long time.

This is stated in his text on the stages of the path; it speaks of reaching pure certainty about how the classic texts present the way to achieve concentration. In that regard, since the general way of teaching the stages of the paths of the three vehicles is demonstrated at length in the noble Asaṅga's five texts on the levels,[58] the texts that teach these practices are very extensive. Among these five, one text gives a detailed explanation, while the others do not. Asaṅga's *Compendium of Determinations* (*Viniścaya-saṃgrahaṇī*) says that his *Śrāvaka Levels* should be used to understand serenity and insight, so it is the *Śrāvaka Levels* that is most extensive. Also, the venerable Maitreya discusses the methods of the nine mental states and the eight antidotes in his *Ornament for the Mahāyāna Sūtras* and *Separation of the Middle from the Extremes*. Following them, such learned Indian masters as Haribhadra, Kamalaśīla, and Ratnākaraśānti wrote much about the process of achieving concentration. On the general sense of concentration the tantras are very consistent with the explanations in these classic texts, except that they use different objects of meditation, such as divine bodies, drops, and syllables. In particular, texts in the sūtra class provide very extensive discussions of problems—such as the five faults of concentration—and ways of clearing them away.

However, those who know how to practice on the basis of those classic texts alone are as rare as stars in the daytime. Those who impose on those texts the stains of their defective understanding derive only a superficial comprehension and maintain that the instructions that reveal the quintessential meaning lie elsewhere. When the time comes for them to put into practice the process of achieving concentration which these texts explain, they do not even research how to do it. **[489]**

The personal instructions of this treatise stress only the practices from the beginning to the end which are derived from the classic texts. Therefore, herein I will explain the methods used to achieve concentration drawing on the classic texts.

This explanation of the meditative process has two sections:

1. How to develop flawless concentration (Chapters 2-4)
2. The stages in which the mental states are thereby developed (Chapter 5)

(1″) How to develop flawless concentration

This has three parts:

1. What to do prior to focusing the attention on an object of meditation
2. What to do while focusing on an object of meditation (Chapters 2-3)
3. What to do after you focus on an object of meditation (Chapter 4)

(a)) What to do prior to focusing the attention on an object of meditation

If you cannot stop the laziness of being disinclined to cultivate concentration and of enjoying things that are not conducive to it, from the outset you will not gain entry into concentration; even if you do attain it once, you will be unable to sustain it, so it will quickly deteriorate. Therefore, it is most crucial to stop laziness in the beginning. When you attain pliancy in which your mind and body are full of delight and bliss, you will stop laziness inasmuch as you will be able to cultivate virtue all day and night without weariness.

To develop this pliancy, you must be able to have continuous enthusiasm for the concentration that causes pliancy. To develop this enthusiasm, you need a continuous, intense yearning that is intent on concentration. As a cause for this yearning you need steadfast confidence in and fascination with the good qualities of concentration. So to start with, cultivate again and again a confidence that is aware of the good qualities of concentration. When you see this process in practice, you will understand this most vital point with the clearest sense of certainty. Maitreya's *Separation of the Middle from the Extremes* states:[59]

> The basis and what is based upon it
> Are the cause and its result.

Here, the "basis" is yearning, which is the basis of endeavor; "what is based upon it" is the endeavor or enthusiasm. The cause of yearning is confident faith in the good qualities of concentration. [490] The result of endeavor is pliancy.

In this context, the good qualities of concentration are as follows: When you reach serenity, your mind is filled with delight and your body filled with bliss, so you are happy in this lifetime. Also, since you have attained physical and mental pliancy, you can turn your attention to any virtuous object of meditation you choose. Since you have quelled uncontrolled distraction toward the wrong sort of objects, you are not constantly involved in wrongdoing and any virtue you do is very powerful. Based on serenity, you can achieve good qualities such as the superknowledges and supernormal powers. In particular, it is on the basis of serenity that you develop the knowledge of insight that knows the real nature, whereby you can quickly cut the root of cyclic existence. If you reflect on any of these good qualities, you will become aware of, and meditate upon, things that strengthen your inclination to cultivate concentration. When this inclination arises, you will be continually prompted from within to cultivate concentration, so it will be easy to attain concentration. Also, since you will cultivate it repeatedly even after attaining it, you will be unlikely to lose it.

(b)) **What to do while focusing on an object of meditation**

This section has two parts:

1. Identifying the object of meditation upon which your attention is set
2. How to focus your mind on the object of meditation (Chapter 3)

(1)) **Identifying the object of meditation upon which your attention is set**

This has two parts:

1. A general presentation of objects of meditation
2. Identifying objects of meditation for this context

(a')) A general presentation of objects of meditation

This has three sections:

1. The objects of meditation themselves
2. Who should meditate on which objects
3. Synonyms of the object of meditation

(1')) The objects of meditation themselves

The Bhagavan stated that yogis have four types of objects of meditation, these being: (1) universal objects of meditation, (2) objects of meditation for purifying your behavior, (3) objects of meditation for expertise, and (4) objects of meditation for purifying afflictions.

(a")) Universal objects of meditation

Universal objects of meditation are of four types: (a) discursive images, (b) non-discursive images, (c) the limits of existence, and (d) achievement of your purpose. [491]

The two types of images (*discursive* and *non-discursive*) are posited in terms of the observer: the first is the object of insight, and the second is the object of meditative serenity. The image is not the actual specifically characterized object upon which your mind is focused, but rather the appearance of that object's aspect to your mind. When you carry out analysis while observing an object, then the image is discursive since analytical thinking is present. When you stabilize your mind without analysis while observing an object, the image is said to be non-discursive since analytical thinking is absent. As for these images, what objects of meditation are they images of? They are the images, or aspects, of the five objects of meditation for purifying behavior, the five objects of meditation for expertise, and the two objects of meditation for purifying afflictions.

The *limits of existence* are posited with reference to the observed object. There are two: The limits of existence for the diversity of phenomena, which are expressed in the statement, "Just this is all there is; there is nothing more"; and the limits of existence for the real nature, expressed in the statement, "This alone is how things exist; they do not exist in any other way." In the case of the diversity of phenomena, this means that the five aggregates include all composite phenomena; the eighteen constituents and twelve sources include all phenomena; and the four truths include everything there is to know; there is nothing else beyond this.[60] In the case of the nature, this means that reason establishes the truth or reality of those objects of meditation.

Achievement of purpose is posited in terms of the result. With either serenity or insight you direct your attention to the images of those objects of meditation. Then you stabilize on them, become accustomed to them, and, by virtue of repeated practice, you become free from your dysfunctional tendencies, undergoing a fundamental transformation. [492]

(b")) Objects of meditation for purifying your behavior

Objects of meditation for purifying behavior are objects that purify behavior in which attachment or the like [hatred, delusion, pride, or discursiveness] is predominant. There are five such objects of meditation. Respectively they are: (a) ugliness, (b) love, (c) dependent-arising, (d) differentiation of constituents, and (e) inhalation and exhalation. (a) Of these, the *objects of meditation on ugliness* consist of the thirty-six uglinesses pertaining to the body,[61] such as head and body hair, and external uglinesses such as a corpse's turning blue.[62] When an aspect of impurity and ugliness arises in your mind, you keep your attention on it. (b) *Love* involves focusing on friends, enemies, and persons toward whom you have neutral feelings, and having an attitude—at the level of meditative equipoise—of providing them with help and happiness. Keeping your attention on these objects of meditation with a loving attitude is called "meditation on love"; love refers both to the subjective attitude and to the object. (c) Regarding the *object of meditation on dependent-arising*: All there is in the past, the present, and the future is dependent-arising in which effects that are mere phenomenal factors simply arise based on mere phenomenal factors. Apart from these, there is no performer of actions or experiencer of their effects. You focus your attention on this fact, and hold it there. (d) As for the *object of meditation on the differentiation of the constituents*: You differentiate the factors of the six constituents—earth, water, fire, air, space, and consciousness. You focus your attention on them and hold it there. (e) Regarding the *object of meditation on inhalation and exhalation*: You focus your attention without distraction by counting and watching the breath move in and out.

(c")) Objects of meditation for expertise

There are also five objects of meditation for expertise, namely expertise in (a) the aggregates, (b) the constituents, (c) the sources, (d) dependent-arising, and (e) what is and is not possible. (a) The *aggregates* are the five aggregates of form and the others [feeling, discrimination, compositional factors, and consciousness]. Expertise in these is knowing that, apart from these aggregates, the self and what pertains to the self do not exist. (b) The *constituents* are the eye and the others of the eighteen constituents. Expertise in them is knowing the causal conditions by which those constituents arise from their own seeds. [493] (c) The *sources* are the eye and the others of the twelve sources. Expertise in these is knowing that the six internal sources are the dominant conditions for the six consciousnesses, that the six external sources are the object-conditions, and that the mind which has just ceased is the immediately preceding condition. (d) *Dependent-arising* is the twelve factors.[63] Expertise in them is knowing that they are impermanent, suffering, and devoid of self. (e) *What is and is not possible* refers to such things as it being possible for a pleasant fruition to arise from a virtuous action, but not possible for a pleasant fruition to arise from a non-virtuous action. Expertise in this is knowing that things are this way. This is a particular case of expertise in dependent-arising; the difference is that you understand diverse causes.[64]

When you use these as objects of meditation for cultivating serenity, you keep your attention on just one of the perspectives in which the aggregates, etc. may be known.

(d")) Objects of meditation for purifying afflictions

Purifying afflictions means either merely reducing the strength of the seeds of the afflictions or else utterly eradicating the seeds. In the former case, the objects of meditation are the comparative coarseness of each lower stage and comparative calmness of each higher stage, proceeding from the level of the desire realm up to the level of Nothingness.[65] In the latter case, the objects of meditation are impermanence and the other of the sixteen aspects of the four noble truths.[66] When you use these as objects of meditation for cultivating serenity, you do not analyze, but instead keep your attention on any one cognition of an aspect of those objects that appears to it.

Kamalaśila's second *Stages of Meditation*[67] states that objects of meditation are three. (1) After you have brought together everything that all twelve branches of scripture say about determining, settling into, and having settled into reality, you stabilize your mind upon it. (2) You observe the aggregates, etc., which include phenomena to some extent. (3) You stabilize your mind on the physical form of the Buddha, which you have seen and heard about.

How do you stabilize your mind on things such as the aggregates? [494] When you understand how all compositional things can be included within the five aggregates, you mentally collect them, gradually, into these five aggregates. Then you observe them and keep your attention on them. Just as discerning wisdom develops when you cultivate differentiation, so when you cultivate collectedness you develop concentration wherein your attention is brought together on the object of meditation without moving toward other objects. This is a personal instruction of the knowledge tradition. Likewise, when you understand how all phenomena can be included within the constituents and sources, you mentally collect them into these categories and keep your attention on this.

Among these four types of objects of meditation, objects of meditation for purifying behavior, as explained, facilitate the stopping of attachment and such in those whose behavior is dominated by attachment and such. They are special objects of meditation because you may readily attain concentration based upon them. Objects of meditation for expertise are conducive to the development of the insight that knows emptiness inasmuch as they refute a personal self that is not included among those phenomena. Therefore, they are excellent objects of meditation for cultivating serenity. Objects of meditation for dispelling afflictions serve as general antidotes to the afflictions, so they have great significance. The universal objects of meditation are not distinct from the aforementioned three.[68] Therefore, since you must achieve concentration using an object of meditative serenity that has a particular purpose, those who achieve concentration using things like pebbles and twigs for objects of meditation are clearly ignorant of the teachings on objects of concentration.

There are those who suppose that if you focus on an object of meditation and keep your attention on it, this is an apprehension of signs. They claim that meditation on emptiness means just stabilizing your mind without any basis, without focusing on any object of meditation. This is a total misunderstanding of how to meditate on emptiness. If you have no consciousness at that time, then neither will you have a concentration that cultivates emptiness. [495] On the other hand, if you have consciousness, then you are conscious of something, so you have to accept that there is an object of consciousness in terms of which consciousness is posited. If there is an object of consciousness, then precisely that is the object of meditation of that mind, because "object," "object of meditation," and "object of consciousness" have the same meaning. In that case, they would have to accept that even their method of concentration would apprehend signs. Thus, their approach is not correct.

Furthermore, whether something constitutes meditation on emptiness is determined by whether it is meditation founded upon the view that knows the way things are; it is not determined by whether there is any conceptualization vis-à-vis the object. This will be demonstrated at length below.[69] Even those who claim to stabilize their minds without an object of meditation must think first, "I will keep my attention such that it does not stray toward any object whatsoever," and then keep their attention in that way. After they have focused like that on the mind itself as an object of meditation, they must be certain to fix on this object without straying in any way. Thus, their own experience contradicts their claim that they have no object of meditation.

In this way, the classic texts on achieving concentration explain that there are many objects of meditation. The purposes of these meditative bases for stabilizing your mind are as explained above, so you should gain expertise in them. Kamalaśila's *Stages of Meditation* explains that the object of meditation of serenity is indeterminate,[70] and Atisha's *Lamp for the Path to Enlightenment* says, "[It is] whatever object or objects of meditation that are appropriate."[71] These statements mean that you are not required to stick with one particular object of meditation; they do not show how to define the range of existing objects of meditation.

(2')) Who should meditate on which objects

As there are various kinds of people, from those with a preponderance of attachment to those with a preponderance of discursiveness, Asaṅga's *Śrāvaka Levels* cites an answer to a question of Revata:[72]

> Revata, if attachment uniquely dominates the behavior of a monk-yogi, a practitioner of yoga, then he focuses his mind on the object of meditation of ugliness. [496] If hatred dominates his behavior, he meditates on love; if ignorance dominates his behavior, then he meditates on the dependent-arising of this condition; if pride dominates his behavior, he focuses his mind on the differentiation of the constituents.[73]

And:

> If discursiveness uniquely dominates his behavior, then he focuses his mind on an awareness of the exhalation and inhalation of the

breath. In this way, he focuses his mind on an appropriate object of meditation.

Asaṅga's *Śrāvaka Levels* also states:[74]

> In this regard, persons whose behavior is dominated by attachment, hatred, ignorance, pride, or discursiveness should, for a while at the outset, just purify those behaviors by contemplating objects of meditation for purifying behavior. After this they will see the stability of their minds, and they will ascertain only their objects of meditation. So they should definitely persevere at using their objects of meditation.

Thus, you certainly should work with these objects of meditation.

If you are a person whose behavior is balanced, or one whose afflictions are slight, then it suffices to keep your attention on whichever of the aforementioned objects of meditation you like; it is not necessary to have a particular one. Asaṅga's *Śrāvaka Levels* states:[75]

> Those whose behavior is balanced should work at whichever object they like so as to attain just mental stability; this is not for the purpose of purifying behavior. Understand that the same applies to those with slight afflictions.

Being dominated by desire—or another of those five afflictions—means that in a previous life you were fully involved in that affliction, became accustomed to it, and expressed it frequently, so that now even if there is a minor object of desire—or another of the five—that affliction arises in a strong and long-lasting form. [497] Balanced behavior means that you were not fully involved in desire and the others in your previous lives, you did not become accustomed to them, and you did not express them frequently. Still, you have not recognized that they are faults and you have not suppressed them, so while desire and such are not predominant or of great duration, it is not as though they do not occur. Having slight afflictions means that you were not fully involved and so on in desire—or another of those five—in your previous lives, and you do see their disadvantages, etc. Therefore, with respect to objects of desire and such that are major, many, or intense, your desire and such arise slowly, while for moderate or minor objects, these afflictions do not arise at all. Also, when desire or another of those five afflictions is predominant, you take a long time to realize stability; with balanced behavior, you do not take an excessively long time; with minor afflictions, you do so very quickly.

An answer to a question of Revata [as cited in the *Śrāvaka Levels*] also explains who works on objects of meditation for expertise:[76]

> Revata, if a monk-yogi, a practitioner of yoga, is confused about the characteristic nature of all composite things, or confused about the thing called person, self, living being, life, that which is re-born, or the nourisher, he should focus his mind on the objects of meditation for expertise in the aggregates. If he is confused about causes, he should focus on the objects of meditation for expertise in the constituents. If he is confused about conditions, he should focus on the objects of meditation for expertise in the sources. If he is confused about impermanence, suffering, and selflessness, he should focus on the objects of meditation for expertise in de-pendent-arising, and on what is and is not possible.

As this states, you mainly use these five objects of meditation to stop confusion.[77]

Which persons should focus their minds on objects of medita-tion for dispelling afflictions is also stated in the same sūtra [an-swering the questions of Revata]:[78]

> If you wish to be free from the attachment of the desire realm, focus your mind on the coarseness of the desire realm and the calm-ness of the form realm; [498] if you wish to be free from the at-tachment of the form realm, focus your mind on the coarseness of the form realm and the calmness of the formless realm. If you wish to become disenchanted with all of the perishing aggregates, and wish to be free from them, then focus your mind on the truth of suffering, the truth of origins, the truth of cessation, and the truth of the path.

You can use these objects of meditation both for analytical medita-tion with insight and for stabilizing meditation with serenity, so they are not exclusively objects of meditation for serenity. Still, since some serve as objects of meditation for newly achieving serenity and oth-ers are used for special purposes after attaining serenity, I have explained them here in the section on the objects of meditation of serenity.

(3')) Synonyms of the object of meditation

There are synonyms for the images or mental appearances of these objects of meditation explained above, these "points upon which the attention is kept," or "meditative bases for concentration," as stated in Asaṅga's *Śrāvaka Levels*:[79]

Also, that image is called "image"; it also is called "sign of concentration," "object in the domain of concentration," "technique of concentration," "door to concentration," "basis of attention," "body of internal conceptualization," and "appearing image." Know these as synonyms of the image which accords with the object that is known.

(b')) Identifying objects of meditation for this context

Now, from among the many objects of meditation I have explained, on which object of meditation should you base yourself so as to achieve serenity? [499] As stated in the sūtra passage cited above, there is no single, definite object; individuals require their particular object of meditation. Specifically, if you are determined to achieve serenity at the least, and if your behavior is dominated by attachment or another affliction, then you need to use a certain type of object of meditation. For if you do not, then you may attain a concentration that approximates serenity, but you will not attain actual serenity. It is said that even if you train with an object of meditation for purifying behavior, you will not achieve serenity unless you do so for a very long time, so how could you ever achieve it by rejecting objects of meditation for purifying behavior? In particular, if you have a predominance of discursiveness, then you definitely have to meditate on the breath.

If you are a person of balanced behavior or a person with slight afflictions, then, as explained before,[80] make your meditative base whichever of the objects of meditation explained above most appeals to you.

Alternatively, Kamalaśīla's middle and last *Stages of Meditation* follow the *Sūtra on the Concentration Which Perceives the Buddha of the Present Face to Face* (*Pratyutpanna-buddha-saṃmukhāvasthita-samādhi-sūtra*) and the *King of Concentrations Sūtra* in stating that you achieve concentration by focusing on the body of the Tathāgata. Also, the master Bodhibhadra explains a multitude [of objects]: [81]

> Here, serenity is twofold: that attained by looking inward and that [based on] an object of meditation viewed outwardly. Of those, looking inward is twofold: focusing on the body and focusing on what is based on the body. Of those, focusing on the body is threefold: focusing on the body itself in the aspect of a deity; focusing on ugliness, such as skeletons; and focusing on special insignia, such as a *khaṭvāṅga*.[82]
>
> Focusing on what is based on the body is fivefold: focusing on the breath, focusing on subtle divine insignia, focusing on the

drops, focusing on the aspects of light rays, and focusing on delight and bliss. [500]

Serenity based on an object of meditation viewed outwardly is twofold: special and common. Of those, the special is twofold: focusing on a deity's body and focusing on a deity's speech.

Atisha's commentary on his own *Lamp for the Path to Enlightenment* (*Bodhi-mārga-pradīpa-pañjikā*) also cites this passage.

In this regard, to keep your attention on the physical form of the Buddha is to recall the Buddha, so it gives rise to limitless merit. When your image of that body is clear and firm, then there is a special intensification of your meditative focus on the field in relation to which you amass merit through prostration, offering, aspirational prayer, etc., as well as on the field in relation to which you purify obscurations through confession, restraint, etc. This kind of meditation serves many purposes. As stated earlier in the extract from the *King of Concentrations Sūtra*,[83] it has advantages such as your not losing your mindfulness of the Buddha as you die. And when you cultivate the mantra path, it heightens deity yoga, etc. The *Sūtra on the Concentration Which Perceives the Buddha of the Present Face to Face* gives a very clear and detailed treatment of these benefits, as well as the method for directing your mind toward the Buddha. Therefore, you should definitely come to know them from there, as Kamalaśīla states in his last *Stages of Meditation*. Fearing verbosity, I do not write of them here. Consequently, it is skill in means when you seek an object of meditation by which you achieve concentration and also fulfill, along the way, some other special purpose.

How do you use something like the bodily form of the Tathāgata as an object of meditation? Kamalaśīla's last *Stages of Meditation* states:[84]

> In that regard, practitioners should first fix their attention on whatever they may have seen and whatever they may have heard about the bodily form of the Tathāgata, and then achieve serenity. The bodily form of the Tathāgata is a golden color like that of refined gold, adorned by the signs and exemplary features, dwells with its retinue, and effects the aims of living beings through various means. By continuously directing their minds toward it, yogis develop a wish for its good qualities and quell laxity, excitement, and so forth. [501] They should continue meditative stabilization for as long as they can see it clearly, as though the Buddha was sitting in front of them.

The *King of Concentrations Sūtra* also says that you should use this kind of object of meditation:[85]

> The glorious protector of the world
> With a body the color of gold—
> The bodhisattva whose mind engages this object
> Is said to be in equipoise.

Of the two ways to do this, newly imagining the Buddha's form and visualizing the Buddha's form as though actually present, the latter has a distinct advantage in developing faith and fits within the context of practices common to both sūtra and tantra vehicles. Therefore, use a visualized image of the Buddha's form as though it already actually exists. When you seek your object of meditation, the basis upon which you first keep your attention, look for an excellent painting or sculpture of the Teacher's body and view it again and again. Remembering its features, firmly familiarize yourself with the mental appearance of the object. Or, seek your object of meditation by reflecting upon the meaning of the eloquent descriptions of the Buddha's form which you have heard from your guru and make this image appear in your mind. Furthermore, do not let the object of meditation have the aspect of a painting or sculpture; rather, learn to have it appear in your mind with the aspect of an actual buddha.

Some set an image before them and immediately meditate on it while staring at it. The master Ye-shay-day's (Ye-shes-sde) rejection of this practice is excellent. He says that concentration is not achieved in the sensory consciousnesses, but in the mental consciousness; thus, the actual object of meditation of a concentration is the actual object of a mental consciousness. Therefore, you must keep your attention on this. He also states what I explained above,[86] that you have to focus your mind on the appearance of the actual concept, or mental image, of the object of meditation.

Furthermore, there are both subtle and gross features of the Buddha's bodily form. It is stated elsewhere that at first you focus on the gross features, and later, when these are solid, you must focus on the subtle. [502] As experience also shows that it is very easy to raise an appearance of the gross features, you must develop your object of meditation in stages starting with the gross features.

An especially important point is that, until you have accomplished satisfactory concentration as explained below, it is never appropriate for you to cultivate meditative concentration by shifting your focus to many different types of objects of meditation. For, if you cultivate concentration by moving to many dissimilar objects of meditation, it will be a great impediment to achieving serenity. Thus, authoritative texts on achieving concentration, such as Asaṅga's texts on the levels and Kamalaśila's three *Stages of Meditation*, explain that when first achieving concentration, you do so in relation to a single object of meditation; they do not say that you shift among many objects of meditation. Āryaśūra also clearly states this [in his *Compendium of the Perfections (Pāramitā-samāsa)*]:[87]

> Solidify your mind's reflection
> By being firm on one object of meditation;
> Letting it flow to many objects
> Leads to a mind disturbed by afflictions.

He says this in the section on achieving meditative stabilization. Also, Atisha's *Lamp for the Path to Enlightenment* states:[88]

> Settle your mind in virtue
> On any single object of meditation.

He makes his point with the phrase "on any single."

Thus, having first focused on one object of meditation and attained serenity, you may then focus on many objects of meditation. Kamalaśila's first *Stages of Meditation* states:[89]

> Only when you have earned concentrated attention should you focus in detail on the particulars of objects, such as the aggregates and constituents. It is in light of the particulars of yogis' meditation on objects such as the eighteen emptinesses that the Buddha states in sūtras such as the *Sūtra Unravelling the Intended Meaning* that there are many aspects of objects of meditation.[90]

Accordingly, the measure for having first found the object of meditation upon which you keep your attention is as follows: Visualize several times in sequence the head, two arms, the rest of the trunk of the body, and the two legs. [503] After that, if when you bring your attention to the body as a whole you can raise before your mind just half of the gross components, then—even without radiant clarity—you should be satisfied with just this and fix your attention upon it. Why? If, dissatisfied with just that, you fail to fix your attention on it and want more clarity instead, then, as you visualize it again and again, the object of meditation will become a bit clearer but you will not obtain a stable concentration; in fact, you will prevent yourself from getting this. Even though the object of meditation is not very clear, if you keep your attention on precisely this partial object of meditation, you will quickly obtain concentration. Since this then intensifies clarity, you will readily achieve clarity. This comes from the instructions of Ye-shay-day; it is of great importance.

As for the manner in which the object of meditation appears, you can describe two sets of four possibilities: for various types of persons, it is easy or difficult to have an image appear, and its appearance may be clear or unclear; moreover, both clear and unclear images may be either stable or unstable. However, as there is considerable variation, you cannot definitely determine what will occur.

When you are practicing deity yoga in the mantra vehicle, you definitely have to establish a clear image of the deity. So until this arises, you must use many methods for developing it. However, in this non-tantric context, if you have great difficulty in making an image of a deity appear, you may adopt any one of the objects of meditation presented above and keep your attention on it because the main purpose is simply to achieve a concentration of meditative serenity. Also, in this non-tantric context, if you practice by focusing on the body of a deity and you keep your attention there even though the image is not appearing, then you will not achieve your desired aim. Thus, you have to keep your attention on an image that does appear.

Keep your attention on the entirety of the body to the extent that it appears. If some parts of the body appear especially clearly, keep your attention on them. When they become unclear, return your attention to the entirety of the body. [504] At that time, there may be uncertainty as to color, as when you want to meditate on gold, but red appears; or uncertainty as to shape, as when you want to meditate on a sitting shape, but a standing shape appears; or uncertainty as to number, as when you want to meditate on one thing, but two things appear; or uncertainty as to size, as when you want to meditate on a large body, but a tiny body appears. As it is utterly inappropriate to pursue such distortions, you must use only the original object of meditation, whatever it may be, as your object of meditation.

3

FOCUSING YOUR MIND

(2)) How to focus your mind on the object of meditation
    (a')) The flawless method
    (b')) Eliminating flawed methods
    (c')) The length of sessions

———————❈———————

(2)) **How to focus your mind on the object of meditation**

This has three parts: (1) presenting the flawless method, (2) eliminating flawed methods, and (3) indicating the length of sessions.

(a')) **The flawless method**

The concentration that you will accomplish here has two special features: vivid intensity—an intense mental clarity—and non-discursive stability, staying one-pointedly on the object of meditation. Some add bliss to these, making three features; others add limpidity as well, making four. However, limpidity is included in the first feature, so it does not have to be listed as a separate item. Delight and bliss which impart a sense of well-being do occur as results of the concentration that you will accomplish here, but they are not concomitant with all of the concentrations which are included in the access to the first meditative stabilization. Also, the concentration of the fourth meditative stabilization—which is said to be the best basis for achieving the good qualities of all three vehicles—is not associated with any physical or mental bliss. Thus, delight and bliss are not counted as features here. [505] While some of the concentrations on the formless levels lack highly vivid intensity, there is nothing wrong with presenting vividness as one of these two features. For, Maitreya's *Ornament for the Mahāyāna Sūtras*[91] refers to "meditative stabilization other than the formless realm." This means that bodhisattvas—except for some powerful bodhisattvas[92]—achieve good qualities by relying on concentrations within the levels of meditative stabilization.

Since the development of this sort of vivid intensity is blocked as long as there is laxity, while one-pointed non-discursiveness is blocked as long as there is excitement, laxity and excitement are the chief obstacles to achieving genuine concentration. So if you do not understand how to identify accurately the subtle and coarse forms of laxity and excitement, or if you do not know how to correctly sustain a concentration which stops these once you have identified them, then it will be impossible for you to develop serenity, not to mention insight. Hence, those who diligently seek concentration should master these techniques.

Laxity and excitement are conditions unfavorable for achieving serenity. Later, I will discuss how to identify these unfavorable conditions and how to actually stop them. Now I shall explain how to develop concentration in a manner conducive to achieving serenity.

Here, concentration refers to your attention remaining one-pointedly on an object of meditation; in addition it must stay with the object continuously. Two things are needed for this: (1) a technique in which your attention is not distracted from whatever it had as its original object of meditation, and (2) an accurate awareness of whether you are distracted and whether you are becoming distracted. The former is mindfulness; the latter is vigilance. Vasubandhu's *Commentary on the "Ornament for the Mahāyāna Sūtras"* (*Mahāyāna-sūtrālaṃkāra-bhāṣya*) states:[93]

> Mindfulness and vigilance bring about close mental focus because the former prevents your attention from wandering from the object of meditation and the latter clearly recognizes that your attention is wandering.

If a lapse in mindfulness leads to forgetting the object of meditation, you will be distracted and will immediately lose the object upon which you are meditating. Therefore, the foundation of cultivating concentration is mindfulness which does not forget the object.

How does such mindfulness focus your mind right on the object of meditation? [506] Once you have at least visualized the object of meditation in the minimal manner as explained above, generate a powerful apprehension of the object that tightly holds it with your attention. After you have set your attention at a high level, stabilize it on the object without newly analyzing anything.

With regard to mindfulness, Asaṅga's *Compendium of Knowledge* says:[94]

> What is mindfulness? In regard to a familiar object, your mind is not forgetful and operates without distraction.

This indicates that mindfulness has three features. (1) Its observed object is "a familiar object," since mindfulness does not occur with regard to a previously unfamiliar object. In this case, the image of a previously ascertained object of meditation appears. (2) Its subjective aspect or manner of apprehension is your mind's not forgetting the object, as indicated by the phrase "your mind is not forgetful." In this case, it is your mind's non-forgetfulness of the object of meditation.

What does non-forgetfulness mean? It is not mentioned in reference to merely being able to remember what your guru taught you about the object of meditation, thinking or saying "The object of meditation is like this" when you cast your mind to it or when someone asks you about it. Rather, it refers to how your attention is fixed on the object of meditation and brings it to mind clearly without even the slightest distraction. If you are distracted, you lose your mindfulness to the extent that you are distracted. Therefore, after you have set your attention on the object of meditation in the manner explained above, you think, "In this way, I have fixed my attention on the object of meditation." Then, without new examination, you sustain the force of that awareness in unbroken continuity. This is the most critical point in the technique of maintaining mindfulness. (3) Its function is to keep your attention from wandering from the object of meditation.

Fixing your attention on an object of meditation in this way and controlling it is said to be like taming an elephant. An elephant trainer ties a wild elephant to a tree or sturdy post with many thick ropes. [507] If it does as the trainer teaches it, then fine; if not, it is subdued and controlled, struck repeatedly with a sharp iron hook. Your mind is like the untamed elephant; you bind it with the rope of mindfulness to the sturdy pillar of an object of meditation such as I explained above. If you cannot keep it there, you must gradually bring it under control by goading it with the iron hook of vigilance. Bhāvaviveka's *Heart of the Middle Way* states:[95]

> The erring elephant of your mind
> Is securely bound by the rope of mindfulness
> To the sturdy pillar of the object of meditation
> And is gradually controlled with the iron hook of intelligence.

Also, Kamalaśīla's second *Stages of Meditation* states:[96]

> With the ropes of mindfulness and vigilance, tie the elephant of your mind to the tree trunk, the object of meditation.

It is not contradictory that the former text likens vigilance to an iron hook while the latter text compares it to a rope. Mindfulness directly and continually fastens your attention to the object of meditation. However, indirectly vigilance also focuses your attention on the object of meditation, for you depend on noticing actual or incipient laxity and excitement with vigilance, and then stabilize your attention on the primary object without falling under their influence. Also, as cited above, the master Vasubandhu[97] says that both mindfulness and vigilance focus your mind on the object of meditation.

It is said that you achieve concentration on the basis of mindfulness and that mindfulness is like a rope that actually fastens your attention to the object of meditation continuously, so mindfulness is the main technique to sustain in achieving concentration.

Also, mindfulness has a way of apprehending its object that carries a sense of certitude. If, while maintaining concentration, you stabilize your mind casually without a solid sense of certainty about the object, then your mind may take on a limpid clarity, but it will not have the vivid intensity of certain knowledge, so you will not develop powerful mindfulness. [508] Therefore, subtle laxity will be unchecked, and only flawed concentration will ensue.

Those who cultivate just non-discursive attention without stabilizing their attention on other objects of meditation, such as a divine body, bring to mind the personal instruction, "Stabilize your mind without thinking of any object at all." Then they must keep their attention from being distracted and wandering. This non-distraction is synonymous with mindfulness that does not forget the object of meditation. Thus, since this meditation is simply the technique of maintaining mindfulness, those who meditate in this way must also rely on a mindfulness that carries the force of certain knowledge.

(b')) Eliminating flawed methods

There are misconceptions to dispel, such as the following.

Wrong position: If you set your consciousness at a high level as you have explained above and then tightly stabilize it without discursiveness, there will indeed not be even the slightest fault of laxity. However, since this increases excitement, you will see that you cannot prolong stability, and your elevated consciousness is brought down. As you will see that relaxing a well-tightened mind quickly leads to stability, this technique is a great personal instruction.

Reply: With a sense of assurance, these words proclaim in a loud voice, "Good relaxation is good meditation." Yet, they fail to differentiate laxity and meditation. Thus, as I explained above,[98] flawless concentration must have two features; the firm stability of nondiscursive attention does not alone suffice.

Wrong position: At that time, laxity is when your mind darkens and becomes clouded; without this, your mind has a limpid clarity, so your concentration is flawless.

Reply: As this statement does not differentiate lethargy and laxity, I will elaborate on them later.[99]

Thus, if you use an intense cognition that is too tight, you may have clarity, but excitement will predominate so that it will be hard to develop stability. [509] If you sustain your meditation after becoming greatly relaxed, then you may have stability, but laxity will predominate so that there is no vivid intensity. It is very hard to find the right balance of tension so as to be neither too taut nor too relaxed, and for this reason it is hard to develop a concentration free from laxity and excitement. With this in mind, the master Candragomin stated in his *Praise of Confession* (*Deśanā-stava*):[100]

> If I use exertion, excitement arises;
> If I abandon it, slackness ensues;
> It is hard to find the right balance in this—
> What should I do with my troubled mind?

The meaning of this is as follows: "Use exertion" means your mind is too tight; when you do this, excitement arises. When you let the tightness go and relax too much, you produce slackness, with your attention remaining inward. So it is difficult to find the proper balance for an even state of mind, free from laxity and excitement. Again, Buddhaśānti's *Commentary on the "Praise of Confession"* (*Deśanā-stava-vṛtti*) says:[101]

> "Exertion" here refers to tightly focusing your mind on virtue with clear enthusiasm.

And:[102]

After you see the problem of incipient excitement, you abandon your exertion; that is, you give up your effort. Thereupon, your attention becomes slack.

Candragomin's *Praise of Confession* also states:[103]

If I strain to engage the object, excitement occurs;
If I relax, slackness develops.
It is hard to find a practice midway between these two—
What should I do with my troubled mind?

Buddhaśānti's commentary on this is clear:[104]

If you strain for a tight focus on the object and exert yourself, your mind becomes excited and distracted, and you thereby destroy your concentration. Therefore, you are not attaining mental stability through exertion. This is problematic, so in order to avoid it you relax your mind, which has been straining to engage the object, and give up your exertion. [510] Then faults such as forgetting the object of meditation lead to slackness and laxity.

Therefore, Candragomin says "it is hard to find" a concentration that is the right balance or midway practice free from the two extremes of laxity and excitement. If getting quite relaxed were adequate, there would not be any problem at all. Since the text says that this leads to laxity, it is obviously improper to use this method to achieve concentration.

It is not enough to have the clarity which is simply the limpid quality of a very relaxed mind; there also must be a degree of tightness in the way you apprehend the object. In his discussion of the method used in the first two of the nine mental states,[105] the noble Asaṅga says:[106]

For stabilizing and properly stabilizing your mind on this object, there is the attention of tight focus.

Also, Kamalaśila's first *Stages of Meditation* says:[107]

After you clear away laxity, firmly hold just the object of meditation.

And Kamalaśila's second *Stages of Meditation* states:[108]

Then, after you have quelled laxity, by all means make it so that your mind very clearly sees just the object of meditation.

When Kamalaśila says "your mind very clearly sees," he does not mean only that the object is clear; he means that your mind's way of apprehending the object is clear and firm.

The above-mentioned way of maintaining mindfulness is extremely important. Without knowing it your meditation will show a great number of faults, such as slipping into great forgetfulness commensurate with the amount of your meditation or dulling the wisdom that differentiates phenomena. Nevertheless you mistakenly presume that you have a solid concentration.

Question: While mindfulness fixes your attention on the object of meditation as explained above, is it appropriate to monitor your meditation and think about whether you are holding the object of meditation well?

Reply: You have to do this, for Kamalaśila's second *Stages of Meditation* states:[109] [511]

> After you have thus set your attention on whatever your chosen object of meditation may be, fix it there continuously. While you stay right with the object, analyze and investigate your mind, thinking: "Is my mind apprehending the object of meditation well? Or is it lax? Or is it distracted by the appearance of external objects?"

It is not that you stop your concentration and then look at your mind. Rather, while maintaining your state of concentration, you just look to see whether your attention is staying where it was previously set on the primary object of meditation and, if it is not, whether there is laxity or excitement. After you have settled into concentration, you monitor this at moderate intervals, neither too often nor too seldom. If you do this while the intensity and force of the previous awareness are not quite gone, it takes place within the perspective of this awareness. This has the purpose of both enabling long-lasting, intense stability, and letting you quickly recognize laxity and excitement.

Accordingly, this is how you sustain your mindfulness, for a necessary cause of powerful and continuous mindfulness is sustaining your meditation by repeatedly reminding yourself, at intervals, of the intended object of meditation. Asaṅga's *Śrāvaka Levels* says:[110]

> In this regard, what is a one-pointed mind? Any continuum of attention that remembers again and again, focuses on a consistently similar object, and is continuous, free of misdeeds, and possessed of delight is called "concentration," as well as "a one-pointed virtuous mind."
>
> What does it remember again and again? You perceive the object of meditation—the characteristic of someone in equipoise—

from the viewpoint of any teaching that you have memorized or heard, and upon which you have received instructions and explications from your gurus. You engage and focus on this object with continuous mindfulness. [512]

Also, Sthiramati's *Explanation of the "Separation of the Middle from the Extremes"* (Madhyānta-vibhāga-ṭīkā) states:[111]

> The statement "Mindfulness means not forgetting the object of meditation" means that you mentally express the instructions on stabilizing your mind.

Therefore, you maintain mindfulness to stop forgetfulness wherein you stray from the object of meditation. Hence, non-forgetfulness of the object of meditation—wherein forgetfulness is stopped—is when you "mentally express" the object of meditation; you bring the object of meditation to mind again and again. For example, when you are anxious about forgetting something you know, it will be hard to forget if you recall it again and again.

Thus, you have to remind yourself of the object of meditation at moderate intervals in order to develop strong mindfulness. The way to strengthen your vigilance, which notices laxity and excitement, is to lock your attention on the object of meditation without distraction, and then to monitor it. Realize that if you repudiate such a procedure by thinking, "This is discursiveness," it will be extremely difficult to develop powerful mindfulness and vigilance.

(c')) The length of sessions

Question: When you fix your attention on the object of meditation with mindfulness, is there a definite length for the session, such that you say, "I will stabilize my mind on the object only until then"?

Reply: On this matter, all earlier gurus of the various Tibetan lineages say that you have to do numerous short sessions. Why? Some say that if you meditate in brief sessions and stop when it is going well, you will still be eager to meditate at the end of each session, while if the session is long, you will become weary. Others explain that if the session is long, it is easy to fall under the sway of laxity and excitement, so it is hard to develop flawless concentration. Asaṅga's *Śrāvaka Levels* and other classic texts do not state the length of sessions clearly. However, Kamalaśīla's third *Stages of Meditation* does say:[112]

> At this stage engage in meditative equipoise for twenty-four minutes, an hour-and-a-half, three hours, or as long as you can. [513]

While this statement occurs in the context of the length of the session for cultivating insight after you have already achieved serenity, it is clearly similar when you are first achieving serenity, so do it this way.

If you practice the techniques of mindfulness and vigilance explained above—reminding yourself of the object of meditation and monitoring your meditation at moderate intervals—it does not matter if the session is a little long. However, usually one of two things will happen when you are a beginner and have a long session. On the one hand you may become distracted due to forgetfulness. In this case, you will not recognize the occurrence of any laxity or excitement quickly but only after a long period of time. On the other hand, though you may not lose your mindfulness, it is easy to fall under the sway of laxity and excitement, and you will not quickly recognize them when they occur. The first situation hinders the development of strong mindfulness; the latter hinders the development of strong vigilance. Hence, it is very difficult to stop laxity and excitement.

In particular, failing to recognize laxity and excitement after you have become distracted due to forgetting the object of meditation is much worse than failing to quickly recognize laxity and excitement while not forgetting the object of meditation. So the techniques for maintaining mindfulness—the previously explained remedies which stop the breakdown of mindfulness ensuing from distraction—are very important.[113]

If you have great forgetfulness ensuing from distraction, as well as vigilance so weak that it does not quickly recognize laxity and excitement, then your session must be short. If it is hard for you to forget the object and you can quickly notice laxity and excitement, it does not matter if the session is a little long. This is the idea behind Kamalaśila's statement above that the duration of a session is indefinite—twenty-four minutes and so forth. In short, since the duration has to comport with your mental capacity, Kamalaśila says "as long as you can."

If temporary injury to your mind or body does not occur, set your mind in equipoise. [514] If such injury does occur, do not persist in meditating, but immediately stop your session and then clear away the impediments in your mental and physical constituents. Then meditate. This is what the adepts intended, so recognize that doing this is an aspect of how long a meditation session should be.

4

DEALING WITH LAXITY
AND EXCITEMENT

(c)) **What to do after you focus on an object of meditation**

This has two sections:

1. What to do when laxity and excitement occur
2. What to do when laxity and excitement are absent

(1)) **What to do when laxity and excitement occur**

This has two parts:

1. Using the remedy for failing to recognize laxity and excitement
2. Using the remedy for failing to try to eliminate them even when they are recognized

(a')) Using the remedy for failing to recognize laxity and excitement

This has two sections: (1) the defining characteristics of laxity and excitement, and (2) the method for developing vigilance that recognizes them during meditation.

(1')) The defining characteristics of laxity and excitement

Excitement is defined in Asaṅga's *Compendium of Knowledge*:[114]

> What is excitement? It is an unquiet state of mind, considered a derivative of attachment, which pursues pleasant objects and acts as an impediment to meditative serenity.

There are three aspects to this definition: (1) Its object is an attractive and pleasant one. (2) Its subjective aspect is that your mind is unquiet and scattered outward. As it is a derivative of attachment, it engages its object with a sense of craving. (3) Its function is to impede stabilization of your mind on its object.

When your attention is inwardly fixed upon its object, excitement—which is attached to form, sound, and so on—pulls your attention helplessly toward these objects and causes distraction. As it says in Candragomin's *Praise of Confession*:[115]

> Just as you are focused on meditative serenity,
> Directing your attention toward it again and again,
> The noose of the afflictions pulls your attention
> Helplessly with the rope of attachment to objects. [515]

Question: Is it excitement when there is scattering in which other afflictions distract your mind away from the object—or, for that matter, when there is scattering toward other virtuous objects?

Reply: Excitement is a derivative of attachment, so being distracted by other afflictions is not excitement; rather, it is the mental process of distraction which is one of the twenty secondary afflictions.[116] Scattering toward virtuous objects may involve any virtuous mind or mental process, so not all scattering is excitement.

Many translations render laxity (*bying ba*) as "slackness" (*zhum pa*), but this "slackness" should not be construed as meaning discouragement (*zhum pa*). As for its definition, most yogis among these snowy peaks seem to consider laxity to be a lethargic state of mind that stays on its object of meditation without scattering elsewhere but lacks limpid clarity. This is incorrect, for lethargy is said to cause laxity, so the two are distinct, as suggested in Kamalaśila's second *Stages of Meditation*:[117]

> If, being oppressed by lethargy and sleepiness, you see your mind become lax, or in danger of laxity....

Also, the *Sūtra Unravelling the Intended Meaning* says:[118]

> If there is laxity due to lethargy and sleepiness, or if you are afflicted by any secondary afflictions in meditative absorption, it is a case of internal mental distraction.

This states that when your mind becomes lax due to lethargy and sleepiness, it is distracted inwardly. Asaṅga's *Compendium of Knowledge* also discusses laxity in the context of the secondary affliction of distraction, but distraction as he explains it may also be virtuous, so it is not necessarily afflictive.

Of lethargy, then, Asaṅga's *Compendium of Knowledge* says:[119]

> What is lethargy? An unserviceable state of mind classified as a derivative of delusion, it works to assist all root afflictions and secondary afflictions.

So, this derivative of delusion is the heaviness and unserviceability of body and mind. Vasubandhu's *Treasury of Knowledge Autocommentary* (*Abhidharma-kośa-bhāṣya*) says:[120] **[516]**

> What is lethargy? The heaviness of the body and the heaviness of the mind which are the unserviceability of the body and the unserviceability of the mind.

Laxity means that your mind's way of apprehending the object of meditation is slack, and it does not apprehend the object with much vividness or firmness. So even if it is limpid, if your mind's way of apprehending the object is not highly vivid, then laxity has set in. Kamalaśīla's second *Stages of Meditation* states:[121]

> When your mind does not see the object vividly—like a person born blind, or a person entering a dark place, or like having one's eyes shut—then recognize that your mind has become lax.

I have not seen a clear presentation of the definition of laxity in the other classic texts.

Laxity may be virtuous or ethically neutral, whereas lethargy is either a nonvirtuous or ethically neutral mental obstruction, and it is invariably a derivative of delusion. Moreover, the classic texts say that to dispel laxity, you must bring to mind pleasant objects such as the body of the Buddha, or meditate on light so as to stimulate your mind. Therefore, you have to stop the object from appearing unclearly, as though darkness were descending on your mind, and you have to put an end to the quality of attention which has become flaccid. You need both a clear object of meditation and a tight way of apprehending the object. Neither a clear object alone nor transparency of the subject alone is enough.

It is easy to recognize excitement, but laxity is hard to comprehend since it is not clearly identified in the authoritative classic texts. It is also very important because in this case it is a major point of misunderstanding concerning flawless concentration. Therefore, you should experience laxity with an exacting awareness, and on that basis examine it well and identify it in accordance with Kamalaśila's *Stages of Meditation*. [517]

(2')) The method for developing vigilance that recognizes laxity and excitement

It is not enough just to have an understanding of laxity and excitement; you have to be able to develop vigilance that accurately detects whether laxity or excitement is present during meditation. Moreover, by gradually developing powerful vigilance, not only must you develop vigilance that recognizes laxity and excitement as soon as they occur, you must also develop a vigilance that recognizes them when they are on the verge of occurring, before they have actually arisen. This is demonstrated by statements in Kamalaśila's last two *Stages of Meditation*:[122]

> If you see your mind become lax, or in danger of laxity...

And:

> You see your mind become excited or in danger of becoming excited.

Until you develop such vigilance, you cannot reliably conclude that you have had flawless meditation—free of laxity and excitement—during a given period of time. This is because, not having developed powerful vigilance, you cannot be sure whether laxity and excitement have occurred. Likewise, in a passage that begins, "There is recognition of laxity and excitement...," Maitreya's *Separation of the Middle from the Extremes*[123] says that you need vigilance in order to recognize laxity and excitement. Accordingly, if you have not developed vigilance such as would preclude any failure to recognize the presence of laxity or excitement, then even if you try to meditate for a long time you will pass the time under the influence of subtle laxity and excitement, failing to sense laxity and excitement while they are occurring.

Question: How do you develop this vigilance?

Reply: Its most important cause is the process of maintaining mindfulness which I explained above.[124] If you can develop continual mindfulness, you will be able to avoid forgetting the object of meditation and becoming distracted. Thus, since this prevents a prolonged failure to sense the presence of laxity and excitement, you can easily recognize laxity and excitement. This will be perfectly evident if you examine in terms of your own experience how long it takes to recognize laxity and excitement when mindfulness is impaired and how quickly you recognize them when it is not impaired. With this in mind, Śāntideva's *Engaging in the Bodhisattva Deeds* states:[125] **[518]**

> When mindfulness dwells
> At the gate of your mind for its protection,
> Then vigilance will appear.

And Sthiramati's *Explanation of the "Separation of the Middle from the Extremes"* states:[126]

> The statement, "There is recognition of laxity and excitement by vigilance if mindfulness does not lapse," indicates that mindfulness, when fully present, is accompanied by vigilance. That is why it says, "if mindfulness does not lapse...."

The following cause of vigilance is distinctive to the way to maintain vigilance. Focus your mind on a visualized image of the body of a deity, etc., or focus on a subjective aspect such as the quality of experience being simply luminous and aware. Then, while you stay mindful as explained above, hold your attention on the object while continuously monitoring whether it is scattering elsewhere. Know that this is critical for the maintenance of vigilance. As Śāntideva's *Engaging in the Bodhisattva Deeds* says:[127]

> Examining again and again
> The states of the body and the mind—
> Just that, in brief,
> Is what it means to preserve vigilance.

Thus, with this method you develop vigilance that notices laxity and excitement when they are on the verge of arising, while with the method for maintaining mindfulness you prevent forgetfulness in which attention is distracted and slips away. Hence, you have to properly distinguish these two. Otherwise, if you practice as is done nowadays—combining all these awarenesses with no understanding of their distinctions—I am afraid that the concentration resulting from a muddled cause will itself be muddled. Therefore, it is very important to make a very precise analysis of this in accordance with each of the major authoritative texts, and then to determine it in your practice. Do not place your hopes on sheer determination, for Āryaśūra's *Compendium of the Perfections* says:[128]

> Using only joyous perseverance, you will end up exhausted.
> If you practice with the aid of wisdom, you will achieve the
> great goal. [519]

(b')) Using the remedy for failing to try to eliminate them even when they are recognized

As explained above, you develop very powerful mindfulness and vigilance through proper use of the methods for maintaining mindfulness and vigilance. Vigilance is then able to notice even very subtle laxity and excitement, so there is no problem recognizing the occurrence of laxity and excitement. However, when you make no effort to stop those two as soon as they arise, your complacency or failure to apply yourself constitutes an extremely serious problem for your concentration. For, if you practice in this way, your mind will form bad habits and then it will be extremely difficult to develop a concentration free of laxity and excitement. Therefore, to remedy a failure to apply yourself to the elimination of laxity and excitement, cultivate the intention called application, or effort.

This section has two parts: (1) intention and the way that it stops laxity and excitement, and (2) the underlying causes of laxity and excitement.

(1')) Intention and the way it stops laxity and excitement

Asaṅga's *Compendium of Knowledge*:[129]

> What is intention? It is the mental activity of applying your mind, having the function of drawing your mind to virtue, nonvirtue, or the ethically neutral.

This is how you should understand it. For example, iron filings are compelled to move under the influence of a magnet. Similarly, the mental process of intention moves and stimulates your mind toward virtue, nonvirtue, or the ethically neutral. So it here refers to an intention that applies your mind to the elimination of laxity or excitement when one of them occurs.

Question: After you have thus aroused your mind to eliminate laxity and excitement, how do you stop laxity and excitement?

Reply: Mental laxity involves a very excessive inward withdrawal, leading to a slippage in the way you apprehend the object of meditation; so you should direct your mind to delightful things that cause it to expand outward. [520] This should be something like a very beautiful image of the Buddha, not something delightful that gives rise to afflictions. Or bring to mind an image of light, such as sunlight. When this clears away laxity, immediately tighten the way you apprehend the object and sustain that in meditation. As Kamalaśila's first *Stages of Meditation* explains:[130]

> How? When you are overcome with lethargy and sleepiness, when there is a lack of clarity in your apprehension of the object of meditation and your mind has become lax, then meditate on the idea of light or bring to mind the most delightful things, such as the qualities of the Buddha. Dispel laxity in this way and firmly hold on to the object of meditation.

In this situation, do not meditate on a disenchanting object because disenchantment causes your mind to withdraw inward.

When you expand your mind by using discerning wisdom to analyze an object of your choice, this also stops laxity. Āryaśūra's *Compendium of the Perfections* says:[131]

> When slack, your mind is stimulated and inspired
> By virtue of the energy of striving for insight.

Thus laxity, or slackness, is as follows. The state of mind the two terms describe is called "laxity" because there is a decline in the way you apprehend the object of meditation. It is called "slackness" because there is an excessive withdrawal inward. You counteract it by stimulating the way you apprehend the object and by making the object of meditation extensive, so as to expand your mind. Bhāvaviveka's *Heart of the Middle Way* states:[132]

> In the case of slackness, expand your mind
> By meditating on an extensive object.

And:

> Further, in the case of slackness, inspire yourself
> By observing the benefits of joyous perseverance.

Also, Śāntideva's *Compendium of Trainings* (*Śikṣā-samuccaya*) states:[133] "If your mind becomes slack, inspire yourself by cultivating delight." The great scholars and adepts are in agreement on this matter.

So here is the most important remedy for stopping laxity: When you reflect on the good qualities of such things as the three jewels, the benefits of the spirit of enlightenment, and the great significance of attaining leisure,[134] it should have a bracing effect on your mind, just as cold water is thrown in the face of a sleeping person. [521] This depends on your having had experience with discerning analytical meditation on these beneficial topics.

If you cultivate a remedy for being accustomed to the underlying causes of laxity—namely, lethargy, sleepiness, and something that induces these two wherein your mind takes on a gloomy aspect—then laxity resulting from these causes will not arise or, if it has arisen, will stop. In this regard, Asaṅga's *Śrāvaka Levels* suggests such activities as going for a walk; holding an image of brightness in your mind and familiarizing yourself with it repeatedly; pursuing any of the six recollections—the Buddha, the teaching, the community, ethical discipline, generosity, and the deities;[135] stimulating your mind by means of other inspiring objects of meditation; orally reciting teachings that discuss the faults of lethargy and sleepiness; gazing in different directions and at the moon and stars; and washing your face with water.

Also, if laxity is very slight and occurs only infrequently, tighten up your apprehension of the object and continue meditating; but if laxity is dense and seems to occur repeatedly, suspend your cultivation of concentration, clear away laxity using any of those remedies, and then resume your meditation.

Whether your object of meditation entails directing your mind inward or outward, if the object is unclear and you have the sense of darkness—slight or dense—descending on your mind, then it will be hard to cut through laxity if you continue to meditate without eliminating it. Therefore, as a remedy for that, repeatedly meditate on the appearance of light. Asaṅga's *Śrāvaka Levels* states:[136]

> Cultivate serenity and insight correctly, with a mind that is bright and radiant, a mind of clear light, free of gloom. On the way to serenity and insight, meditate on a sense of brightness in this way. [522] If you do, then even if at the outset your interest in an object of meditation is dull and brightness is fading, the cause and condition of having accustomed yourself to that meditation will clarify your interest in the object of meditation and lead to great brightness. If there is clarity and great brightness at the outset, clarity and brightness will later become still more vast.

So since he says you should cultivate brightness even when the object of meditation is clear from the beginning, this is all the more true when it is unclear. Asaṅga's *Śrāvaka Levels* also describes how to hold the sign of brightness in meditation:[137]

> Hold in meditation the sign of brightness from the light of an oil-lamp, the light of a bonfire, or the orb of the sun.

Meditate on the sign of brightness not only while cultivating concentration, but on other occasions as well.

In the case of excitement, out of attachment your attention pursues objects such as forms and sounds; so in response to that, bring to mind disillusioning things that cause your attention to be drawn inward. As soon as this calms the excitement, settle your mind on the earlier object of meditation. Kamalaśila's first *Stages of Meditation* states:[138]

> When you see that your mind is occasionally becoming excited as you recall previous excitement, play, and so forth, calm the excitement by bringing to mind disillusioning things, such as impermanence. Then strive to engage the object of meditation without your mind becoming involved in activity.

And Bhāvaviveka's *Heart of the Middle Way* states:[139]

> Calm excitement by bringing to mind
> Impermanence and so forth.

And:[140]

> Pull your mind back from distraction by noting
> The faults of the distracting objects.

Also, Śāntideva's *Compendium of Trainings* states:[141] "If excitement occurs, calm it by bringing impermanence to mind." [523]

So, if very strong or prolonged excitement arises, it is crucial that you relax the meditation for a while and cultivate a sense of disenchantment, rather than attempting to pull in your mind and direct it back to the object of meditation every time it becomes scattered. For excitement that is not so dominant, draw in the scattered attention, and fix your attention upon the object of meditation. This is because Āryaśūra's *Compendium of the Perfections* states:[142]

> When your mind becomes excited stop this disturbance
> By calming it and stabilizing your attention.

And Asanga's texts on the levels say that the sūtra passage, "you focus your mind," refers to a remedy for excitement.

It is generally said that if your mind is excited, you should focus on the object of meditation, while if it is lax, you should think about a delightful object. Asanga's *Śrāvaka Levels* states:[143]

> Thus, once your mind has become withdrawn inward and you note that there is slackness or the threat of slackness, maintain and

gladden your mind by thinking of any inspiring things. This is maintaining your mind. How do you settle your mind? While maintaining your mind, when you note that your mind is excited or that there is the threat of excitement, withdraw your mind inward and settle in a calming stabilization.

When your mind is excited, do not bring to mind inspiring and delightful objects because this will cause your mind to be distracted outward.

(2')) The underlying causes of laxity and excitement

Asaṅga's *Levels of Yogic Deeds* states:[144]

> What are the signs of laxity? Not restraining the sensory faculties; not eating in moderation; not making an effort to practice rather than sleeping during the early and later parts of the night; ongoing lack of vigilance; deluded behavior; over-sleeping; being unskillful; being lazy in one's aspirations, joyous perseverance, intention, and analysis; giving only partial attention to serenity without accustoming yourself to it and fully refining it; letting your mind stay as though in darkness; and not delighting in focusing on the object of meditation. [524]

Here, "signs of laxity" should be understood as the causes of laxity. The word "lazy" applies to joyous perseverance, intention, and analysis, as well as to aspirations. The same text also states:[145]

> What are the signs of excitement? The first four points listed above for the signs of laxity—not restraining the sensory faculties, etc.; behaving with attachment; having a disquieted manner; lacking a sense of disenchantment; being unskillful; having a great sense of grasping in your aspiration, etc.; failing to accustom yourself to joyous perseverance; meditating in an unbalanced way without refining your apprehension of the object of meditation; and being distracted by any sort of exciting topic, such as thoughts about relatives.

The "signs of excitement" are the causes of excitement. "Great grasping" is an excessive mental hold on a delightful object. "Aspiration, etc." refers to the four points [aspiration, joyous perseverance, intention, and analysis] explained earlier.

Thus the four practices of which restraint of the sensory faculties is the first, which were discussed earlier in the section on practice between meditation sessions,[146] are important for stopping both laxity and excitement. Moreover, if you recognize those causes and try to stop them, this is obviously very helpful for interrupting laxity and excitement. Therefore, use vigilance to notice even subtle laxity and excitement. You should stop laxity and excitement in every possible way, not tolerating them in any form. Maitreya's *Separation of the Middle from the Extremes* says that failing to do this is a fault of concentration called "non-application." [525]

Some may gradually give up, thinking, "Slight excitement and distraction persist even though I cut them off at the outset, so I shall not cut them off." Or if laxity and excitement are not strong and do not persist for long periods, they may think, "Since they are weak and of brief duration, I do not accumulate karmic obstructions. So I do not need to cut them off." Those who think this way and fail to apply themselves to the elimination of these hindrances do not know the right way to achieve concentration, yet pretend that they do. They deceive those who aspire to concentration, for their approach places them outside the tradition of methods for attaining concentration laid down by teachers such as the venerable Maitreya.

Moreover, in terms of counteracting laxity and excitement, at the outset you will most often be interrupted by excitement and distraction, so strive to eliminate them. If, by working on this, you stop gross excitement and distraction, then you will get a little bit of stability; at this point, make an effort to guard against laxity. If you are on guard against laxity with a heightened awareness, then excitement—more subtle than before—may again interrupt your stability. So strive to eliminate this; if you do stop it, then stability will increase. Then laxity will again arise, so try to eliminate laxity.

In summary, withdraw your mind from scattering and excitement, inwardly fixing it upon the object of meditation, and seek stability. Each time stability occurs, take great precautions against laxity and bring forth a vivid intensity. You will achieve flawless concentration by alternating between these two. Do not expect to attain stability by means of mere limpidity, which lacks the vividness that goes along with an intense way of apprehending the object.

(2)) What to do when laxity and excitement are absent

By continuing to meditate after eliminating even subtle laxity and excitement, as explained above, your mind will enter a state of equipoise that is free from the imbalances of either laxity or excitement. [526] At this point, it is a fault of concentration to apply or exert yourself, so cultivate equanimity as a remedy for this. Kamalaśila's second *Stages of Meditation* says:[147]

> When laxity and excitement have gone and you see that your attention is calmly remaining on the object of meditation, relax your

effort and abide in equanimity; then remain this way for as long as you please.

Question: How can it be that applying yourself, or making an effort, turns into a problem?

Reply: Through meditation, turning your attention inward when your mind is excited and stimulating your mind when it is lax, you gain confidence that laxity and excitement will not occur during each suitable meditation session. At this point you are still extremely wary of laxity and excitement, just as at the outset. Sustaining this is the problem. Your mind will become distracted, so at that time you must know to relax, as stated in Kamalaśīla's second and third *Stages of Meditation*:[148] "If you exert yourself when your mind has entered a state of equipoise, then your mind will be distracted." This entails relaxing the effort, but not sacrificing the intensity of the way you apprehend your object.

Therefore, this cultivation of equanimity is not to be done every time laxity and excitement are absent, but once you have reduced the force of laxity and excitement; for when you have not done so, there is no equanimity.

Question: What sort of equanimity is this?

Reply: Generally, three types of equanimity[149] are taught: (1) the feeling of impartiality, (2) the impartiality that is one among the four immeasurables, and (3) equanimity with respect to application. This is equanimity with respect to application. Its nature is to be understood in accordance with this passage from Asaṅga's *Śrāvaka Levels*:[150] [527]

> What is equanimity? As your mind attends to objects of meditation associated with serenity and insight, it is focusing with calm settling, spontaneous mental engagement, a sense of mental well-being, effortless mental functioning after becoming serviceable, and a mental balance free from the afflictions.

When you achieve such equanimity—on those occasions when laxity and excitement are absent as you cultivate concentration—stay with this equanimity and let your mind rest without exerting strong effort. The signs of this sort of attention are described in the same text:[151]

> What are the signs of equanimity? The object of meditation places your mind in equanimity; your mind is not overflowing with excessive joyous perseverance with respect to the object of meditation.

The time for cultivating equanimity is also set forth in that text:[152]

When is the time for equanimity? In terms of serenity and insight, when your mind is free of laxity and excitement.

The above explanations of the method for developing flawless concentration are in accord with the venerable Maitreya's teachings in the *Separation of the Middle from the Extremes*:[153]

> Staying with that joyous perseverance,
> Your mind becomes serviceable, and you attain all goals.
> This occurs as a result of eliminating the five faults
> And relying on the eight antidotes.
> The five faults are laziness,
> Forgetting the instructions,
> Laxity and excitement,
> Non-application, and application.
> The eight antidotes are the basis [yearning], that based on it [effort],
> The cause [confidence], the effect [pliancy],
> Not forgetting the object of meditation,
> Recognizing laxity and excitement,
> Application to eliminate them,
> And calmly stabilizing your mind when they have been quelled.

In those verses, "Staying with that" refers to keeping up the output of joyous perseverance for the sake of dispelling unfavorable conditions. With this, a concentration in which your mind is serviceable arises. Moreover, since this is the foundation, or basis, of supernormal powers which achieve all goals—superknowledge and so forth—you attain all goals.

What do you do to develop such concentration? [528] It develops as a result of using the eight antidotes in order to eliminate the five faults. These are the five faults: at the time of preparation, *laziness* is a fault because you do not apply yourself at concentration. When you are working at concentration, *forgetting the instructions* is a fault because when you forget the object upon which you were instructed to meditate, your mind is not set in equipoise upon the object of meditation. When it is set in meditative equipoise, *laxity and excitement* are faults because they make your mind unserviceable. When laxity and excitement occur, lack of effort [*non-application*] is a fault because it does not quell those two. When laxity and excitement are absent, the fault is the intention of *application*. Kamalaśīla's three *Stages of Meditation* point out that there are five faults if laxity and excitement are treated as one, six if they are listed separately.

Among the remedies for those faults, the eight antidotes, there are four remedies for laziness—confidence, yearning, effort, and pliancy. Then the remedies for forgetfulness, laxity and excitement, non-application, and application are, respectively, mindfulness, vigilance that recognizes laxity and excitement, the intention of application, and calmly established equanimity. I explained these extensively above.[154]

These are the most excellent instructions for achieving concentration. They are set forth in the great master Kamalaśila's three *Stages of Meditation*, as well as many expositions on achieving concentration by other great Indian scholars. They are also explained in the discussion on achieving serenity in Atisha's commentary on his own *Lamp for the Path to Enlightenment*. Earlier gurus of the stages of the path have conveyed a rough idea of these points, yet those wishing to cultivate meditative stabilization have not understood how to proceed. Thus, I have set this forth at length.

That mindfulness and vigilance remove laxity and excitement from your mind's one-pointed concentration is a common theme to all personal instructions on this practice. [529] So do not think, "This is a teaching particular to the vehicle of dialectics,[155] but it is not necessary in the mantra vehicle." For it is common to the mantra vehicle as well, since this is also stated in the class of the highest yoga tantras. The second chapter of the first section of the glorious *Integration Tantra (Saṃpuṭi)* states:[156]

> The concentration of yearning, the foundation of the supernormal abilities associated with remedial application, is based in solitude; it is based in freedom from attachment; and it is based in cessation. There is thorough transformation by means of correct elimination. With this yearning you meditate without being very slack or elated....

It also describes the three concentrations of enthusiasm, of analysis, and of the mind in the same way. Serviceable concentration, as explained above, is the basis for attaining qualities such as supernormal abilities. Therefore, since it is like a foundation, it is called the foundation of supernormal abilities. Texts such as Sthiramati's *Explanation of the "Separation of the Middle from the Extremes"* explain that there are four avenues to accomplish this: (1) achieving it through fierce yearning, (2) achieving it through prolonged joyous perseverance, (3) achieving concentration by discriminating examination of the object of meditation—these first three are called, respectively, yearning concentration, enthusiastic concentration, and analytical concentration—and (4) achieving one-pointedness of mind based on having in your mind seeds of earlier concentration; this is called mental concentration. "Very slack" refers to excessive relaxation, and "very elated" refers to excessive tightness. The point is that you should sustain a meditation which lacks these two.

5

ATTAINING SERENITY

(2") The stages in which the mental states develop

In this section there are three parts:

1. The actual stages in which the mental states develop
2. The process of achieving them with the six forces
3. How the four attentions are involved in this

(a)) The actual stages in which the mental states develop

These are the nine mental states:

1. *Mental placement:* [530] This entails thoroughly withdrawing your attention from all outside objects and directing it inwardly to the object of meditation. Maitreya's *Ornament for the Mahāyāna Sūtras* states:[157] "After you have directed your attention to the object of meditation...."

2. *Continuous placement:* Your attention that was initially directed to the object of meditation does not stray elsewhere, but is continuously set upon the object of meditation. The *Ornament for the Mahāyāna Sūtras:* "Its continuity is not distracted."

3. *Patched placement:* If your attention is drawn away by forgetfulness and distracted outward, you recognize this and again fix it upon the object of meditation. The *Ornament for the Mahāyāna Sūtras:* "Swiftly recognizing distraction, it is patched up again."

4. *Close placement:* Kamalaśila's first *Stages of Meditation* comments that with the previous mental state you recognize distraction and eliminate it; with this mental state you have eliminated distraction and with effort place your attention upon the object of meditation.[158] Ratnākaraśānti's *Instructions for the Perfection of Wisdom* asserts that your attention, which is by nature expansive, is repeatedly drawn in and refined, establishing ever greater stability.[159] This is in accord with the statement [from the *Ornament for the Mahāyāna Sūtras*]: "The wise withdraw their attention inward to ever greater levels." Asaṅga's *Śrāvaka Levels* explains that first mindfulness is applied, and your attention does not stray outside.[160] As the force of mindfulness develops, forgetfulness does not create outward distraction.

5. *Taming:* Reflecting upon the advantages of concentration, you take delight in concentration. The *Ornament for the Mahāyāna Sūtras:* "Then, because you see the advantages, your mind is tamed in concentration." The *Śrāvaka Levels* comments that if your mind is distracted by the signs of any of the five sensory objects of visual form and so on, of the three mental poisons [attachment, hostility, and ignorance], or of a man or a woman, you regard these ten signs as disadvantageous from the outset and do not let them scatter your mind.

6. *Pacification:* Regarding distraction as a fault, you quell any dislike for concentration. The *Ornament for the Mahāyāna Sūtras:* "Because you see the faults of distraction, you quell dislike for the meditation." [531] The *Śrāvaka Levels* asserts that if your attention is disturbed by thoughts such as those concerning sensory objects and by secondary afflictions such as obstructions involving attraction to the sensory, you regard these from the beginning as disadvantageous, and do not allow your attention to be drawn to your thoughts and secondary afflictions.

7. *Complete pacification:* This entails the fine pacification of the occurrence of attachment, melancholy, lethargy, sleepiness, etc. The *Ornament for the Mahāyāna Sūtras:* "As soon as attachment, melancholy, etc. arise, they are pacified." The *Śrāvaka Levels* says that if

the thoughts and secondary afflictions mentioned earlier arise as a result of forgetfulness, you do not submit to all that appear, but eliminate them.

8. *One-pointed attention:* This entails exerting effort so that you engage the object of meditation effortlessly. The *Ornament for the Mahāyāna Sūtras*: "Then one endowed with restraint and enthusiasm applies remedies for the obstacles to his or her mind and naturally achieves the ninth mental state." This is to be understood from the statement in the *Śrāvaka Levels*: "By means of application you have no hindrance, and, since you continuously establish a flow of concentration, you make a single channel." Another term applied to the eighth mental state is "single channeling," the meaning of which is easily understood.

9. *Balanced placement:* According to Kamalaśīla's *Stages of Meditation*, this refers to the equanimity that occurs when your mind becomes balanced; Ratnākaraśānti's *Instructions for the Perfection of Wisdom* says this refers to spontaneous, natural attention and the attainment of independence as a result of familiarity with single channeling.[161] The *Ornament for the Mahāyāna Sūtras* states: "There is non-application due to familiarity with that." The *Śrāvaka Levels* says your mind is "concentrated," and the meaning of this is clearly stated in the same text:[162]

> As a consequence of dedication, familiarization, and frequent practice, you reach the path of both spontaneous and natural attention. [532] With no application and with spontaneity, your mind enters into a flow of concentration that is without distraction. In this way it is concentrated.

The names of the nine mental states are in accord with the lines in Kamalaśīla's first *Stages of Meditation*:[163] "This path of meditative serenity is explained in the Perfection of Wisdom sūtras and so on...."

(b)) **The process of achieving them with the six forces**

There are six forces: the force of hearing, the force of reflection, the force of mindfulness, the force of vigilance, the force of enthusiasm, and the force of thorough acquaintance. The method of accomplishing the mental states with these forces is as follows:

1. With *the force of hearing,* you accomplish mental placement. The reason for this is that due to following the instructions that you have merely heard from someone else about focusing on the object of meditation, at first you simply fix your attention upon the object. But this is not a case of familiarity due to your own repeated reflection.

2. With *the force of reflection*, you accomplish the mental state of continual placement; for, as a consequence of the practice of repeatedly reflecting on the continuation of the initial fixation of attention upon the object of meditation, for the first time you achieve the ability to maintain a little continuity.

3. With *the force of mindfulness*, you accomplish the mental states of patched placement and of close placement; for, in the case of patched placement, when your attention is distracted away from the object of meditation, you are mindful of the previous object of meditation and your attention is drawn back in; and in the case of close placement, you generate the power of mindfulness from the beginning, and this prevents your attention from being distracted away from the object of meditation.

4. With *the force of vigilance*, you accomplish the mental states of taming and of pacification; for, with vigilance you recognize the faults of being scattered toward thoughts and the signs of the secondary afflictions, and by regarding them as faults, you do not let scattering toward these two occur. [533]

5. With *the force of enthusiasm*, you accomplish the mental states of complete pacification and of one-pointed attention; for, by striving to eliminate even subtle thoughts and secondary afflictions, you do not submit to them; and by so doing, laxity, excitement, etc. are unable to interfere with your concentration, and you achieve continuous concentration.

6. With *the force of acquaintance*, you accomplish the mental state of balanced placement; for, with the force of great familiarity with the above, you develop effortless, natural concentration.

These accord exactly with the intended meaning of Asaṅga's *Śrāvaka Levels*; so, although there are alternative explanations, do not rely on them.

The achievement of the ninth mental state can be understood in terms of an analogy: In the case of those who are extremely familiar with reciting scriptures and so on, if the initial motivation to recite arises and they begin, even though their mind is occasionally distracted elsewhere, the recitation continues effortlessly, without interruption. In a similar fashion, once your mind is settled with mindfulness fixed upon the object of meditation, even if you do not continually cultivate mindfulness and vigilance, your concentration is able to focus continually, for long periods of time, without being interrupted by scattering. Since effort is not needed to maintain a continuous stream of mindfulness and vigilance, this is said to be without application, or effort.

For that to arise, in an earlier phase of practice you continually and energetically cultivate mindfulness and vigilance. During that phase, it is necessary to produce a concentration that can be sustained throughout long meditation sessions, without its being able to be disturbed by such hindrances as laxity and excitement. This is the eighth mental state. This and the ninth state are similar in that they cannot be hindered by factors such as laxity and excitement that are incompatible with concentration. However, in this eighth state, you must uninterruptedly cultivate mindfulness and vigilance, so it is said to be associated with application, or effort. [534] For this to arise, you must stop even subtle laxity, excitement, etc. as soon as they occur, without submitting to them; so the seventh mental state is necessary.

For this to arise, you must recognize that the distraction of thoughts and the secondary afflictions is a disadvantage, and you must have intense vigilance that monitors your attention so that it does not disperse to them. So the fifth and sixth mental states are necessary, for those two are accomplished with the strengthening of vigilance.

Furthermore, for such mental states to arise, you must have mindfulness that swiftly recalls the object of meditation when you are distracted from it, and mindfulness that prevents distraction from the object of meditation from the very outset. So the third and fourth mental states are necessary, for you accomplish these two with those two kinds of mindfulness.

For this to arise, your attention must first of all be fixed upon the object of meditation, and you must have an undistracted continuity of this fixation. So the first two mental states arise before the others.

Therefore, in summary, first of all follow the personal instructions that you have heard, and correctly apply the method for setting your attention in a balanced fashion. Then repeatedly reflect on the way of setting your attention, and as you are able to bring together a little continuity, sustain a continuous stream of attention. Then if your mindfulness declines and you become distracted, swiftly draw your attention back in and quickly become mindful that you have forgotten the object of meditation. Then generate powerful mindfulness and bring forth the force of mindfulness that prevents distraction away from the object of meditation from the outset. By accomplishing forceful mindfulness and by seeing the faults of laxity, excitement, etc., which distract the attention away from the object of meditation, develop intense vigilance to monitor your attention. Then when you are distracted by even subtle foregetfulness, recognize this immediately and stop it short; and upon eliminating it, generate the power of effort to lengthen the flow of attention that is uninterrupted by hindrances. Once that has arisen, you master familiarity by meditating with effort, and you accomplish the ninth mental state, in which your concentration becomes effortless. [535] Therefore, until yogis attain the ninth mental state, they must exert effort to apply their minds to concentration; but upon attaining the ninth mental state, even if they expend no effort for the purpose of settling the mind in meditative equipoise, their minds automatically become concentrated.

Even in the case that this ninth mental state is attained, if pliancy is not achieved, then—as will be explained later[164]—if you are not even defined as attaining meditative serenity, how much less are you defined as achieving insight. Nevertheless, there are those who assert that when you achieve such concentration that is adorned with bliss, clarity, and non-discursive awareness, you have brought forth a non-discursive, sublime wisdom that integrates meditative equipoise and the post-equipoise state. Further, as will be discussed later on, there are a great many people who specifically confuse this ninth mental state described in Asaṅga's *Śrāvaka Levels* with the culmination of the stage of completion in highest yoga tantra.

(c)) How the four attentions are involved in this

The *Śrāvaka Levels* states:[165]

> With respect to these nine mental states, know that there are four types of attention: (1) tight focus, (2) intermittent focus, (3) uninterrupted focus, and (4) spontaneous focus. Now in the first two mental states of mental placement and correct mental placement [i.e., continuous placement], there is the attention of tight focus. In the next five mental states of withdrawn mental placement [i.e., patched placement], close placement, taming, pacification, and complete pacification, there is the attention of intermittent focus. In the eighth mental state of single channeling [i.e., one-pointed attention], there is the attention of uninterrupted focus. In the ninth state of concentrated awareness [i.e., balanced placement], there is the attention of effortless [i.e., spontaneous] focus.

During the first two mental states the attention must be strenuously tight, so this is tight focus. Then during the phases of the next five mental states there is interference by laxity and excitement and you are unable to maintain long meditation sessions; so this is intermittent focus. [536] Then since in the eighth mental state you are able to sustain long meditation sessions without interference by laxity and excitement, there is uninterrupted focus. Then since in the ninth mental state there are no interruptions and no need for continuous exertion, you apply the attention of effortless focus.

Qualm: In this case, during the first two mental states there is interrupted focus, and during the intermediate five mental states there is a need for tight focus; so why does one not speak of the attention of interrupted focus for the first two, and of the attention of tight focus for the intermediate five mental states?

Reply: In the first two mental states there are occasions when your mind is and is not concentrated, with considerably longer periods in the latter state; whereas in the intermediate five states the duration of concentration is much longer, so the designation of "interruption to concentration" is used for the latter and not for the former. Therefore, although those two sets of mental states are similar in terms of the presence of tight focus, they are dissimilar in terms of the presence and absence of interrupted focus; so the five mental states are not included in the attention of tight focus.

Thus, after you have established yourself in the preconditions explained earlier,[166] you will achieve serenity if you cultivate continual joyous perseverance for accomplishing concentration. But if after you practice this only a few times you discard the practice again, it is said that you will not accomplish serenity. Thus Āryaśūra's *Compendium of the Perfections* states:[167]

> With constant yoga
> Strive to accomplish meditative stabilization.
> If you repeatedly slack off,
> Fire will not arise from friction.
> Likewise, do not stop striving at the method of yoga,
> Until you reach a special state.

(c′) **The measure of successful cultivation of serenity**

Here there are three sections:

1. A presentation of the dividing line between accomplishing and not accomplishing meditative serenity
2. A general presentation of the way to proceed along the path on the basis of meditative serenity [537] (Chapter 6)
3. A specific presentation of the way to proceed along the mundane path (Chapter 6)

(1′) A presentation of the dividing line between accomplishing and not accomplishing meditative serenity

This has two sections: (1) a presentation of the actual meaning and (2) the marks associated with attention, and the elimination of qualms.

(a″) A presentation of the actual meaning

Qualm: Once you have properly understood the means of cultivating concentration as explained previously[168] and then sustained them in meditation, the nine mental states arise in sequence; and in the ninth state you are able to meditate for long sessions free of subtle laxity and excitement. Given that you have then achieved a concentration that becomes focused spontaneously without resorting to the effort of continual cultivation of mindfulness and vigilance, have you achieved meditative serenity or not?

Reply: I shall explain. In the achievement of this concentration there are those who do and those who do not achieve pliancy. So if pliancy is not achieved, this would be an approximation of meditative serenity, but would not be genuine serenity. Thus it is called an attention that approximates meditative serenity. This is clearly stated in the *Sūtra Unravelling the Intended Meaning*:[169]

> Bhagavan, when bodhisattvas direct their attention inward and focus it upon their minds, what is this attention called for as long as physical pliancy and mental pliancy are not achieved? Maitreya, this is not meditative serenity. You should say that it is associated with an aspiration that approximates meditative serenity.

Maitreya's *Ornament for the Mahāyāna Sūtras* also states:[170]

> As a consequence of familiarity, there is non-application.
> Then upon achieving great pliancy
> Of the body and mind,
> You are said to have attention.

In this instance, attention refers to meditative serenity, as will be explained below in a citation from Asaṅga's *Śrāvaka Levels*.[171]

Furthermore, Kamalaśīla's second *Stages of Meditation* states that you must achieve both pliancy and the freedom to stabilize on the object of meditation:[172]

> For you who have cultivated meditative serenity in this way, when your body and mind become pliant and you have mastery over your mind in directing it as you wish, at that time know that you have accomplished serenity. [538]

Thus Kamalaśila's first *Stages of Meditation* states:[173]

> When your attention is focused on the object of meditation for as long as you wish, without resort to an antidote, know that you have perfected serenity.

The second *Stages of Meditation* clearly indicates that the above citation also refers to the presence of pliancy.

Furthermore, the equanimity explained in Maitreya's *Separation of the Middle from the Extremes* among the eight antidotes has the same meaning as the ninth mental state referred to here. It states that this alone does not suffice and you need pliancy as well. Ratnākaraśānti's *Instructions for the Perfection of Wisdom* very clearly states:[174]

> The bodhisattvas, dwelling alone in solitary places, direct their attention to their intended object. Freeing themselves of mental conversation, they frequently direct their attention to the mental image. Until physical and mental pliancy arise, this is an attention that approximates serenity; but when they do arise, it is serenity.

All these citations also establish the meaning of the *Sūtra Unravelling the Intended Meaning*.[175]

Question: Well then, which of the nine levels incorporates the concentration in which pliancy has not yet arisen?

Reply: This concentration is included in the level of the desire realm. This is because it is included in one of the nine levels of the three realms,[176] and it is not at or above access to the first meditative stabilization. To achieve this access, it is certainly necessary to achieve serenity. Although there is such concentration without pliancy in the level of the desire realm, it is a concentration that is a level without meditative equipoise. The reason why it is not presented as a level of equipoise is that it is not accomplished with lack of regret, supreme delight and bliss, and with pliancy. This is stated in Asaṅga's *Levels of Yogic Deeds*:[177]

> Why is it that this concentration alone is called the level of meditative equipoise, and one-pointedness of the desire realm is not? [539] Here is the reason: this concentration is accomplished with lack of regret, supreme delight, pliancy, and bliss. The concentration which functions in the desire realm is not like the concentration that does not function there, but it is not the case that in the desire realm there is no concentration on a correct phenomenon.

Thus, without having achieved pliancy, even when mindfulness is not continually maintained, your mind can automatically become non-discursive, and you can integrate this with all activities of moving, walking, lying down, and sitting. This approximation of concentration is called a one-pointed mind of the desire realm, but understand that it is not fit to be presented as genuine meditative serenity.

Question: Well then, what are the means of achieving pliancy, and upon achieving it, how does it lead to serenity?

Reply: Pliancy is to be understood in accordance with the explanation in Asaṅga's *Compendium of Knowledge:*[178]

> What is pliancy? It is a serviceability of the body and mind due to the cessation of the continuum of physical and mental dysfunctions, and it has the function of dispelling all obstructions.

Physical and mental dysfunctions are the unfitness of your body and mind for being employed to cultivate virtue at will. Their remedies, physical and mental pliancy, entail great serviceability in terms of applying your body and mind to wholesome actions, for you are free of dysfunctions of both the body and the mind.

Moreover, physical dysfunction, which is included in the category of afflictions, interferes with your delight in eliminating afflictions. When you try to eliminate your afflictions, your body becomes unserviceable with a sense of heaviness and so on. Once you are free of this, your body becomes buoyant and light; this is a serviceable body. Likewise, mental dysfunction, which is included in the category of afflictions, interferes with your delight in eliminating afflictions. [540] When you try to eliminate your afflictions, you cannot experience pleasure in focusing on a virtuous object. Once you are free of this, your mind focuses on the object of meditation without resistance; this is a serviceable mind. Thus the master Sthiramati states [in *Explanation of the "Thirty Stanzas" (Trimśikā-bhāṣya)*]:[179]

> The serviceability of the body is that from which lightness and buoyancy arise in your physical actions. The serviceability of the mind is the cause of the cheerfulness and lightness of the mind in engaging in perfect attention. If you are endowed with this transformed quality that arises from your mind, you focus on the object of meditation without resistance. Therefore, this is called the serviceability of the mind.

In short, due to the unserviceability of the body and mind, even when you want to strive to eliminate afflictions, you do so arduously and with distaste, like someone unable to engage in work. When pliancy is achieved, this tendency stops, and your body and mind become very easy to employ. Such complete physical and mental serviceability arises to a slight degree from the time that you start to cultivate concentration. This gradually increases until it finally turns into pliancy and one-pointed meditative serenity. At first this is difficult to recognize due to its subtlety, but later on it becomes easy to recognize. Asaṅga's *Śrāvaka Levels* states:[180]

> At the very beginning when you begin the correct training, the occurrence of mental and physical pliancy and mental and physical serviceability is subtle and difficult to discern.

And:[181]

> As that one-pointed mind and mental and physical pliancy increase, in the manner of a chain reaction, they lead to a one-pointed mind and mental and physical pliancy that are obvious and easy to discern.

The portent of the occurrence of easily discernible, perfected pliancy is this: [541] persons who are striving to cultivate concentration experience a sense of heaviness and numbness of the brain, but it is not an unpleasant heaviness.[182] As soon as this occurs, they are freed of the mental dysfunction that obstructs their delight in eliminating afflictions, and mental pliancy, which is the remedy for this dysfunction, arises for the first time. The *Śrāvaka Levels* states:[183]

> The portent of the proximate occurrence of obvious, easily discernible one-pointedness of mind and mental and physical pliancy is a sensation of the brain becoming heavy; but this is not a harmful characteristic. As soon as this happens, you eliminate the mental dysfunction that belongs to the category of afflictions and that obstructs your delight in eliminating afflictions; and the mental serviceability and mental pliancy which are the remedy for this dysfunction arise.

Then due to the power of the arising of the pliancy that makes your mind serviceable, an energy that is a cause for physical pliancy courses through your body. Once this energy has pervasively coursed throughout the parts of your body, you are freed of physical dysfunction, and physical pliancy, which is the remedy for physical dysfunction, arises. Once this saturates the entire body, there is an experience of being as if filled with the power of this serviceable energy. The *Śrāvaka Levels* states:[184]

> Due to its [pliancy's] occurrence, energy-wind[185]—included among the great elements—that is conducive to the arising of

physical pliancy courses through the body. When it flows, you are freed of the physical dysfunction that belongs to the category of afflictions and that obstructs your delight in eliminating afflictions; and physical pliancy, the remedy for this affliction, saturates the entire body, so that it seems as if you are filled with this energy.

Now, physical pliancy is a very pleasant sensation within the body, not a mental process. [542] As the master Sthiramati states, citing sūtra:[186]

> If a distinctive physical sensation is qualified by delight, recognize this to be physical pliancy. If your mind is delighted, your body becomes pliant.

Thus, when physical pliancy initially occurs, due to the power of energy there arises a great sense of well-being in your body, and on this basis there also arises in your mind a most exceptional experience of that pleasure. Thereafter, the force of this initial occurrence of pliancy gradually subsides, but this is not a case of pliancy becoming exhausted. Rather, this pliancy is coarse and excessively agitates your mind; so with its disappearance, there occurs a pliancy, tenuous like a shadow, that is compatible with steady concentration. Once the rapturous delight of your mind has disappeared, your mind stabilizes firmly upon the object of meditation, and you achieve meditative serenity, which is free of the turbulence caused by great delight. The *Śrāvaka Levels* states:[187]

> When this first arises, you experience delight, a great sense of bliss, attention to unsurpassed delight, and manifest delight. Following this, the force of pliancy that first arose slowly becomes very refined, and your body becomes endowed with shadow-like pliancy. You eliminate delight, your mind becomes stabilized with meditative serenity, and you focus on the object of meditation with exceptional serenity.

Once such things happen, "You are said to have attention,"[188] you achieve serenity and you are included among the ranks of "those who have achieved attention." [543] For, by achieving serenity which is included in the access to the first stabilization, you achieve the smallest type of attention on the level of meditative equipoise.[189] This accords with the statement in the *Śrāvaka Levels*:[190]

> Thereafter, the novice yogi is endowed with attention and is included in the ranks of those who are called "attentive." Why? Because this person has achieved the small type of attention on the level of meditative equipoise that first experiences the form realm. Therefore, this person is called "attentive."

The level of meditative equipoise is a synonym for the level of the two higher realms [the form and formless realms].

(b″) The marks associated with attention, and the elimination of qualms

These are the marks and signs to be known by yourself and others as "the criteria for having achieved attention." You who have achieved such attention have these marks:

1. The achievement in small measure of these four: your mind belongs to the level of form, physical pliancy, mental pliancy, and one-pointedness of mind.

2. The ability to purify afflictions either by means of the path bearing the aspects of calmness and coarseness, or the path bearing the aspects of the truths.

3. Once your mind is established inwardly, meditative equipoise and physical and mental pliancy arise ever so swiftly.

4. For the most part, the five obstructions,[191] such as sensual desire, do not occur.

5. When you rise from meditative equipoise, you still possess physical and mental pliancy to some extent.

Thus the *Śrāvaka Levels* says:[192]

> These are the marks of a novice who is endowed with attention: You achieve the small degree of a mind that experiences the form realm, physical pliancy, mental pliancy, and the small degree of one-pointedness of mind. You have the opportunity and ability to practice with objects of meditation that purify afflictions. Your mind-stream becomes smooth, and you are enveloped by meditative serenity.

And:[193] [544]

> When your mind is perfectly drawn inward, settled and focused, mental and physical pliancy occur ever so swiftly; you are not afflicted by physical dysfunction, and for the most part the obstructions do not operate.

And:[194]

> Even when you rise from meditation and move about, you still have a certain degree of physical and mental pliancy. Recognize such experiences to be purified characteristics and signs of possessing attention.

After you have achieved attention bearing such characteristics, it is very easy for the path of serenity to be thoroughly purified as follows: After you have achieved equipoise in meditative serenity, in which your mind is one-pointed, you are swiftly able to induce physical and mental pliancy so that pliancy increases. Commensurate with the increase of pliancy, one-pointed serenity increases, so that they mutually enhance each other. The *Śrāvaka Levels*:[195]

> Just as your physical and mental pliancy increase, so does your mental one-pointedness upon the object of meditation increase; and just as your mental one-pointedness increases, so does your physical and mental pliancy increase. These two phenomena—mental one-pointedness and pliancy—are based upon each other and are dependent upon each other.

In summary, when your mind is serviceable, energy and mind focus as one, so the energy becomes serviceable. At that time, an extraordinary physical pliancy occurs, and when this happens, exceptional concentration arises in your mind. This, in turn, brings forth an exceptionally serviceable energy. Therefore, the process of physical and mental pliancy is as explained above. [545]

The elimination of qualms is as follows.

Qualm: Accordingly, it is said of the non-discursive ninth mental state that even without continual effort at mindfulness and vigilance, your mind becomes concentrated. Moreover, you are endowed with an intensity of clarity that prevents even subtle laxity. And, as in the earlier presentation of physical pliancy,[196] there is concentration that yields outstanding well-being in your body and mind due to the power of serviceable energy. As explained in the above section on the marks associated with attention,[197] for the most part there is no movement of the secondary afflictions of sensual desire and so on; and even when you rise from meditative equipoise, you have the quality of not being parted from pliancy. In terms of the five paths, where does this occur?[198]

Reply: In the past as well as the present there have been a great number of people who assert that when such concentration arises it is generally to be placed on the Mahāyāna path. Specifically, they assert this as a contemplation in which the characteristics of the completion stage of the highest yoga tantra are perfected. They draw this conclusion upon noting the occurrence of a great experience of bliss in the body and mind, based on a feeling as if one's entire body were filled with ecstasy due to the energy corresponding to the arising of pliancy, as well the attributes of non-discursive awareness and great clarity. However, when this is analyzed on the basis of the classic texts of the venerable Maitreya, the noble

Asaṅga, and so on, and the authoritative texts, such as the Madhyamaka *Stages of Meditation*,[199] that clearly set forth the stages of concentration, it is not possible to place this kind of concentration even on the Hīnayāna path, let alone the Mahāyāna. For the *Śrāvaka Levels* states that even the mundane paths which look to the aspects of calmness and coarseness for accomplishing the actual first stabilization are accomplished on the basis of this concentration. [546] Therefore, non-Buddhist sages, who, by means of mundane paths, free themselves from attachment to the level of Nothingness[200] and lower levels, must proceed to higher paths on the basis of this concentration. So this is a concentration common to both non-Buddhists and Buddhists.

Furthermore, if this concentration is imbued with the view that correctly knows selflessness and with the attitude of the determination to be free which properly ascertains the faults of the whole of cyclic existence, is repelled by the cycle of existence, and diligently strives for liberation, it turns into the path to liberation. If it is imbued with the precious spirit of enlightenment, it turns into the Mahāyāna path. For example, if the generosity of giving a single morsel of food to an animal and observing even one type of ethical discipline are imbued with these attitudes, they turn into the collection of merit on the paths to liberation and omniscience respectively. Nevertheless, in the case of this question you do not investigate whether it becomes a path of liberation and omniscience in terms of its being imbued with other paths; rather you investigate which path it becomes by the very nature of the concentration itself.

Although there are inconsistencies between the Madhyamaka and Cittamātrin ways of establishing the object of the view of insight, in general there are no inconsistencies in their identifications of serenity and insight or in the way they develop knowledge of these in their mind-streams. Therefore, the noble Asaṅga states in his *Bodhisattva Levels*, *Compendium of Determinations*, *Compendium of Knowledge*, and *Śrāvaka Levels* that within the context of the individual practices of serenity and insight, when serenity is accomplished, it is accomplished through the stages of the nine mental states. Moreover, since this is elaborately set forth in the *Śrāvaka Levels*, these nine concentrations are not asserted as the means for accomplishing insight—in those treatises insight is explained separately from the nine mental states, and the means of accomplishing it are also explained separately in Asaṅga's *Śrāvaka Levels*.

Similarly, the Madhyamaka *Stages of Meditation* texts and Ratnākaraśānti's *Instructions for the Perfection of Wisdom* also separately discuss the path of serenity consisting of nine mental states and the path of insight. [547] There are also no discrepancies between the statements in the teachings of Maitreya and the commentaries by Asaṅga, so all the great trailblazers are of one mind in this regard.

Qualm: Although bliss and clarity are present in the concentration which is explained in the *Śrāvaka Levels*, it is mere serenity since there is no profound non-discursiveness awareness. But if non-discursive awareness is present, it becomes concentration on emptiness.

Reply: By "concentration on emptiness" are you referring to investigating the meaning of "profound" in the phrase "profound non-discursive awareness" by using your discerning wisdom to establish this definitively in theory and then focusing on this without discursiveness? Or are you referring simply to settling in non-discursive awareness and not analyzing anything? In the first case I also assert such a practice to be concentration on emptiness. If you assert likewise, there is a distinction between those who have and those who do not have an understanding of the view of the way things are. Those individuals who have the view and sustain a non-discursive awareness upon settling in this view are practicing the profound concentration on emptiness. The meditation of those who lack an understanding of this view and meditate by not thinking about anything is not profound meditation on emptiness. It is valid to claim this distinction. Do not declare that all types of meditation in which you do not think about anything are meditative stabilization on the objectless, or on the signless, or on emptiness.

Qualm: Regardless of whether or not you have the view that comprehends emptiness, all meditation in which your mind is focused on not thinking about anything and on not analyzing anything is concentration on emptiness.

Reply: In that case you would be forced to assert that even the concentrations along the way to meditative serenity, mentioned previously in passages from Asaṅga's *Śrāvaka Levels*,[201] are concentrations on emptiness. For in those, too, when settled in concentration—apart from a few occasions of monitoring and so on when the strength of mindfulness and vigilance has decreased—you sustain the meditation without the slightest discursive thought of "this is this" or "this is not this." [548] Therefore, the *Sūtra Unravelling the Intended Meaning* says that the concentrations for achieving serenity attend to an image that is without discursive thought.[202]

Furthermore, within the context of serenity and insight, Asaṅga's *Śrāvaka Levels* refers to serenity in this way:[203]

At that time, this [concentration] attends to an image without discursive thought, and it exclusively focuses mindfulness one-pointedly upon the object. It does not examine it, nor classify it, nor investigate it, nor ponder it, nor analyze it.

And the same text states:[204]

When you achieve the mind of serenity in this way, signs, thoughts, or secondary afflictions may appear, manifest, or become the object, because of forgetfulness or the fault of lack of habituation. Do not fall immediately under the influence of the faults that you have previously observed; neither recall them nor pay attention to them. In this way, because you are neither being mindful of this object nor attending to it, it dissolves; and when it is dispelled, you will settle in the absence of the appearance of these obstructions.

This is stated in a passage concerning the practice of meditative serenity alone. In passages concerning the practice of serenity, the authoritative treatises speak only of meditation that is focused without analytical activity. So, to knowledgeable people the contention that all meditation without any discursive thought at all constitutes the practice of meditation on emptiness is laughable. In particular, this citation from Asaṅga's *Śrāvaka Levels* also perfectly refutes the assertion that all references to meditation with no mindfulness or attention is meditation on emptiness.

Furthermore, Kamalaśīla's first *Stages of Meditation* says:[205] [549]

The nature of serenity is nothing more than a one-pointed mind. This is the general characteristic of all meditative serenity.

Ratnākaraśānti's *Instructions for the Perfection of Wisdom* also states:[206] "Focusing on the mind which is perceiving various things, reject mental conversation and cultivate serenity." Mental conversation is the discursive thought, "This is this." Moreover, after earlier citing numerous sūtras and treatises by the great trailblazers, including the discussion in the *Cloud of Jewels Sūtra*[207] concerning serenity as mental one-pointedness, I have already explained numerous times that serenity entails no discursive thought whatsoever.

Therefore, there is a non-discursive awareness that meditates on emptiness as well as a non-discursive awareness that lacks even the slightest cognition of emptiness. So do not regard every occurrence of bliss, clarity, and non-discursive awareness as meditation on emptiness. These comments disclose only a portion of this subject; so strive diligently and understand the ways of accomplishing serenity and insight as elucidated by Maitreya, Asaṅga, and so on. If you fail to do so, you will mistake certain concentrations that are focused non-discursively—but without even reaching serenity—for the insight which cuts the root of cyclic existence. And, after you have arrogantly held this to be an awareness without a truly existent object, as time goes by you will certainly deceive yourself and others. The treatises of authoritative scholars and adepts assert that when you newly practice serenity, you exclusively focus your attention non-discursively in stabilizing meditation; and when you first practice insight, you meditate by means of analysis with discerning wisdom. Once you hold that all thought consists of grasping to true existence and discard it altogether, your understanding is turned directly away from the authoritative treatises, and you do not reach an errorless view of selflessness. Nevertheless, the notion that the absence of thought constitutes meditation on the profound object of insight is simply the unadulterated system of the Chinese master Ha-shang. Take a careful look at Kamalaśila's three *Stages of Meditation*, and you will understand. [550]

6

SERENITY AS PART OF THE PATH

(2') A general presentation of the way to proceed along the path on the basis of meditative serenity

Question: Should you simply sustain a non-discursive awareness characterized by clarity, non-discursiveness, etc., by achieving attention entailing non-discursive concentration as explained previously?

Reply: Producing such concentration in your mind-stream is for the purpose of generating insight that overcomes afflictions. Hence, if you do not generate insight on the basis of this concentration, you will be unable to eliminate even the afflictions of the desire realm, no matter how much you grow accustomed to that concentration. In that case, what need is there even to mention eliminating all afflictions? Therefore, cultivate insight.

Furthermore, there are two kinds of insight: the insight proceeding by the mundane path, which eliminates manifest afflictions, and the insight proceeding by the supramundane path, which eradicates the seeds of afflictions. There is no means of proceeding on a higher path other than these two. Asaṅga's *Śrāvaka Levels* states:[208]

> Thus, the yogi who has achieved attention and has entered the small delight of elimination of afflictions has two ways to progress, and no others. What are these two? They are the mundane and the supramundane.

Therefore, one who has achieved meditative serenity, or attention, may cultivate either the insight of the mundane path or the insight that proceeds by the supramundane path. Whichever you wish to cultivate, you must frequently cultivate the serenity achieved previously; and when you practice in this way, pliancy and mental one-pointedness greatly increase, and serenity also becomes much more stable. Moreover, you become knowledgeable about the signs of serenity and insight, and thereafter you strive at whichever of the two paths you want. [551] The *Śrāvaka Levels*:[209]

> In regard to this, the novice yogis who are endowed with attention reflect, "I shall proceed by either the mundane or the supramundane path," and they frequently apply themselves to this attention. Commensurate with how much they pass the days and nights in frequent practice, their pliancy and mental one-pointedness increase, expand, and are broadened. When their attention becomes firm, stable, and solid, when it engages pure objects at will, and when it is imbued with the signs associated with serenity and insight, at that time they strive at their practice along the mundane path or the supramundane path, whichever they wish to follow.

Mundane insight consists of meditation bearing the aspects of calmness and coarseness, in which you observe the coarseness of the lower levels and the calmness of the higher levels. Supramundane insight, as stated in the *Śrāvaka Levels*, consists of meditation which observes the sixteen aspects of the four noble truths, including impermanence, and so on.[210] Principally you cultivate the view which is the knowledge of the selflessness of the person.

Question: What kind of person achieves the attention of serenity explained previously and does not proceed by the supramundane path in that lifetime, but proceeds by the mundane path?

Reply: The *Śrāvaka Levels* states:[211]

> What persons proceed in this life solely by the mundane path and not by the supramundane path? There are the following four types of persons: (1) all those who are not Buddhists; (2) those who

adhere to this [Buddhist] teaching but, while they have practiced serenity well, are of dull faculties; (3) similarly, those who are of sharp faculties, but whose roots of virtue have not matured; and (4) bodhisattvas who wish to achieve enlightenment in the future, but not in this life. [552]

In that regard, all non-Buddhist yogis who have achieved the meditative serenity explained earlier do not use discerning wisdom to sustain an analysis of the selflessness of the person, for they are not drawn to selflessness. Therefore, they either sustain non-discursive meditative serenity alone, or they cultivate just the insight bearing the aspects of calmness and coarseness. In this way, they proceed solely by the mundane path.

If you are a practitioner of this teaching, a Buddhist, but have dull faculties and have previously been deeply habituated to the stabilizing meditation of serenity alone, you will not be interested in meditation which investigates the meaning of selflessness with discerning wisdom. Or, even if you are interested, due to an inability to understand the meaning of selflessness, you will proceed in this life solely by the mundane path. This is because you either sustain the stability of serenity alone, or you cultivate just the insight bearing the aspects of calmness and coarseness.

Even if you are a Buddhist of sharp faculties who has comprehended the meaning of selflessness, if your roots of virtue for perceptually knowing the truth have not matured, in this life you will still be unable to generate the supramundane, undefiled, noble path. In this case, it is said that you will "proceed by the mundane path alone," but not that you are unable to cultivate insight focused on selflessness.

Consider bodhisattvas who are bound to one more birth before buddhahood and who during their next lifetime, their final rebirth in cyclic existence, will produce in their mind-streams the four paths, beginning with the path of preparation. While they are still bound to one more birth, they are unable to generate the noble path. So it is said that in this lifetime they "proceed by the mundane path," but not that they fail to know the meaning of selflessness. Vasubandhu's *Treasury of Knowledge* (*Abhidharma-kośa*) states:[212]

> For Our Teacher and the rhinoceros-like *pratyekabuddhas*
> All paths, from preparation to enlightenment,
> Are on the one last meditative stabilization.
> Prior to that are the aids to liberation [the path of accumulation].
> [553]

This accords with the way of achieving buddhahood taught in the Hīnayāna treatises, but it is not the Mahāyāna interpretation of the noble master Asaṅga.

Therefore, non-Buddhists who eliminate manifest afflictions by meditating on the path bearing the aspects of calmness and coarseness, as well as Buddhists who radically eliminate afflictions by meditating on the meaning of selflessness, must first of all achieve the concentration of meditative serenity explained earlier. So the serenity explained above is needed by non-Buddhist and Buddhist yogis as the basis for eliminating afflictions. Furthermore, yogis of either the Mahāyāna or the Hīnayāna must also achieve this concentration; and even among the Mahāyāna practitioners, all yogis of both the mantra and perfection vehicles must also achieve meditative serenity. So this serenity is extremely important as the basis for proceeding along the paths of all yogis.

Moreover, the serenity explained in the tantric texts contains certain differences in methods for generating concentration and in objects of meditation, such as focusing on a divine form, on hand implements of the chosen deity, or on syllables. But apart from those, they are entirely alike in terms of the need to eliminate the five faults of concentration, including laziness and so on; in terms of the means of cultivating their antidotes, such as mindfulness and vigilance, and so on; and in terms of the achievement of the nine mental states and the ensuing occurrence of pliancy, etc. So this concentration is very widespread. With this in mind, the *Sūtra Unravelling the Intended Meaning* states that all Mahāyāna and Hīnayāna concentrations are included within the concentrations of serenity and insight.[213] Thus, you who wish to be skilled in concentration should become skilled in serenity and insight.

Although there are many purposes for developing this concentration (the attention of serenity), the chief purpose is for the sake of developing the knowledge of insight. [554] Moreover, in terms of insight there are two kinds: (1) that which bears the aspects of calmness and coarseness, which eliminates only manifest afflictions, and which is common to Buddhists and non-Buddhists; and (2) that which is common to Buddhists, both Mahāyāna practitioners and Hīnayāna practitioners; that is, insight bearing the aspect of the reality of selflessness, which utterly eliminates the seeds of the afflictions. This last is a unique quality of Buddhists. The former is a luxury, not something indispensable; while the latter is an indispensable element. So those aspiring for freedom should produce the insight that comprehends the reality of selflessness.

Furthermore, even if you do not achieve the higher meditative stabilizations of the form realm or the meditative absorptions of the formless realm, but do achieve the serenity explained previously, which is included in the level of access to the first meditative stabilization, then you can achieve liberation—freedom from all the fetters of cyclic existence—by cultivating insight based on that serenity. By means of mundane insight developed on the basis of the serenity explained earlier, you can achieve the "mind of the Peak of Cyclic Existence," which has eliminated all of the manifest afflictions of the formless level of Nothingness and below.[214] But if you do not know the reality of selflessness and meditate upon it, you will not be liberated from cyclic existence. Thus, Mātṛceṭa's "Praise that Falls Short," [the first chapter of his] *Praise in Honor of One Worthy of Honor (Varṇāha-varṇa-stotra)* says:[215]

> Those opposed to your teaching
> Are blinded by delusion.
> Even after venturing to the peak of cyclic existence,
> Suffering occurs again, and cyclic existence is maintained.
> Those who follow your teaching—
> Even if they do not achieve actual meditative stabilization—
> Turn away from cyclic existence,
> While under the steady gaze of the eyes of Māra.[216]

Therefore, the meditative serenity that serves as the basis for the insight that achieves the noble paths of all stream-enterers and once-returners is the serenity explained earlier, which is included in the access to the first meditative stabilization. [555] Similarly, know that all arhats who simultaneously eliminate the afflictions become arhats by cultivating insight on the basis of the meditative serenity explained earlier. If you do not first establish in your mind-stream the concentration of serenity explained previously, it is not possible for the actual knowledge of insight which is focused on either the real nature or the diversity of all phenomena to arise. This will be discussed later on.[217]

Therefore, while yogis in the highest yoga tantra tradition may not develop the insight bearing the aspects of calmness and coarseness which focuses on the diversity of all phenomena, or the serenity generated by this insight, they must develop serenity. Moreover, the point at which serenity first arises, in terms of the stage of generation and the stage of completion, is during the first of these two.

In summary, you must first develop serenity and then on this basis you may proceed on a graduated path up to the Peak of

Cyclic Existence by means of insight bearing the aspects of calmness and coarseness; or you may proceed along the five paths of liberation or omniscience by means of insight bearing the aspect of the reality of selflessness. This constitutes the general seal of the Conqueror's teachings, so no yogi can depart from it.

The preceding is a general presentation of the way to proceed from high to higher paths on the basis of meditative serenity.

(3') A specific presentation of the way to proceed along the mundane path

Here there are two sections: (1) the need to achieve meditative serenity before proceeding on the path bearing the aspects of calmness and coarseness, and (2) on the basis of meditative serenity, the way to freedom from attachment to the desire realm.

(a") The need to achieve meditative serenity before proceeding on the path bearing the aspects of calmness and coarseness

One who cultivates the path bearing the aspects of calmness and coarseness by way of discernment of characteristics[218] must first achieve the meditative serenity explained earlier, for the *Ornament for the Mahāyāna Sūtras* says:[219]

> Upon increasing this concentration,
> And by increasing it further,
> The yogi achieves actual meditative stabilization. [556]

This states that one who has achieved the previously explained ninth mental state, together with pliancy, increases this concentration and thereby achieves actual meditative stabilization.

Moreover, from the time of the ninth mental state up until you achieve the attention [of the discernment of characteristics], you are said to attain a "beginner at attention [first attainment of serenity]." Once you have achieved the attention of the discernment of characteristics, and you cultivate it out of a desire to purify afflictions, you are said to attain a "beginner at purifying afflictions." So one who cultivates the discernment of characteristics first achieves attention [serenity]. The *Śrāvaka Levels* states:[220]

> A "beginner at attention" is a beginner while not attaining attention with respect to one-pointedness [on the aspects of calmness and coarseness] and until reaching one-pointedness. A "beginner at purifying afflictions" occurs after attaining this attention and begins with the attainment of the attention of the discernment of

characteristics—an attention which desires to purify the mind
from the afflictions and is a familiarization with this practice.

Also at the beginning of the fourth section it is said that you cultivate the mundane and supramundane paths of detachment after
you have achieved attention [serenity].

This very extensive explanation in the *Śrāvaka Levels* of the process of eliminating afflictions by first accomplishing the serenity
explained above and then achieving mundane and supramundane
insight does not clearly appear in other treatises on knowledge.
Former scholars who were learned in the earlier higher and lower
texts on knowledge[221] also have not clearly articulated this process
of eliminating afflictions on the basis of first accomplishing one-
pointed serenity.

Therefore, if you have not understood well this explanation in
the *Śrāvaka Levels*, you might have the following mistaken idea: "The
lowest stage on the path of the meditative stabilizations of the form
realm and the meditative absorptions of the formless realm is the
access to the first stabilization. [557] And the first of the six types of
attention explained with respect to this is the discernment of characteristics. Therefore, the discernment of characteristics is a state
of mind at the beginning of the access." It is very incorrect to hold
such a view, for these reasons: (1) without achieving serenity you
have no way to produce access to the first meditative stabilization;
(2) if you do not achieve this access you will not achieve serenity;
and (3) since discernment of characteristics consists of analytical
meditation, by cultivating it you will not be able to newly accomplish the serenity that you have not achieved earlier. According to
the quotation from the *Levels of Yogic Deeds* cited earlier,[222] there is
no pliancy in one-pointedness within the desire realm; and the *Sūtra
Unravelling the Intended Meaning* and so on state that if you do not
achieve pliancy, you will not accomplish serenity.[223] Thus, if you
do not achieve the first access state, you will not achieve serenity.

Therefore, the first of the six types of attention of the first access
state [the six causal attentions in the list of seven attentions mentioned below] is the entrance to cultivating the insight included in
the access state, but it is not right at the beginning of the first access
state, for it must be preceded by the serenity that is included in the
access state. All states of concentration prior to the achievement
of the concentrations included in the first access state are solely
mental one-pointedness in the desire realm. So if you adhere to

the explanations in the classic texts, there are very few who achieve even serenity, let alone insight.

(b″) On the basis of meditative serenity, the way to freedom from attachment to the desire realm

Once you have become familiar with just the meditative serenity explained earlier, which bears the many attributes of clarity, non-discursive awareness, etc., if you do not cultivate either of the two kinds of insight, you will not be able to suspend even the manifest afflictions of the desire realm. In that case, what need is there to mention eliminating the seeds of afflictions and cognitive obscurations? [558] Therefore, if you wish to achieve the first stabilization, which is free of attachment to the desire realm, cultivate insight on the basis of that serenity.

Qualm: Well, why does this not contradict the earlier statement that if you become accustomed to serenity alone, you will suppress manifest afflictions?[224]

Reply: There is no problem, for the earlier explanation subsumed mundane insight under the category of meditative serenity; but this explanation refers to the serenity that is included in the first access state and that precedes both types of insight. Moreover, with respect to the insight that accomplishes freedom from attachment, there are the two ways of freeing yourself, one by means of insight bearing the aspect of the truths and the other by the insight that bears the aspects of calmness and coarseness. This present discussion is a presentation of the way to accomplish freedom from attachment by way of the latter of these two paths.

With regard to this, the persons who cultivate it[225] are both non-Buddhists, who utterly lack the view of selflessness, and followers of this teaching [Buddhists] who have the view of selflessness. The type of path they cultivate in order to eliminate the afflictions accords with the teachings of the *Śrāvaka Levels*:[226]

> For the sake of freedom from the desire realm, diligent yogis use the seven types of attention and subsequently achieve their freedom. The seven types of attention are: the attention of (1) the discernment of characteristics, (2) arisal from belief, (3) isolation, (4) delight or withdrawal, (5) analysis, (6) final application, and (7) the result of final application.

Among those, the final one is the attention at the time of entering the actual state of meditative stabilization upon being freed from attachment to the desire realm; so this is what is to be accomplished, while the former six are what accomplishes it.

Question: If in this case you are not eliminating the afflictions through meditation on the meaning of selflessness, then what kind of thing are you establishing and then meditating on to eliminate the afflictions? [559]

Reply: Although other manifest afflictions of the desire realm are eliminated with this path bearing the aspects of calmness and coarseness, the phrase "to free yourself from attachment to the desire realm" refers chiefly to eliminating attachment by way of its antidote. Moreover, attachment refers here to the yearning for and attachment to the five sensory objects of the desire realm. The antidote to this is to regard sensory objects as disadvantageous in a multitude of ways. By thus adhering to the opposite of the mode of apprehension of attachment and then accustoming yourself to it, you become free from attachment to the desire realm.

Furthermore, you may have the firm certainty of the discernment of characteristics, an unmistaken discernment of the faults of the desire realm and the good qualities of the first meditative stabilization. Nevertheless, if you have not already accomplished serenity, you will not be able to eliminate afflictions no matter how familiar you become with distinguishing between those faults and good qualities. Moreover, even if you have achieved serenity, if you do not analyze with discernment, however much you cultivate serenity, you will not be able to eliminate afflictions. Thus, you must eliminate them by way of cultivating both serenity and insight. This is the procedure for every elimination of afflictions.

In that case, the seven types of attention are described as follows:

1. The knowledge of characteristics [*the discernment of characteristics*] in which one distinguishes between the faults and advantages of the lower and higher levels entails the integration of study and reflection by means of mental states arisen from study on some occasions and those arisen from reflection on other occasions.

2. By familiarizing yourself in this way, you will exclusively believe in the objects of calmness and coarseness by way of meditation that transcends study and reflection; and this is the *attention arisen from belief.* In this regard the *Śrāvaka Levels* states,[227] "Focusing on that very sign [coarseness and calmness], you cultivate serenity and insight"; and even in the passage concerning the sixth attention there is reference to cultivating serenity and insight. The passage on the first attention speaks of focusing on the six elements, including the meaning,[228] and in other passages this focusing is frequently referred to as insight. Hence, even though this does not entail cultivating the view of selflessness, it is insight. [560]

Thus, in the context of these types of attention you eliminate afflictions after you have meditated by way of both serenity and insight. Here is how you cultivate the two: you cultivate insight by repeatedly analyzing the distinct objects of calmness and coarseness, and at the conclusion of this analysis you cultivate serenity by one-pointedly focusing on these objects of calmness and coarseness. The second and first types of attention in such meditation are the antidote of disillusionment.

3. When on the basis of familiarizing yourself with the alternating cultivation of serenity and insight in that way, you give rise to the antidote to the great afflictions of the desire realm, this is called *isolated attention.*

4. Further, the *attention of delight or withdrawal* is when you are able to eliminate middling afflictions by means of the alternating cultivation of serenity and insight.

5. Then, when you see that the desire realm's afflictions that obstruct your endeavors in virtue are not activated either while abiding in concentration or when you have risen from it, do not have the coarse thought, "Now I have eliminated the afflictions." Rather, analyze, "Is the attachment of sensual attraction not being activated while I am not freed of it? Or, is it not activated after I have been freed from it?" Then in order to test this, watch attachment arise when you focus on a very beautiful object of attachment. Thereafter, your interest in meditation for the sake of eliminating this attachment is *analytical attention.* This gets rid of the conceit of thinking that you have eliminated that which has not been eliminated.

6. Then again you both analytically discriminate the objects of calmness and coarseness as before and focus one-pointedly at the conclusion of the analysis. The *attention of final application* is when by meditating in this way you give rise to the antidote to the small afflictions of the desire realm. The third, fourth and sixth types of attention are antidotes that eliminate afflictions.

7. Thus, when you have eliminated the small afflictions, you have overcome all the manifest afflictions of the desire realm, and for the time being they are not activated in the slightest degree. But you have not completely destroyed the seeds of those afflictions. [561] By this means you are freed from attachment to states up to Nothingness, but since you are unable to stop even the manifest afflictions of the Peak of Cyclic Existence, you cannot transcend the cycle of existence. However, on the basis of meditative stabilization you also achieve the five kinds of superknowledge,[229] but I shall not

discuss them due to fear of verbosity. Since this is elaborated upon in Asaṅga's *Śrāvaka Levels,* look there.[230]

Nowadays there is no one who uses these methods to accomplish the actual meditative stabilizations and so on, so there is no one to lead you astray. Nevertheless, if you generate an understanding that is not confined to a mere general verbal description of them, it is very helpful for avoiding the pitfalls of concentrations other than these.

Such concentrations of the four meditative stabilizations of the form realm and the four meditative absorptions of the formless realm, as well as the five kinds of superknowledge, are shared with non-Buddhists. So, even if you achieve such extraordinary concentrations, not only will you not be liberated from the cycle of existence by these alone, they even bind you to the cycle of existence. Therefore, seek discerning insight and the view of selflessness, and do not be satisfied with serenity alone.

Even if you lack extensive knowledge of the means of accomplishing the actual first stabilization and so on, you should certainly look carefully into the heart of the following discussions and come to know at least something of the teachings themselves, free of your own fabrications: (1) the discussion given above concerning the nine ways of focusing your mind, set forth in the previously cited Madhyamaka *Stages of Meditation,* that are the means of accomplishing the aforementioned "serenity," or "attention" that comes from the profound Perfection of Wisdom sūtras, etc.; (2) their intended meaning as expounded in Maitreya's *Ornament for the Mahāyāna Sūtras;* (3) the noble Asaṅga's summary discussions of them in his *Bodhisattva Levels, Compendium of Knowledge,* and *Compendium of Determinations,* and extensive explanation of them in his *Śrāvaka Levels* in accordance with the indication in his *Compendium of Bases (Vastusaṃgraha)*[231] that both serenity and insight are discussed in the *Śrāvaka Levels;* (4) the discussions of their meaning in the Madhyamaka *Stages of Meditation* and Ratnākaraśānti's *Instructions for the Perfection of Wisdom;* and also (5) the way to accomplish serenity through the eight antidotes and the ways to eliminate the five faults, in Maitreya's *Separation of the Middle from the Extremes.* [562]

Some practitioners of meditative stabilization are not even familiar with the mere names of the meditations. Some become familiar with just the words when they study the classics, but they do not properly understand the meaning. When they then get around to practice they see no need for those treatises, discard them as being of no account, and sustain their meditation. Consequently, when they achieve a state of concentration that is fit to be included in the category of serenity, they maintain that it is concentration on emptiness, which is an indication that they have not discerned the point of the practice with careful understanding. When they achieve merely the ninth mental state, which is a concentration common to both Buddhists and non-Buddhists, they claim to have experienced the completion stage of highest yoga tantra with its complete characteristics. Many of these persons, after they have mingled meditative equipoise with the post-meditation state, mistakenly assert that this experience is uninterrupted, non-discursive wisdom.

When you gain proper certainty concerning the previous explanations, you will not be deceived by the mere designation of such enticing terms as meditation on the objectless, the signless, and the definitive meaning. By knowing the extent of the meanings of these concentrations, you will recognize what are and are not deviations from the path. Therefore, become skilled in the stages of accomplishing concentration taught in those authoritative treatises.

Here I say:

> Profound are the descriptions of the stages for achieving
>   concentration
> Well taught in the sūtras and the great commentaries.
> Those of little intelligence do not precisely comprehend them,
> Projecting the faults of their own minds upon others.

> Thinking, "There are no instructions there for sustaining non-
>   discursive awareness,"
> They do not look for them in texts that have them,
> And they think they have found them
> After diligently seeking them where they do not exist.

> Such people fail to distinguish between
> Even the concentrations of Buddhists and non-Buddhists.
> What need, then, is there to mention
> Their precisely distinguishing the differences

> Between concentrations of the Mahāyāna and Hīnayāna [563]
> And of the Vajrayāna and Pāramitāyāna!
> Seeing this situation, I have explained in simple words
> The way to sustain concentration as taught in the classics.

> O friends who have trained for many years in the classics,
> Do not discard your precious gem
> In favor of others' costume jewelry,
> But recognize you have something of great value!

There is nothing apart from the meaning of the instructions
In the treatises you have studied. Knowing this,
The Master of the Sages said, "There is bliss in the forest
For those of great learning." Analyze these words.

May even those meditators who place their hopes in sheer
    determination,
Though they have not first acquired a proper discernment
Of how to practice and the measure of success
For the path of a fully non-discursive, focused serenity,

Come to know precisely the way to sustain
Meditation in reliance on the learned.
Otherwise, there is less harm if they take for awhile
A refreshing break from the teachings of the Conqueror.

This explanation of the way to achieve serenity
Using the treatises of Maitreya and Asaṅga
Is for the sake of preserving for a long time
The teachings of the Conqueror.

Among the stages of the path of a person of great capacity, this concludes the explanation of how those who are training in the deeds of bodhisattvas train in serenity, which is meditative stabilization.

PART TWO: INSIGHT

7

WHY INSIGHT IS NEEDED

(ii) How to train in insight

————————— ⚅ —————————

(ii) **How to train in insight**

[564] As I have explained,[232] meditative serenity has the features of
(1) *non-discursiveness*—i.e., when your attention is intentionally set
on a single object of meditation, it stays there; (2) *clarity*—i.e., it is
free from laxity; and (3) *benefit*—i.e., delight and bliss. However,
you should not be satisfied with just this. Rather, developing the
wisdom that properly determines the meaning of reality, you must
cultivate insight. Otherwise, since mere concentration is something
Buddhists have in common even with non-Buddhists,[233] its cultivation—as with non-Buddhist paths—will not get rid of the seeds
of the afflictions. Hence it will not free you from cyclic existence.
As Kamalaśīla's first *Stages of Meditation* says:[234]

> After you have thus stabilized your mind on an object of medita-
> tion, you should analyze it with wisdom—it is the dawn of knowl-
> edge that obliterates the seeds of confusion. If you do not do this,
> you cannot abandon the afflictions with concentration alone, just
> as non-Buddhists cannot. [The *King of Concentrations*] *Sūtra* says:[235]
>
>> Although worldly persons cultivate concentration,
>> They do not destroy the notion of self. [565]
>> Afflictions return and disturb them,
>> As they did Udraka,[236] who cultivated concentration in this
>>   way.

The phrase "Although worldly persons cultivate concentration" means that worldly persons cultivate a concentration with features such as non-discursiveness and clarity, as explained above. The line "They do not destroy the notion of self" means that despite cultivating that concentration, they cannot eliminate the conception of self. "Afflictions return and disturb them" indicates that worldly persons will still produce afflictions because they have not eliminated the conception of self.

What kind of meditation leads to liberation? As cited earlier,[237] the very next [verse of the *King of Concentrations Sūtra*] says:

> If you analytically discern the lack of self in phenomena
> And if you cultivate that analysis in meditation
> This will cause the result, attainment of nirvāṇa;
> There is no peace through any other means.

The first line sets out the condition—if, after you have analytically discerned phenomena which are selfless, you develop the wisdom that understands the meaning of selflessness. The second line, "And if you cultivate that analysis in meditation," refers to sustaining and cultivating in meditation the philosophical view of selflessness that you have gained. The third line, "This will cause the result, attainment of nirvāṇa," means that this is the cause of attaining the goal—nirvāṇa, or liberation. Liberation is attained through cultivating that wisdom. Can you also attain liberation without that wisdom, by cultivating some other path? The fourth line of this passage says, "There is no peace through any other means," meaning that even were you to cultivate another path, you would not quell suffering and the afflictions without that wisdom.

This scripture very clearly teaches that only the wisdom of selflessness severs the root of cyclic existence; Kamalaśila quotes it in his second *Stages of Meditation*[238] in order to discredit the assertions of the Chinese abbot Ha-shang. Therefore, you must have certain knowledge of this. For even non-Buddhist sages have many good qualities—such as concentration and the superknowledges—but, since they do not have the view of selflessness, they cannot escape cyclic existence at all. In this way the *Scriptural Collection of the Bodhisattvas*, cited earlier, says:[239] [566]

> One who is satisfied with mere concentration, not understanding the reality explained in the scriptures, might develop an inflated sense of pride, mistaking mere concentration for the path of meditation on the profound meaning. Consequently, such a person will not become free from cyclic existence. It was with this

in mind that I said, "One who listens to others will be free from aging and death."

The Teacher himself explains clearly what he meant: "listening to others" means to hear the explanation of selflessness from another person. Therefore, it is unquestionable that the Buddha spoke of listening to others in order to refute the idea that you can develop the view of selflessness from within yourself, without the study and reflection that go along with listening to an excellent external spiritual guide explain the meaning of selflessness.

Generally, among all the Conqueror's scriptures there are some that explicitly teach about reality, and even those that do not explicitly teach it nonetheless indirectly point toward it. The darkness of confusion is not overcome until the knowledge of reality dawns, but it is overcome when that knowledge arises. Therefore, meditative serenity—one-pointedness of mind—does not in itself become pure sublime wisdom, nor does it overcome the darkness of confusion. Hence there is no doubt that you must seek wisdom; you should think, "I will seek the wisdom that discerns the meaning of selflessness—reality." Kamalaśila's second *Stages of Meditation* says:[240]

> Then, having achieved serenity, you should cultivate insight. You should think, "All the sayings of the Bhagavan were spoken well; directly or indirectly, they all elucidate and point to reality. If I know reality, I will escape all of the entanglements of dogmatic views, just as darkness is cleared away by the dawn. Meditative serenity alone does not lead to pure, sublime wisdom; nor will it clear away the darkness of the obscurations. However, if I use wisdom to meditate well on reality, I will reach pure, sublime wisdom and know reality. Only through wisdom can I really get rid of the obscurations. [567] Therefore, I will remain in serenity and use wisdom to pursue reality. I will not be satisfied with meditative serenity alone." What is this reality? Ultimately all things are empty of the two selves—the self of persons and the self of phenomena.

Of all the perfections, it is the perfection of wisdom that knows reality. Since you cannot know it by means of meditative stabilization or the other perfections, you should develop wisdom without mistaking mere meditative stabilization for the perfection of wisdom. The *Sūtra Unravelling the Intended Meaning* says:[241]

> "Bhagavan, through what perfection should bodhisattvas apprehend the absence of an essence in phenomena?"

"Avalokiteśvara, they should apprehend it through the perfection of wisdom."

As quoted earlier, the *Sūtra of Cultivating Faith in the Mahāyāna* also makes the same point: "I do not say that those who have faith in the Mahāyāna of bodhisattvas, unless they have wisdom, are delivered—no matter what Mahāyāna practices they may do." [242]

8

Relying on Definitive Sources

(a') Fulfilling the prerequisites for insight
  (1') Identifying scriptures of provisional meaning and definitive meaning
  (2') The history of commentary on Nāgārjuna's intended meaning

Since insight is needed, the second section[243] concerns how to train in insight. It has four parts:

1. Fulfilling the prerequisites for insight (Chapters 8-24)
2. Classifications of insight (Chapter 25)
3. How to cultivate insight in meditation (Chapters 25-26)
4. The measure of achieving insight through meditation (Chapter 26)

(a') Fulfilling the prerequisites for insight

You should listen to the stainless textual systems, relying on a scholar who accurately understands the key points of the scriptures. An indispensable prerequisite for insight is to use the wisdom gained through study and reflection to develop knowledge of reality. For without a decisive *view* of how things exist, you cannot develop *insight* that knows the real nature, emptiness. Also, in seeking such a view you must rely not on that which has provisional meaning, but rather on that which is definitive. [568] Therefore, you should differentiate between the provisional and the definitive, and you should then internalize the meaning of the definitive scriptures.

Moreover, if you do not rely upon the treatises by authoritative trailblazers commenting on the Buddha's thought, you are like a blind person headed toward danger without a guide. Hence, you must rely on accurate commentaries on the Buddha's thought. On what sort of commentator should you depend? You should rely on the one whom the Bhagavan Buddha himself very clearly prophesied in many sūtras and tantras as a commentator on the heart of the teaching, the profound reality beyond all extremes of existence and nonexistence. He is the noble Nāgārjuna, renowned in this world and in those beyond. Therefore, rely upon his texts as you seek the view that is the knowledge of emptiness.

With regard to these prerequisites for insight, there are three parts:

1. Identifying scriptures of provisional and definitive meaning
2. The history of commentary on Nāgārjuna's intended meaning
3. How to determine the philosophical view of emptiness (Chapters 9-24)

(1') Identifying scriptures of provisional meaning and definitive meaning

Those who wish to know reality must rely on the Conqueror's scriptures. However, due to the diversity of ideas among the Buddha's disciples, the scriptures vary. Hence you might wonder what sort of scripture you should rely upon in seeking the meaning of the profound reality. You must know reality in reliance upon scriptures of definitive meaning.

What sort of scripture is definitive and what sort is provisional? This is determined by way of the subjects that they discuss. Those that teach the ultimate are considered scriptures of definitive meaning and those that teach conventionalities are considered scriptures of provisional meaning. In that vein, the *Teachings of Akṣayamati Sūtra (Akṣayamati-nirdeśa-sūtra)* says:[244]

> What are sūtras of definitive meaning? What are sūtras of provisional meaning? Those sūtras that teach so as to establish conventionalities are called provisional. Those sūtras that teach so as to establish the ultimate are called definitive. **[569]** Those sūtras that teach by way of various words and letters are called provisional. Those sūtras that teach the profound reality, which is difficult to understand and difficult to know, are called definitive.

Question: How does a sūtra teach conventionalities so as to be classified as provisional? And how does a sūtra teach the ultimate so as to be classified as definitive?

Reply: This also is indicated very clearly in the [*Teachings of Akṣayamati*] *Sūtra*. It says:[245]

> Sūtras called provisional are those that teach as though there were an owner where there is none, using various expressions—self, sentient being, living being, nourished being, creature, person, humankind, human, agent, experiencer.
>
> Sūtras called definitive are those that teach the doors of liberation—emptiness, signlessness, wishlessness, no composition, no production, no creation, no sentient beings, no living beings, no persons, and no owners.

This means that the definitive are those that teach selflessness, no production, and such by eliminating elaborations, while the provisional are those that teach self and so forth. Therefore, you should understand that no self, no production, and such are the ultimate, while production and so forth are the conventional. The *King of Concentrations Sūtra* also says:[246]

> Understand as instances of definitive sūtras those that teach
> In accordance with the emptiness explained by the Sugata.
> Understand as of provisional meaning all those teachings
> That posit a "sentient being," "person," or "living being."

Also, Kamalaśīla's *Illumination of the Middle Way* (*Madhyamakāloka*) says:[247]

> Therefore, you should understand that only those that discuss the ultimate are of definitive meaning; the others are of provisional meaning. Also, the *Ornament for the Light of Wisdom that Introduces the Object of All Buddhas* (*Sarva-buddha-viṣayāvatāra-jñānālokālaṃkāra*) says, "The definitive object is the ultimate." [570] And also the *Teachings of Akṣayamati Sūtra* teaches that the absence of production and so forth "are definitive." Consequently, it is certain that only the absence of production and so forth are called "ultimates."

Therefore, the collections of Madhyamaka arguments[248] as well as the commentaries on them are considered texts that precisely teach the definitive because they demonstrate at length the meaning of the ultimate that is free from all the masses of elaborations, such as production and cessation.

Why are teachings called "provisional" or "definitive"? A text is called definitive, or of definitive meaning, because it cannot be interpreted to mean something else. Its meaning is the end-point of the process of making determinations insofar as it is the meaning of reality itself. No one else can interpret it as having some further or different meaning because it is backed up by valid proofs. Thus Kamalaśila's *Illumination of the Middle Way* says:[249]

> What is a text of definitive meaning? It is one that gives an explanation in terms of the ultimate and is supported by valid cognition, for it cannot be interpreted by someone else as having any other contrary meaning.

Implicitly, this statement allows you to understand the provisional. The provisional, or that which requires interpretation, is a text that cannot be taken to mean exactly what it says; rather, you must explain what it intends, interpreting it as having some other meaning. Or, it is a text that can be taken literally, but in which this literal meaning is not the final reality, and you must still seek that reality as something other than the conventional phenomena to which the text refers.

Qualm: Since sūtras of definitive meaning are literal, when statements such as "production does not exist" and "persons do not exist" appear in those sūtras, one must conclude that production and persons do not exist at all; [571] otherwise those sūtras would not be literal, and it would absurdly follow that they are provisional.

Reply: This does not seem tenable because there are many definitive sūtras in which the Buddha, the teacher who makes these statements, adds the qualification "ultimately" when refuting production and so forth. If he adds such a qualification once, then we must add it even where it does not occur because it is a common attribute of all such refutations. Since the absence of ultimate existence is the reality of phenomena, how could a sūtra teaching this not be definitive?

Otherwise, if these sūtras did refute production in a general sense, then, as far as particulars, they would also refute words, and hence even the definitive sūtras that teach this could not make their presentations.

Therefore, you should understand that a sūtra or a treatise may still be definitive even if what it teaches in a few isolated phrases cannot be read literally when stripped from the context of the general system surrounding it in that scripture. You also should understand that even when the teaching of the very words of a text *can* be taken literally, the text may still be provisional.

(2′) The history of commentary on Nāgārjuna's intended meaning

Nāgārjuna gave flawless commentary on scriptures—e.g., the Perfection of Wisdom sūtras—that teach that all phenomena are without any intrinsically existent production, cessation, and so forth. What is the history of commentary on Nāgārjuna's thought? Both the father [Nāgārjuna] and his spiritual son [Āryadeva] are sources for the other Mādhyamikas; even great Mādhyamikas such as the masters Buddhapālita, Bhāvaviveka, Candrakīrti, and Śāntarakṣita took Āryadeva to be as authoritative as the master [Nāgārjuna]. Therefore, earlier Tibetan scholars used the term "Mādhyamikas of the fundamental texts" for those two and the term "partisan Mādhyamikas" for the others.

In the past, there were some Tibetan teachers who said that when Mādhyamikas are described in terms of how they posit conventionalities, there are two types: [572] Sautrāntika-Mādhyamikas, who assert that external objects exist conventionally, and Yogācāra-Mādhyamikas, who assert that external objects do not exist conventionally. Mādhyamikas are also of two types when described in terms of how they assert the ultimate: the Proponents of Rationally Established Illusion assert that a composite of appearance and emptiness is an ultimate truth, and the Proponents of Thorough Non-Abiding assert that the mere elimination of elaborations with regard to appearances is an ultimate truth. These earlier teachers asserted that within this second typology, the first type includes masters such as Śāntarakṣita and Kamalaśīla. There were also some Indian masters who used the terms "illusionlike" and "thoroughly non-abiding" to refer to different types of Mādhyamikas.

Broadly speaking, there were some Indian and Tibetan masters who claimed to be Mādhyamikas who used this kind of terminology for dividing Mādhyamikas. However, here I aim to establish only the systems of the great Mādhyamikas who are followers of the master Nāgārjuna. Who could explain every subtle distinction? Moreover, the great translator Lo-den-shay-rap (Blo-ldan-shes-rab) makes an excellent point when he says that this presentation of two types of Mādhyamikas, distinguished according to how they assert the ultimate, is simply something to impress fools. For, those who make such a distinction seem be claiming that for Proponents of Rationally Established Illusion such as Śāntarakṣita and Kamalaśīla the mere object that is understood by an inferential reasoning consciousness *is* an ultimate truth, whereas both Śāntarakṣita's

Ornament for the Middle Way (*Madhyamakālaṃkāra*) and Kamalaśīla's *Illumination of the Middle Way* say that the object understood by a reasoning consciousness *is designated* "ultimate" due to its being concordant with an ultimate truth.

Also, the other great Mādhyamikas do not accept as an ultimate truth the mere object that is arrived at when reason eliminates elaborations with regard to an appearance.[250] Therefore, this division is not a good approach.

As to the history of commentary on Nāgārjuna's thought, the master Ye-shay-day explains that the masters—the noble [Nāgārjuna] and his spiritual son [Āryadeva]—did not make clear in their Madhyamaka treatises whether external objects exist; later, the master Bhāvaviveka refuted the system of Vijñaptimātra and presented a system in which external objects exist conventionally. [573] Then the master Śāntarakṣita set forth a different Madhyamaka system that teaches, based on Yogācāra texts, that external objects do not exist conventionally; it also teaches that the mind ultimately lacks intrinsic existence. Thus, two forms of Madhyamaka arose; the former is called Sautrāntika-Madhyamaka and the latter Yogācāra-Madhyamaka.

It is evident that this sequence of events as explained by Ye-shay-day is correct. However, while the master Candrakīrti does assert that external objects exist conventionally, he does not do so in a manner congruent with the claims of other tenet systems. Thus it is unsuitable to call him a "Sautrāntika-Mādhyamika." Similarly, the claim that he is in accord with the Vaibhāṣikas is also very unreasonable.

Scholars of the later dissemination of Buddhist teachings to the snowy land of Tibet use the terms "Prāsaṅgika" and "Svātantrika" for different types of Mādhyamikas. Since this agrees with Candrakīrti's *Clear Words* (*Prasanna-padā*), you should not suppose that it is their own fabrication.[251]

Therefore, all Mādhyamikas are included within two types—those who do and those who do not assert external objects in conventional terms. If they are distinguished in terms of how they develop within their mind-streams the view that is certain knowledge of emptiness, the ultimate, then again they are all included within two types—Prāsaṅgikas and Svātantrikas.

Following whom did those masters seek to understand what the noble Nāgārjuna and his spiritual son Āryadeva intended? The Great Elder [Atisha] considered the system of the master Candrakīrti to be the main Madhyamaka system. Seeing this, the great gurus of the past who followed Atisha in giving personal instructions on these stages of the path also took Candrakīrti's system as the main system.

The master Candrakīrti saw that among the commentators on Nāgārjuna's *Fundamental Treatise on the Middle Way* (*Mūla-madhyamaka-kārikā*),[252] it was the master Buddhapālita who had fully elucidated what the noble Nāgārjuna intended. So he commented on the noble Nāgārjuna's intended meaning using his system as a basis; he also took many good explanations from the master Bhāvaviveka, while refuting those that seemed a little inaccurate. Inasmuch as the commentaries of master Buddhapālita and the glorious Candrakīrti are seen to be excellent explanations of the texts of the noble Nāgārjuna and his spiritual son Āryadeva, I will follow them in making determinations about what the noble Nāgārjuna intended. [574]

9

THE STAGES OF ENTRY INTO REALITY

(3') How to determine the philosophical view of emptiness
    (a") The stages of entry into reality

(3') **How to determine the philosophical view of emptiness**
This has two parts:

    1. The stages of entry into reality
    2. The actual determination of reality (Chapters 10-24)

(a") **The stages of entry into reality**
Question: Nirvāṇa is the reality one seeks to attain, but what is nirvāṇa? If "entry into reality" means a method for attaining it, then how do you enter?

    Reply: The reality that you seek to attain—the embodiment of truth—is the total extinction of conceptions of both the self and that which belongs to the self, specifically by stopping all the various internal and external phenomena from appearing as though they were reality itself—which they are not—along with the latent predispositions for such false appearances.

    The stages by which you enter that reality are as follows: First, having contemplated in dismay the faults and disadvantages of cyclic existence, you should develop a wish to be done with it. Then, understanding that you will not overcome it unless you overcome its cause, you research its roots, considering what might be the root cause of cyclic existence. You will thereby become certain from the depths of your heart that the reifying view of the perishing aggregates, or ignorance, acts as the root of cyclic existence. You then need to develop a sincere wish to eliminate that.

Next, see that overcoming the reifying view of the perishing aggregates depends upon developing the wisdom that knows that the self, as thus conceived, does not exist. You will then see that you have to refute that self. Be certain in that refutation, relying upon scriptures and lines of reasoning that contradict its existence and prove its nonexistence. This is an indispensable technique for anyone who seeks liberation. After you have thus arrived at the philosophical view that discerns that the self and that which belongs to the self lack even a shred of intrinsic nature, you should accustom yourself to that; this will lead to the attainment of the embodiment of truth. [575] Candrakīrti's *Clear Words* says:[253]

> *Question:* You say that all of these afflictions, karma, bodies, agents, and effects are not reality. Still, though they are not reality, they appear to the childish in the guise of reality—like a phantom city and so forth. If this is so, then what is reality and how do you enter that reality?
>
> *Reply:* Reality is the total extinction of the conceptions of both the self and that which belongs to the self in regard to the internal and the external, this being a result of the non-apprehension of internal and external things. As for entry into reality, look in the *Commentary on the "Middle Way"* (*Madhyamakāvatāra*), which says:
>
> > In their minds, yogis perceive that all afflictions
> > And all faults arise from the reifying view of the perishing
> > aggregates,
> > And, knowing that the self is the object of that view,
> > They refute the self.

Candrakīrti's *Clear Words* also says:[254]

> Yogis who wish to enter reality and who wish to eliminate all afflictions and faults examine the question, "What does this cyclic existence have as its root?" When they thoroughly investigate this, they see that cyclic existence has as its root the reifying view of the perishing aggregates, and they see that the self is the object observed by that reifying view of the perishing aggregates. They see that not observing the self leads to eliminating the reifying view of the perishing aggregates, and that through eliminating that, all afflictions and faults are overcome. Hence, at the very

beginning they examine only the self, asking, "What is the 'self' that is the object of the conception of self?"

Scripture sets forth many arguments refuting the intrinsic existence of a limitless number of individual things. However, when yogis initially engage in practice, they meditate in an abridged way, determining that both the self and that which belongs to the self lack intrinsic nature. The master Buddhapālita says that this is the meaning of the eighteenth chapter of Nāgārjuna's *Fundamental Treatise.* [576] The master Candrakīrti bases his own commentary on this statement by Buddhapālita. Also, the teachings on the selflessness of the person in Candrakīrti's *Commentary on the "Middle Way"* are just extended explanations of the eighteenth chapter of Nāgārjuna's *Fundamental Treatise.*

Qualm: Are you not teaching how to enter the reality of the Mahāyāna? In that case, the reality that one seeks to attain cannot be the mere extinction of the conceptions of both the self and that which belongs to it.[255]

Also, since a simple determination that both the self and that which belongs to it lack intrinsic nature does not entail a determination that *objects,* as distinct from persons, lack self, it is wrong to posit it as the path for entering into reality.

Reply: There is no problem here, for there are two types of total extinction of the conceptions of both the self and that which belongs to it. Even Hīnayānists may have the first type, the utter elimination of the afflictions so that those afflictions will never recur; however, the second is a buddha's embodiment of truth. It is the elimination—through utter non-apprehension—of all signs which are elaborations of external and internal phenomena.

Also, when you know that the self does not exist intrinsically, you also overcome the conception that the aggregates which are its components exist intrinsically—just as when a chariot is burned, the wheels and such that are its parts are also burned. Candrakīrti's *Clear Words* says:[256]

> The self is imputed dependently; it is what those who have the error of ignorance cling to fiercely; it is regarded as the appropriator of the five aggregates. Those who seek liberation analyze whether this self has the character of the aggregates. When those who seek liberation have analyzed it in every way, they do not observe a self, and thus [Nāgārjuna's *Fundamental Treatise*] says:
>
> > If the self does not exist
> > How could that which belongs to the self exist?

Because they do not observe the self, they also do not at all observe the aggregates which belong to the self—the basis on which the self is designated. [577] When a chariot is burned, its parts also are burned and thus are not observed; similarly, when yogis know that the self does not exist, they will know that what belongs to the self, the things that are the aggregates, are also devoid of self.

Thus Candrakīrti says that when you know that the self lacks intrinsic nature, you also know that the self's aggregates lack self— that is to say, they lack intrinsic nature.

Also, Candrakīrti's *Explanation of the "Middle Way" Commentary (Madhyamakāvatāra-bhāṣya)* says:[257]

> Śrāvakas and pratyekabuddhas following Hīnayāna tenets are inaccurate because they apprehend an essence in things such as form. Therefore, they do not know even the selflessness of persons. This is because they hold conceptions of the aggregates, the basis that is designated as the self. [Nāgārjuna's *Precious Garland (Ratnāvalī)*] says:[258]
>
> > As long as you conceive of the aggregates,
> > You will conceive of them as "I."

Thus he says that if you do not know that the aggregates lack intrinsic nature, you do not know the selflessness of the person.

Qualm: If the same awareness that knows that the person lacks intrinsic existence also knows that the aggregates lack intrinsic existence, then there is a fallacy—the two awarenesses that know the two types of selflessness would be the same. However, since objects and persons are distinct, the awarenesses that know that they lack intrinsic existence are also distinct, as in the case of the awarenesses that know the impermanence of a pot and that of a pillar. If the awareness that knows that the person lacks intrinsic existence does *not* know that the aggregates lack intrinsic existence, then how can Candrakīrti claim that one will know that the aggregates lack intrinsic existence when one knows the selflessness of the person?

Reply: Since we do not assert this, I will answer your final question. The awareness that knows that the person lacks intrinsic existence does not think, "The aggregates do not intrinsically exist." However, without relying on anything else, that very awareness can induce certain knowledge that the aggregates lack intrinsic existence, thereby eliminating the reification of intrinsic existence that has been superimposed upon the aggregates. Therefore, Candrakīrti says that when you know that the person lacks intrinsic existence, you also know that the aggregates lack intrinsic existence. [578] Also, *Buddhapālita's Commentary on the "Fundamental Treatise"* (*Buddhapālita-mūla-madhyamaka-vṛtti*) says:[259]

> What the so-called self possesses is called "that which belongs to the self." That self does not exist; if it does not exist, how can it be right to speak of what belongs to it?

This is how you should understand it. For example, when reflecting that the son of a barren woman does not exist, that very awareness does not think, "His ears and such do not exist." However, that awareness can eliminate any reifying thought that might imagine that his ears exist. Similarly, when you know that the self does not exist in reality, you stop any notion that its eyes and such exist in reality.

Objection: There are Buddhist essentialists[260] who hold that the person exists as an imputation; they do not assert that the person exists ultimately. Therefore, even they would know that eyes and such lack intrinsic existence.

Reply: You are arguing that since they assert that gross objects such as eyes and seedlings exist as imputations, they would know that those objects lack intrinsic existence. If you accept that this is so, then you contradict your own assertion that these are essentialists, proponents of true existence. If essentialists did know the absence of intrinsic existence, then it would not be necessary for Mādhyamikas to prove to them that seedlings lack true existence. Further, the process of completing a virtuous or nonvirtuous action is a continuum, and if essentialists accepted that a continuum lacks intrinsic existence, then why would they challenge the Madhyamaka position that a continuum, like a dream, lacks true existence? Yet this is what we find in Haribhadra's *Little Commentary on the "Ornament for Clear Knowledge"* (*Abhisamayālaṃkāra-vivṛtti*):[261]

> [The essentialists say to us Mādhyamikas:] If all phenomena are like dreams, then the ten nonvirtues, giving, and so forth would not exist. Hence even when you are not asleep, it would be as though you were.

Therefore, there is a huge disparity between an essentialist system and a Madhyamaka system with respect to whether things exist, either ultimately or conventionally. What they consider conventional existence amounts to ultimate existence from a Madhyamaka perspective and what they consider ultimately existent exists only conventionally according to Madhyamaka. [579]

There is nothing contradictory about this. Hence, you need to draw distinctions.

Furthermore, although the imputedly existent person of these Buddhist essentialists and the imputedly existent person of the master Candrakīrti are similar in name, their meanings are not the same. For, Candrakīrti maintains that these Buddhist essentialists do not have the view which is the knowledge of the selflessness of the person. This is because he asserts that if you have not known the selflessness of objects, then you have not known the selflessness of the person. Therefore, Candrakīrti asserts that they will continue to apprehend the person as substantially existent as long as they do not give up the tenet that the aggregates are substantially existent. Hence essentialists do not know that the person does not ultimately exist.

10

MISIDENTIFYING THE OBJECT TO BE NEGATED

(b″) The actual determination of reality
    (1″) Identifying the object to be negated by reason
        (a)) Why the object of negation must be carefully identified
        (b)) Refuting other systems that refute without identifying the object to be
            negated
            (1)) Refuting an overly broad identification of the object to be negated
                (a′)) Stating others' assertions
                (b′)) Showing that those assertions are wrong
                    (1′)) Showing that those systems contradict the unique feature of
                        Madhyamaka
                    (a″)) Identifying the distinguishing feature of Madhyamaka

(b″) The actual determination of reality

The section on actually determining the view of reality has three parts:

1. Identifying the object to be negated by reason (Chapters 10-17)
2. Whether to carry out that refutation with a Svātantrika procedure or with a Prāsaṅgika procedure (Chapters 18-21)
3. How to use that procedure to generate the right philosophical view within your mind-stream (Chapters 22-24)

(1″) Identifying the object to be negated by reason

This has three parts:

1. Why the object of negation must be carefully identified
2. Refuting other systems that refute without identifying the object to be negated (Chapters 10-16)
3. How our system identifies the object of negation (Chapter 17)

(a)) Why the object of negation must be carefully identified

In order to be sure that a certain person is not present, you must know the absent person. Likewise, in order to be certain of the meaning of "selflessness" or "the lack of intrinsic existence," you must carefully identify the self, or intrinsic nature, that does not exist. For, if you do not have a clear concept of the object to be negated, you will also not have accurate knowledge of its negation. For Śāntideva's *Engaging in the Bodhisattva Deeds* says:[262]

> Without contacting the entity that is imputed
> You will not apprehend the absence of that entity.

There is limitless diversity among objects of negation, but they come together at the root; when you refute this, you refute all objects of negation. [580] Moreover, if you leave some remainder, failing to refute the deepest and most subtle core of the object of negation, then you will fall to an extreme of true existence. You will cling to the idea of real things, whereby you will not be able to escape cyclic existence. If you fail to limit the object of negation and overextend your refutation, then you will lose confidence in the causal progressions of dependent-arising, thereby falling to a nihilistic extreme. This nihilistic view will lead you to rebirth in a miserable realm. Therefore, it is crucial to identify the object of negation carefully, for if it is not identified, you will certainly develop either a nihilistic view or an eternalistic view.

(b)) Refuting other systems that refute without identifying the object to be negated

This has two parts:

1. Refuting an overly broad identification of the object to be negated (Chapters 10-15)
2. Refuting an overly restricted identification of the object to be negated (Chapter 16)

(1)) Refuting an overly broad identification of the object to be negated

This has two parts:

1. Stating others' assertions
2. Showing that those assertions are wrong (Chapters 10-15)

(a')) Stating others' assertions

Most of those who today claim to teach the meaning of Madhyamaka say that all phenomena ranging from forms through omniscient consciousness are refuted by rational analysis of whether production and such exist as their own reality. For when reason analyzes anything that is put forward, there is not even a particle that can withstand analysis. Also, all four possible ways that something could be produced—as an existent effect, a nonexistent effect, and so forth—are refuted, and there is nothing that is not included in those four.

Moreover, these persons assert that a noble being's sublime wisdom which perceives reality perceives production, cessation, bondage, freedom, and so forth as not existing in the least. Therefore, since things must be just as this sublime wisdom knows them, production and such do not exist.

When we assert that production and such do exist, these persons ask, "Are these capable of withstanding rational analysis of their reality? If so, then there would be things that can withstand rational analysis, and thus there would be truly existent things. If not, then how is it possible for something that has been rationally refuted to exist?"

Similarly, when we hold that production and such exist, these persons ask, "Does valid cognition establish them?" [581] If we claim that it does, they reply that since the sublime wisdom perceiving reality perceives production as nonexistent, it is impossible for that wisdom to establish production. Further, if we argue that production is established by conventional visual consciousnesses and such, they reply that it is impossible for such conventional consciousnesses to be valid cognitions that establish production, because scriptural sources refute the claim that those conventional consciousnesses are valid cognitions. The *King of Concentrations Sūtra* says:[263]

> The eye, ear, and nose consciousnesses are not valid
> cognitions.

The tongue, body, and mental consciousnesses are also not
    valid cognitions.
If these sensory consciousnesses were valid cognitions,
Of what use to anyone would the noble beings' path be?

Also, Candrakīrti's *Commentary on the "Middle Way"* says,[264] "The
world is not valid in any way." They argue that we cannot say that
production exists without valid establishment, for we ourselves do
not assert this and it is not reasonable.

They also argue that if we are to assert production, since it cannot be asserted ultimately in Madhyamaka, we will have to assert
it conventionally, but that is unreasonable because Candrakīrti's
Commentary on the "Middle Way" says:[265]

The argument which shows that production from self and from
    other
Are untenable in the context of ultimate reality
Also shows that production is untenable even conventionally.
As this is so, what argument will demonstrate the production
    you believe in?

Thus, they say that the argument refuting ultimate production also
refutes conventional production.

Furthermore, these persons say that if we assert that production
exists despite the lack of an effect which is produced from any of
the four—itself, something other, and so forth—then, when we try
to carry out the Madhyamaka refutation of production through
investigating those four alternatives, we will fail.[266] For we ourselves would have already allowed a type of production which is
not among those four.

Also they say that if there were production from any of those four,
then it would have to be production from a cause which is something other than the effect, for we do not accept the remaining three
[production from self, both self and other, or causelessly]. However,
this is not reasonable because Candrakīrti's *Commentary on the
"Middle Way"* says,[267] "Production from another does not exist even
in the world."

Therefore these persons say that you should not add the qualifying word "ultimate" when refuting production, for Candrakīrti's
Clear Words refutes the addition of this qualification. Among those
who argue in this way, there are some who say that they do not
accept production and such even conventionally, while others accept that production and such do exist conventionally. [582] However, all of them stick out their necks and argue: "It is undeniable

that the system of the master Candrakīrti is a rational refutation of essential or intrinsic nature, for he refutes intrinsic existence in terms of both truths. Thus, if something does not intrinsically exist, how else could it exist? Therefore, adding the qualification 'ultimate' to the object of negation is the procedure only in the Svātantrika-Madhyamaka system."

(b')) **Showing that those assertions are wrong**

This has two parts:

1. Showing that those systems contradict the unique feature of Madhyamaka (Chapters 10-11)
2. Showing that the Madhyamaka critique does not eradicate conventional existence (Chapters 12-15)

(1')) **Showing that those systems contradict the unique feature of Madhyamaka**

This has three parts:

1. Identifying the distinguishing feature of Madhyamaka (Chapters 10-11)
2. Showing that those systems contradict this distinguishing feature (Chapter 11)
3. How a Mādhyamika responds to those who negate the distinguishing feature of Madhyamaka (Chapter 11)

(a")) **Identifying the distinguishing feature of Madhyamaka**

Nāgārjuna's *Sixty Stanzas of Reasoning* (*Yukti-ṣaṣṭikā*) says:[268]

> Through this virtue may all beings
> Amass the collections of merit and wisdom
> And attain the two sublime embodiments
> That arise from merit and wisdom.

What this means is that disciples who progress by way of the supreme Mahāyāna vehicle will attain, upon reaching their goal, both the sublime embodiment of truth and the sublime embodiment of form. This attainment, as explained earlier,[269] is based on their having amassed along the path immeasurable collections of merit and sublime wisdom, collections within which method and wisdom are inseparable. That, in turn, definitely relies upon attaining certain knowledge of the diversity of phenomena. This profound knowledge understands that the relationship of cause and effect—*conventional* cause and effect—is such that specific beneficial and harmful effects arise from specific causes. At the same time, amassing the collections of merit and wisdom also definitely relies on attaining certain knowledge of the real nature of phenomena. This means reaching a profound certainty that all phenomena lack even a particle of essential or intrinsic nature. Certain knowledge of *both* diversity and the real nature is needed because without them it is impossible to practice the whole path, both method and wisdom, from the depths of your heart. [583]

This is the key to the path that leads to the attainment of the two embodiments when the result is reached; whether you get it right depends on how you establish your philosophical view of the basic situation. The way to establish that view is to reach certain knowledge of the two truths as I have just explained them.[270] Except for Mādhyamikas, other people do not understand how to explain these two truths as non-contradictory; they see them as a mass of contradictions. However, experts possessed of subtlety, wisdom, and vast intelligence—experts called Mādhyamikas — have used their mastery of techniques for knowing the two truths to establish them without even the slightest trace of contradiction. In this way they reach the final meaning of what the Conqueror taught. This gives them a wonderful sense of respect for our Teacher and his teaching. Out of that respect they speak with utter sincerity, raising their voices again and again: "You who are wise, the meaning of emptiness—emptiness of intrinsic existence—is dependent-arising; it does not mean that things do not exist, it does not mean that they are empty of the capacity to function."

Scholars who are Buddhist essentialists may have great training in many topics of learning, but they do not accept the Madhyamaka view, and their dispute with the Mādhyamikas is as follows: "If all phenomena are empty, lacking any essential or intrinsic nature, then all of the teachings on cyclic existence and nirvāṇa—bondage, freedom, and so forth—are untenable." Nāgārjuna's *Fundamental Treatise* states their view:[271]

> If all these were empty,
> There would be no arising and no disintegration;
> It would follow that for you
> The four noble truths would not exist.

They say that if this is empty of intrinsic existence, then production, disintegration, and the four truths would not be tenable. Nāgārjuna's *Refutation of Objections* (*Vigraha-vyāvartanī*) also states an essentialist's objection:[272]

> If all things
> Are completely without intrinsic nature,
> Then your words also lack intrinsic nature
> And cannot refute intrinsic existence. [584]

They say that if words lack intrinsic nature, then they can neither refute intrinsic nature nor prove its absence. They argue from the supposition that if there is no intrinsic nature, then the agents and objects of production are not tenable, and neither are the processes of refutation and proof. Hence they dispute with us on the grounds that the arguments which refute intrinsic existence will refute all functionality. Therefore, when essentialists and Mādhyamikas debate about their disparate tenets, they debate exclusively about whether all the teachings about cyclic existence and nirvāṇa can be appropriate for that which is empty of intrinsic existence.

Hence, the distinguishing feature of Madhyamaka is the admissibility of all the teachings about cyclic existence and nirvāṇa— the agents and objects of production, refutation, proof, and so forth—in the absence of even a particle of essential or intrinsic nature. The twenty-fourth chapter of Nāgārjuna's *Fundamental Treatise* says:[273]

> The *reductio* expressing the fallacy that all is untenable
> Is not right about emptiness;
> Thus, forsaking emptiness, as you have,
> Is not right for me.
>
> For those to whom emptiness makes sense
> Everything makes sense;
> For those to whom emptiness does not make sense
> Nothing makes sense.

Nāgārjuna says that fallacies adduced by the essentialists, such as, "If all these are empty, there would be no arising and no disintegration...," do not apply to those who advocate the absence of intrinsic nature. Moreover, he also says that things such as production and disintegration are tenable within the position of emptiness of intrinsic existence, whereas they are not tenable within the position that phenomena are not empty of intrinsic existence. Candrakīrti's *Clear Words* cites that passage and explains:[274]

> Not only does the fallacy expressed in the *reductio* stated by the essentialists simply not apply to our position, but it is also the case that within our position all of the teachings on the four noble truths, etc. are quite correct. In order to indicate this, Nāgārjuna said, "For those to whom emptiness makes sense...."

The twenty-sixth chapter of Nāgārjuna's *Fundamental Treatise* teaches the stages of production in the forward progression of the twelve factors of dependent-arising and the stages of their cessation in the reverse progression.[275] [585] The other twenty-five chapters mainly refute intrinsic existence. The twenty-fourth chapter analyzes the four noble truths. It demonstrates at length that none of the teachings about cyclic existence and nirvāṇa—arising, disintegration, etc.—makes sense in the context of non-emptiness of intrinsic existence, and how all of those do make sense within the context of emptiness of intrinsic existence. Hence, you must know how to carry the implications of this twenty-fourth chapter over to the other chapters.

Therefore, those who currently claim to teach the meaning of Madhyamaka are actually giving the position of the essentialists when they hold that all causes and effects—such as the agents and objects of production—are impossible in the absence of intrinsic existence. Thus, Nāgārjuna the Protector holds that one must seek the emptiness of intrinsic existence and the middle way on the very basis of the teachings of cause and effect—that is, the production and cessation of specific effects in dependence upon specific causes and conditions. The twenty-fourth chapter [of Nāgārjuna's *Fundamental Treatise*] says:[276]

> That which arises dependently
> We explain as emptiness.
> This [emptiness] is dependent designation;
> This is the middle way.

> Because there is no phenomenon
> That is not a dependent-arising,
> There is no phenomenon
> That is not empty.

Thus, Nāgārjuna says that dependent-arisings are necessarily empty of intrinsic existence. Do not turn this statement on its head by claiming that what is produced in dependence on causes and conditions must intrinsically exist. Similarly, Nāgārjuna's *Refutation of Objections* says:[277]

> For whomever emptiness makes sense,
> Everything makes sense;
> For whomever emptiness makes no sense,
> Nothing makes any sense.

> I bow down to the Buddha,
> The unequaled supreme teacher,

Who taught that emptiness, dependent-arising,
And the middle way hold a single meaning.

Also, Nāgārjuna's *Seventy Stanzas on Emptiness* (*Śūnyatā-saptati*) says:[278]

The unequaled Tathāgata taught
That because all things
Are empty of intrinsic existence,
Things are dependent-arisings. [586]

Also, Nāgārjuna's *Sixty Stanzas of Reasoning* says:[279]

Those who cling to the self or to the world
As though these were not contingent
Are captivated by extreme views
Of permanence and impermanence.

Those who claim that dependent things
Exist in reality—
How can they avoid the fallacies
Of permanence and so forth?

Those who hold that contingent things,
Like a moon reflected in water,
Are neither real nor unreal—
They are not captivated by such wrong views.

Also, Nāgārjuna's *Praise of the Transcendent One* (*Lokātīta-stava*) says:[280]

Logicians claim that suffering
Is produced from itself, or from something other,
Or from both of those, or without a cause;
You said it arises dependently.

You hold that whatever arises
Dependently is empty;
There is nothing to match your roar,
"Things do not exist on their own!"

Thus Nāgārjuna says that it is precisely because of being dependent-arisings that phenomena are empty of intrinsic existence. This explanation that dependent-arising is the meaning of emptiness—that is to say, the absence of intrinsic existence—is the unique system of Nāgārjuna the Protector.

Therefore, dependent-arising does not mean accepting emptiness—the absence of intrinsic existence—for oneself as a Mādhyamika, while leaving teachings on dependently arisen cause and effect to others because one is uncomfortable with having them in one's own system. For Nāgārjuna's statement in the *Fundamental Treatise*, "For those to whom emptiness makes sense…,"[281] means that all of the dependent-arisings of cyclic existence and nirvāṇa are admissible in a system that teaches the absence of intrinsic existence.

11

DEPENDENT-ARISING AND EMPTINESS

(b″)) How those systems contradict this distinguishing feature of Madhyamaka
(c″)) How a Mādhyamika responds to those who negate the distinguishing feature of
Madhyamaka

How is it that all of cyclic existence and nirvāṇa is possible in a system that asserts emptiness? As I will explain below, proponents of the view that all things are empty of intrinsic existence argue that this is possible by reason of things' arising in dependence on causes and conditions. [587]

This being the case, dependent-arising is tenable within emptiness of intrinsic existence, and when dependent-arising is tenable, suffering is also tenable—for suffering may be attributed only to what arises in dependence on causes and conditions; it cannot be attributed to what does not arise dependently. When true suffering exists, then the origins from which it arises, the cessation that is the stopping of that suffering, and the paths leading to those cessations are tenable; thus, all four truths exist. When the four truths exist, then it is possible to understand, to eliminate, and to actualize the first three truths respectively, and it is possible to cultivate true paths; when such practices exist, then everything—the three jewels and so forth—is tenable. As Candrakīrti's *Clear Words* says:[282]

> For those to whom this emptiness of intrinsic existence of all things
> makes sense, everything that has been mentioned also makes

sense. Why? Because we call dependent-arising "emptiness"...
thus, dependent-arising makes sense in a system in which emptiness makes sense... and the four noble truths are reasonable for
those to whom dependent-arising makes sense. Why? Because
only what arises dependently can be suffering, not what does not
arise dependently. Since what arises dependently lacks intrinsic
nature, it is empty.

Once there is suffering, then the origins of suffering, the cessation of suffering, and the paths leading to the cessation of suffering
also make sense. Therefore, thorough understanding of suffering,
elimination of origins, actualization of cessation, and cultivation of
paths also make sense. When there is thorough understanding, etc.
of the truths—suffering, etc.—then it makes sense that there will
be spiritual results. Once there are results, then it makes sense that
there are people who have achieved those results; this in turn implies the possibility of people who are approaching those results.
Once there are people who are approaching and achieving these
results, then the community is possible. [588]

When the noble truths exist, then the sublime teaching also
makes sense, and when the sublime teaching and community
exist, then buddhas are possible as well. Therefore, the three jewels also make sense.

All profound knowledge of everything mundane and supramundane makes sense. Proper and improper conduct, the results
of that [happy and miserable rebirths], and all worldly conventions make sense as well. Therefore, in that way, Nāgārjuna says,[283]

> For those to whom emptiness makes sense
> Everything makes sense....

If emptiness did not make sense, then dependent-arising would
not exist, and so nothing would make sense.

Therefore, you should understand that "what makes sense" and
"what does not make sense" here refer to whether those things exist.

As cited earlier,[284] an objection by essentialists appears in
Nāgārjuna's *Refutation of Objections*:

> If all things
> Are completely without intrinsic nature,
> Then your words also lack intrinsic nature
> And thus cannot refute intrinsic existence.

The master Nāgārjuna clearly answers that functionality is tenable
within the context of the absence of intrinsic existence. The *Refutation of Objections*:[285]

We propound that the dependent-arising
Of things is called "emptiness";
That which arises dependently
Has no intrinsic nature.

Also, Nāgārjuna's own *Commentary on the "Refutation of Objections"* (*Vigraha-vyavārtinī-vṛtti*) here says:[286]

> Failing to comprehend the emptiness of things, you essentialists look for something to criticize, and argue against the Mādhyamikas, saying, "Your words lack intrinsic nature and therefore cannot refute the intrinsic existence of things." Here in Madhyamaka, the dependent-arising of things is emptiness. Why? Because they lack intrinsic nature. Those things that arise dependently are not associated with intrinsic nature because they lack intrinsic nature. Why? Because they rely on causes and conditions. [589] If things had intrinsic nature, then they would exist even without causes and conditions; since such is not the case, they lack intrinsic nature. Therefore, we speak of them as "empty."
>
> Similarly, my words also are dependent-arisings and therefore are without intrinsic nature. Because they lack intrinsic nature, it is reasonable to say that they are "empty." Because things such as pots and cloth are dependent-arisings, they are empty of intrinsic nature. Yet a pot can receive and hold honey, water, and soup; a cloth can protect one from the cold, wind, and sun.[287] And so it is with my words. Because they are dependent-arisings, they lack intrinsic nature; yet they are fully capable of establishing that things lack intrinsic existence. Therefore, it is inappropriate for you to give the argument, "Because your words lack intrinsic nature, it is not tenable that they refute the intrinsic existence of all things."

Thus Nāgārjuna speaks very clearly about the pervasion that whatever relies on causes and conditions lacks intrinsic nature and the counter-pervasion that whatever has intrinsic nature does not rely on causes and conditions; he very clearly says that words without intrinsic nature can carry out refutations and proofs. Is it even necessary to point out that dependent-arising—the production and cessation of afflicted and pure phenomena in dependence on causes and conditions—is located right together with the absence of intrinsic existence? Dependent-arising is the best reason to use in order to know the absence of intrinsic existence. You should be aware that only the Mādhyamika experts have this unique approach.

If you hold that dependent production and dependent cessation would have to be essentially existent, and you use the arguments against intrinsic existence to refute the dependent-arising of production and cessation, then those arguments—like a god transformed into a demon—will be a tremendous obstacle to finding an accurate understanding of Madhyamaka. [590] In that case, when you develop a sense of certainty that phenomena lack even a particle of essential or intrinsic nature, you will then have no basis for developing certain knowledge of the relationship between cause and effect within your own system; you will have to posit those as others see them, etc. Or, if you do develop a sense of certainty about cause and effect within your own system, then it will be impossible for your system to foster certain knowledge of the absence of intrinsic existence. You will have to find some other way to construe what the Buddha meant in speaking of the absence of intrinsic existence. If this is the case, then you must understand that you have not yet found the Madhyamaka view.

What will help you to find the right view? As a basis, you should be pure in upholding your ethical commitments. Then strive in many ways to accumulate the collections of merit and wisdom and clear away obscurations. Rely on the learned, making efforts to study and to reflect upon their instructions.

Since certainty about appearances and certainty about emptiness almost never develop together, it is extremely difficult to find the Madhyamaka view. This is what Nāgārjuna meant in the twenty-fourth chapter of the *Fundamental Treatise*:[288]

> Therefore, knowing that those of limited intelligence
> Would have difficulty understanding the depths of his teaching,
> The mind of the Sage turned away
> From giving this teaching.

Nāgārjuna's *Precious Garland* says:[289]

> When the impurity of this body—
> Which is coarse, directly observable,
> And continuously appearing—
> Does not stay with the mind,
>
> Then how could the excellent teaching—
> Which has no basis, is not immediately apparent,
> And is most subtle and profound—
> Easily come to mind?
>
> Realizing that because of its profundity
> This teaching is difficult to understand,
> The Sage, when he became a buddha,
> Turned away from giving this teaching.

Thus, treatises and scriptures state that it is very difficult to understand the profound view.

Failing to reach such knowledge of both appearances and emptiness, some mistake the meaning of statements in certain authoritative texts that demonstrate the absence of intrinsic existence via rational analysis of whether pots and such are one with or different from their parts. [591] Analyzing whether something such as a pot is any of its parts—such as its lip or neck—they do not find it to be any of those; this leads them to a sense of certainty that "there is no pot here." Then, applying the same analysis to the analyzer, they become certain that "there is also no analyzer here." They then wonder, "If the analyzer is not to be found, then who is it that knows that pots and such do not exist?" So they say, "Things are neither existent nor nonexistent." If the false certainty brought on by this sort of counterfeit reasoning were considered a case of finding the Madhyamaka view, then gaining that view would seem to be the easiest thing in the world.

Therefore, the intelligent should develop an unshakable certainty that *the very meaning of emptiness is dependent-arising*. This is what is said in the definitive scriptures and in the pure Madhyamaka texts, the treatises that comment on the intended meaning of those definitive scriptures. This is the distinguishing feature of the Mādhyamika experts. Specifically, this is the subtle point that the noble Nāgārjuna and his spiritual son Āryadeva had in mind and upon which the master Buddhapālita and the glorious Candrakīrti gave fully comprehensive commentary. This is how dependent-arising bestows certain knowledge of the absence of intrinsic existence; this is how it dawns on you that it is things which are devoid of intrinsic existence that are causes and effects.

(b")) How those systems contradict this distinguishing feature of Madhyamaka

Thus, the system of Nāgārjuna the Protector is that phenomena do not have even a particle of essential or intrinsic nature. Also, if there were intrinsic existence, then all of the teachings on cyclic existence and nirvāṇa would be impossible. Since it is inappropriate not to give those teachings, all the teachings on bondage, freedom, etc. should be set forth. Thus, you definitely must assert the absence of intrinsic existence.

However, you misinterpreters of Madhyamaka seem to say, "As things have no essential or intrinsic nature, then what else is there? [592] Therefore, it is not necessary to add a qualification such as 'ultimate' when refuting bondage, freedom, production, cessation, etc. Bondage, etc. are refuted by the arguments that refute intrinsic existence."

If you say this, think about how you should not contradict that which allows you—in the absence of intrinsic existence—to posit bondage, freedom, arising, disintegration, and so forth.

Objection: The master Candrakīrti holds that teachings on cyclic existence and nirvāṇa—bondage, freedom, etc.—are made conventionally, and we also accept these conventionally. Hence, there is no fault.

Reply: This is not reasonable. For you also accept the master Candrakīrti's assertion that phenomena have no essential or intrinsic nature even conventionally. The argument refuting intrinsic existence must refute it even conventionally and you claim that the argument refuting intrinsic existence also refutes bondage, freedom, and so forth. Therefore, it is quite clear that in your system bondage, freedom, and so forth are refuted even conventionally.

In brief, if you claim that the absence of intrinsic existence contradicts bondage, freedom, production, cessation, etc., then it will be impossible—in terms of either truth—to give the full and correct teachings on nirvāṇa and cyclic existence within emptiness, the emptiness of intrinsic existence. You have therefore denied the unique feature of Madhyamaka.

If you claim that the absence of intrinsic existence does not contradict bondage and such, then you are left without any good reason with which to support your claim that—without having to add any qualification such as "ultimate" to what is negated—the argument refuting intrinsic existence also refutes production, cessation, bondage, freedom, etc. Therefore, if the argument refuting intrinsic existence refutes cause and effect, then you are asserting that production, disintegration, and such are impossible in the absence of intrinsic existence. In that case, it is quite clear that your position does not differ in the slightest from the essentialist argument set forth in the twenty-fourth chapter [of Nāgārjuna's *Fundamental Treatise*]:[290]

> If these were all empty,
> There would be neither arising nor disintegration;
> It follows that for you
> The noble truths would not exist.

Nor does your position differ at all from the essentialist argument set forth in Nāgārjuna's *Refutation of Objections*:[291]

> If all things
> Are completely without intrinsic nature, [593]
> Then your words also lack intrinsic nature
> And thus cannot refute intrinsic existence.

Objection: Production, disintegration, and so forth are possible neither within emptiness of intrinsic existence nor within non-emptiness of intrinsic existence; since we assert neither emptiness of intrinsic existence nor non-emptiness of intrinsic existence, we have no fault.

Reply: This reading of the Madhyamaka texts is utterly inappropriate, as Candrakīrti's *Clear Words* proves:[292]

> We avoid the fallacy that arising, disintegration, and such would not be tenable. What is more, the four truths, etc. are tenable.

Also, Nāgārjuna's *Fundamental Treatise* makes a clear distinction between the tenability of the four truths in the context of emptiness of intrinsic existence and their untenability in the context of non-emptiness. Further, Candrakīrti's *Commentary on the "Middle Way"* says:[293]

> Empty things, such as reflections, depend on a collection of
>   causes—
> It is not as though this were not well known.
> From those empty reflections and so forth
> Arise consciousnesses that bear their image.
> Similarly, even though all things are empty,
> From those empty things, effects are definitely produced.

Moreover, when reason refutes bondage, freedom, and so forth, according to your assertion it is not suitable to refute those ultimately and thus they must be refuted conventionally. In that case, one would be refuting all teachings on cyclic existence and nirvāṇa even conventionally. Such a Madhyamaka is without precedent.

(c")) How a Mādhyamika responds to those who negate the distinguishing feature of Madhyamaka

To the objection, "If things were empty of intrinsic existence, the causes and effects of cyclic existence and nirvāṇa could not be set forth," Nāgārjuna the Protector responds that since the fallacy that the Mādhyamikas were going to adduce has been advanced against them, they will turn it around and use it against the objectors. The twenty-fourth chapter of Nāgārjuna's *Fundamental Treatise* says:[294]

You take your own fallacies [594]
And turn them into ours,
Like someone who while riding on a horse,
Forgets that very horse.

If you regard things
As existing intrinsically,
Then you regard all things
As having no causes or conditions.

Also:[295]

If all these phenomena were not empty
There would be neither arising nor disintegration;
It would follow that for you essentialists
The four noble truths would not exist.

And there are other such passages.

Therefore, it is clear that those who argue, "If there is no essential or intrinsic existence, then what else is there?" have unquestionably failed to distinguish between a seedling's lack of intrinsic existence and a seedling's lack of existence. Because of that, they have also failed to distinguish between the existence of a seedling and the existence of a seedling by way of its own essence. Therefore, they clearly hold that whatever exists must exist essentially, and if something is not essentially existent, then it does not exist. Otherwise, why would they claim that the arguments refuting essential existence refute mere existence and mere production and cessation, etc.? They claim that insofar as seedlings and such are asserted to exist, they must exist essentially and they claim that if seedlings utterly lack essential existence, they must be utterly nonexistent. In taking these positions, they undeniably fall to both extremes of permanence and of annihilation. Thus, their perspective is no different from that of the essentialists. For, Candrakīrti's *Commentary on [Āryadeva's] "Four Hundred Stanzas"* (*Bodhisattva-yoga-caryā-catuḥ-śataka-ṭīkā*) says clearly:[296]

The essentialists say that whenever things exist, there is essence. As they see it, without essence these things would be completely nonexistent—like the horn of a donkey. Therefore these essentialists cannot avoid being proponents of both extremes of permanence and of annihilation. Consequently, it is difficult to reconcile all of their explicit assertions.

The glorious Candrakīrti distinguishes intrinsic existence from existence; he also distinguishes the absence of intrinsic existence from nonexistence. [595] Unless you know this you will no doubt fall to both extremes, and thus you will not know the meaning of the middle way which is without extremes. For when it turns out that a phenomenon utterly lacks essential existence, for you it will be utterly nonexistent; then, since there will be no way at all to posit cause and effect within emptiness—emptiness of intrinsic existence—you will fall to an extreme of annihilation. Also, once you accept that a phenomenon exists, you will have to assert that it essentially exists. In that case it will be impossible for you to treat cause and effect as similar to illusions in the sense that they appear to exist intrinsically whereas they do not. Consequently, you will fall to the extreme of permanence.

Therefore, to avoid falling to the extreme of existence, you must realize that from the outset all phenomena lack even a particle of essential existence. And to escape the extreme of nonexistence, you must develop definite knowledge that things such as seedlings nevertheless have the power to perform their own functions; that is, they do not turn into non-things which are empty of the capacity to perform functions.

A clear differentiation between the absence of intrinsic existence and nonexistence is also set forth in Candrakīrti's *Clear Words*:[297]

> *Objection*: This claim that things lack intrinsic existence will wipe out everything the Bhagavan said, such as, "You experience the fruition of the karma that you yourself have done." By making this claim, you mistakenly deny karma and its effects. Therefore, you are the supreme nihilists.
>
> *Reply*: We are not nihilists. We refute both the proposition of existence and the proposition of nonexistence; we illuminate the path free from these two, the path that leads to the city of nirvāṇa. We also do not claim, "Karma, agents, effects, and so forth do not exist." What do we say? We posit that these lack intrinsic nature.
>
> *Objection*: There is still a defect in your position because it is not tenable for things that lack intrinsic nature to function. [596]
>
> *Reply*: Again, there is no such defect, because functionality is not attested in that which has intrinsic nature; functionality is attested only in that which lacks intrinsic nature.

The essentialist's position is that the denial of intrinsic nature prevents karma from giving rise to effects. This is no different from the assertion [by Tibetans who claim to be Mādhyamikas] that the arguments which refute intrinsic existence refute cause and effect.

The Mādhyamika and the essentialist agree that if one denies cause and effect, one becomes the most extreme sort of nihilist.

However, the Mādhyamika does not deny cause and effect. Still, the essentialist calls the Mādhyamika a "nihilist" or "annihilationist," supposing that if you refute intrinsic nature, then you certainly must also refute cause and effect. Most Tibetans who claim to be Mādhyamikas seem to agree with the essentialist's assertion that if an argument refutes intrinsic nature, it must also refute cause and effect. Yet unlike essentialists, these Tibetans seem pleased that reason refutes cause and effect, taking this to be the Madhyamaka system.

In answer to this objection, Candrakīrti responds: "We are not nihilists; we eliminate the propositions of existence and nonexistence; we illuminate the path to liberation." The rest of the passage shows how he avoids the positions of existence and nonexistence. By saying, "We do not claim that karma, effects, and so forth are nonexistent," Candrakīrti avoids the nihilistic position. We would be nihilists if we asserted that cause, effect, and so forth do not exist, but we do not assert this. In response to the question, "Well, what do you hold?" Candrakīrti says, "We posit, or assert, that these—karma, effects, and so forth—lack intrinsic nature." He thereby avoids the position of existence.

The statement, "There is still a defect in your position because it is not tenable for that which lacks intrinsic nature to function," indicates the essentialist's objection—[597] "You Mādhyamikas say, 'We do not propound nonexistence; we propound an absence of intrinsic nature,' but you still cannot escape the fallacy that we have already stated: Without intrinsic nature, cause and effect are not tenable." Those essentialists raise this objection because in their system there is no difference between the absence of intrinsic nature and nonexistence. In reply, Candrakīrti says that functions—such as causes giving rise to effects—are impossible in the context of intrinsic existence and are possible only in the absence of intrinsic existence.

Also, Candrakīrti's *Commentary on the "Four Hundred Stanzas"* says:[298]

> We are not proponents of nonexistence, for we are proponents of dependent-arising. Are we proponents of real things? No, because we are proponents only of dependent-arising. What do we propound? We propound dependent-arising. What is the meaning of dependent-arising? It means the absence of intrinsic existence; it means no intrinsically existent production; it means the arising of effects whose nature is similar to a magician's illusion, a

mirage, a reflection, a phantom city, an emanation, or a dream; it means emptiness and selflessness.

Candrakīrti shows that by asserting dependent-arising you can avoid the two extremes, the position that things exist and the position that things do not exist. He avoids the position that things exist by explaining that dependent-arising means no intrinsically existent production, and he avoids the position that things do not exist by indicating that dependent-arising refers to the arising of effects that are like a magician's illusion.

Therefore, "thing" may refer either to "intrinsic existence" or to "the capacity to perform a function."[299] Between these two, the "thing" in "the essentialist position that things exist" refers only to intrinsic existence; "thing" in "the position that things do not exist" refers to things that perform functions. For in avoiding those two extremes, Candrakīrti refutes intrinsic existence and indicates that there do exist causes and effects that are like a magician's illusions.

Moreover, Candrakīrti's *Commentary on the "Four Hundred Stanzas"* says:[300] [598]

> *Question:* Do you Mādhyamikas claim that there are no memory consciousnesses that have as their objects the things of the past?
> *Reply:* Who would claim that such do not exist? We do not eliminate dependent-arising. The master Āryadeva himself gives a precise statement of how memory exists:
>
> > Therefore, the arising of what we call "memory"
> > Is only an unreal subject with an unreal object.
>
> Therefore, what memory observes is something in the past. If the past thing essentially existed, then the memory of it would be observing an object that essentially exists. Therefore, that memory would be essentially existent. But insofar as that past thing lacks intrinsic existence, the memory observing it also lacks intrinsic existence. Therefore, Āryadeva has established that the past object and the memory of it are unreal. "Unreal" means only "lacking intrinsic existence" and "dependent-arising"; it does not mean the nonexistence of things that can perform functions. A past thing is not entirely nonexistent because it is an object of memory and its effects can be seen. It also does not essentially exist, for if it did it would have to be permanent and it would have to be directly apprehensible.

Candrakīrti says that these—past objects and such—are not utterly nonexistent and are also not essentially existent; he explains that unreal or false means being a dependent-arising and does not mean that things do not exist.

Therefore, if you claim that these phenomena are essentially existent, then you are a proponent of real things; you have fallen to the extreme of intrinsic existence. However, to hold that these phenomena are simply existent does not make you a proponent of real things or a proponent of real existence. Similarly, if you hold that internal and external things are non-things, devoid of the capacity to perform functions, then you are propounding the nonexistence of things, and you have fallen to the extreme of nonexistence. However, you do not fall to an extreme of nonexistence by saying that things lack intrinsic existence.

Some [Tibetans who claim to be Mādhyamikas] do not distinguish utter nonexistence from the absence of intrinsic existence, and do not distinguish essential existence from mere existence. [599] They hope to avoid falling to the extremes of existence and nonexistence simply by saying, "We do not claim that things are nonexistent (*med pa*); we say that they are not existent (*yod pa ma yin pa*). We do not claim that things exist (*yod pa*); we say that they are not nonexistent (*med pa ma yin pa*)."

This is nothing but a mass of contradictions; it does not in the least explain the meaning of the middle way. For when they refute others, they perform the refutation via an investigation of whether or not something intrinsically exists. Therefore, they have to limit the possibilities to two [i.e., it intrinsically exists or it does not]; yet in making their own assertions they claim there is something that is neither of those two. Why should they have to limit the possibilities to two when they investigate something to see whether or not it intrinsically exists? Because if there were a third possibility beyond those two, it would not be reasonable to investigate the question, "Which is it, intrinsically existent or not intrinsically existent?" It would be as though there were a color and someone asked, "Is it blue or is it yellow?"

Limiting things to two possibilities—either they intrinsically exist or they do not—derives from the universal limitation that anything imaginable either exists or does not exist. Similarly, the limitation that what truly exists must either truly exist as single or truly exist as plural is based on the universal limitation that anything must be either single or plural. When there is such a limitation, any further alternative is necessarily precluded; hence, it is utter nonsense to assert a phenomenon that is neither of those two. As Nāgārjuna's *Refutation of Objections* says:[301]

If the absence of intrinsic nature were refuted,
Then the presence of intrinsic nature would be proven.

Moreover, there will always be some doubt in the minds of those who make these claims because they have no way of making a definitive list that excludes any further alternative. This is because as they see it the exclusion of one possibility—such as "exists" or "does not exist"—does not entail the other possibility.

If they accept that there are some cases—such as "is" (*yin*) and "is not" (*min*)—which exclude any further alternatives, then they should know that it is exactly the same in the case of "exists" (*yod*) and "does not exist" (*med*).[302] **[600]** Evidently their position is an overly literal misunderstanding of Madhyamaka texts that say, "is not existent and is not nonexistent." Therefore, if—as they claim— it is inappropriate to say "exists" or "does not exist," then it would also be wrong to say, "is not existent and is not nonexistent" be- cause those Madhyamaka texts say that you should reject all four possibilities.

Therefore, Nāgārjuna's *Fundamental Treatise* does not refer to simple existence and nonexistence when it states:[303]

To say "it exists" is a conception of permanence;
To say "it does not exist" is a view of annihilation.
Hence the learned should not dwell
In either existence or nonexistence.

This clearly means that the person who claims that things intrinsi- cally exist will have views of permanence and annihilation. Candrakīrti's *Clear Words* explains that in this passage the concep- tion of existence and nonexistence refers to the view that things exist and the view that things do not exist. It then says:[304]

Why is it that when you have the view that things exist and the view that things do not exist, it follows that you have views of permanence and of annihilation? As Nāgārjuna's *Fundamental Treatise* says:

Whatever exists intrinsically is permanent
Since it does not become nonexistent.
If you say that an intrinsically existent thing that arose
  before
Is now nonexistent, that entails an extreme of annihilation.

Since intrinsic existence is not overcome, something that is said to be intrinsically existent would never become nonexistent; thus the assertion that something is intrinsically existent entails a view of permanence. Also, a view of annihilation is entailed by the assertion that there was intrinsic nature in things at an earlier time, but it has now been destroyed and no longer exists.

Candrakīrti calls the assertion of intrinsic existence a view of permanence, and says that if you assert the later destruction of what was formerly intrinsically existent, such is a view of nihilism. He does not say this of mere existence and mere disintegration.

Also *Buddhapālita's Commentary on the "Fundamental Treatise"* clearly explains that when Nāgārjuna says, "Whatever exists intrinsically is permanent," and so forth, he is indicating the type of permanence and the type of annihilation he meant when he explained that to say "exists" or to say "does not exist" is to have views of permanence or annihilation.[305]

In brief, if you claim that the emptiness which is the absence of intrinsic existence is not the sublime emptiness taught by the Buddha and you refute it, then you will be reborn in a miserable realm due to having abandoned the true teaching, the perfection of wisdom. [601] If you take an interest in the absence of intrinsic existence, but think, "If there is no intrinsic existence, what is there?" and then claim that all phenomena do not exist at all, you will still fall into the chasm of a view of annihilation. Similarly, [Nāgārjuna's *Fundamental Treatise*] says:[306]

> If they view emptiness in the wrong way,
> Those of limited intelligence will be ruined.

Commenting on this, Candrakīrti's *Clear Words* says:[307]

> If, on the one hand, you were to think, "All is empty, that is, does not exist," then you would be viewing emptiness in the wrong way. In this vein [Nāgārjuna's *Precious Garland*] says:
>
> > If this teaching is misunderstood
> > It ruins the unwise, for
> > They sink into the filth
> > Of nihilistic views.
>
> On the other hand, suppose that you do not deny all phenomena, but then say, "We have seen these things; how could they be empty? Therefore, an absence of intrinsic existence is not what emptiness means." In that case, you have definitely abandoned emptiness. After you have abandoned emptiness in this way, you will definitely be reborn in a miserable realm due to this action of depriving yourself of the true teaching. As Nāgārjuna's *Precious Garland* says:[308]

> Further, if they misunderstand this,
> Fools who take pride in their supposed wisdom
> Will destroy themselves by abandoning it
> And fall head-first to the Unrelenting Hell.

Qualm: If we had claimed that there were real things, and then later viewed them as nonexistent, then we would have a view of annihilation. However, we do not accept their existence from the outset. What is annihilated so as to make this a view of annihilation? For [Nāgārjuna's *Fundamental Treatise*] says:[309]

> If you say that what arose before
> Is now nonexistent, that entails annihilation.

Thus Nāgārjuna says that such is a view of annihilation. Also, Candrakīrti's *Clear Words* says:[310]

> Yogis do not fall to the two extremes if they know that conventional truths—which are produced only by ignorance—lack intrinsic existence, and then know that the emptiness of those has the character of the ultimate. [602] They think, "How could something which has now become nonexistent have existed then?" Since they do not regard earlier things as having had intrinsic nature, they do not think that such later become nonexistent.

Reply: This is not reasonable. Your supposition is that in order to have a view of annihilation, one must assert the earlier existence of whatever thing is annihilated later. In that case, it would absurdly follow that even the Lokāyata proponents of materialism[311] would not have a view of annihilation. For it is not their claim that past and future lives, karma and its effects, etc. once existed and later became nonexistent; they do not accept such as having existed in the first place. Therefore, when Nāgārjuna said, "If you say that what arose before is now nonexistent, that entails annihilation," he meant that proponents of existence who assert that things have an essential or intrinsic nature will unquestionably have views of permanence or annihilation. For, if they claim that this intrinsic nature never changes, then they will have a view of permanence; if they claim that it once existed and was later destroyed, then they will have a view of annihilation. Mādhyamikas do not accept the existence of even a particle of essential or intrinsic nature; this fact proves that they lack one type of view of annihilation, the type in which it is held that an intrinsic nature that once existed is later destroyed. It does not prove that they have eliminated *all* views of annihilation.

In a different way, Mādhyamikas are also unlike those who have the other type of view of annihilation, a view in which it is held that karma and its effects do not exist. This is set forth at length in Candrakīrti's *Clear Words*, as follows. Mādhyamikas and nihilists have different theses since those who have a view of annihilation hold that karma and its effects, as well as other worlds beyond this lifetime, do not exist, whereas Mādhyamikas hold that such things lack intrinsic existence. Mādhyamikas propound that things such as karma and its effects lack intrinsic existence by reason of their being dependent-arisings; nihilists do not assert that karma and its effects are dependent-arisings, so they do not use dependent-arising as a reason in support of their thesis. [603] Instead, to support their claim that karma and its effects are nonexistent, the reason they give is that the living beings who are here now were not seen arriving in this life from a former one, and are not seen leaving it for a future one. Hence there is an enormous difference between nihilists and Mādhyamikas in their reasons. Candrakīrti's *Clear Words* says:[312]

> Some say that Mādhyamikas are no different from nihilists. Why? Because Mādhyamikas propound that virtuous and nonvirtuous actions, agents, and effects, as well as all the worlds of this and other lifetimes are empty of intrinsic existence, while nihilists also propound that those are nonexistent. Hence they argue that Mādhyamikas do not differ from nihilists.
>
> Such is not the case, for Mādhyamikas propound dependent-arising and propound that because of being dependent-arisings, everything—this world, other worlds, and so forth—lacks intrinsic existence. The nihilists' understanding that things such as other worlds beyond this lifetime are not real is not reached via knowledge that those things are empty of intrinsic existence due to being dependent-arisings. What do they claim? They regard the aspects of the things in this world as naturally existent;[313] they do not see them come to this world from another or go to another world from this one, so they deny the existence of other things [e.g., former and future lives] which are in fact like the things seen in this world.

Qualm: Even though Mādhyamikas and nihilists cite different reasons, their views of the absence of intrinsic existence are the same because they are alike in realizing that karma and its effects and the worlds of past and future lifetimes lack essential or intrinsic existence.

Reply: Even in this they differ. For nihilists hold that the absence of intrinsic existence is utter nonexistence, and thus they do not accept karma, etc. as either of the two truths. Mādhyamikas, however, accept conventionally the existence of such things as karma and its effects. Candrakīrti's *Clear Words* says:[314] **[604]**

> *Qualm:* Even so, their views are similar in one way because nihilists consider the absence of an essence in things to be nonexistence.
>
> *Reply:* This is not so. They are not similar because Mādhyamikas assert that things without essence exist conventionally; these nihilists do not assert them at all.

This shows that those who claim to be Mādhyamikas, yet do not accept the existence of karma and its effects even conventionally, in fact have a view similar to that of the Lokāyata nihilists.

What reason does the master Candrakīrti give for the difference between Mādhyamikas and nihilists? He does not say, "Because they have assertions, whereas we do not." He does not say, "They assert that those are nonexistent, whereas we do not say that they are nonexistent (*med pa*); rather, we hold that they are not existent (*yod pa ma yin*)."[315] Instead, he says that Mādhyamikas propound that karma and such lack intrinsic existence; he says that Mādhyamikas cite dependent-arising as the reason for that lack of intrinsic existence; he says that Mādhyamikas do accept those teachings on karma and such in conventional terms.

Qualm: You propose that things such as karma and its effects lack essential or intrinsic existence. Those nihilists also assert that such things lack intrinsic existence inasmuch as they assert that they are nonexistent. Therefore they agree with the Mādhyamikas about the lack of intrinsic existence.

Reply: Again, there is a very great difference. For example, suppose someone who does not know who stole some jewels deceptively states, "That person committed the robbery." Another person—who saw the thief steal the jewels—also says, "That person committed the robbery." As it happens, they identify the same thief who has actually stolen the jewels. Yet they are not alike, for one spoke deceptively and the other honestly. In this vein, Candrakīrti's *Clear Words* says:[316]

> *Objection:* Mādhyamikas and nihilists agree about real things.
>
> *Reply:* Even if they agree that real things do not exist, they are still not the same because the way that they know that is different.

For example, suppose someone does not really know that a certain person committed a robbery, but out of animosity toward that person dishonestly proclaims, "This person committed the robbery." **[605]** Another person makes the same accusation having actually seen that robbery. Even though there is no difference between those two with regard to the fact, still there is a difference in the two accusers, for of the one it is said, "That one speaks dishonestly," and of the other, "That one speaks honestly." A careful investigation of the first person will lead to disgrace and reproach, but such is not the case with the second.

Similarly, here also, when the understanding and the utterances of the Mādhyamikas, who accurately know the nature of things, are compared to those of nihilists, who do not accurately know the nature of things, what they know and say are not alike.

Some persons, in understanding the absence of intrinsic existence, think that reason refutes such things as karma and its effects; thus they conclude that cause and effect cannot be posited in their own system. Candrakīrti totally refutes the proposition that such persons, though wrong about the class of appearances, i.e., conventionalities, have gained an accurate view of the class of emptiness.

Therefore, do not take emptiness to mean being empty of the capacity to perform functions. Instead, you must have a way to posit the dependent-arising of causes and effects despite the absence of intrinsic existence. Candrakīrti's *Commentary on the "Four Hundred Stanzas"* says:[317]

> In that case, regarding any object,
>
> > When it is produced, it does not come;
> > Likewise, when it ceases, it does not go.
>
> It definitely does not intrinsically exist. If it does not intrinsically exist, then what is there? Dependent-arisings—entities caused by the afflicted and the pure—do exist.

This clearly answers the question, "If there is no intrinsic existence, then what does exist?"

The master Buddhapālita also gives an answer that clearly distinguishes existence from essential existence; *Buddhapālita's Commentary on the "Fundamental Treatise,"* commenting on the twentieth chapter of Nāgārjuna's text, says:[318]

> *Objection*: If time does not exist, and causes, effects, and collections of causes and conditions also do not exist, then what else could exist? **[606]** Therefore, the Madhyamaka position is simply a nihilistic argument.

Reply: It is not so. It is utterly impossible for time and such to exist essentially, as you imagine. However, they are established as dependent designations.

Thus he refutes this, saying that it is impossible for there to be essential existence as the essentialists claim. He also says that dependent-arisings exist: "They are established as dependent designations."

Thus, you will overcome countless wrong ideas if you distinguish intrinsic existence and the absence of intrinsic existence from existence and nonexistence. Moreover, you will not mistake the arguments refuting intrinsic existence for refutations of existence itself. Therefore, since the main answers that Mādhyamikas give to scholars who are essentialists proceed from this set of distinctions, I have given a bit of explanation.

12

RATIONAL ANALYSIS

(2')) Showing that the Madhyamaka critique does not eradicate conventional existence
(a")) You cannot eradicate conventional phenomena by refuting them through investigating whether they are capable of withstanding rational analysis

———— ⚬ ————

(2')) Showing that the Madhyamaka critique does not eradicate conventional existence

This has four parts:

1. You cannot eradicate conventional phenomena by refuting them through investigating whether they are capable of withstanding rational analysis
2. You cannot eradicate conventional phenomena by refuting them through investigating whether valid cognition establishes them (Chapters 13-14)
3. You cannot eradicate conventional phenomena by refuting them through investigating whether they are produced in one of four alternative ways [from self, other, both, or neither] (Chapter 15)
4. A refutation of all four parts of the tetralemma—things exist, things do not exist, and so forth—is not a legitimate critique of conventional phenomena (Chapter 15)

(a")) You cannot eradicate conventional phenomena by refuting them through investigating whether they are capable of withstanding rational analysis

A proper analysis of whether these phenomena—forms and such—exist, or are produced, in an objective sense is what we call "a line of reasoning that analyzes reality," or "a line of reasoning that analyzes the final status of being." Since we Mādhyamikas do not assert that the production of forms and such can withstand analysis by such reasoning, our position avoids the fallacy that there are truly existent things.

Question: If these things cannot withstand rational analysis, then how is it possible for something to exist when reason has refuted it?

Reply: You are mistakenly conflating the inability to withstand rational analysis with invalidation by reason. [607] Many who have made this error claim that production and such exist even though rational analysis of reality refutes them. This is reckless chatter, so we do not agree.

To ask whether something can withstand rational analysis is to ask whether it is found by a line of reasoning that analyzes reality. Candrakīrti's *Commentary on the "Four Hundred Stanzas"* says:[319]

> ...because our analysis is intent upon seeking intrinsic nature.

So this is seeking to discover whether forms and so forth have an intrinsic nature that is produced, ceases, and so forth. Thus, the analysis searches to see whether forms and so forth have production and cessation that exist essentially; it is not that this line of reasoning searches for *mere* production and cessation. Therefore, this line of reasoning is said to "analyze reality" because it analyzes whether production, cessation, and so forth are established in reality.[320]

When such a line of reasoning analyzes or searches for production and so forth, it does not find a trace of them; they are "unable to withstand analysis." However, the fact that this line of reasoning does not find them does not entail that it refutes them. Rather, reason refutes something that—if it did exist—would have to be established by reason, but which reason does not establish. Conventional consciousnesses establish the production and cessation of forms and such; although forms and such exist, reasoning consciousnesses do not establish them. Therefore, while reason does not find forms and such, how could it refute them? For example, a visual consciousness does not find sounds, but this does not refute them. This is similar.

Therefore, if production, cessation, and so forth existed essentially, i.e., were established in reality, then reason would have to find them because it accurately analyzes whether forms and such have essentially existent production and cessation. Since such analysis does not find production and so forth, it refutes production, cessation, and so forth that exist essentially, that is, in reality. For if they existed essentially, that analysis would have to find them, but it does not. [608] For example, when a searcher who is certain to find a pot in the east if it is there searches in the east for a pot and does not find it, this refutes the existence of a pot in the east. Yet how could it refute the mere existence of a pot? Similarly, Madhyamaka analysis is certain to find essentially existent production if such exists; when it does not find production, this constitutes a refutation of intrinsically or essentially existent production. How could it refute mere production? In this vein, Candrakīrti's *Commentary on the "Four Hundred Stanzas"* is clear:[321]

> Therefore, when reason analyzes in this way, there is no essential nature that exists in the sensory faculties, objects, or consciousnesses; hence, they have no essential existence. If they essentially existed, then under analysis by reason their status as essentially existent would be seen even more clearly, but it is not. Therefore, they are established as "empty of intrinsic nature."

Candrakīrti repeatedly allows that these conventionalities, such as forms and sounds, do exist. However, they are not in the least established by reasoning that analyzes reality, that is, analyzes whether they have intrinsic nature. Thus the scrutiny of reason is not applied to them. Also, Candrakīrti often says that it is those who are incompetent at positing conventionalities who claim that conventionalities are destroyed when, upon rational analysis, reason does not find them.

If reasoning that analyzes whether they have intrinsic nature could refute them, then you would have to apply intense rational scrutiny to these conventionalities, i.e., forms, feelings, and so forth. However, the texts of this master completely refute such efforts. Therefore, it is those who have wandered very far from the middle way who claim that something is invalidated when it is not found by reasoning that analyzes whether it has intrinsic nature.

Similarly, the meditative equipoise of a noble being does not see the production and cessation of forms and so forth, but how could it see production, cessation, and so forth as nonexistent? [609] Also, reasoning that analyzes whether things have intrinsic nature does not find production and so forth, but it does not consider production, cessation, and so forth to be nonexistent.

Therefore, even some earlier scholars,[322] not to mention those today, seem to have erred by not differentiating, and instead considering identical, the following pairs: (1) something unable to withstand rational analysis *vs.* something invalidated by reason; (2) the non-perception of production and cessation by a noble being's wisdom of meditative equipoise *vs.* the perception of production and cessation as nonexistent by a noble being's wisdom of meditative equipoise; and (3) the non-discovery of production and cessation by a reasoning consciousness which analyzes whether they intrinsically exist *vs.* the discovery that production and cessation are nonexistent. Therefore, the intelligent should analyze this in detail and make careful distinctions!

In saying this, we do not assert that conventional consciousness is more powerful than knowledge of the ultimate; nor do we assert that conventional consciousness contradicts knowledge of the ultimate. However, you claim that rational analysis of reality refutes conventional forms, feelings, and so forth when it analyzes them and does not find them. It does not refute them. In fact, mundane knowledge will contradict any attempt to refute conventional phenomena. Candrakīrti's *Commentary on the "Middle Way"* says:[323]

> If you think that the world does not contradict you,
> Then refute something that is based right in the world.
> You and the world can argue about it
> And afterwards I will follow the stronger party.

Candrakīrti's *Explanation of the "Middle Way" Commentary* says:[324]

> We have endured great hardship in order to overturn worldly conventionalities. Please, you eliminate worldly conventionalities. If the world does not contradict you, then we will join you. However, the world does contradict you. [610]

The statement, "We have endured great hardship in order to overturn worldly conventionalities," refers to striving at the path in order to purify mistaken subjects, such as visual consciousnesses, and mistaken appearances of objects, such as forms. Hence we do not assert that these are objects that are refuted by reason. Rather, we consider them objects that are negated by the cultivation of the path.

The statement, "Please, you eliminate worldly conventionalities," answers those Cittamātrins who draw the following parallel: "If you Mādhyamikas refute substantially existent dependent entities, then we will use reason to refute your conventionalities." Candrakīrti replies, "We can refute the intrinsic existence of dependent entities; if you can use reason to give a similar refutation of conventionalities, then we will go along with you." He means that if reason *could* refute conventionalities, we would want that, as it would render unnecessary the hardships involved in cultivating the path in order to overcome them. Therefore, this passage shows that reason does not refute conventionalities.

Since it does not refute them, Candrakīrti says that what is commonly known in the world contradicts any attempt to refute them. Hence, conventional knowledge contradicts any apparently reasonable argument to that effect. We therefore assert that conventional knowledge is more powerful than those arguments. Consequently, when essentialists use rational analysis to refute conventional phenomena such as external objects, reason does not find those conventional phenomena, but it does not contradict them.

Objection: When we say that we do not refute forms and so forth in conventional terms, we mean that they are not refuted in the eyes of ordinary worldly people, such as shepherds. However, rational analysis of reality does refute them.

Reply: Your position is quite unacceptable. Reflective individuals may wonder whether rational analysis of reality refutes these, yet they never doubt that such things remain unrefuted for those whose minds have not been affected by tenets. Moreover, if rational analysis of reality did refute them, then that refutation would have to be done in conventional terms.[325]

The master Candrakīrti also clearly states that rational analysis of reality does not refute all forms of production. [611] His *Commentary on the "Four Hundred Stanzas"* says:[326]

> *Incorrect position*: Āryadeva means that compounded phenomena lack production because this analysis refutes all forms of production.
>
> *Reply:* In that case, the production of compounded phenomena would not be like a magician's illusion. Rather, we would make it understood using examples such as the son of a barren woman. Wary of the absurd implication that dependent-arisings would not exist, we avoid such comparisons. Instead, we compare the production of things to a magician's illusion and so forth, examples that do not contradict dependent-arising.

The phrase "this analysis" refers to rational analysis of reality. "Refutes all forms of production" means refuting all production of any kind without adding any qualification to the object to be negated. The passage referring to the barren woman should be understood as follows: If reason refuted all production, then production—like the son of a barren woman, the horns of a hare, and such—would be a non-thing, empty of all function. In that case, there would be the fallacy that dependent-arisings would not exist. We are wary of that. Hence we do not say that it is like the non-production of something devoid of the capacity to perform functions, such as the son of a barren woman. We say that production is like a magician's illusion and so forth. Therefore, we refute truly existent or intrinsically existent production.

Also, Candrakīrti's *Commentary on the "Four Hundred Stanzas"* says:[327]

> *Objection*: If eyes and such do not exist, then how can the sensory faculties of organs such as the eye be considered things that result from karma?
>
> *Reply*: Would we refute that it is the nature of these to result from karma?
>
> *Objection*: Since you are demonstrating the refutation of eyes and such, how could you not refute that?
>
> *Reply*: Because our analysis is intent upon seeking intrinsic nature. We refute here that things exist essentially; we do not refute that eyes and such are products and are dependently arisen results of karma. [612] Therefore, they exist. Hence, when eyes and such are explained only as results of karma, they do exist.

Hence Candrakīrti very clearly states exactly what reason does and does not refute. Therefore, once he makes these distinctions in one passage, they must be applied, even when they are not stated, in all similar passages throughout the text.

Therefore, reason refutes essential existence—objective existence found on the side of the thing itself; it does not refute mere existence. Since he says that reason is intent on seeking intrinsic nature, reason seeks to discover whether something intrinsically exists. Therefore, this means that a refutation by such analysis is a refutation of intrinsic existence. Hence, distinguish these two.[328]

Candrakīrti does not refute that such instances are results of karma; moreover, he says that Mādhyamikas must assert this. The continuation of that passage says: Therefore, the learned do not subject worldly objects to the analysis just explained, i.e., the analysis congruent with the perception of reality. Instead, they accept that worldly objects are simply the inconceivable results of karma. They accept the whole world as though it were an emanation projected by another emanation.

So when you present the two truths, does the line of reasoning that establishes the ultimate contradict the presentation of the conventional? If it does, then your presentation of the two truths contradicts itself. In that case, how can you have perfected the skill of positing the two truths? If, on the other hand, there is no trace of internal contradiction in your presentation of the two truths, then it is a contradiction to claim that the line of reasoning that establishes the ultimate refutes the presentation of conventionalities. Candrakīrti's *Clear Words* also says:[329]

> Unskilled in ultimate and conventional truths, you sometimes apply analytical standards inappropriately and destroy the conventional. [613] Because we are skilled in positing conventional truths, we stay with the world's position, and we use its conventional standards to overturn the standards that you set so as to eliminate the category of conventionalities. Like the elders of the world, we drive out only you who deviate from the traditional standards of the world; we do not drive out conventionalities.

Thus he says that he refutes only proponents of tenets that deviate from conventionalities; he does not refute conventionalities. He also says that it is those who are unskilled in positing the two truths who destroy conventionalities by using analysis, i.e., rational analysis of reality. Thus, this master did not at all intend to use reason to refute conventional forms and such.

In brief, while one person may try to find contradictions in another person's presentation of the two truths, I hold that there is no one from any Indian Buddhist tenet system, Madhyamaka or otherwise, who says, "In my own presentation of the two truths, reasoning directed at the ultimate eradicates conventional objects."

13

VALID ESTABLISHMENT

(b″)) You cannot eradicate conventional phenomena by refuting them through investigating whether valid cognition establishes them

———— ·❧· ————

(b″)) You cannot eradicate conventional phenomena by refuting them through investigating whether valid cognition establishes them

As to assertions about forms and such, we do not hold that valid cognition does not establish them; valid cognition does establish them.

Qualm: Then how can Candrakīrti's *Commentary on the "Middle Way"* be correct when it says, "The world is not valid in any way"?[330]

Reply: That passage refutes the notion that the world's visual consciousnesses and such are valid with regard to reality. It does not refute their validity regarding all objects. In this vein, Candrakīrti's *Explanation of the "Middle Way" Commentary* says:[331]

Accordingly, only noble beings are authorities on the contemplation of reality; those who are not noble beings are not. [614] Those who are not noble beings would be authorities on reality if our acceptance of the world's critique meant that we accept the validity of the world's perception of our analysis of reality. [The *Commentary on the "Middle Way"* says]:

If the world were an authority, it would see reality.
Then what need would there be for those others called noble beings?

What would the noble path accomplish?
It is not right that fools should be authorities.

In the commentary following that [*Explanation of the "Middle Way"
Commentary*], Candrakīrti says:[332]

Because mere visual consciousness and such would ascertain reality, it would be fruitless to work at ethics or to study, reflect, and
meditate in order to understand the noble path. However, this is
not the case. Therefore [the *Commentary on the "Middle Way"* says]:

Because the world is not valid in any way,
The world has no critique in the context of reality.

Also Candrakīrti's *Commentary on [Nāgārjuna's] "Sixty Stanzas of
Reasoning"* (*Yukti-ṣaṣṭikā-vṛtti*) says:[333]

To view those forms and such as simply existing is not to see reality. In order to establish this, the Bhagavan said, "The eye, ear,
and nose consciousnesses are not valid cognitions."

Since Candrakīrti cites such scripture, it is extremely clear that what
he refutes is that visual consciousnesses and such are valid with
regard to a special object—reality—and not that they are valid with
regard to other objects.

If it is not taken in this way, his statements would be inconsistent. Suppose Candrakīrti meant, "If visual consciousnesses and
such were valid regarding conventional objects such as forms and
sounds, then it would absurdly follow that there is no need to strive
at the noble path in order to perceive reality." This would be as
senseless as saying that if visual consciousness is aware of form, it
follows that the ear is not needed to hear sounds. On the other hand,
suppose he meant, "If the visual consciousness were valid with
regard to forms, then it would absurdly follow that it is pointless
to strive at the noble path in order to perceive things such as forms
and sounds." We completely agree with this, so what unwanted
absurdity does it demonstrate?

Qualm: Candrakīrti's *Commentary on the "Four Hundred Stanzas"*
says:[334]

It is quite inconsistent to call sensory consciousness "perception"
and also to consider it valid with regard to other things. As the
world sees it, a valid cognition is simply a non-deceptive consciousness; [615] however, the Bhagavan said that even consciousness, because it is composite, has a false and deceptive quality and
is like a magician's illusion. That which has a false and deceptive
quality and is like a magician's illusion is not non-deceptive because

it exists in one way but appears in another. It is not right to designate such as a valid cognition because it would then absurdly follow that all consciousnesses would be valid cognitions.

How do you interpret this general refutation of the position that visual consciousnesses and such are valid cognitions?

Reply: Unlike the passage, "Eye, ear, and nose are not valid," this passage has been a source of grave doubt. Therefore, I will explain it in detail.

This refutation of the position that the visual consciousnesses and such are both perceptions and valid cognitions is a refutation of the assertions of the logicians. Therefore, let us start by considering what they assert. Candrakīrti's *Commentary on the "Four Hundred Stanzas"* says:[335]

> Because these logicians are utterly unpracticed in the sensibilities of the world, you must train them from the very beginning, like young children. Hence, in order to teach them, you question them closely, asking, "What is a perception in your system?" They answer, "A consciousness is a perception." "What sort of consciousness?" "One that is free from conceptuality." "What is this conceptuality?" "It is the fluctuation of the discrimination that is involved in the superimposition of names and types to objects. Because they are free from that, the five sensory consciousnesses engage only the inexpressible intrinsic character of their objects. They are therefore called 'perceptions'."

Hence the logicians hold that a perception is a consciousness that is free from conceptuality and non-mistaken. It is non-mistaken in that it apprehends the intrinsic character of the object just as it is. [616] Thus, since all five sensory perceptions comprehend the intrinsic character of their objects, the intrinsic characteristics of forms, sounds, and so forth are the objects comprehended by those five perceptions. Therefore, it is in relation to the intrinsic character of these five objects that they consider such perceptions to be valid.

As we will explain,[336] the master Candrakīrti does not accept even conventionally that anything exists essentially or by way of its intrinsic character. Thus, how could he accept this claim that the sensory consciousnesses are valid with regard to the intrinsic character of their objects? Therefore, this refutation of the claim that sensory consciousnesses are valid is a refutation of the view that they are valid with regard to the intrinsic character of the five objects.

This refutation is made by way of the Bhagavan's statement that consciousness is false and deceptive. The statement that it is deceptive refutes its being non-deceptive, and this in turn refutes its validity because "that which is non-deceptive" is the definition of "valid cognition." In what sense is it deceptive? As Candrakīrti puts it, "it exists in one way but appears in another." This means that the five objects—forms, sounds, and so forth—are not established by way of their intrinsic character, but appear to the sensory consciousnesses as though they were. Therefore, those sensory consciousnesses are not valid with regard to the intrinsic character of their objects.

In brief, what Candrakīrti intended in this passage is that the sensory consciousnesses are not valid with regard to the intrinsic character of the five objects because they are deceived in relation to the appearance of intrinsic character in the five objects. This is because those five objects are empty of intrinsic character, yet appear to have it. For example, it is like a consciousness that perceives two moons.

On this point, essentialists claim that if forms, sounds, and so forth did not exist intrinsically—that is, were not established by way of their intrinsic character—they would be non-things, devoid of all capacity to perform functions. They therefore assert that if the sensory consciousnesses are not valid perceptual cognitions of the intrinsic character of the five objects, then there can be no valid cognition of the five objects; if the sensory consciousnesses are valid cognitions of the five objects, then they will be valid cognitions of the intrinsic character of those objects.

According to the master Candrakīrti, if something were established by way of its intrinsic character, or essence, it would be something true. [617] Hence a valid cognition that posited such a truly existent object would have to be valid regarding the object's intrinsic character. However, because objects are false, the valid cognition that posits them does not have to be valid regarding their intrinsic character. For, Candrakīrti's *Commentary on the "Four Hundred Stanzas"* says:[337]

> It is not reasonable that worldly perception should cancel perception of reality, because worldly perception is valid only for the world, and because the objects it observes have a false and deceptive quality.

Therefore, since Candrakīrti is refuting the logician's position that sensory consciousnesses are valid regarding the intrinsic character of objects, he need not refute the position that they are simply valid cognitions.

Consequently, Candrakīrti is *not* giving a general refutation of the position that there are valid cognitions among conventional consciousnesses. If he were, then it would not be reasonable for him to say, "As the world sees it, a valid cognition is simply a non-deceptive consciousness,"[338] because he would have refuted the validity of every sort of conventional consciousness. Also, this would contradict Candrakīrti's *Clear Words,* where he presents direct, inferential, scriptural, and analogical valid cognitions, saying, "We therefore posit that the world knows objects with four valid cognitions."[339]

Candrakīrti refutes essentially existent valid cognitions and objects of comprehension; he does not refute valid cognitions and objects of comprehension that are contingently posited dependent-arisings. That same text [the *Clear Words*] says:[340]

> Those are established through mutual dependence. When valid cognitions exist, then there are things that are the objects of comprehension. When there are things that are objects of comprehension, then there are valid cognitions. However, neither valid cognitions nor objects of comprehension exist essentially.

Therefore, if a sensory consciousness is unimpaired—that is, no eye disease or other internal or external cause of error is affecting it—then it is accurate in conventional terms. It is mistaken in terms of appearance because, under the influence of ignorance, it apprehends its object as though it were intrinsically existent—which it is not. Yet this does not contradict its conventional accuracy. [618] Candrakīrti's *Commentary on the "Middle Way"* says:[341]

> Also, perceivers of falsities are of two types:
> Those with clear sensory faculties and those with impaired
> sensory faculties.
> A consciousness with an impaired sensory faculty
> Is considered wrong in relation to a consciousness with a good
> sensory faculty.
> Those objects known by the world
> And apprehended with the six unimpaired sensory faculties
> Are true for the world. The rest
> Are posited as unreal for the world.

Thus conventional consciousnesses and their objects are of two types: accurate in relation to conventional consciousness and inaccurate in relation to conventional consciousness.

With regard to internal conditions that impair the sensory faculties, Candrakīrti's *Explanation of the "Middle Way" Commentary* says:[342]

Eye disease, jaundice, and so forth, as well as eating datura[343] and so forth, are internal conditions that impair the sensory faculties.

With regard to external conditions that impair the sensory faculties, that same text says:[344]

External conditions that impair the sensory faculties include sesame oil, water, mirrors, sounds spoken from within caves and such, as well as sunlight at certain times and places. Even in the absence of internal conditions that impair the sensory faculties, these cause the apprehension of reflections, echoes, the water of a mirage, and so forth. You should understand that this is also the case with the medicine, mantra, and such used by conjurers and so forth. As for what impairs the mental sensory faculty, there are those just mentioned as well as incorrect tenets, etc., and false inference.

Thus he says that bad tenets and false reasoning are conditions that degrade the mental consciousness. He says that conditions such as sleep also degrade the mental consciousnesses associated with dreams and so forth. [619] Therefore, you should not consider the impairment of being affected by ignorance as a cause of impairment in this context—even though the object apprehended by ignorance does not exist even conventionally, as will be explained below.

Qualm: If the five sensory consciousnesses that are unimpaired by causes of error other than ignorance are non-mistaken conventionally, then the intrinsic character that appears to them must exist conventionally. However, the master Candrakīrti does not assert such. Therefore, we must assert that the sensory consciousnesses are mistaken; in that case it is not feasible for those consciousnesses to be valid cognitions that posit things such as forms and sounds in conventional terms. Why? In conventional terms, they are mistaken with regard to forms.

Reply: On this point, the master Bhāvaviveka asserts that it is the nature of forms and such to exist conventionally by way of their intrinsic character. The Cittamātrins argue that imaginary constructs lack characteristic nature because it is not their nature to exist by way of intrinsic character. To refute them, Bhāvaviveka investigates the agents and objects involved in the process of imaginary construction. He says that if they assert that the terms and minds that construct entities and features lack intrinsic character conventionally, then they are inappropriately denying the existence of contingent entities. Therefore, it is clear that Bhāvaviveka asserts that contingent entities have intrinsic character conventionally. Along the same lines, Bhāvaviveka's *Lamp for [Nāgārjuna's] "Fundamental Treatise"* (*Prajñā-pradīpa-mūla-madhyamaka-vṛtti*) comments on the twenty-fifth chapter of Nāgārjuna's text as follows:[345]

> If you say that the very nature of a construct—the mental and verbal expression "form"—does not exist, then you are mistakenly denying things, for you are mistakenly denying mental and verbal expressions.

In his *Explanatory Commentary on [Bhāvaviveka's] "Lamp for the 'Fundamental Treatise'"* (*Prajñā-pradīpa-ṭīkā*), on this, the master Avalokitavrata says:[346]

> This statement by Bhāvaviveka indicates the following: As to the nature of the imaginary construct, the Yogācārins say that it has no nature inasmuch as it has no characteristic nature. In the case of entities and attributes such as "form," what is the nature that constructs mental expressions, i.e., conceptions, and verbal expressions, i.e., conventions? [620] If you say that there is no such nature because they have no characteristic nature, this is unsuitable, since you would be inappropriately denying even conventional existence in things that are contingent.

He says that if you assert that those contingent entities that are included among the imputing terms and minds lack characteristic nature even conventionally, then it is an inappropriate denial.

"Character" in the phrase "lack characteristic nature" refers to intrinsic character or intrinsic nature. Cittamātrins assert that imputations do not have such character, but that contingent entities do, and therefore exist intrinsically. Nonetheless, because contingent entities arise from other things, they have no self-produced nature and hence Cittamātrins hold that they lack nature in this sense. The Buddha explained it this way in the *Sūtra Unravelling the Intended Meaning*; he said that there was an ulterior meaning behind the statements in the Perfection of Wisdom sūtras which say that all phenomena lack nature.[347] In this regard, the master Kamalaśīla said in his *Illumination of the Middle Way*:[348]

> By indicating the intended meanings of the three types of naturelessness, that sūtra [the *Sūtra Unravelling the Intended Meaning*] teaches the middle way free from the two extremes. Consequently, the system it sets up is strictly definitive.

Kamalaśīla's argument is that [the *Sūtra Unravelling the Intended Meaning*] teaches the meaning of the middle way by showing that the ultimate nature that is superimposed upon contingent entities is an imaginary construct, and is thus nonexistent, while also teaching that contingent entities have intrinsic character conventionally—thus avoiding an inappropriate negation. Hence the master Kamalaśīla also asserts that objects have intrinsic character conventionally.

Candrakīrti's *Explanation of the "Middle Way" Commentary* says:[349]

> For example, a snake is an imaginary construct when conceived in relation to a rope, but is perfectly real when conceived in relation to an actual snake. Similarly, a nature is an imaginary construct when conceived with regard to contingent entities, which are dependently arisen fabrications. However, as the object of a buddha, it is considered perfectly real. Understand the presentation of the three natures in this way; then explain what the *Sūtra Unravelling the Intended Meaning* means. [621]

He states this as commentary on these lines from his *Commentary on the "Middle Way"*:[350]

> Any sūtra that explains something that is not reality,
> And sets forth the provisional, should be understood as such
>   and interpreted.

Thus, it is obvious that he considers the *Sūtra Unravelling the Intended Meaning's* presentation of the three natures to be provisional. In his own system, the imaginary refers to the intrinsic existence of the contingent; hence, Candrakīrti does not assert that contingent entities have intrinsic character or intrinsic nature even conventionally.

The Cittamātrins accept the nonexistence of characteristic nature only for imaginaries, but do not assert that with regard to the contingent and the perfectly real. Thus, they assert that these two have essential character, intrinsic nature. It appears that this assertion is based mainly on the *Sūtra Unravelling the Intended Meaning*. Because of this, they assert that the contingent and the perfectly real exist ultimately. The masters Buddhapālita and Candrakīrti assert that if something were to exist by way of its intrinsic character, then it would have to be truly existent; masters such as Bhāvaviveka assert that this alone does not imply that something ultimately exists.

Furthermore, the Cittamātrins say that individual, minute particles are not the objects of the sensory consciousnesses because they do not appear to them; an aggregation of many minute particles is also not an object of the sensory consciousnesses because it does not substantially exist. They say that this is like the appearance of two moons. In answering the first proposition, Bhāvaviveka's *Blaze of Reasons (Tarka-jvālā)* says:[351]

> If you are proving that a minute particle alone, not in a composite, is not an object of a sensory consciousness, then you are proving that which is already established.

As an answer to the latter position, he says:[352]

> Are you claiming that an aggregation of minute particles of one type in one place is not the cause of a sensory consciousness, giving as your reason, "because such aggregations do not substantially exist"? If you are, then I simply do not accept your reason. Why? It is as follows. Various minute particles of a single type coalesce and contribute to that aggregation, thus constituting the parts of an object. From this there arises a mind to which an image appears, the image of an aggregation of minute particles. [622] We hold that, like minute particles, pots and such are also substantially existent, for they are composites of minute particles of a single type.
>
> It is the nature of a minute particle to be an aggregation of eight substances, yet you explicitly assert that it is substantially existent. Likewise, therefore, pots and such—which have natures of being aggregations—are also substantially existent. A non-aggregate singularity does not exist.

Thus it appears that he asserts that each of the minute particles of a composite is a cause of a sensory consciousness and is substantially existent. Since he evidently asserts that each of these is the ultimate of minute particles, he implicitly accepts that partless particles are the perceptual condition for the arising of a sensory consciousness. Therefore, Bhāvaviveka asserts that sensory consciousnesses are non-mistaken if they are affected by neither the internal nor the external causes of error explained earlier.[353] At the conventional level, he agrees with the Sautrāntikas in his assertions about the perceptual condition for the arising of a consciousness.

Candrakīrti's *Explanation of the "Middle Way" Commentary* says:[354]

> Some say that the Mādhyamikas accept in conventional terms exactly what the Sautrāntikas advocate ultimately. You should understand that those who say this speak out of sheer ignorance of the reality explained in Nāgārjuna's *Fundamental Treatise*. Also, there are those who think that Mādhyamikas accept in conventional terms what the Vaibhāṣikas advocate ultimately. Those who think this understand nothing at all of the reality set forth in the

Fundamental Treatise. For supramundane teachings cannot be likened to worldly teachings in this manner. The learned should know that our system is unique.

Thus he does not accept even conventionally the partless subjects and objects that are posited by the distinctive tenets of these schools. Candrakīrti's *Commentary on the "Four Hundred Stanzas"* says:[355]

It is not right for Buddhist schools to assert substantially existent minute particles as do the Vaiśeṣikas.

Thus he says that he does not assert partless particles. [623]

Candrakīrti is referring to things such as partless particles when he says that the Mādhyamikas do not assert in conventional terms what the two schools, Vaibhāṣika and Sautrāntika, assert ultimately. He does not mean that Mādhyamikas reject, even conventionally, everything those two assert as true, for while Vaibhāṣikas and Sautrāntikas assert that things like forms and sounds are true, Mādhyamikas do accept the mere existence of these conventionally.

In the *Commentary on the "Four Hundred Stanzas,"*[356] Candrakīrti refutes the assertion that each minute particle within a collection of minute particles in a sensory faculty is a cause of a sensory consciousness. He argues that the sensory faculties are not established either as being just those minute particles or as being something other than them. Thus, the bases of the sensory consciousnesses are sensory faculties that are ascribed in dependence upon those minute particles. Likewise, in the case of objects, he says that the objects of sensory consciousnesses exist as constructs that are contingently constructed. He also asserts that the consciousness is designated as direct [in the sense of perceiving], but the object of consciousness is actually what is direct [that is, directly before consciousness]. Therefore, although the master Candrakīrti and the master Bhāvaviveka are alike in accepting external objects, they seem to differ in how they posit the sensory faculties and their objects.

Earlier, while refuting that the sensory consciousnesses are valid with regard to intrinsic character, Candrakīrti's *Commentary on the "Four Hundred Stanzas"* said that the object of a sensory consciousness is deceptive "because it exists in one way but appears in another."[357] Thus, things like forms and sounds appear to sensory consciousnesses as though they existed by way of their own intrinsic character, but the intrinsic character that appears to them does not exist even conventionally. Therefore, Candrakīrti asserts that these sensory consciousnesses are mistaken even conventionally.

Still, it is not impossible for sensory consciousnesses to be valid cognitions that posit objects such as forms, sounds, and so forth conventionally. The reason why those sensory consciousnesses are posited as mistaken is that there is no object that exists by way of intrinsic character such as appears to them. The nonexistence of such an object is established by a reasoning consciousness analyzing whether things exist intrinsically; it is not at all established by conventional valid cognition. Therefore, in terms of conventional consciousnesses, they are not mistaken.

As for consciousnesses that perceive things such as a double moon or a reflection, objects such as those which appear to them— two moons, a reflected face, and the like—do not exist; [624] this is established by conventional valid cognition itself without relying on a reasoning consciousness. Thus, it is appropriate that these wrong sensory consciousnesses and the five valid sensory consciousnesses be differentiated as incorrect conventional consciousnesses and correct conventional consciousnesses.

Qualm: We allow that it makes a difference whether a consciousness is known as mistaken in dependence upon reasoning consciousness or conventional valid cognition. However, just as the referent of a perception of a reflected image as a face does not exist, so also the referent of a perception of anything as having intrinsic character does not exist. Just as forms and such which are empty of intrinsic character do exist, so also a reflection that is empty of being a face exists. For this reason, one cannot differentiate those perceptions in terms of their accuracy even in relation to ordinary conventional awareness.

Reply: Indeed, something that exists by way of its intrinsic character and an object in a reflection that exists in accordance with its appearance as a face are alike in not existing conventionally. Also, forms and reflections are alike in existing conventionally. However, Candrakīrti's *Explanation of the "Middle Way" Commentary* says:[358]

> Some dependently arisen things—such as reflections and echoes— are false and appear to be false even to the ignorant. Some things— blue and other forms as well as minds, feelings, etc.—appear to be true. The final nature of things [that is, emptiness] does not appear in any way to those who are ignorant. Therefore, that nature [i.e., emptiness] and whatever is false even conventionally are not conventional truths.

He thus makes the distinction that blue and so forth are posited as conventional truths, while reflections and such are not. If someone were to challenge this distinction, how could we reply? This is what I think: Although forms and reflections are alike in appearing to conventional consciousnesses, even a worldly consciousness can know that reflections and such are false; thus, they are not posited as truths for the world, that is, for a conventional consciousness. [625] Blue and such are falsities, but a worldly consciousness cannot understand them as falsities; hence, Candrakīrti posits them as truths for the world, that is, for a conventional consciousness.

It is thus possible to distinguish objects as true and false in terms of conventional consciousness. It is likewise possible to distinguish subjects as accurate and inaccurate in terms of conventional consciousness.

Qualm: If a sensory consciousness is accurate in terms of conventional consciousness, this contradicts its being mistaken conventionally.

Reply: There is the "conventional" in terms of which the sensory consciousnesses are mistaken when we say that they are mistaken conventionally. Then again, there is the "conventional" consciousness in relation to which those unimpaired sensory consciousnesses are posited as accurate. If these two were the same, then there would be a contradiction. However, as these two usages of "conventional" are distinct, what contradiction is there?

How are they distinct? Reason refutes the essential or intrinsic existence of forms and such. It cannot do this ultimately [because nothing can be done ultimately in this system which refutes ultimate existence], so it must do it conventionally. For that kind of conventional consciousness, the sensory consciousnesses are mistaken. Apart from that, the sensory consciousnesses are not mistaken as seen by ordinary conventional consciousnesses; thus there is no contradiction. For example, it is like the worldly convention, "Some are here; some are not here." The term "some" is the same, but no one supposes that the some who are here and the some who are not here are the same. So also, the "non-mistaken" quality of the sensory consciousnesses is posited in terms of an ordinary worldly consciousness; Mādhyamikas do not assert them to be non-mistaken. It is like the statement by Candrakīrti, "Those... are true for the world."[359]

Therefore, the Mādhyamikas posit the sensory consciousnesses as mistaken. Nonetheless, it is not a contradiction that these sensory consciousnesses posit their false objects. Rather, if a true object were posited, it would be contradictory for us to claim that it was posited by a mistaken subject. Conventionally, we assert that all phenomena are like a magician's illusion and are, therefore, false in conventional terms. Still, it is not contradictory to posit them as conventional truths (*kun rdzob bden pa, saṃvṛti-satya*). [Candrakīrti's *Commentary on the "Middle Way"*] says,[360] "Because ignorance obscures the nature of phenomena, we call it the concealer (*kun rdzob, saṃvṛti*)." Hence there is no contradiction in something being true for the concealer (*kun rdzob, saṃvṛti*), that is, ignorance, and false for the conventional consciousness (*kun rdzob, saṃvṛti*) with which we refute the essential existence in phenomena. [**626**]

The statement [in Candrakīrti's *Explanation of the "Middle Way" Commentary*] "whatever is false even conventionally is not a conventional truth"[361] refers to a conventional valid cognition which realizes that things like a reflection's being an actual face are false. It cannot refer simply to forms and such being false in conventional terms.

14

CONVENTIONAL EXISTENCE

In this way, we Mādhyamikas posit conventionally, within our own system, many presentations of cyclic existence and nirvāṇa; we also refute the conventional existence of constructs that are put forward as unique assertions by essentialists. As this is extremely difficult, accurate knowledge of the presentation of the two truths scarcely exists.

Misunderstanding may arise as follows. When we refute the conventional existence of the constructs that the essentialists assert, we must carry out the refutation using rational analysis. Moreover, in taking their own stance on matters such as the existence of conventional production and cessation, reflective individuals will decide what to assert according to what can be proven, and proof is based in a sequence of reasoning. Taking this into consideration, some feel that under rational analysis the proposed conventions of production, etc. and the imaginary constructs of essentialists have the same status as either contradicted or not contradicted by reason. Thus, if they deny the conventional existence of constructs such as a divine creator or a primal essence,[362] then they must also deny the conventional existence of forms and such; if they hold that forms do exist conventionally, then they would also have to accept the existence of a divine creator. They see those two as equivalent. They say that it is inappropriate for their own system to identify or to assert of any phenomenon, "This is such and such; this is not such and such." They presume that in this they have found the Madhyamaka reality. Further, in accordance with such understanding, they hold that stabilizing your mind without apprehending anything at all is cultivation of the genuine Madhyamaka view. [627] There are a great many who assert this.

It is evident that such talk does not please the learned. For, having failed to identify the object negated by reason as explained above, those who say this use the arguments that refute intrinsic existence to destroy all presentations of conventionalities. Consequently, theirs is a highly inaccurate position; it treats the correct view and the wrong view as the same in the degree to which they are mistaken or non-mistaken. As a result, prolonged habituation to such a view does not bring you the least bit closer to the correct view. In fact, it takes you farther away from it, for such a wrong view stands in stark contradiction to the path of dependent-arising, the path in which all of the teachings on the dependent-arisings of cyclic existence and nirvāṇa are tenable within our system. Therefore, Candrakīrti's *Commentary on the "Middle Way"* says:[363]

> The self as it is imagined by the non-Buddhist philosophers
> Who are disturbed by the sleep of ignorance,
> And things that are ascribed to mirages,
> Magicians' illusions, and so forth, do not exist even for the
>   world.

He says that what is imagined in the unique assertions of non-Buddhist philosophers—or, according to the earlier citation,[364] in the unique assertions of Buddhist essentialists—does not exist even conventionally in our Madhyamaka system. I will explain this point.

How does one determine whether something exists conventionally? We hold that something exists conventionally (1) if it is known to a conventional consciousness; (2) if no other conventional valid cognition contradicts its being as it is thus known; and (3) if reason that accurately analyzes reality—that is, analyzes whether something intrinsically exists—does not contradict it. We hold that what fails to meet those criteria does not exist.

In a sense, conventional consciousness operates in a non-inquisitive manner. It operates only within the context of how a given phenomenon appears to it, without analyzing, "Is this how the object actually exists, or does it just appear this way to my mind?" [628] It is called non-analytical consciousness, but it is not the case that it is utterly non-inquisitive. It operates within the context of how things appear, how they are known, to a worldly or conventional consciousness. It does not operate via analysis of how things actually exist. Therefore, it is called mundane knowledge. This kind of consciousness occurs in all persons, whether or not they have become involved in philosophical tenet systems. Thus, no matter whose mind-stream it occurs in, this is called "mundane knowledge" or "non-analytical consciousness."

Do not suppose that it exists only in the mind-streams of those worldly persons who are not involved in philosophical tenet systems. Those who are involved in such systems may often have minds that analyze, "Is conventional knowledge accurate?" or "Does this object exist this way in reality?" Still, how could *all* of their consciousnesses analyze how things actually exist? Therefore, if you want to understand what worldly knowledge is, you cannot ask only those worldly elders who hold no philosophical tenets. However, it is sufficient to consider how non-analytical minds operate in the mind-streams of the two parties in a debate. What these consciousnesses know is the perceptual or experiential basis for the construction of conventional language.

Ordinary people do not understand karma and its effects, the levels and paths, or such matters, but they hear about and experience them, thereby taking them as objects. As this is so, they appear even to ordinary consciousnesses that are not analyzing how things actually exist. We thus avoid the fallacy that these would not be things that the world knows.

Other conventional valid cognitions do not contradict that which exists conventionally. For example, a consciousness that does not analyze how things actually exist may think that a rope is a snake or that a mirage is water. However, conventional valid cognition does contradict the objects apprehended by such consciousnesses, so those objects do not exist even conventionally.

A reasoning consciousness that accurately analyzes whether something intrinsically exists does not contradict that which exists conventionally. [629] What is posited conventionally must be established by conventional valid cognition. In addition, reasoning consciousnesses that accurately analyze whether it intrinsically exists definitely must not contradict it in any way. Whatever such reasoning establishes as existing must exist essentially, so it is contradictory for such to be a conventional object. Because of this, it is wrong to confuse (1) not being contradicted by a reasoning consciousness and (2) being established by a reasoning consciousness. Such confusion is the basis for the misconception that the following two propositions stand equally, either both true or both false:

1. Pleasure and pain arise conventionally from virtue and nonvirtue.

2. Pleasure and pain arise from a divine creator and a primal essence.

This misconception is incorrect. The two propositions are equivalent to the extent that a line of reasoning that accurately analyzes whether things intrinsically exist will establish neither, but the two are not alike in all respects—one is contradicted by reason and the other is not.

A partless object and subject, a self, a primal essence, a divine creator—such things are imaginary constructs put forward in the unique assertions of Buddhist and non-Buddhist essentialists. When they posit such, they do so after rational analysis of whether such things essentially exist; they think that this sort of rational analysis will discover these things. Thus, because they assert that these things can withstand rational analysis, they have to accept that others outside of their schools can perform such rational analysis in order to discover whether these things intrinsically exist. When analyzed in this way, such things cannot withstand the pressure of inquiry by impeccable reasoning. Thus, when reason does not find them, they stand refuted—for if they did exist, such reasoning would have to find them.

We posit forms, sound, and such only as they are known to conventional consciousnesses that are not impaired by internal or external causes of error. [630] We do not assert them as part of a system in which an analysis of whether they are mere conventions or instead have objective existence will find that they are essentially or intrinsically existent. Thus, rational analysis of whether they intrinsically exist is irrelevant because we do not assert that these objects can withstand rational analysis. For example, if someone claims, "This is a sheep," it is inappropriate to analyze this claim by asking, "Is it a horse or is it an elephant?" This is similar.

There are things that have been "known to the world" from beginningless time, and yet do not exist even conventionally inasmuch as reason contradicts them. As examples, one can cite the essence that ignorance superimposes on things, the essentially existent "I" and "mine" conceived by the reifying view of the perishing aggregates, or the object of the conception that yesterday's mountain is today's mountain. Therefore, it is not the case that Mādhyamikas conventionally accept *everything* that is known to the world.

Some argue that in terms of conventional existence, forms, sounds, and so forth are not equivalent to the constructs of non-Buddhist philosophers for the reason that the former are known to all the world whereas the latter are known only to advocates of philosophical tenets. Those who hold this position have failed to make careful distinctions. Otherwise, they would see the many unwanted implications of their argument, such as: In conventional terms, forms and such could not be like illusions; rather, at the conventional level they would have to exist essentially. Also, Candrakīrti's *Commentary on [Nāgārjuna's] "Sixty Stanzas of Reasoning"* says:[365]

> The inaccurate are those that apprehend these things in cyclic existence only as blissful and so forth, because even conventionally these things do not have this nature. The accurate are those that apprehend these things as suffering and so forth because these things have such a nature conventionally.

He explains that although the permanence and so forth of the things of cyclic existence is "common knowledge" in the world, such conceptions are inaccurate even conventionally. [631] Also, even though their impermanence and so forth are not known to all the world, such conceptions are accurate.

Thus, a conceptual consciousness which apprehends the aggregates as impermanent and so forth is mistaken with regard to its appearing object, but we call it accurate, or non-mistaken, insofar as what it discerns is not contradicted by valid cognition. Sensory consciousnesses are mistaken with regard to their appearing objects, and we do not call them non-mistaken since they have no other factor that is non-mistaken. All sensory consciousnesses are alike in being mistaken with regard to what appears to them. However, sensory consciousnesses such as those to which a reflection appears are incorrect conventional consciousnesses; other, unimpaired sensory consciousnesses are correct conventional consciousnesses. This is based on whether there is an object compatible with what appears to the worldly perspective of that sensory consciousness.

Since the objects conceived by conceptual consciousnesses that apprehend the aggregates as permanent and so forth do not exist conventionally, reason can refute them. However, the referent objects of the conceptions of the aggregates as impermanent, etc. do exist conventionally; hence, reason cannot refute them. There is no ultimate or essential permanence and so forth; likewise, there is no ultimate or essential impermanence and so forth. Therefore the conceptions of those eight as existing in reality are identical in their degree of accuracy.[366] Thinking of this, the Buddha said [in the Perfection of Wisdom sūtras] that you are meditating on signs of true existence whether you meditate upon forms as permanent or impermanent, as blissful or painful, as having self or not having self.

Qualm: Ignorance superimposes intrinsic nature on things. For you to use reason to overcome its perspective, yet not to refute conventional objects—this is a contradiction, because Candrakīrti's *Commentary on the "Middle Way"* says:[367]

> The Sage said that because ignorance obscures the nature of
> phenomena,
> It is a "concealer" (*kun rdzob, saṃvṛti*).
> The fabrications that it perceives as true
> Are called "truths-for-a-concealer" (*kun rdzob bden pa, saṃvṛti-satya*).

Thus Candrakīrti says that forms, sounds, and so forth are posited as conventional truths (*kun rdzob bden pa, saṃvṛti-satya*) through the force of ignorance.

Reply: There is no fault here. [632] When we posit things such as forms and sounds as conventional truths, "truth" means that they are true through the force of a particular thought. Since that thought must be considered a conception of true existence, forms, sounds, and so forth are truths for the ignorance that superimposes intrinsic existence on them. Therefore, Candrakīrti refers to the two types of arhats who have eliminated afflicted ignorance and to bodhisattvas on the eighth level and above when he says, "They see these appearances as fabrications and not as true because they do not have an exaggerating conception of true existence."[368] For this reason, Candrakīrti says that for those who do not have the conception of true existence, forms and so forth are "mere conventionalities."

Therefore, the *truth* of forms, sounds, and such is posited in the perspective of ignorance, but ignorance does not posit things such as forms and sounds. For example, from the perspective of a wrong consciousness that apprehends a rope as a snake, the rope is a snake, but this wrong consciousness does not posit the rope. Since the minds that posit things like form and sound are the six unimpaired consciousnesses associated with the eye, etc., the objects they establish do exist conventionally, and thus reason does not refute them. However, even conventionally they do not exist as ignorance apprehends them. This is because ignorance superimposes an essential or intrinsic nature on things, and this intrinsic nature does not exist even conventionally. Therefore, reason conventionally refutes what ignorance apprehends; if it did not, then you could not prove that, at the conventional level, things are like illusions.

Ignorance superimposes an intrinsic nature on things; from this, attachment, hostility, and so forth arise, further superimposing features such as attractiveness or unattractiveness upon that intrinsic nature. Therefore, reason can also be used to eradicate the way that attachment and such apprehend objects. Candrakīrti's *Commentary on the "Four Hundred Stanzas"* says:[369]

> Attachment and so forth superimpose features such as attractiveness or unattractiveness only upon the intrinsic nature of things that ignorance has superimposed. **[633]** Therefore they do not work apart from ignorance; they depend upon ignorance. This is because ignorance is the main affliction.

These are the innate afflictions that have operated from beginningless time. However, because reason can eradicate the way that they apprehend things, their referent objects do not exist even conventionally. Therefore, objects of innate minds are of two types: those that reason can refute and those that reason cannot refute. The objects of the innate conventional valid cognitions that posit things like form and sound do exist conventionally; hence, reason does not refute them.

Accordingly, since we refute essential or intrinsic existence even conventionally in the system of the masters Buddhapālita and Candrakīrti, it seems to be very difficult to posit conventional objects. If you do not understand how to posit these well, without contradiction, then you will not be fully certain about the practices in the performance class.[370] It seems that this causes most individuals to fall into an overly negative view. Therefore, the intelligent should master this system's procedure for positing conventionalities. At this point, I am afraid I may have said more than enough about this; I will not elaborate any further.

15

Production Is Not Refuted

(c″)) You cannot eradicate conventional phenomena by refuting them through investigating whether they are produced in one of four alternative ways
(d″)) A refutation of all four parts of the tetralemma is not a legitimate critique of conventional phenomena

———————— ❧ ————————

(c″)) You cannot eradicate conventional phenomena by refuting them through investigating whether they are produced in one of four alternative ways

Objection: Madhyamaka refutes production from self, from another, and from both, as well as causeless production. Does this refute production? If you claim that it does, then since these four alternative types of production do not exist even conventionally in this Madhyamaka system, there is no need to add any qualifying phrase to the refutation of production. If you claim that it does not, then your refutation of the four alternatives of production fails to refute ultimate production.

Reply: We do not accept the former of these two positions, so I will explain the answer to the latter.

Those who assert ultimate production must assert that it withstands analysis by reasoning that analyzes reality. As this is so, they must use reason to analyze production so as to discover which it is among the four alternatives—production from self, other, and so forth. [634] Hence, those who assert ultimate production are definitely required to assert that it can be analytically fixed within one of the four alternatives.

Because we assert mere production—the arising of particular effects in dependence on particular causes and conditions—we do not assert real production. Since we do not assert real production, why would we use reasoning that analyzes reality to analyze production as to which it is—production from self, other, and so forth? For, we are not required to assert that production withstands rational analysis.

Moreover, dependent production itself refutes the four alternative types of production. As Candrakīrti's *Commentary on the "Middle Way"* says:[371]

> Because things arise dependently
> These mistaken conceptions cannot bear scrutiny.
> Therefore, the reasoning of dependent-arising
> Cuts all the entanglements of bad views.

Therefore, Candrakīrti asserts that dependent production refutes the four alternative types of production. However, you claim that if there is no production from among the four alternative types, then even mere production does not exist. Hence it seems that what you propose is the opposite of what Candrakīrti asserts. Candrakīrti's *Commentary on the "Middle Way"* also says:[372]

> Because things are not produced
> Causelessly, or from causes such as a divine creator,
> Or from self, other, or both self and other,
> They are produced dependently.

However, according to you, it would be contradictory for Candrakīrti to say this. Therefore, dependently produced dependent-arisings are free from the four extreme types of production. So do not ask, "That which is free from extremes—which of the four extremes is it?" Once again, these opponents go wrong by not distinguishing "no intrinsic production" from "no production."

Qualm: How do you explain the statement in Candrakīrti's *Commentary on the "Middle Way"*:[373]

> The argument which shows that production from self and
>   from other
> Are untenable in the context of ultimate reality
> Also shows that production is untenable even conventionally.

Reply: This means that if you assert substantially existent production, or production that exists by way of its intrinsic character, then those arguments refute it even conventionally. It does not at all indicate a refutation of mere production, for in the transition to that passage, [Candrakīrti's *Explanation of the "Middle Way" Commentary*] says:[374] [635]

> *Objection*: The things that serve as the causes of afflicted and pure phenomena must produce substantially existent entities.
> *Reply*: If this were so, then the very words of your statement would not remain. Why?

At this point Candrakīrti gives the verse cited above, "The argument which shows that production from self and from other...." Commenting on that verse, he says:[375]

> You must therefore admit, albeit unwillingly, that production by way of intrinsic character does not exist in terms of either of the two truths.

Thus, insofar as essentially existent production is ultimate production, when others assert it—even if they assert it conventionally— you must refute its propriety just as you refute ultimate production. Since this is the excellent assertion of the master Candrakīrti, you should not assert essentially existent production even conventionally. Candrakīrti's *Commentary on the "Middle Way"* says:[376]

> The self-generation of the son of a barren woman
> Exists neither in reality nor in the world.
> Similarly, all these things lack essential production
> Both for the world and in reality.

Some hold that the lack of intrinsic production—production's lack of intrinsic existence—must mean that production does not exist. They argue that dependent production and the absence of intrinsic production are contradictory. Candrakīrti says [in the *Commentary on the "Sixty Stanzas of Reasoning"*] that those who say this have no ears or heart. In saying that they have no ears, he means that they do not hear the qualification "intrinsic" when we refer to the lack of intrinsic production; they hold that we have said, "lack of production." In saying that they have no heart, he means that even if they hear it they have no comprehension of the meaning of the word "intrinsic." Nāgārjuna's *Sixty Stanzas of Reasoning* says:[377]

> The supreme knower of reality
> Said that dependent production is not production.

Commenting on that passage, Candrakīrti's *Commentary on the "Sixty Stanzas of Reasoning"* says:[378]

When you see dependent-arising, you do not perceive things as intrinsically existent. This is because the dependently produced is not intrinsically produced, like a reflection. [636]

Objection: Is it not the case that the dependently produced is only produced? How can you say that it is not produced? If you say that something is not produced, then you should not say that it is dependently produced. Therefore, because these are mutually exclusive, your position is incorrect.

Reply: Poor thing! With neither ears nor heart, you still argue. This puts us in a difficult situation. We contend that dependently produced things are, like reflections, not produced intrinsically. As this is the case, how can your objection stand a chance?

Thus you should cherish these distinctions.

Also, the *Question of the Nāga King Anavatapta (Anavatapta-nāga-rāja-paripṛcchā-sūtra)* says:[379]

Whatever is produced from conditions is not produced;
It is not intrinsically produced.
Whatever depends upon conditions, I consider empty;
One who knows emptiness is diligent.

After the Buddha has stated in the first line, "Whatever is produced from conditions is not produced," he indicates with the second line the manner of non-production, "It is not intrinsically produced." Thus, adding a qualifying phrase to the object of negation, the Buddha says that things are not produced intrinsically. Some hear these words and do not understand them; they say, "Only the produced is not produced; only the dependent does not depend." They evidently think that aggressively advocating this mass of contradictions constitutes an advanced view.

This is also stated very clearly in the *Descent into Laṅka Sūtra (Laṅkāvatāra-sūtra)* as quoted by Candrakīrti in his *Clear Words*:[380]

Mahāmati, thinking that they are not produced intrinsically, I said that all phenomena are not produced.

This actually answers the question whether the qualification "ultimately" should be added to the refutation of production and so forth. However, I will answer this question more specifically below.[381]

These points explained above indicate that none of the refutations set forth by opponents can refute this procedure for positing things such as cause and effect in the absence of intrinsic existence. [637] In general, the height of false refutation is an argument that obliterates the analysis that was supposed to refute the opponent, leaving no trace. Thus, your statement is the height of false refutation. This is because the method you use to refute your opponent's position, analyzing whether reason contradicts it and so forth, can be turned against you and used to refute your critique.

Qualm: You assert the existence of forms and such, so the analysis of them in terms of the four alternatives does bear upon your position. We, however, have no position of our own, so such analysis does not apply to us.

Reply: This argument cannot avoid those fallacies. I will explain this later in the section on whether the view is established through *reductio ad absurdum* arguments or through autonomous syllogisms.[382]

(d")) A refutation of all four parts of the tetralemma is not a legitimate critique of conventional phenomena

Qualm: The Madhyamaka texts refute all four parts of the tetralemma—a thing or intrinsic nature (1) exists, (2) does not exist, (3) both exists and does not exist, and (4) neither exists nor does not exist. Reason refutes everything, as there are no phenomena that are not included among these four.

Reply: As indicated earlier, "thing" has two meanings.[383] Between these two, we refute the assertion that things essentially exist in terms of both truths; however, at the conventional level we do not refute things that can perform functions. As for non-things, if you hold that non-compounded phenomena are essentially existent non-things, then we also refute such non-things. We likewise refute something that is both such a thing and such a non-thing, and we also refute something that essentially exists as neither. Thus, you should understand that all methods for refuting the tetralemma are like this, involving some qualifier such as "essentially."

Suppose that you refute the tetralemma without affixing any such qualification. You refute the position that things exist and you refute the position that things do not exist; you then say, [**638**] "It is not the case that they both exist and do not exist." If you now continue with the refutation, saying, "It is also not the case that they are neither existent nor nonexistent," then you explicitly contradict your own position. If you then stubbornly insist, "Even so, there is no fallacy," then the debate is over because we do not debate with the obstinate.

Furthermore, when you refute essential or intrinsic nature, or self, with regard to the aggregates, this gives rise to a wisdom consciousness thinking, "Intrinsic nature, or self, does not exist." If you also refute the lack of intrinsic nature that is the object of that wisdom consciousness, then you are refuting the Madhyamaka view. This is because you have refuted the object of the wisdom consciousness that knows that phenomena lack intrinsic nature.

This is what I ask of those who claim to refute both intrinsic nature and the absence of intrinsic nature: Please tell me how you refute the absence of intrinsic nature that is the object of the wisdom consciousness ascertaining that the aggregates do not intrinsically exist.

Qualm: Nāgārjuna's *Fundamental Treatise* says:[384]

> If there were the slightest trace which is non-empty,
> Then a trace of emptiness would exist as well;
> As there is no trace that is non-empty,
> How could there be a trace of emptiness?

Therefore, because there is nothing that is not empty, the emptiness that is the absence of intrinsic existence also does not exist.

Reply: Here in the *Fundamental Treatise*, "empty" and "non-empty" refer to being empty and not empty of intrinsic nature, and they are used in this way throughout the entire text, from beginning to end. Thus "not empty of intrinsic nature" means "having intrinsic nature." What could be more ridiculous than your position that since there is no intrinsic nature, the emptiness that is the absence of intrinsic nature also does not exist!

Furthermore, the definite knowledge which apprehends that something such as a seedling lacks essential or intrinsic nature apprehends that there is no intrinsic nature in the seedling. It does not think, "This absence of intrinsic nature exists," nor does it think, "This absence of intrinsic nature does not exist." Close your eyes, turn inward, and know this; it is very easy to understand. It would not be appropriate to apprehend the absence of intrinsic nature as existing in that way.[385] [639]

Suppose that this did mean that it is proper to use reason to refute the existence of emptiness in order to overcome the conception that the absence of intrinsic nature exists. You would still have to hold that you are refuting the object of some other mind which apprehends the absence of intrinsic nature as something that exists; it would be quite wrong to refute the object of the wisdom that realizes that a seedling does not intrinsically exist.

When we refute the essential or intrinsic nature of a seedling, we have definite knowledge that the seedling does not intrinsically exist. Then, even if some other awareness apprehends that absence of intrinsic nature as existing, reason does not refute the object of that other mind. However, if that mind holds that emptiness exists essentially, then reason does refute that.

Qualm: How could someone develop an apprehension that the absence of intrinsic nature intrinsically exists?

Reply: In perceiving the seedling's lack of intrinsic nature, you do not establish this lack as the seedling's intrinsic nature. Still, you might develop the idea that the absence of intrinsic nature is the intrinsic nature of that seedling. For example, in the absence of a pot, you would not develop the idea, "The truth is that there is a pot," but you might develop the idea, "The truth is that there is no pot."

Accordingly, since there is nothing at all that is not empty of intrinsic existence, it is perfectly reasonable to say that even the emptiness which is a seedling's lack of intrinsic nature lacks essential existence. Candrakīrti's *Commentary on the "Four Hundred Stanzas"* speaks of refuting the essential existence of emptiness:[386]

> If that which is called emptiness did have some essential existence, then things would have intrinsic nature. However, it does not. In order to indicate this, Āryadeva's *Four Hundred Stanzas* (*Catuḥ-śataka*) says:
>
> > As there is nothing that is not empty,
> > From what can emptiness arise?
> > As there is nothing to oppose,
> > How can there be a remedy?

If you disagree, and you refute the existence of the emptiness which is the absence of intrinsic nature, then the absence of intrinsic nature would not exist. In that case, since essential or intrinsic nature *would* exist, it would be totally inappropriate to refute intrinsic nature. [640] For, in this vein, Nāgārjuna's *Refutation of Objections* says:[387]

> How could the absence of intrinsic nature in my words
> Refute my claim that things lack intrinsic nature?
> If the absence of intrinsic nature were refuted,
> Then the presence of intrinsic nature would be proven.

And, Nāgārjuna's *Commentary on the "Refutation of Objections,"* commenting on that, says very clearly:[388]

> *Objection*: Just as someone might stop sound with the sound, "Don't make a sound," so the absence of intrinsic existence in your words refutes your claim that there is no intrinsic nature in things.
> *Reply*: The example is correct, but your point is not. Here, words that have no intrinsic nature do refute the intrinsic existence of

things. If the absence of intrinsic nature in words could refute the absence of intrinsic nature in things, then this would refute the absence of intrinsic nature itself. Therefore, things would have intrinsic nature, and because of having intrinsic nature, they would not be empty.

Therefore—just after the passage in the *Fundamental Treatise* cited above,[389] "How could there be a trace of emptiness?"—Nāgārjuna says:[390]

> The Conqueror said that emptiness
> Eradicates all dogmatic views;
> As for those who take a dogmatic view of emptiness,
> He said that they are incurable.

Again, having a dogmatic view of emptiness does not mean taking the view that things are empty of intrinsic nature. It means thinking of emptiness, emptiness of intrinsic nature, as truly existent or viewing it as a real thing. For, *Buddhapālita's Commentary on the "Fundamental Treatise"* says this very clearly, giving an example:[391]

> It is possible to overcome the misconceptions of those who think that things exist essentially. [641] You can explain emptiness and show them that things are empty of essence, saying, "As these are dependent-arisings, they are designated as this or that thing through the force of causes and conditions; things do not exist essentially." However, there is no way to overcome the misconceptions of those who think that emptiness is a real thing. For example, if you tell someone, "I have nothing," and that person then says, "Give me that nothing," how could you make that person understand that you have nothing?

If it is not taken in this way, the example would also be inappropriate. Suppose you say to me, "Give me some money," and I reply, "I have no money." If you conclude, "This person has no money," then there is no problem. However, if you think of "no money" as a kind of money, then there is no way that I can assure you that I have no money. In just the same way, suppose you ask, "Do things have intrinsic nature or not?" and I say, "They do not have intrinsic nature." If you then think, "Things do not have intrinsic nature," how could that be a problem? I wanted you to get this idea. However, if you think that things' lack of intrinsic nature is itself intrinsically existent, then this is a problem. According to your interpretation, when you hear me say that I have no money and then develop the idea, "This person has no money," then even that idea must be refuted. So it would be wonderful for you to rely on what I have said.

Also, in the *Clear Words* Candrakīrti speaks of clinging to emptiness as a real thing;[392] hence, he is not refuting emptiness itself, and there is no fault in simply having the view of emptiness. The *Verse Summary of the Perfection of Wisdom in Eight Thousand Lines* (*Ratnaguṇa-sañcaya-gāthā*) says:[393]

A bodhisattva who thinks, "The aggregates are empty," is meditating on signs and lacks faith in the realm of non-production.

Also, Nāgārjuna's *Precious Garland* says:[394]

Therefore the Great Sage refuted
Views of self and selflessness.

Although these and other scriptures and treatises say that it is wrong to have a view of emptiness or selflessness, you should understand them as I have explained above. Otherwise, they would contradict a great many statements in other texts. In the *Heart Sūtra* (*Prajñāpāramitāhṛdaya-sūtra*), Śāriputra asks Avalokiteśvara how one who wishes to practice the profound perfection of wisdom should train. In reply, Avalokiteśvara says:[395] **[642]**

A bodhisattva should correctly view these five aggregates as empty of intrinsic existence.

The *Verse Summary of the Perfection of Wisdom in Eight Thousand Lines* says:[396]

One who knows that phenomena do not intrinsically exist is practicing the supreme perfection of wisdom.

Candrakīrti's *Commentary on the "Middle Way"* says:[397]

Consequently, a yogi views the emptiness of the self
And that which belongs to the self, and thereby becomes free.

Therefore, the root of all problems is the ignorance that superimposes intrinsic existence. There is only one consciousness that can uproot it by apprehending things in a way that explicitly contradicts it. That consciousness is the wisdom that knows selflessness, the absence of intrinsic existence. As this is so, if you refute this way of apprehending things, then you will have to admit, albeit unwillingly, that you are refuting the view of reality.

At the point where Āryadeva's *Four Hundred Stanzas* says, "There is no second door to peace," Candrakīrti's *Commentary on the "Four Hundred Stanzas"* says:[398]

The extinction of attachment is the cause of attaining nirvāṇa and, except for the view of the absence of intrinsic existence, there is no other teaching that can cause that extinction of attachment. Thus, selflessness—characterized by the absence of intrinsic existence—is the one and only door to peace. As a gateway to the city of nirvāṇa, it is alone, and nothing can match it.

Although there are the three doors of liberation called "emptiness," "signlessness," and "wishlessness," still only the view of selflessness takes priority. If you know phenomena without exception as selfless and thereby extinguish every attachment to all things, then how could you ever long for anything or apprehend signs in anything? Because of this, selflessness alone is the one and only door to peace. [643] Therefore, the *Equipment for Enlightenment (Byang chub kyi tshogs)* explains:[399]

> Because phenomena do not intrinsically exist, they are empty.
> Further, because phenomena are empty, what use are signs?
> Inasmuch as they have overcome all signs
> Why would the learned wish for such phenomena?

Thus Candrakīrti clears up the apparent contradiction between scriptural explanations that there are three doors to liberation and other texts which explain that the view of emptiness of intrinsic existence is the only door to liberation. He uses scripture and reason to prove that just this view is the door to liberation.

Why should the mere negation of intrinsic nature imply the refutation of the object of wisdom? It should not, for such knowledge remedies the conceptions of the two selves as signs and it lacks even a trace of such a misconception. If you regard as defective even such a conception, and refute all conceptuality of any sort—good or bad—then it is evident that you want to set up the system of the Chinese abbot Ha-shang.

16

NOT NEGATING ENOUGH

(2)) Refuting an overly restricted identification of the object to be negated

------------- ৪|৪ -------------

(2)) Refuting an overly restricted identification of the object to be negated

Opponent: The object to be negated is an intrinsic nature that has three attributes: (1) causes and conditions do not bring it into being, (2) its condition is immutable, and (3) it is posited without depending on some other phenomenon. For, Nāgārjuna's *Fundamental Treatise* says:[400]

> It is not reasonable that a nature
> Should arise from causes and conditions.
> If it did arise from causes and conditions
> Then a nature would be something that is made.
>
> How could it be suitable
> For a nature to be something that is made?
> A nature is not fabricated
> And does not depend on another.

Reply: In general, if someone claims that internal and external things—e.g., seedlings—have "intrinsic nature" in this sense, then Mādhyamikas indeed must refute such. However, here, identifying the object to be negated means identifying the fundamental object of negation. When you refute the fundamental object of negation, then the Madhyamaka view—knowledge that phenomena lack intrinsic nature—develops in your mind-stream. **[644]**

Fallacies arise if we follow this opponent's interpretation. Since the partisans of non-Madhyamaka Buddhist schools have already established that compounded phenomena are produced by causes and conditions and are mutable, we should not have to demonstrate to them the absence of intrinsic nature. They also should have recognized that things lack intrinsic nature. So how can this be the unique Madhyamaka object of negation?

Many Madhyamaka texts adduce arguments such as: If things existed essentially, then they could not depend on causes and conditions, they would have to be immutable, and so forth. However, these statements indicate fallacies that would be entailed if things existed essentially; they do not identify the object of negation on its own terms.

It is the case that if something existed ultimately, existed in reality, or truly existed, then it could not depend on causes and conditions, and so forth; however, that is not what ultimate existence means. For example, even though being a pot entails being impermanent, impermanence is not the proper meaning of pot; rather you have to say that it means a "bulbous splay-based thing able to perform the function of holding water."

Likewise, if something existed ultimately, etc., it would have to be a partless thing; still, here in Madhyamaka we do not suggest that "partless thing" is the fundamental object of negation. Since partless things are merely imputed from the unique perspective of advocates of philosophical tenets, such notions are not the fundamental cause that binds embodied beings in cyclic existence. Further, even if you determined that those partless things lack intrinsic nature and then meditated on that, this would not at all counter the ignorant conception which has operated from beginningless time. Therefore, even optimal and direct knowledge of that would not overcome the innate afflictions.

Thus, when making philosophical determinations, make your principal task to determine that an object as conceived by innate ignorance does not exist. Ancillary to that, refute objects of acquired misconceptions. **[645]** If you do not understand this, and fail to eradicate the perspective of innate ignorance, then, when you refute a personal self, you will only refute a self that is permanent, unitary, and independent. When you refute an objective self, you will only refute things that are imputed by the advocates of philosophical tenets—such as objects that are partless particles, partless moments of experience, or a natural substrate (*pradhāna*) with three *guṇas* ("strands") asserted by the Sāṃkhyas. This is completely inappropriate. If you think otherwise, then when you make philosophical determinations, you will establish nothing more than this shallow selflessness. As philosophical determinations are made for the purposes of meditation, when you meditate you will have to meditate only on this. Therefore, even if you actualized such a selflessness in meditation and consummated your cultivation of it, nothing would come of it. It would be extremely absurd to claim that you can overcome innate afflictions by seeing as nonexistent the two selves imputed by acquired misconceptions.[401] Candrakīrti's *Commentary on the "Middle Way"* says:[402]

> When knowing selflessness, some eliminate a permanent self,
> But we do not consider this the basis of the conception of "I."
> It is therefore astonishing to claim that knowing this selflessness
> Expunges and uproots the view of self.

Also, Candrakīrti's *Explanation of the "Middle Way" Commentary* says:[403]

> To elucidate this very point, the irrelevance of such to innate afflictions, by way of an example:
>
> > Someone sees a snake living in the wall of his house.
> > To ease his concern, someone else says, "There is no
> >   elephant here."
> > Alas, to others it is ridiculous
> > To suppose that this would dispel the fear of the snake.

Candrakīrti refers to the selflessness of the person, but it is the same for the selflessness of objects; he could have added:

> When knowing selflessness, some eliminate an acquired
>   conception of self,
> But we do not consider this the basis of ignorance.
> It is therefore astonishing to claim that knowing this selflessness
> Expunges and uproots ignorance. **[646]**

Question: In the statement by Nāgārjuna set forth above,[404] he says that the defining characteristics of a "nature" are not being fabricated and not depending upon something else. Was he speaking hypothetically or does such a nature exist?

Reply: The Buddha posits a "nature," saying, "This is the reality of phenomena."[405] It is not fabricated and does not depend on something else. Candrakīrti's *Explanation of the "Middle Way" Commentary* establishes that it exists, citing a sūtra source:[406]

> Is there a nature that has such qualifications as the master Nāgārjuna claims? Yes, it is the "reality" of which the Bhagavan spoke extensively, saying, "Whether *tathāgatas* appear or not, the reality of phenomena remains."[407] What is this "reality"? It is the nature of things such as these eyes. And, what is their nature? It is that in them which is neither fabricated nor dependent upon something else; it is their identity as known by knowledge free from the impairment of ignorance. Does it exist or not? If it did not exist, for what purpose would bodhisattvas cultivate the path of the perfections? Why would bodhisattvas undergo hundreds of hardships in order to know reality?

Question: Did you not previously argue that all phenomena lack intrinsic nature?

Reply: Even phenomena that are not internal mental constructs lack even a particle of essential or intrinsic nature. Have we not given this answer several times? Therefore, what need is there to speak of other phenomena in terms of such a nature? Even reality, the ultimate truth, has no intrinsic nature at all. For, Candrakīrti's *Clear Words* says:[408]

> The "final nature" is the unfabricated fundamental entity which is ineluctably present in fire in the past, present, and future; [647] it is not the later occurrence of something that was not there before; it does not depend on causes and conditions like the heat of water, or here and there, or long and short. Does fire have such a nature? It neither essentially has it nor essentially lacks it. Nevertheless, to avoid frightening listeners, I reify it and say, "It exists conventionally."

Thus Candrakīrti refutes the view that this nature exists essentially; he says that it exists conventionally.

Objection: He does not assert that it exists, for he says that he reifies it in order to avoid frightening listeners.

Reply: That is not reasonable. He also spoke of other phenomena, having imputed them for that same reason. So if the final nature did not exist, those other phenomena also would not exist. As cited earlier, Candrakīrti proves that the final nature exists, making the argument that if it did not exist, then it would absurdly follow that pure conduct is senseless. Also, Candrakīrti's *Explanation of the "Middle Way" Commentary* says:[409]

Not only does the master Nāgārjuna assert this nature, others also can be made to accept it. Thus he posits this nature as established for both parties to the debate.

If it were otherwise, then you would have to hold that in Madhyamaka it is impossible to attain freedom. This is because (1) Candrakīrti says that to attain nirvāṇa means to perceive nirvāṇa, and he says that nirvāṇa is considered a true cessation and that true cessations are ultimate truths; and (2) ultimate truths would not exist. In his *Commentary on the Sixty Stanzas of Reasoning*, Candrakīrti takes pains to prove that when you attain nirvāṇa, you must perceive the ultimate truth of cessation. [648]

Accordingly, compounded phenomena such as eyes are not natures in the sense of being essentially existent, nor are they natures when reality is posited as the final nature. So they are neither sort of nature. Ultimate truths are natures when reality is posited as the final nature, but what establishes them as such natures is that they are non-fabricated and do not depend upon something else. They do not at all exist as natures in the sense of being essentially existent. Thus, they exist merely conventionally.

"Fabricated" means "produced" in the sense of a new occurrence of something that did not exist before; "to depend upon something else" means to depend on causes and conditions.

Since forms and so forth are neither type of nature, when you speak of cultivating the path in order to view the final nature, "nature" has the sense of reality. Therefore, Candrakīrti says that pure conduct is not senseless. Moreover, he explains that his utter lack of an assertion that phenomena have a nature in the sense of essential existence does not contradict his incidental assertion of a final nature.[410] Candrakīrti's *Explanation of the "Middle Way" Commentary* says:[411]

> *Objection*: Alas, utterly wrong! You do not assert real things at all, but also incidentally assert a nature that is non-fabricated and does not depend upon something else. You are saying things that are blatantly contradictory.
>
> *Reply*: In saying this, you miss the point of the *Fundamental Treatise*. This is what it means: If eyes and such—dependent-arisings that are evident to ordinary childish beings—were their own nature, then pure conduct would be senseless because even inaccurate consciousnesses could know that nature. Because they are not their own nature, pure conduct for the sake of viewing that nature does have a purpose. Further, I say that this nature, as

compared to conventional truths, is non-fabricated and does not depend upon something else. **[649]** Only something that ordinary childish beings do not see is suitable to be the nature. Therefore, the ultimate is neither a thing nor a non-thing; by nature, it is simply peace.

Here "thing" and "non-thing" refer to essential existence and utter nonexistence, as explained above in the section on dualism.[412]

Now when you as an ordinary being determine that phenomena lack even a particle of essential or intrinsic nature, you find that emptiness—emptiness of intrinsic nature—is an attribute of the phenomena, such as form, that serve as its substrata. Thus, it is not contradictory for both substrata and attribute to be objects of a single mind. Since you have not stopped dualistic appearance, that emptiness is a nominal rather than actual ultimate truth.

By accustoming yourself to that view which knows the absence of intrinsic nature, you will know it by perceiving it. For such a consciousness, all mistaken appearances stop. Mistaken appearance here means the appearance of intrinsic existence where there is no intrinsic existence. Therefore, since the consciousness directly perceiving that reality does not perceive substrata such as forms, neither that reality nor its substrata exist from the perspective of that mind. So emptiness and forms, etc. must be posited as reality and substrata from the perspective of some other mind, a conventional mind.

As this is so, an ultimate truth is posited where, in addition to the stilling of all elaborations of essential existence, there is also a sheer stoppage of all elaborations of mistaken appearances, appearances of intrinsic existence where there is none. Thus, while we assert a final nature, how could we be forced to accept an essentially existent nature? Candrakīrti's *Clear Words* says:[413]

> Driven by the impairment of ignorance, ordinary beings perceive a certain aspect in things. As noble beings who are free from the impairment of ignorance do not see that mistaken aspect, there is something else that serves as their object. That very entity is posited as the final nature of those things.

Also:[414] **[650]**

> Things' lack of intrinsically existent production is not anything. Thus, since it is just a non-thing, it has no essence. Therefore, it is not the intrinsic nature of things.

Some [Tibetans] do not posit ultimate truth as the sheer elimination of the elaborations of the objects of negation, e.g., the two selves. Instead they hold that, as the object of a mind that non-mistakenly knows how things exist, the ultimate appears to exist under its own power—just as things such as blue and yellow appear to an ordinary mind. Ascertaining that it does exist in that way is the view that knows the profound. They also claim that it is a misstep with regard to the correct view to regard external and internal phenomena—the bases with regard to which living beings cling to the two selves—as lacking intrinsic existence.

These assertions stand outside the sphere of all the scriptures, Hīnayāna and Mahāyāna. They accept that it is necessary to stop the conception of self, the root that binds all living beings in cyclic existence. They then assert that you do not stop the conception of self by realizing that there is no intrinsic existence in the substrata it apprehends as a self; rather, you stop it by knowing as truly existent some other unrelated phenomenon. This is no different from the following scenario: Suppose that there is no snake in the east, but someone thinks that there is and is terrified. You say to the distressed person, "You cannot stop your idea that there is a snake by thinking, 'In the east there is no snake at all.' Rather you should think, 'There is a tree in the west.' That will stop your idea that there is a snake and will end your distress."

Hence, you who wish the good for yourselves should stay far away from such wrong views. You should work on the method for eradicating the way that ignorance apprehends things, this ignorance being the root of all that binds you and degrades you in cyclic existence. Regarding this method, the texts of the father, the noble Nāgārjuna, and his spiritual son Āryadeva clearly set forth vast collections of arguments that build deep and certain knowledge of the definitive scriptures and how it is that the meaning of these scriptures cannot be otherwise interpreted.[415] **[651]** Relying on these texts by Nāgārjuna and Āryadeva, cross to the other side of the ocean of cyclic existence.

To avoid missteps in reaching the Madhyamaka view, it is most crucial to refute wrong ideas about the object of negation. For that reason I have given an extended explanation.

17

THE ACTUAL OBJECT TO BE NEGATED

(c)) How our system identifies the object of negation
    (1)) The actual identification of the object to be negated
    (2)) When to add qualifications to other objects of negation
    (3)) Whether to add the qualification "ultimate" to the object of negation

---

(c)) **How our system identifies the object of negation**

This has three parts:

1. The actual identification of the object to be negated
2. When to add qualifications to other objects of negation
3. Whether to add the qualification "ultimate" to the object of negation

(1)) **The actual identification of the object to be negated**

In general, with regard to objects of negation, there are objects negated by the path and objects negated by reason. As to the first of these, Maitreya's *Separation of the Middle from the Extremes* says:[416]

> There are teachings on afflictive obscuration
> And on cognitive obscuration.
> We hold that all obscurations are among these,
> And when they are gone, you are free.

Thus, there are afflictive obscurations and cognitive obscurations. These objects of negation do occur among objects of knowledge, for, if they did not exist, then all embodied beings would escape cyclic existence without exertion.

As for objects negated by reason, Nāgārjuna's *Refutation of Objections* says:[417]

> Someone thinks that an emanated
> Woman is a woman.
> Another emanation stops this wrong conception—
> This is like that.

In his *Commentary on the "Refutation of Objections"* he says:[418]

> A woman emanated by some being is empty of the nature of being a woman, but someone else wrongly thinks, "This is ultimately a woman." Therefore, due to that wrong conception, attachment arises. The Tathāgata or a *śrāvaka* of the Tathāgata emanates another emanation, and thereby stops that person's wrong conception.
>
> Similarly, my words, which are empty like an emanation, stop any apprehension that anything exists intrinsically. All things, like the emanated woman, are empty and do not intrinsically exist. [652]

Thus he speaks of misconceptions as objects of negation and he also treats the intrinsic nature that they apprehend as an object of negation, making two kinds of objects to be negated. However, the primary object of negation is the latter. For, in order to stop an inaccurate consciousness, you must first refute the object which that consciousness apprehends. For instance, dependent-arising refutes the essential or intrinsic existence of persons and phenomena.

This latter object of negation cannot be among objects of knowledge because, if it did exist, then it could not be refuted. Still, there are mistaken superimpositions that apprehend it as existing, so you must refute it. This refutation is not like destroying a pot with a hammer; rather, it is a matter of developing certain knowledge that recognizes the nonexistent *as* nonexistent. When you develop certain knowledge that it does not exist, the mistaken consciousness that apprehends it as existing will stop.

Similarly, using reason to establish something is not a matter of newly establishing something that did not exist before, like a seed producing a seedling. Rather, it is the development of certain knowledge that recognizes a phenomenon as it is. Nāgārjuna's *Refutation of Objections* says:[419]

> What use is it to establish the negation
> Of what does not exist anyway, even without words?

To answer that, the words "does not exist"
Cause understanding; they do not eliminate.

In his *Commentary* on that Nāgārjuna says:[420]

> *Qualm*: If you are establishing the negation of something that
> does not exist even without words, without saying anything, then
> what is the use of your words, "All things lack intrinsic nature"?
>
> *Reply*: The words, "All things lack intrinsic nature," do not
> cause things to lack intrinsic nature, but, in the absence of intrin-
> sic nature, they do make it understood that things lack intrinsic
> nature.
>
> For example, even though Devadatta is not in the house,
> someone says, "Devadatta is in the house." Someone else, in or-
> der to show that Devadatta is not there says, "Devadatta is not
> there." [653] Those words do not cause Devadatta not to be there,
> but merely indicate that Devadatta is not in the house. Similarly,
> the words, "Things lack intrinsic nature," do not cause things to
> lack intrinsic nature. All things lack intrinsic nature, like creatures
> in a magical illusion. However, childish beings are confused about
> the absence of real essence in all things, so we make them under-
> stand that there is no intrinsic nature in the things that they, con-
> fused by ignorance, reify as having intrinsic nature. Therefore,
> what you have said—that if there is no intrinsic nature, what use
> are the words, "There is no intrinsic existence," inasmuch as things
> would be established as without intrinsic nature even without any
> words, without saying anything—is not reasonable.

You should understand this in accordance with this very clear
statement.

Some hold that to conduct the extensive rational analysis required for refutations and proofs is to meander among mere conventional words, for all phenomena are devoid of refutation and
proof, in that, if something exists, it cannot be refuted, and, if it does
not exist, it need not be refuted. This is a nonsensical collection of
contradictions, showing neither general awareness of how reason
establishes and negates things nor general awareness of how the
path establishes and negates things. For, you claim that refutation
and proof should not be done, while you yourself are refuting your
opponent's use of analysis that involves refutation and proof, citing
as your reason, "If something exists, it cannot be refuted, and if it
does not exist, it need not be refuted." Furthermore, your stated reason is not an appropriate refutation of an opponent who holds that
it is necessary to conduct refutation and proof because according to

you, if something exists, it cannot be refuted, and if it does not exist, it need not be refuted.

We carry out refutations with excellent reasoning so as to stop inaccurate and mistaken conceptions; proof by reasoning is a technique for developing accurate and certain knowledge. [654] Therefore, those who wish to stop the various inaccurate awarenesses and to develop the various accurate awarenesses should pursue the collections of arguments by authors such as Nāgārjuna and should develop minds that have accurate and certain knowledge of refutation and proof.

Question: If, as you say, refutation by means of reasoning is done in order to develop accurate and certain knowledge by eradicating inaccurate cognitive processes, then reason will cancel out an object as it is apprehended by a certain kind of mind. What is that mind?

Reply: In general, there are a limitless number of conceptual consciousnesses that apprehend the object of negation; however, you should carefully identify the incorrect conceptual consciousness that is the root of all faults and defects and you should eradicate its referent object. For, if that is stopped, then all faults and defects will be stopped.

Moreover, the remedies set forth in sūtra for other afflictions, such as attachment, cure a portion of the afflictions, whereas the remedies set forth for ignorance cure all afflictions. Therefore, ignorance is the basis of all faults and defects. Candrakīrti's *Clear Words* says:[421]

> The teachings of the buddhas—the sets of sūtras and so forth—
>   are based on the two truths.
> In nine types they rightly proclaim the vast remedies which
>   correspond to worldly behavior.
> Among these, those said to eliminate attachment do not
>   extinguish hostility,
> Those said to eliminate hostility do not extinguish attachment,
> And those said to extinguish pride and so forth do not over-
>   come other defilements.
> Therefore they are not broadly effective, and those scriptures
>   are not of great significance.
> Those said to extinguish delusion overcome all afflictions;
> The conquerors have said that all afflictions are based upon
>   delusion.

What is this delusion like? It is ignorance, which in this context is an awareness that mistakenly superimposes intrinsic nature; it apprehends internal and external phenomena as existing by way of their own intrinsic character. [655] Candrakīrti's *Commentary on the "Four Hundred Stanzas"* says:[422]

It is said that one becomes attached to things by the power of an afflictive misunderstanding, a consciousness that superimposes an essence of things, and that one stops cyclic existence by totally stopping that which serves as the seed for the process of cyclic existence. In order to indicate this, the *Four Hundred* says:

> The seed of worldly existence is a consciousness;
> Objects are its sphere of activity.
> When you see that objects lack self,
> You negate the seed of worldly existence.

Hence, Āryadeva holds that by seeing objects as lacking intrinsic nature, you totally stop the seed of cyclic existence, the consciousness that causes attachment. This stops cyclic existence for *śrāvakas*, *pratyekabuddhas*, and bodhisattvas who have attained forbearance with regard to the teaching of non-production.

This is also called the conception of true existence. For Āryadeva's *Four Hundred* says:

> Just as the tactile sensory faculty pervades the body,
> Delusion lies within all the afflictions.
> Therefore, by destroying delusion
> You will destroy all afflictions.

Commenting on this verse, Candrakīrti's *Commentary on the "Four Hundred Stanzas"* says:[423]

Because of confusion brought on by the thought that things truly exist as they appear, delusion acts to superimpose upon things an essence of true existence.

Qualm: If, as you say, ignorance is the root of cyclic existence, then it would be incorrect for Candrakīrti to explain in the *Commentary on the "Middle Way"* and in the *Clear Words* that the view of the perishing aggregates as "I" and "mine" is the root of cyclic existence. For, there cannot be two primary causes of cyclic existence.

Reply: In the section on the person of medium capacity, I have already explained what other masters say about how to assert ignorance and the view of the perishing aggregates.[424] Therefore, here I will explain the assertions of the master Candrakīrti. Other Mādhyamikas consider the conception of things as truly existent to be a cognitive obscuration; he asserts that such a conception is ignorance and, what is more, he asserts that it is afflictive ignorance.

For, as cited above,[425] his *Commentary on the "Four Hundred Stanzas"* explains that the conception of true existence is afflictive. [656] Also, his *Explanation of the "Middle Way" Commentary* says:[426]

> Because this causes living beings to be confused in their view of the actual state of things, it is delusion; ignorance mistakenly superimposes upon things an essence that they do not have. It is constituted so as to block perception of their nature. It is a concealer.

Also:[427]

> Thus, conventional truths are posited through the force of the afflictive ignorance which is included within the factors of cyclic existence.

Thus, because he explains that it is the first of the twelve factors of dependent-arising, it is an affliction and not a cognitive obscuration. What are the cognitive obscurations? This will be explained below.[428]

Therefore, he explains that the ignorance which is the first of the twelve factors is the root of cyclic existence and, within that, he also explains that the view of the perishing aggregates is the root of cyclic existence. Since ignorance is the general category and the view of the perishing aggregates is an instance, there is no contradiction.

Ignorance is the opposite of knowledge, and this does not refer to just any knowledge, but to the wisdom that knows the reality that is selflessness. The opposite of that cannot simply be the nonexistence of that wisdom, nor can it simply be something other than that wisdom; therefore, it is a conception that is that wisdom's contradictory equivalent. This is the superimposition of self. There are two types: the superimposition of an objective self and the superimposition of a personal self. Thus, both the conception of a personal self and the conception of an objective self are ignorance. Therefore, when he indicates that the view of the perishing aggregates is the root of all other afflictions, this does not mean that ignorance is not the root.

Also, [Nāgārjuna's *Precious Garland*] says,[429] "As long as you conceive of the aggregates, you will conceive of them as 'I'." This means that the ignorance that is confusion in regard to an objective self causes confusion with regard to a personal self. [657] Since this places the internal divisions of ignorance in a cause-and-effect relationship, it does not contradict the teaching that the view of the perishing aggregates is the root of all afflictions other than ignorance.

If you do not understand this way of explaining what the master Candrakīrti intended, then it is very difficult to dispel the false impression that he contradicted himself by explaining the root of cyclic existence in two different ways.

Nāgārjuna the Protector also accepts this system of identifying ignorance. For, his *Seventy Stanzas on Emptiness* says:[430]

> The Teacher said that ignorance
> Is the conception that, in reality,
> Things are produced from causes and conditions.
> From this, the twelve factors arise.
>
> Through seeing reality, you know
> That things are empty; ignorance does not arise.
> This is the cessation of ignorance.
> Because of this, the twelve factors cease.

Also, the twenty-sixth chapter of his *Fundamental Treatise* says:[431]

> When ignorance is stopped
> Compositional activity will not arise at all.
> That which stops ignorance
> Is knowing and meditating on reality.
>
> By stopping this and that earlier factor of dependent-arising,
> This and that later factor will not arise.
> In this way you thoroughly stop
> The whole mass of suffering.

This and the other passage just cited are in agreement and fit together very well with the line in Nāgārjuna's *Precious Garland*, "As long as you conceive of the aggregates...,"[432] which says that the root of cyclic existence is the conception of the aggregates as intrinsically existent.

The noble Āryadeva also asserts this, as is clearly indicated by the passages cited earlier, "Just as the tactile sensory faculty pervades the body..." and also, "The root of cyclic existence is a consciousness...."[433]

When the master Nāgārjuna refutes the object of negation in the *Fundamental Treatise*, he gives all of his diverse arguments so as to refute an intrinsic nature—delusion's reification of phenomena as essentially existent—and to show that phenomena lack essence. Thus, Nāgārjuna gives a wide range of arguments only for the sake of eradicating the way that ignorance apprehends things. *Buddhapālita's Commentary on the "Fundamental Treatise"* says:[434]

What is the purpose of teaching dependent-arising? [658] The master Nāgārjuna, whose very nature is compassion, saw that living beings are beset by various sufferings and assumed the task of teaching the reality of things just as it is so that they might be free. He therefore began teaching dependent-arising. For, it is said:

> Seeing what is not real, you are bound;
> Seeing the real, you are free.

What is the reality of things just as it is? It is the absence of essence. Unskilled persons whose eye of intelligence is obscured by the darkness of delusion conceive of an essence in things and then generate attachment and hostility with regard to them. When the illumination of the knowledge of dependent-arising clears away the darkness of delusion and the eye of wisdom sees the absence of essence in things, then there is no foundation for the other afflictions, and attachment and hostility do not develop.

Also, in the transition to the twenty-sixth chapter, that same text says:[435]

> *Question*: You have already explained entry into the ultimate through the Mahāyāna texts. Now explain entry into the ultimate through the texts of *śrāvakas*.
> *Reply*: [The *Fundamental Treatise*] says, "Through obscuration by ignorance, cyclic existence recurs...."

And, in the transition to the twenty-seventh chapter, Buddhapālita says:[436]

> *Question*: Now illustrate the absence of wrong views using scriptures that accord with the vehicle of *śrāvakas*.
> *Reply*: [The *Fundamental Treatise*] says, "In the past, I arose...."

These statements make it clear that the master Buddhapālita also asserts that the ignorance which is the first of the twelve factors of dependent-arising is the superimposition of intrinsic nature on things and that even *śrāvakas* and *pratyekabuddhas* know the selflessness of objects. [659] Therefore, you should understand that the great proof for showing that *śrāvakas* and *pratyekabuddhas* know that objects lack intrinsic nature is the fact that the conception of an objective self is counted as the ignorance that is among the twelve factors of dependent-arising.

Āryadeva's *Four Hundred Stanzas* says,[437] "Conceptuality sees and you are bound; it should be stopped here." Even the conceptuality mentioned in that statement does not refer to all conceptual consciousnesses whatsoever, but rather to conceptual consciousnesses that superimpose essential existence on phenomena. For, commenting on that passage, Candrakīrti's *Commentary on the "Four Hundred Stanzas"* says,[438] "A conceptual consciousness superimposes an incorrect sense of intrinsic existence." Further, he asserts that it is afflictive ignorance. Hence, while there are those who claim that reason refutes the object of every conceptual consciousness that thinks, "This is such and such," they have done no detailed investigation of this matter.

If it were otherwise, then, since for ordinary beings the meaning of reality is hidden, they would have no way of apprehending the meaning of emptiness with a non-conceptual consciousness. Also, if the objects of every conceptual consciousness were contradicted by reason, then even the objects of certain knowledge would be like the intrinsic nature superimposed by a mistaken, wrong consciousness. This would imply that there is no correct view leading to the state of nirvāṇa, whereby it would be pointless to do any study or reflection on the Madhyamaka texts. For, Āryadeva's *Four Hundred Stanzas* says:[439]

> Seeing what is not emptiness as if it were emptiness,
> Some say, "I will attain nirvāṇa," but they will not.
> The *tathāgatas* said that
> You do not reach nirvāṇa through wrong views.

Based on just this [intrinsic nature], the referent object of the way that ignorance apprehends things as explained above, essentialist schools—Buddhist and non-Buddhist—reify many different things. When you negate the referent of ignorance's cognitive process, you completely stop all of these tenet-driven reifications, as though you cut a tree at its root. [660] Therefore, those who have the faculty of wisdom should understand that the referent object of innate ignorance is the basic object of negation and should not devote themselves merely to refuting imaginary constructs that are imputed only by the advocates of philosophical tenets.

Refuting the object of negation in this way is not an idle pursuit. You see that living beings are bound in cyclic existence by a wrong conceptual consciousness that has the object of negation as its object and you then refute its object. What binds all living beings in cyclic existence is innate ignorance; acquired ignorance exists only among those who advocate philosophical tenets, so it cannot be the root of cyclic existence. It is extremely important to gain specific and certain knowledge of this point.

Hence, the ultimate wrong conceptual consciousness that conceives the object of negation is the innate ignorance which is the first of the twelve factors of dependent-arising. Acquired objects of negation are merely superimpositions based on this. Thus, it is not at all the case that reason negates all of the cognitive processes through which non-conceptual consciousnesses—e.g., sensory consciousnesses—apprehend things. Therefore, only conceptual mental consciousnesses have cognitive processes that are negated by reason; more specifically, reason refutes the cognitive processes of the two conceptions of self and the cognitive processes of those conceptual consciousnesses that superimpose further attributes on objects that have been imputed by those two conceptions of self. It is not that reason refutes the cognitive processes of all conceptual consciousnesses of any kind.

Question: How does ignorance superimpose intrinsic nature?

Reply: In general, there appear in Candrakīrti's texts many usages of verbal conventions such as "nature" or "essence" with regard to objects that exist only conventionally. However, here in the case of reification by ignorance, there is, with regard to objects, be they persons or other phenomena, a conception that those phenomena have ontological status—a way of existing—in and of themselves, without being posited through the force of an awareness. The referent object that is thus apprehended by that ignorant conception, the independent ontological status of those phenomena, is identified as a hypothetical "self" or "intrinsic nature." **[661]** For, Āryadeva's *Four Hundred Stanzas* says:[440]

> All of this is without its own power;
> Therefore there is no self.

Commenting on this, Candrakīrti's *Commentary on the "Four Hundred Stanzas"* says:[441]

> It is that which exists essentially, intrinsically, autonomously, and without depending on another....

Thus, he says that those are synonyms. "Without depending on another" does not mean not depending on causes and conditions. Instead, "other" refers to a subject, i.e., a conventional consciousness, and something is said not to depend on another due to not being posited through the force of that conventional consciousness.

Therefore, "autonomously" refers to the nature of an object that has its own unique ontological status or manner of being. It is just this that is called "essence" or "intrinsic nature." Take, for example, the case of an imaginary snake that is mistakenly ascribed to a rope. If we leave aside how it is ascribed from the perspective that apprehends a snake and try to analyze what the snake is like in terms of its own nature, since a snake is simply not present in that object, its features cannot be analyzed. It is similar with regard to these phenomena. Suppose that we leave aside analysis of how they appear—i.e., how they appear to a conventional awareness—and analyze the objects themselves, asking, "What is the manner of being of these phenomena?" We find they are not established in any way. Ignorance does not apprehend phenomena in this way; it apprehends each phenomenon as having a manner of being such that it can be understood in and of itself, without being posited through the force of a conventional consciousness. Candrakīrti's *Commentary on the "Four Hundred Stanzas"* says:[442]

> Without any doubt, what exists only through the presence of conceptual thought, and does not exist without conceptual thought, definitely does not exist essentially—as in the case of a snake that is imputed to a coiled rope.

Thus Candrakīrti states how phenomena do not essentially exist.

Therefore, what exists objectively in terms of its own essence without being posited through the power of a subjective mind is called "self" or "intrinsic nature." [662] The absence of this quality in the person is called the selflessness of the person; its absence in phenomena such as eyes, ears, and so forth is called the selflessness of objects. Hence, one may implicitly understand that the conceptions of that intrinsic nature as present in persons and objects are the conceptions of the two selves. It is as Candrakīrti's *Commentary on the "Four Hundred Stanzas"* says:[443]

> "Self" is an essence of things that does not depend on others; it is an intrinsic nature. The nonexistence of that is selflessness. Because of the division into objects and persons, it is understood as twofold: a "selflessness of objects" and a "selflessness of persons."

Qualm: The conception of persons as existing by way of their intrinsic character cannot be a conception of a personal self. For if it were, then even observing persons other than oneself and conceiving of them as existing by way of their own intrinsic characteristic would be a conception of a personal self. If you admit this, then, while it must be a view of the perishing aggregates, it cannot be a view of the perishing aggregates insofar as it is not a conception that thinks, "I."

Reply: As explained earlier, Candrakīrti says that an intrinsic nature in persons is a self of persons, so one must accept that a conception of the person as intrinsically existent is a conception of a self of persons. However, a conception of a self of persons is not necessarily a view of the perishing aggregates.

What is needed in order to have a conception of self that is a view of the perishing aggregates? In the case of the conception of self that is an *acquired* view of the perishing aggregates, there is no definite rule, as there are many—including some among the Saṃmitīya schools—who do, as a result of their philosophies, apprehend a self when they observe the aggregates. However, in the case of the *innate* view of the perishing aggregates, Candrakīrti's *Commentary on the "Middle Way"* refutes that the aggregates are the observed object and his *Explanation of the "Middle Way" Commentary* says that the dependently imputed self is the observed object.⁴⁴⁴ Hence, an innate view of the perishing aggregates does not take the aggregates as its object of observation, but rather observes the mere person. Moreover, it must be a person who is a basis for the arising of the thought "I." Thus, a person of another continuum of mental and physical aggregates is not the object of observation. [663]

With regard to how that object of observation is apprehended, Candrakīrti's *Explanation of the "Middle Way" Commentary* says:⁴⁴⁵

> Concerning that, a view of the perishing aggregates operates within thoughts of "I" and "mine."

Thus, it is not simply a conception of intrinsic existence, i.e., existence by way of intrinsic character; it must be a conception thinking "I." The *Explanation of the "Middle Way" Commentary* also says:⁴⁴⁶

> Just the view of the perishing aggregates is to be eliminated, and it is eliminated upon understanding the selflessness of the self.

Thus Candrakīrti says that you eliminate the view of the perishing aggregates by knowing the selflessness—the non-intrinsic existence—of the self that is its object of observation, thereby contradicting the way that it is apprehended by the view of the perishing aggregates. Hence, the view of the perishing aggregates must apprehend the opposite of that wisdom which knows selflessness. Moreover, since a view of the perishing aggregates is a conception of the person as essentially existent, it is a conception of an "I" that exists by way of its intrinsic character.

Using this as an example, you should be able to understand the view of the perishing aggregates that is a conception of "mine."

Even when they do not conceive "I" or "mine," conceptions of the person as substantially existent are still cases of ignorance that misconceives a self of persons, so it is not the case that they are not afflictions.

As in the passage just cited, "self" refers to mere essential or intrinsic existence and also refers to the object of an awareness that simply thinks, "I." Of these two, the former is the object negated by reason, whereas the latter is accepted conventionally, so it is not refuted. Therefore, this passage indicates that you do not refute the object which is observed by the innate view of the perishing aggregates. However, the way that its aspect is apprehended is as an essentially existent "I," so it is not that you do not refute that way of apprehending. For example, you do not refute the sound that is the object observed by a conception that sound is permanent, but you do refute the permanent sound that is the referent object of that conception. It is not a contradiction; this case is similar.

The noble father Nāgārjuna, his spiritual son Āryadeva, and the two masters [Buddhapālita and Candrakīrti] preface their refutations by saying, "If things existed intrinsically," "If things existed essentially," "If things existed by way of their own intrinsic character," and "If things existed substantially." You should understand that the "intrinsic nature" and so forth mentioned in those texts is as indicated above. [664] Also, you should understand that the words indicating that those various things do not exist mean that they do not exist as they are conceived by ignorance.

(2)) When to add qualifications to other objects of negation

When you say that utter nonexistents such as the horns of a rabbit and the son of a barren woman do not exist, you need not attach a qualification such as "intrinsically." Similarly, there are things that, although existent among objects of knowledge, exist at some times and places and do not exist at other times and places. When you say that these do not exist at a particular time or place, there is also no need to add that qualification. Furthermore, when refuting imaginary constructs from the unique assertions of Buddhist or non-Buddhist essentialists—things that Mādhyamikas do not accept as conventionally existent—there is no need to newly attach the qualification "essentially" or "intrinsically" to the objects, except in the occasional situation when you should add it, taking into account the opponents' perspective. This is because those proponents of tenets have already asserted the essential existence of those objects.

In any other case whatsoever, where Mādhyamikas do conventionally posit the object, if you fail to add a qualification when refuting it, then the fallacies you adduce will equally apply to your own critique, and hence it will be only a sham of a refutation. Thus, it must be added.

Moreover, as explained earlier,[447] neither a reasoning consciousness which analyzes whether something exists intrinsically nor a conventional valid cognition can contradict what the Mādhyamikas posit conventionally. For, if either did, it would be utterly untenable to make the distinction that we do not conventionally assert things such as a divine creator and yet we do assert forms, sounds, and such. Hence, there would be no way to make presentations of the mundane or supramundane such as, "This is the path; that is not the path," or "This tenet is correct; that is not correct." [665] Consequently, the distinguishing feature that all the presentations of cyclic existence and nirvāṇa are tenable within the emptiness of intrinsic existence would be impossible.

To a skillful philosopher, it is ridiculous to claim that something is refuted even though such valid cognitions do not contradict it. Therefore, when stating that you refute those phenomena such as forms, you should be sure to add a qualifying phrase. Candrakīrti's *Commentary on the "Four Hundred Stanzas"* and *Commentary on "Sixty Stanzas of Reasoning"* very often add a qualifying phrase when refuting the object to be negated. Such phrases frequently appear in Nāgārjuna's *Fundamental Treatise*, in *Buddhapālita's Commentary on the "Fundamental Treatise,"* and in Candrakīrti's *Clear Words* and *Commentary on the "Middle Way"* along with his *Explanation of the "Middle Way" Commentary*. Thus, those authors regard the repetition of qualifying phrases as excessive verbiage, and they thought that the significance of their having added them at certain points would make it easily understood even when they did not. You should add it even where they did not because there is not the slightest difference between the places where they did add it and the places where they did not.

Furthermore, they frequently add the qualification of analysis, saying, "When analyzed, it does not exist." As explained above, this means that if something existed essentially, it would have to be found by a reasoning consciousness which analyzes the way it exists; however, it is not found, and therefore, an essentially existent object does not exist. Hence, you should realize that this makes the same point as saying, "It does not exist essentially or intrinsically." For, it is as Candrakīrti's *Commentary on the "Four Hundred Stanzas"* says:[448]

Since they are deceptive—like the wheel of a firebrand, an emanation, or such—these things become non-things. If they did not, then under exacting rational analysis their essences would be very clearly observable, as in the case of a goldsmith analyzing gold. However, their causes are strictly erroneous, so that when the fire of analysis burns them, they can never be anything but essenceless. [666]

(3)) Whether to add the qualification "ultimate" to the object of negation

It is quite unreasonable to claim that adding the qualification "ultimate" to the object of negation is the procedure only in Svātantrika-Madhyamaka. Candrakīrti's *Explanation of the "Middle Way" Commentary* cites the *Perfection of Wisdom Sūtra [in Twenty-five Thousand Lines (Pañca-viṃśatisāhasrikā-prajñāpāramitā)]*:[449]

> "Venerable Subhuti, is it that there is no attainment and no clear knowledge?"
>
> Subhuti answered, "Venerable Śāriputra, there is attainment and there is also clear knowledge, but not in a dualistic sense. Venerable Śāriputra, attainment and clear knowledge exist as worldly conventions. Also stream-enterers, once-returners, never-returners, arhats, *pratyekabuddhas*, and bodhisattvas exist as worldly conventions. Ultimately, however, there is no attainment and there is no clear knowledge."

Candrakīrti's *Explanation of the "Middle Way" Commentary* says that you should follow this statement. Do you claim that this is a Svātantrika sūtra? It is evident that there are a great many such cases where definitive sūtras add the qualification "ultimate." Also, Nāgārjuna's *Seventy Stanzas on Emptiness* says:[450]

> Through the force of worldly convention,
> And not through the force of reality,
> The Buddha spoke of duration, production, and cessation;
> Of existence and nonexistence; of what is low, moderate, or
>   supreme.

Also, Nāgārjuna's *Precious Garland* says:[451]

> It is said that both the self and that which belongs to the self
>   exist.
> They do not exist in an ultimate sense.

Also:

> How can something be true
> When the seed that produces it is false?

Also:[452]

> Similarly, production and disintegration
> Appear in this illusory world,
> But ultimately there is no production
> And no disintegration.

Thus, such texts often make statements in which they attach "ultimately," "truly," or "in reality" to the negation; even when they do not add those, they very frequently add a qualification that something "does not exist essentially," "does not exist intrinsically," or "does not exist by way of its intrinsic character." [667]

Also, *Buddhapālita's Commentary on the "Fundamental Treatise"* says:[453]

> Nāgārjuna's *Fundamental Treatise*:
>
>> The teachings given by the buddhas
>> Rely wholly on the two truths—
>> Worldly conventional truths
>> And ultimate truths.
>
> Thus, with the truth of worldly convention, you say, "A pot exists," or "A bamboo mat exists"; and with that same conventional sense you indicate that they are impermanent—"The pot broke," "The bamboo mat burned." When you begin to contemplate reality, pots and bamboo mats are untenable in that they are dependently imputed objects. In that case, how can it be tenable to regard them as broken or burned?
>
> Furthermore, you indicate the impermanence of even the Tathāgata through the force of the worldly conventions: "The Tathāgata has grown old," and "The Tathāgata has passed from sorrow." When you contemplate the ultimate, even the Tathāgata is not tenable; in that case, how can his growing old and passing from sorrow be tenable?

Also, the master Candrakīrti says that he refutes true production but does not refute mere production. His *Commentary on "Sixty Stanzas of Reasoning"* says:[454]

> We do not propound that an apprehension of a reflection—dependently produced and seen strictly as false—is not produced in any way. However, we say that it does not occur in terms of the nature, and we do propound that it is not produced in that sense. What is the nature in terms of which we say that it is not produced? A nature that you can clearly hold as a truth. However, it is not that it is not produced as something false, because we do assert that it arises as that dependently.

Thus, he does not refute production that is false, like an illusion; he does refute true production. He says that it is not contradictory to be both produced dependently and not produced intrinsically. That same text says:[455]

> Therefore, in this way production and non-production have a different scope, so how can they contradict one another? [668]

Also:[456]

> We contend that dependently produced things are, like reflections, not produced intrinsically. As this is the case, how can your objection stand a chance?

He says this in reply to an objection that it is contradictory for something to be dependently produced and yet not produced intrinsically. Also, Candrakīrti's *Commentary on the "Middle Way"* says:[457]

> Therefore, through such a process you should understand that primordially
> Things are not produced in reality, but are produced in the world.

Thus he attaches the qualification "in reality" to "not produced." The *Commentary on the "Middle Way"* also says:[458]

> Just as these things—pots and such—do not exist in reality
> But do exist in terms of what the world understands,
> So it is for all things.
> Therefore, it does not follow that they are like the son of a barren woman.

Thus he says that all internal and external things do not exist in reality but do exist conventionally. Hence, he does not omit the qualification "ultimately" in the negation.

In brief, if you in no way accept the addition of the qualification "ultimately" to the negation, then you will have no way to distinguish the two truths, and you will not be able to say, "Ultimately, it is such and such; conventionally, it is such and such." There is no explanation of such a Madhyamaka anywhere, so it is simply a wrong idea.

Candrakīrti's *Clear Words* refutes the addition of the qualification "ultimately" to the negation in the context of refuting production from self, not in the context of refuting mere production. This is very clear in that commentary. Also, as Candrakīrti's *Explanation of the "Middle Way" Commentary* says:[459]

The master Nāgārjuna refutes production from self in general without using a qualification, saying, "There is no production from self." There is someone [i.e., Bhāvaviveka] who uses the qualification, "Things are not produced from self *ultimately* because of existing, like a living being." I think that this use of the qualification "ultimately" is senseless.

Consequently, we do not distinguish Svātantrika-Madhyamaka and Prāsaṅgika-Madhyamaka by way of whether they add the qualification "ultimately" to the negation. [669] Instead, they differ in whether they refute essential or intrinsic existence conventionally. Hence, when refuting the essential or intrinsic existence of internal and external phenomena, Prāsaṅgikas say that it is unnecessary to add on new qualifications such as "ultimately," "in reality," or "truly." This is because if there were essential or intrinsic existence, it would have to be established as an ultimate, etc. Svātantrikas say that if you do not attach "ultimate" or the like to them then they cannot be refuted, so they add "ultimately," "in reality," or "truly." However, neither Madhyamaka system asserts that you can refute [conventionally existent things, such as] production, cessation, bondage, release, and so forth without adding some qualification such as "ultimately" or "essentially."

What is the meaning of "does not exist ultimately" (*don dam par med pa*)? Here, "object" (*don*) means something knowable, and "highest" (*dam pa*) means supreme; an ultimate (*don dam*) is a common locus of both. In another way, "highest" refers to a non-conceptual sublime wisdom and the ultimate is the object of the highest (*don dam*) because it is the object or domain of that. In yet another way, the wisdom concordant with the non-conceptual sublime wisdom that directly knows the ultimate is called the ultimate.

[Bhāvaviveka's *Heart of the Middle Way*] says:[460]

Earth and such
Are not elements ultimately.

Commenting on this, his *Blaze of Reasons* says:[461]

Regarding the term "ultimate" (*don dam pa, paramārtha*), it is an "object" (*don, artha*) because it is something to be known; it is synonymous with "something to be examined" and "something to be understood." "Highest" (*dam pa, parama*) is a term that means "supreme." Joined in the compound "highest object" (*don dam, paramārtha*), this means that because emptiness is an object and also the highest, it is the ultimate.

In another way, ultimate means "object of the highest" (*dam pa'i don, paramasya artha*). Because emptiness is the object of the highest—a non-conceptual sublime wisdom—it is the ultimate.

In another way, it means that which is "concordant with the ultimate." Because that ultimate exists for a wisdom that is concordant with direct knowledge of the ultimate, it is said to be concordant with the ultimate. [670]

When they say that something "does not exist ultimately" or "is nonexistent ultimately," it has the last of these three meanings, because that same text says:[462]

> *Qualm*: The ultimate is beyond all awarenesses, but the refutation of an essence of things is in the realm of letters. Thus, would not the refutation be nonexistent for that reason?
>
> *Reply*: There are two types of ultimate. One of these operates without conceptual activity; it is supramundane, stainless, and without elaborations. The second operates with conceptual activity and is concordant with the collections of merit and wisdom; it is called "sublime wisdom in the world" and it does involve elaborations. Here we hold this latter to be the qualifier in the thesis, "does not exist ultimately," so there is no fallacy.

Take this as referring to wisdom based on study and reflection that properly analyzes reality and to consciousnesses above that; it does not refer only to a noble being's post-equipoise condition.

Also, Kamalaśīla's *Illumination of the Middle Way* says:[463]

> The meaning of a statement such as "Production does not exist ultimately" is as follows: All consciousnesses that arise from study, reflection, and meditation on reality are accurate subjects. They are therefore called "ultimate" in that they are the ultimate of those consciousnesses. They differ in whether they work directly or indirectly, but the force of their thought makes it understood that all these things are strictly not produced. Therefore, we explain the phrase, "Production does not exist ultimately," as meaning that knowledge of reality does not establish that these things are produced.

This seems to agree with what is stated [in Bhāvaviveka's *Blaze of Reasons*]. Also, Kamalaśīla's *Commentary on the Difficult Points of [Śāntarakṣita's] "Ornament for the Middle Way"* (*Madhyamakālaṃkārapañjikā*) says:[464]

> To the qualm, "In what way is it that things do not exist intrinsically?" Śāntarakṣita said, "In reality." [671] The term "reality" refers to the status of things just as they are, something that is

known by an inference based on facts. This is the same as saying that things are empty when you analyze them just as they are. This explains the phrases "in reality," "ultimately," and so forth.

In another way, terms such as "reality" may refer only to knowledge of reality because that is what it observes. Knowledge of reality, not conventional knowledge, provides the understanding that allows us to say that things do not exist intrinsically.

Both Bhāvaviveka's *Lamp for [Nāgārjuna's] "Fundamental Treatise"* and his *Blaze of Reasons* often add qualifications such as "in reality" to the absence of intrinsic existence. In particular, the *Lamp for the "Fundamental Treatise,"* commenting on the fifteenth chapter of the *Fundamental Treatise*, says:[465]

> *Objection:* If things have no essence, how can they be things? If they are things, then they are not without essence. Thus, you have the fallacy of mistakenly denying those objects with the very words within your thesis.

The objection is that within the thesis, "Things do not have essence," Bhāvaviveka contradicts his own words. In that same text he replies:[466]

> We did not claim that things ultimately have essence and then advance the thesis of essencelessness. Therefore, we do not on that account mistakenly deny the object of our thesis. Thus, since this is not a case where the meaning of the reason is not established, we have no fault.

He holds that he does not mistakenly deny things due to his assertion that things lack essence *ultimately*; so it is clear that he asserts that it *would* be a mistaken denial to say that they lack essence— that is, do not essentially exist— *conventionally*. That same text also says:[467]

> Ultimately, internal things lack essence because they are produced and also because this distinctive statement of their being produced indicates that they are contingent upon the dependent.[468] For example, they are like the human beings, etc. that a conjurer has emanated. [672]

Thus he definitely adds the qualification "ultimately" in the refutation of intrinsic existence.

With regard to this, all of these masters agree that something's not existing ultimately means that when a reasoning consciousness properly analyzing its ontological status places it under scrutiny, that consciousness does not establish its existence. Therefore, even the texts of Bhāvaviveka, in positing conventionalities, say such things as, "Without engaging in analysis that accords with perception of reality..."; when refuting intrinsic existence they often say, "...does not exist under rational analysis." Thus, these statements and those of the former masters are similar.

However, these masters do not agree as to whether something that exists essentially must be held capable of withstanding scrutiny by rational analysis of its ontological status. As I have explained at length above, the two masters Buddhapālita and Candrakīrti hold that something that exists essentially must be able to withstand scrutiny by rational analysis of reality, and hence must also be established ultimately.

18

MISINTERPRETATIONS OF THE SVĀTANTRIKA/PRĀSAṄGIKA DISTINCTION

(2″) Whether to carry out that refutation with a Svātantrika procedure or with a Prāsaṅgika procedure
  (a)) The meaning of Svātantrika and Prāsaṅgika
    (1)) The refutation of others' positions
      (a')) What others believe
        [(1')) The first misinterpretation]
        [(2')) The second misinterpretation]
        [(3')) The third misinterpretation]
        [(4')) The fourth misinterpretation]

(2″) Whether to carry out that refutation with a Svātantrika procedure or with a Prāsaṅgika procedure

Should you refute the object of negation with a Svātantrika procedure or with a Prāsaṅgika procedure? This has two parts:

1. The meaning of Svātantrika and Prāsaṅgika (Chapters 18-21)
2. Which system to follow so as to develop the right philosophical view in your mind-stream (Chapter 21)

(a)) The meaning of Svātantrika and Prāsaṅgika

It is not clear that the commentary of the master Buddhapālita sets up a Prāsaṅgika system, distinguishing Prāsaṅgika from Svātantrika.

Nonetheless, consider his commentary on the opening lines of the *Fundamental Treatise*:[469]

> There is no sense in which anything
> Has ever been produced
> Either from itself, from something else,
> From both, or without a cause.

Here he negates the four types of production by pointing out the faults of other systems. The master Bhāvaviveka refutes him, claiming that Buddhapālita's arguments have no power to establish his own position or to repudiate the positions of others. [673] Now the master Candrakīrti extensively comments on why Buddhapālita's own system does not suffer from such faults, and in so doing he states that Mādhyamikas should employ *reductio ad absurdum* (*prasaṅga*) arguments, not autonomous (*svatantra*) arguments, as their method for instilling the Madhyamaka view in others. In this way Candrakīrti elucidates the Prāsaṅgika position through a refutation of autonomous argument.

This section on how to posit such a Svātantrika/Prāsaṅgika distinction has two parts:

1. The refutation of others' positions (Chapters 18-19)
2. Setting forth our own position (Chapters 20-21)

(1)) The refutation of others' positions

This section has two parts:

1. Stating what others believe
2. Refuting those positions (Chapter 19)

(a')) What others believe

There have been many ways of defining *reductio* arguments and autonomous arguments; who could explain all of them? That is why I focus on only a few of them.

[(1')) The first misinterpretation][470]

Jayānanda advocates the following position. In his *Explanation of [Candrakīrti's] "Commentary on the 'Middle Way'"* (*Madhyamakāvatara-ṭīkā*) he says:[471]

> *Question*: If you consider *reductio ad absurdum* argument to be a syllogistic reasoning, then does valid cognition establish it? If so, then it would be established for *both* parties, so how can you say that it is "what the other party asserts"? If not, then since it

would be inappropriate for the other party to assert what is not established, how can you say that it is "what the other party asserts"?

Reply: Some might answer, "Whatever valid cognition establishes is established for both sides," but that is precisely what we do *not* know. When one party posits something as a probative reason, even though valid cognition may establish it for the one who posits the syllogism, how can that person be certain that valid cognition establishes it for the other party? After all, the particulars of another person's mind are objects of neither perception nor inference. And how can you be certain that valid cognition establishes it even for yourself, for it is possible that you could be deceived, inasmuch as you have been under the influence of error for an exceedingly long time. Therefore, I accept the nature of things on the strength of both the proponent and opponent accepting such as valid. Hence, I refute the positions of others in terms of their own assertions. [674]

The proponent of any syllogism does not know whether the opponents have established the reason for themselves by means of a valid cognition. This is because neither of the two types of valid cognition [valid sense-type cognition and valid cognition based on a reason] give the proponent access to what the opponent is thinking. You cannot be certain that valid cognition establishes the reason even for yourself, for even when you determine that you have established it by valid cognition, it is possible that you have been deceived. Therefore, since there are no validly established reasons, the debate is founded on what the parties accept as valid. Hence, it is proper to refute opponents in terms of what they accept, even though valid cognition does not establish anything for either party. This is how he explains it.

And again, this same *Explanation of [Candrakīrti's] "Commentary on the 'Middle Way'"* continues:[472]

According to the partisans of autonomous reasoning, what makes something an autonomous probative reason is that valid cognition establishes the pervasion between the reason and the probandum. Yet that pervasion is not established. A valid cognition that establishes a pervasion is either a perception or an inference. Let us take them one at a time.

A perception cannot establish the pervasion. Through what is perceived and what is not perceived, you can know that there is a necessary conditional relationship between fire and smoke in a kitchen, so that if one exists, the other will also, and if one does not exist, neither will the other. However, you cannot deduce the existence of fire from the existence of smoke in *all* places.

Nor can you use inference to establish the pervasion, for that too is limited to certain domains. The domain of inference is not universal because knowledge that something is impermanent, for example, will arise only when there is a reason related to the probandum and not in all places and times. Therefore, the pervasion is established only by way of what the world accepts, and not by means of a valid cognition. Hence, how can it be wrong to use *reductio* syllogistic reasoning to refute the opposition?

So if valid cognitions did establish pervasions—such as the presence of fire wherever there is smoke or the impermanence of all that is produced—then autonomous arguments would be acceptable, but they do not. [675] If valid cognitions established pervasions, then the pervasions concerning the existence of fire wherever there is smoke and impermanence wherever there is production would have to be established in all places and times. However, since perception and inference establish those pervasions only in relation to specific domains, such as kitchens and pots, the scope of those pervasions is limited. Therefore, mere acceptance and not valid cognition must establish even the pervasions. This is what Jayānanda says. Evidently he believes that if a proof uses a reason for which valid cognition has established the three criteria, then it is an autonomous argument; if a proof is made just on the basis of the parties accepting the fulfillment of the three criteria,[473] then it is a *reductio* argument.

[(2')) The second misinterpretation]

Some translators, students of that scholar [Jayānanda], argue as follows:[474] Mādhyamikas have no theses of their own. They only refute what others believe. Since the elements of a syllogism such as the subject are not agreed upon—that is, accepted by both parties—autonomous arguments are not tenable. The only result of reasoned analysis is that others give up their tenets. Apart from this, since Mādhyamikas have no beliefs of their own, the autonomous syllogism should not be used under any circumstances. Therefore, only *reductio* arguments are permissible. Indeed, since those *reductio* arguments which establish a positive position ultimately derive from autonomous syllogisms, only *reductio*s that negate the position of opponents are permissible. Since this latter type of *reductio* is a *reductio* in which both the reason and the pervasion are merely accepted by both parties or derived from the mere assertions of the parties, correct valid cognition does not establish the reason and pervasion. It is based on such a *reductio* that they eliminate the claims or elaborations of others, and they do this with four types of arguments.

Of these, the *"reductio* argument expressing a contradiction" works in the following way. The opponents accept that production, for example, is purposeful and finite, and they also believe that things are produced from themselves. But if a thing is produced from itself, since that would mean that something that already exists is being produced, production would be purposeless and endless, and it would be incorrect to hold that it is purposeful and finite. If they accept that, then it would be incorrect for them to accept that things are produced from themselves. When the contradictions are assembled in this way, the only result is that the opponents understand them and abandon this tenet. [676]

"Inference based on what others accept" refutes the opponent using a subject, a reason, and so forth that are accepted by that opponent. For example, the seedling that you accept as produced from itself is not produced from itself because it is its own very self. Even though the Mādhyamikas state that it is not produced from itself, this is merely a refutation of the others' claim that things arise from themselves; it does not establish for the Mādhyamikas themselves the nonexistence of production from self, and hence the Mādhyamikas have no theses.

The argument called "the similarity of probative reason and probandum" involves showing how none of the examples or signs that the opponents state in order to prove their position can be proven relevant to that position.

The "argument from the parallelism of similar reasons" involves parallelism between indistinguishable reasons, such that if you accept one, you accept the other.

Objection: Well then, do you or do you not believe such refutations of what the opponent accepts? If you do, then that in itself constitutes your thesis and there would be an autonomous reason proving that position. If you do not, it is pointless for you to give arguments that refute what the other party accepts.

Reply by the followers of Jayānanda: When you analyze the ultimate, if you accept a predicate such as "lacks intrinsic existence" or "is not produced," then you have to accept autonomous theses and reasons. However, since we do not accept such predicates, we have no fault. If simply believing something means that you have a thesis, then everyone would have theses about everything.

That is how [the followers of Jayānanda] explain their position. Evidently they believe that even though they have nothing to prove from their own side, they can merely refute others' positions; that even though they have beliefs, they have no theses; and that they have no position of their own, avoiding theses such as the absence of intrinsic existence when analyzing the ultimate. Apparently, they consider as Svātantrikas those who do not believe that there is nothing at all that can be asserted and who therefore, when analyzing the ultimate, assert the predicate "lacks intrinsic nature" and establish that as their own position. Those who do not assert such predicates, but engage only in the refutation of what others accept, they consider Prāsaṅgikas.

[(3')) The third misinterpretation][475] [677]

According to those who today consider themselves Prāsaṅgika-Mādhyamikas, there is nothing to accept even conventionally in one's own system, neither as regards the ultimate nor as regards the conventional. If you have such a thesis, then you have to accept the examples and reasons that prove it, and in that case you are a Svātantrika. Therefore, Prāsaṅgikas have no system of their own at all. For, Nāgārjuna's *Refutation of Objections* states:[476]

> If I had any thesis,
> Then I would suffer from that fault,
> But as I have no theses,
> I alone am without faults.

> If sensory perception and so forth
> Could actually perceive something
> Then there would be something to prove or to refute.
> But as they do not, I cannot be faulted.

Also, Nāgārjuna's *Sixty Stanzas of Reasoning* says:[477]

> Mahātmas have no positions,
> They have no arguments.
> How can those who have no positions themselves
> Have positions *vis-à-vis* others?

Also, Āryadeva's *Four Hundred Stanzas* says:[478]

> No matter how long you try
> You can never rebut
> Those who have no position
> In regard to existence, nonexistence, or both.

All of these are sources showing that a Mādhyamika has no position or thesis. The *Clear Words* states:[479]

> If you are a Mādhyamika, it is not right to make an autonomous argument, for we do not accept the positions of others.

And also:[480]

> The opposite of the absurd consequence in a *reductio* pertains to
> the opponent, but not to ourselves, for we have no theses.

Also, Candrakīrti's *Commentary on the "Middle Way"* states:[481]

> Does a refutation work to refute by contacting what it refutes?
> Or does it refute without making contact?
> This problem is inevitable for those who have positions,
> But since I do not, this *reductio* argument does not apply to me.

These passages state that because Mādhyamikas have no position,
those faults do not apply to them. Therefore, all Madhyamaka expositions are put forward only in terms of the perspective of the
other party. [678] For, as Candrakīrti's *Commentary on the "Middle
Way"* states:[482]

> While you accept real dependent entities
> I do not accept them even conventionally;
> For effect, I say they exist even though they do not.
> Taking the perspective of the world, I speak of a self.

What is more, Nāgārjuna's *Refutation of Objections* says:[483]

> Since there is nothing to be refuted,
> I refute nothing.
> Therefore, in saying that I refute something,
> You insult me.

So there is no such thing as even refuting some other position. That
is what they say.

[(4')) The fourth misinterpretation][484]

Some earlier Mādhyamikas, Tibetan scholars who follow the master
Candrakīrti, argue as follows: We completely reject these systems that
claim that Mādhyamikas have no positions of their own and no valid
cognitions to establish them. Our own system is as follows. We refute both the perceptual and inferential "valid cognitions based on
real fact"[485] of those who put forward presentations of valid cognition and the objects it cognizes in terms of intrinsic character that can
withstand rational analysis. Accepting conventionally, without analysis, the valid cognitions and cognized objects familiar to the world,
we Mādhyamikas demonstrate that things lack true existence with
sound reasoning by making a proof statement to the opponent. Even
so, we are not Svātantrikas, for we posit the lack of true existence by
means of valid cognitions that are familiar to the world, unanalyzed.

19

REFUTING MISINTERPRETATIONS OF THE SVĀTANTRIKA/PRĀSAṄGIKA DISTINCTION

(b')) Refuting those positions

(1')) Refuting the first misinterpretation

In the system of Jayānanda's *Explanation of [Candrakīrti's] "Commentary on the 'Middle Way',"* valid cognition does not establish the reason and the pervasion. Jayānanda claims that valid cognition does not establish the reason, but his justification is deficient for the following reasons: (1) Even in a system that holds that both proponent and opponent must have previously established the reason with valid cognition, something does not cease to be considered a reason simply because the proponent is not certain that the reason is established for the opponent. Hence, Jayānanda's rationale does not vitiate against the necessity of the opponent's establishing the reason by means of a valid cognition. [679] (2) If you claim that you do not know whether a reason is established for an opponent because you do not know the mind of the opponent, then it follows that you cannot even be certain that the other party has accepted a particular point; therefore, it would be impossible to refute opponents in terms of what they accept, etc. Why? Even if you have perceptual certainty about the opponents' words when they say, "This is what we accept," following your logic you would not have certain knowledge that they actually accept what they have stated because you do not know the minds of other beings.

The justification that Jayānanda gives for why valid cognition does not establish the *pervasion* is also inadequate. The kitchen is the object based upon which you understand the pervasion, "in the kitchen, when there is smoke there is fire." The thing understood with respect to that basis is the bare pervasion, "when there is smoke, there is fire." It is certainly not that you are to apprehend the pervasion, "where there is kitchen smoke, there is kitchen fire." Hence, how could it be that you apprehend a pervasion limited to a particular time and place? Or else, if the pervasion were limited in that way, since kitchen would not work as the basis for ascertaining such a limited pervasion, you would have to adduce some other basis in relation to which ascertainment of the limited pervasion is needed. For example, impermanence—a predicated quality that is ascertained with respect to sound—must apply to both sound and pots. A form of impermanence that is sound's alone cannot be posited as the predicated quality. This same line of reasoning demonstrates that it is incorrect to hold that the inference establishing the pervasion is not a valid cognition.

He also claims that only the proponent's and opponent's acceptance of the pervasion establishes it inasmuch as valid cognition does not establish it. This also is incorrect. Why? If you treat the mere acceptance of a position as justification for it, then you cannot refute the opponent, for the opponent's assertion of a point would establish it, and neither side has any valid cognition that can refute it.

Question: But what if you were to distinguish between different types of acceptance, wherein one type could and the other could not establish the reason, pervasion, etc.?

Reply: If you justify such a distinction by the mere fact that it has been asserted, then your argument resembles what you are trying to prove and you have not advanced your position. If, however, you make the distinction on the basis of whether there is a valid cognition to back up an assertion, then you have strayed from your belief that there are no valid cognitions.

(2')) **Refuting the second misinterpretation [680]**

You hold that avoiding autonomous theses means that when analyzing reality you do not assert the thesis that there is no intrinsic nature. But in not accepting that thesis, is it because the thesis is not established by the reasoned knowledge analyzing whether there is intrinsic nature? Or, in not accepting that thesis, do you adduce the reason that this is an occasion in which reality is being analyzed? Which do you hold?

In the first case, if reasoned knowledge does not establish the referent of the thesis, the lack of intrinsic nature, then reasoned knowledge could also not refute the referent of the thesis "intrinsic nature exists," for similar reasons. And it is utterly incorrect of you to think that the referent of the thesis "intrinsic nature exists" is not refuted when reality is being analyzed, for the following reasons: (1) You claimed previously that reasoned analysis refutes the others' systems. (2) Non-analytical [i.e., conventional] knowledge cannot refute others' systems. (3) Otherwise, if analysis did not refute the thesis "intrinsic nature exists," then why would you have to specify, "We accept no thesis *in our own system*"? For in that case you would not even accept *reductio* arguments that refute the others' systems.

When you use a *reductio* argument to eliminate the tenets of the other party, then the refutation of the existence of intrinsic nature should itself establish the absence of intrinsic nature. I made this point above in regard to a previously cited passage from the *Refutation of Objections* and its commentary.[486] There is no third alternative. Were this not the case, someone might claim just the opposite of your position, saying, "I am establishing the absence of intrinsic nature; I am not refuting the existence of intrinsic nature." What response could you give? If you think that affirming the absence of intrinsic nature must, without a doubt, negate intrinsic nature, then it should also be the case that negating the existence of intrinsic nature must, without a doubt, similarly affirm the absence of intrinsic nature.

If you think that theses such as the absence of intrinsic nature are improper because this is an occasion in which reality is being analyzed, give your justification for this now. [681] You may suppose that one cannot accept such beliefs because something that exists when reality is being analyzed must ultimately exist, but this conclusion is incorrect. If you reject the very occasion during which reality is being analyzed, then you will have to accept the impossibility of a time period during which a Mādhyamika analyzes things with reason. But if you admit to such an occasion, then you definitely must also accept the existence of the analyzer, the analyzing reasoning, the basis of the analysis, the opponent with whom you are analyzing, etc. Hence, why is it necessary for everything that exists at that time to exist ultimately? Nor is it satisfactory to claim that insofar as a mere *reductio* involves only what is asserted by the opponent, or what can ultimately be derived from those assertions, you are constructing a *reductio* even though there are no valid cognitions. Therefore, I refute your view just as I refuted the first system above.

Moreover, it is not appropriate to claim that you have no assertions while reality is being analyzed, but that you do have assertions conventionally. This is because the occasion during which reality is analyzed cannot be an ultimate thing; hence, it must be a conventionality, and that contradicts your thesis. Also, if not existing while reality is being analyzed means not existing ultimately, then having no assertions while reality is being analyzed could not be a distinguishing characteristic of Prāsaṅgika—for no Mādhyamikas of any sort hold that they have assertions ultimately.

(3′)) Refuting the third misinterpretation

As previously explained, those who claim that the Mādhyamikas have no theses, even conventionally, have not properly identified the object that reason negates. Hence, they refute the opponent with arguments that refute intrinsic nature, and then, when the situation is reversed, they see those arguments as applying in exactly the same way to their own system as well. In setting forth their own system they have no idea of how to avoid error. Hence, all dependent-arisings—whether of cyclic existence or nirvāṇa—end up having an ontological status like that of non-Buddhists' fabrications such as a divine creator. Therefore, that interpretation slanders the Mādhyamikas and merits utter contempt. [682] I have already explained at length the refutation of that position.

Those who analyze whether Mādhyamikas assert anything must agree that a Mādhyamika is posited as one who has the "middle way." Hence, they will have to accept that a Mādhyamika understands the meaning of dependent-arising—that ultimately not even a particle exists, while conventionally all is like illusion. So there *is* something to assert. Moreover, you must posit this by refuting the vile claims that are the reverse of those positions, namely, the belief that things ultimately exist and the belief that they do not exist even conventionally. Therefore, there *is* valid cognition that knows what is proven and what is refuted, and there is a discourse in which Mādhyamikas, based on their own knowledge, accurately teach others. Because of this, and because the opponents have no philosophically coherent response to the points that they set forth, this system is exceedingly pure.

Accordingly, even if you do not know how to set forth the perfect system of Mādhyamika scholars, you should at least not slander it by claiming that it does not exist. The very acceptance of the reasoning of dependent-arising cuts through all of the entanglements of wrong views. The intelligent who heed this will avoid all contradiction in setting forth the Madhyamaka system and will not trust those who spread such lies. Candrakīrti's *Clear Words* states:[487]

> Thus, our position is completely pure of any logical flaw and definitely does not contradict any traditional presentation of conventional or ultimate reality, while your position has obvious and severe flaws and does contradict those traditional presentations. Through utter foolishness, you do not see these faults and good points accurately. Those faults that you attribute to me are yours.

The Madhyamaka system mentioned in this previously cited passage is an irrefutable presentation deriving both from valid cognitions that determine what is ultimate and from conventional valid cognitions. [683] Hence you can be certain that it is completely pure of logical flaw and that it allows you to make a complete exposition of cyclic existence and nirvāṇa. Or else, if the claim "Mādhyamikas have no system of their own" were considered irrefutable, then the claim "Everything that you say is a lie" could also not be refuted even to the slightest degree, for similar reasons.

Objection: Those who claim to assert nothing are not subject to analysis as to whether or not they have any assertions. So, because we accept nothing at all, no one can refute us.

Reply: This too is untenable. For if it were tenable, then even in the case of those who claim, "All claims are false," one could not show that they have contradicted their own words because their claim that all words are false would by your logic preclude analysis of the veracity of those very words. It is also not tenable because Candrakīrti's *Commentary on the "Middle Way"* states:[488]

> If there were some self that existed in reality, then it would be something
> That exists with the body, as does the mind; it would not be ineffable.

In response to the Vatsiputriyas' belief that there is a substantially existent self that cannot be described as either the same as or different from the aggregates, this passage says that if the self exists substantially, it must be susceptible to description either as the same as or as different from the aggregates. But if you are right, then it would be possible for the Vatsiputriyas to answer, "You cannot engage in an analysis of that kind."

Suppose you argue that you can engage in analysis as follows: "If the Vatsiputriyas claim that the person substantially exists, it is incorrect for them to hold that the person cannot be described in terms of those aggregates, as this would contradict their view that the person is neither the same as the aggregates nor different from them." If you do make this argument, then by the same token the very statement, "If I assert nothing, I have no assertion," constitutes a sincere claim. You might argue that the following two situations are similar: (1) saying, "We have no wealth," and receiving the reply, "Give me that wealth which is no wealth"; and (2) saying, "We accept nothing," and receiving the reply, "The acceptance of nothing is itself accepting something." [684] However, in making this argument you misunderstand our position. We are *not* claiming that not having assertions is itself an assertion. Well then, what are we saying? We are demonstrating that by sincerely claiming that you assert nothing you necessarily assert that you assert nothing. As a result, you inevitably cancel out your own words.

If claims like the ones you make do not belong to the Madhyamaka system, then you contradict yourself by proving them through the citation of passages from the works of the noble Nāgārjuna and his spiritual son Āryadeva. Also, such claims cannot be considered the system of Candrakīrti, nor the system of any other Buddhist. Thus, they fall outside of the teaching.

Those who claim to advocate the Madhyamaka system, and in particular the system of Candrakīrti, contradict themselves by claiming to have no system of their own. Likewise, it is also incorrect to claim that everything that you set forth is posited only in terms of the perspective of others, in this way hoping to free yourself from asserting anything. When you say that you must assert the existence of things such as form only in terms of the perspective of others, you may not be asserting the existence of things such as form, but you certainly must be asserting that you posit form and such in terms of the perspective of others, so you have not freed yourself from all assertions. You have to assert that at that time there is (1) another person in terms of whose perspective you posit things, and (2) yourself, the one who posits them. Therefore, the claim that you accept things only in terms of the perspective of others not only fails to imply that you have no system of your own, it actually vitiates against such a notion.

Objection: We do not even claim that we have no system or that we assert theses only in terms of the perspective of others. However, from your point of view it appears that we make these claims.

Reply: This position denies sensory experience that even the Lokāyatas cannot deny. When you do not even experience what you yourself claim, how surprising that you should know what *we* have heard. If you do deny the evidence of sensory experience, then why do you need to insist that you have no assertion? For no matter what you claim, you can deny it later and thus never be faulted. [685]

Opponent: We posit even *reductio* arguments only in terms of the perspective of others. We do not accept them in our own system.

Reply: Then what does it mean for you to repudiate the Svātantrika system and to have faith in the system of Candrakīrti, the textual founder of the Prāsaṅgika system? For, just as the autonomous syllogism is inadmissible in your own system, so too *reductio* arguments are inadmissible; just as *reductio* arguments are admissible in terms of the perspective of others, you also end up using autonomous syllogisms, as needed, in terms of the perspective of others.

We cannot call those persons Cittamātrins who accept mind-only philosophy in terms of the perspective of others, but who do not accept it in their own system. Likewise, we cannot call those persons Prāsaṅgikas who, while not allowing in their own system *reductio* arguments that establish the meaning of the middle way, nonetheless posit them in terms of the perspective of others. And since those who advocate this position are also not Svātantrikas, this clearly shows that they are not Mādhyamikas.

[Candrakīrti's *Commentary on the "Middle Way"*] states:[489]

> I say they exist for the effect, even though they do not.
> Taking the perspective of the world, I speak of a self.

You cannot use this as a source to prove that all positions are taken only in terms of the perspective of others. Why? One posits phenomena as lacking essential or intrinsic nature only in the purview of reasoned knowledge that properly analyzes whether such a nature exists. One does not posit this in the purview of an ordinary conventional consciousness. Why? Were that ordinary consciousness able to establish the lack of intrinsic nature, then reasoned knowledge would be pointless, which is absurd. Also, since that same text says, "I say they exist… taking the perspective of the world," it means that the existence of forms and such is posited in terms of the perspective of the world.

When that text, in the lines prior to those just cited, states that we do not accept the conventional, it means that we do not accept dependent entities as Cittamātra accepts them; it does not mean that we do not in our own system accept the conventional, for it says "real dependent entities such as you accept." This stanza responds to a Cittamātrin argument given in a transitional passage of the commentary on that text:[490] **[686]** "If you use what is valid or reasonable to refute dependent entities, I will use your arguments to refute what you consider the conventional." Hence, the meaning is this: You Cittamātrins believe dependent entities to be things that can withstand rational analysis. I do not accept such conventional phenomena. Hence, we disagree as to whether one can use reason to refute them.

We do not take the expression "taking the perspective of the world" to refer to the perspective of others who do not belong to our own system; rather it refers to unimpaired conventional consciousnesses. This is because the existence of conventional objects must always be posited within the purview of such a consciousness and because the valid cognitions that posit conventionalities exist even in the Mādhyamika's own mind-stream. Therefore, we take the words "even though they do not exist" to refer to their lack of existence by way of intrinsic character. So the passage should be glossed as, "I tell them they exist, even though they do not exist by way of their intrinsic character." It is inappropriate to gloss it as, "I say they exist even though they do not exist." This is because this passage represents our way of positing conventional objects in which existence by way of intrinsic character is not possible even conventionally. Also, in the portion of the commentary to his *Commentary on the "Middle Way"* that explains that passage, Candrakīrti states that "I accept whatever exists or does not exist for the world just as the world does." Thus, that passage cannot be taken to mean that things do not exist. Therefore, since there are many such instances in which the text states that even though things do not ultimately exist, they nonetheless exist conventionally, there is not the slightest fault in taking the existence that is affirmed and the existence that is denied as having different meanings in the passage, "I say they exist even though they do not."

Objection: You still have to explain what Nāgārjuna's *Refutation of Objections* means when it says that Mādhyamikas have no positions and theses.[491] If you adopt the thesis, "the seedling has no essential or intrinsic nature," then you also have to accept the reason, "because it is a dependently arisen thing," and the example, "for example, like a reflected image." [687] Accordingly, you accept that a syllogistic statement creates for the opponent (1) a reason that has bearing on the subject and has the two forms of pervasion,[492] (2) a probandum that the reason proves, and (3) an inference that understands that probandum. This being the case, then—aside from simply hating the *name* "autonomous syllogism"—why do you go to the trouble of refuting autonomous syllogisms?

Reply: The *Refutation of Objections* does explain that we have no theses and positions, just as you have cited it, but since there are also many passages that state that it is necessary to posit assertions, how can simply citing that one passage prove that Mādhyamikas have no positions?

It is quite true, however, that there has been concern that anyone who holds the absence of intrinsic existence as a thesis is a Svātantrika. This is because this is an exceedingly subtle and difficult point. Our response to that will be explained when we set forth our own position.[493]

As for Nāgārjuna's statement in the *Refutation of Objections* that he has no thesis, Mādhyamikas say that things lack intrinsic nature. The essentialists argue that if the words of such a thesis have intrinsic nature, then it is incorrect to say that all phenomena lack intrinsic nature; if those words lack intrinsic nature, then they cannot repudiate the existence of intrinsic nature. However, something without intrinsic nature *can* function to prove or to disprove; according to previously cited passages from the *Refutation of Objections* and its commentary, this is admissible.[494] Therefore, the issue as to having or not having theses is not an argument about whether Nāgārjuna has them *in general*. It is instead an argument as to whether the words of the thesis "all things lack intrinsic nature" have intrinsic nature. Hence, the meaning of the lines from the *Refutation of Objections* is this: If I accepted that the words of such a thesis had an intrinsic nature, then I could be faulted for contradicting the thesis that all things lack intrinsic nature, but because I do not accept that, I cannot be faulted. That is why these lines cannot be taken as proving that Mādhyamikas have no theses, for there is a very great difference between the absence of intrinsic existence and nonexistence.

The verse of the *Refutation of Objections*—"If sensory perception and so forth…"—does state that sensory perception and such have no perception at all.[495] [688] However, according to the previously cited passage from the *Clear Words*,[496] this means that valid cognition and the phenomena it perceives are not essentially existent perceived objects and perceiving agents. It does not mean that there are no dependently arisen valid cognitions or phenomena that they perceive. In [the essentialists'] opinion, even if the intrinsic character of things as established by sensory perception *could* be refuted, the Mādhyamikas' claim that all things are empty of intrinsic nature would still require that sensory perception and the objects perceived by it be empty of intrinsic nature inasmuch as they are included among "things." In that case, sensory perception and the objects perceived by it would in their view be nonexistent; hence one cannot refute the intrinsic character of things. That passage from the *Refutation of Objections* which states that sensory perception lacks perception is given in answer to this essentialist view, a view which it states in these lines: [497]

> If the things perceived by sensory perception
> Were then repudiated,
> The sensory perception by which things are perceived
> Would itself be nonexistent.

The *Commentary* to those lines states:[498]

> Nor is it possible to claim that perception observes all things and then to repudiate them by stating, "All things are empty." Why? Valid sensory perception is included among "all things," and is therefore empty. That which perceives things would also be empty. Therefore, there would be no perception by valid cognition. What cannot perceive also cannot refute, and hence the claim that all things are empty is not valid.

As for the lines from Āryadeva's *Four Hundred Stanzas*, "You can never rebut…,"[499] Candrakīrti's commentary teaches us that one cannot refute the advocates of emptiness, no matter how long one tries. Since you claim that you do not even assert emptiness, how can you cite this passage in support of having no assertion at all? Candrakīrti's *Explanation of the "Middle Way" Commentary* quotes those four lines in the following passage:[500]

> It is incorrect for those who advocate the position that things exist only as designations to advocate dualism. [689] Therefore, those who advance critiques and responses grounded in dualism

against the Madhyamaka never find the slightest foothold. As Āryadeva's *Four Hundred Stanzas* says,

> No matter how long you try
> You can never rebut
> Those who have no position
> In regard to existence, nonexistence, or both.

Hence, Candrakīrti uses this passage to explain that neither the essentialists, who hold that things exist essentially, nor the nihilists, who believe in the total repudiation of the functioning of things such as form, can refute those who accept imputed existence while repudiating essential or substantial existence. Consequently, that passage cannot be used as a source for the claim that Mādhyamikas have no position of their own. It is quite clear that the positions of existence, nonexistence, and so forth refer to instances of dualistically advocated positions. Hence, they are to be explained just as they were previously in our treatment of the refutation of the tetralemma and the way to refute the advocates of existence and nonexistence.[501]

Candrakīrti's commentary on Nāgārjuna's *"Sixty Stanzas of Reasoning"* passage, "Mahātmas have no positions...," states:[502]

> Since there are no such real things, neither one's own position nor those of others can occur. The afflictions of those who see this will definitely stop.

This commentary gives the nonexistence of real things as the reason for having no position. Moreover, "real thing" here must be taken to refer to intrinsic character or intrinsic nature, for to construe it as referring to functionality would contradict the statement that seeing its nonexistence stops the afflictions. Therefore, insofar as Mādhyamikas have no positions in which they accept intrinsically existing things, this text says that they have no positions. This is because Candrakīrti's *Commentary on the "Sixty Stanzas of Reasoning,"* in the passage preceding this verse, identifies the assertion of real things as the reification of intrinsic character in things. Candrakīrti's *Commentary* and its root text say:[503]

> As for those who have not fathomed this reality—dependent-arising—and who believe completely in the intrinsic character of things:
>
>> If they assert a real thing, it is absolutely certain
>> That they will cling to stubborn
>> And pernicious views which will

Give rise to attachment and hostility.
Disputation will be the result of those views. [**690**]

Therefore, these scriptural passages do not teach that the Mādhyamikas have no system of their own. Hence, this is also how you should understand the meaning of the *Clear Words* passage that says, "...because we do not accept others' positions...," citing the *Refutation of Objections* and the *Four Hundred Stanzas*.[504]

"To be refuted" in the *Refutation of Objections* passage that states, "Since there is nothing to be refuted, I refute nothing,"[505] might be interpreted in two ways. If we take "what is to be refuted" as referring to the object of the reification of things as intrinsically existent, it makes no sense for Nāgārjuna to say that because intrinsic existence does not exist, he refutes nothing. Hence, we must take it as referring to the reifying consciousness that is refuted. Candrakīrti's commentary on that passage says that even the refuting agent does not exist; hence the nonexistence of both what is refuted and the refuting agent refers to the nonexistence of a refuted object and a refuting agent that exist by way of intrinsic character. [The *Commentary on the "Refutation of Objections"*][506] states that the essentialist, taking the refuting agent and object of refutation to exist in that way, that is, by way of their intrinsic character, insults us by saying that we do that kind of refutation.

Nāgārjuna does assert that both the refuted object and the refuting agent are like illusions. Why? His *Refutation of Objections* states:[507]

An emanation can send out an emanation,
And an illusory being can use illusion
To stop illusion.
This refutation works in the same way.

It also states that if the apprehension of a mirage as water intrinsically existed it would not occur in dependence upon its causes and conditions, and no one could overcome that apprehension:[508]

If that apprehension intrinsically existed,
It could not arise dependently.
Can any apprehension that arises dependently
Help but be empty?

If an apprehension intrinsically existed,
Who could overcome it?
The same procedure works for everything else.
That is why there is no reply to it.

The *Clear Words* passage that states, "The opposite of the absurd consequence in a *reductio* pertains to the opponent, but not to ourselves, for we have no theses,"[509] can also not be taken as a source to prove that Mādhyamikas have no system of their own, for that passage means that they have no autonomous theses.

What about the *Commentary on the "Middle Way"* passage in which Candrakīrti says that he has no positions?[510] [691] In his own system Candrakīrti holds that neither his refutation nor the position he is refuting exist intrinsically. Therefore, when he uses reasoned analysis to refute the other party's belief that causes *intrinsically* give rise to their effects, asking whether causes give rise to effects through contact with them or without contact with them, this refutation does not apply to Candrakīrti himself because he does not have to assert things that can withstand rational analysis. This is what that passage means. It does not at all imply that we have no system of our own, for Candrakīrti's *Explanation of the "Middle Way" Commentary* comments on that passage:[511]

> We do not fall into a similar absurdity in our own system because, from our perspective, the refutation does not refute what it refutes by contacting it, nor does the refutation refute what it refutes without contacting it. This is because neither the refutation nor what it refutes intrinsically exist. Therefore, we do not consider whether they make contact.

Why is the rational analysis proposed by the essentialists not applicable to the Madhyamaka refutation? He says it is because the refutation and what it refutes do not intrinsically exist; he does not say that it is because Mādhyamikas have no assertions. In support he cites the *Perfection of Wisdom Sūtra in Twenty-five Thousand Lines* where Śāriputra investigates and asks Subhuti about what kind of phenomenon, produced or unproduced, brings about the attainment of an unproduced phenomenon. After Śāriputra has refuted that either kind brings it about, he then asks, "Is it that there is no attainment and no clear knowledge?" and Subhuti says, as in the earlier citation,[512] that these two do exist, but not dualistically. Using this as an example, Candrakīrti's *Explanation of the "Middle Way" Commentary* gives this explanation:[513]

> Because it would lead to such dualistic absurdities, the sūtra denies that a produced or unproduced phenomenon brings about attainment. Moreover, as dualistic analysis is inappropriate in the absence of real things, attainment is accepted without analysis, according to the conventions of the world. Likewise, it is neither

that a refutation and what it refutes come into contact nor is it that
they do not come into contact. **[692]** Nonetheless, you should realize that conventionally a refutation refutes what is to be refuted.

This clearly states that when analyzed in terms of contact or non-
contact, refutation does not exist in either way. But since this analysis
does not deny the existence of refutation, Mādhyamikas must accept that conventionally there are refutations of the positions taken
by others.

What is more, Candrakīrti also accepts the fact that a syllogistic
reason establishes the probandum. How so? In another passage that
immediately follows the one cited above, his *Commentary on the
"Middle Way"* and *Explanation of the "Middle Way" Commentary*
state:[514]

> You can see the details of the orb of the sun,
> Such as an eclipse, even in a reflection of the sun.
> It is unreasonable to ask whether the sun and its image
>   come into contact,
> Yet this does occur in a merely conventional and dependent
>   way.
>
> A reflection is not something that is true, but in order to
>   make your face beautiful
> You treat it as existing; likewise, the reasonings
> That have the power to cleanse wisdom's countenance
> Induce understanding of the point to be proven, even
>   though they are "improper" [according to essentialist
>   logic].

This is how it should be understood: Since a reflected image does
not exist in the least, it is totally impossible to consider whether it
is produced through contact or without contact with the orb of the
sun. Nonetheless, when you see in a reflection a nearby form that
is a causal condition for that reflection, you ascertain the object that
you are seeking to understand. Likewise, a refutation that is empty
of intrinsic nature refutes what is to be refuted, and a reasoning that
is "improper"[515] and is empty of intrinsic nature proves the point
that is to be proven. Since this does not lead to absurdities of a di-
chotomizing analysis, it is incorrect for you to claim that our own
words suffer from absurdities similar to that which we find in your
position. This is how you should understand it.

Thus, this is how Candrakīrti explains his answer that the arguments
we used against others cannot be turned around and used against
us. He does not say that we have no system of our own. **[693]**

Moreover, while analysis of whether a cause produces an effect with or without contact refutes those who accept intrinsic existence, Candrakīrti gives our assertion of the absence of intrinsic existence as the reason why this fault does not apply to us. This is how he avoids that fallacy. He does not avoid it by saying that we have no system of our own. For, the *Explanation of the "Middle Way" Commentary* states:[516]

> How do we explain production? It is because both cause and effect are like illusions that this is not a fault for us; the things of the world exist. That analysis is applicable to those who maintain that cause and effect respectively are intrinsically characterized as the producer and the produced thing. But what about someone who maintains that since things are generated by false imputation, they are like illusions in that it is not their intrinsic nature to be produced? What about someone who holds that things lack intrinsic nature but are the objects of mental construction—like the falling hair that may appear to a person with eye disease? That person has no conception of intrinsic production. Therefore, there is no opportunity to fault us in the way just explained. Also, since the things of the world do exist when left unanalyzed, everything is established.

He gives the acceptance of intrinsic character as the reason why the fault applies to the other position, and the belief that things are like illusions as the reason why we do not have this fault. Understanding this, you should realize how to present the Madhyamaka system as being free from fault.

In general, there are innumerable instances of definitive scriptures and Madhyamaka treatises that make statements such as, "This is that way and not this way," or "Such things exist and such things do not." Hence, why should it be necessary to cite special scriptural passages to prove that these statements represent the assertions of their authors? If it were necessary, then when explaining the meaning of passages where expressions like, "I accept such and such," and, "I believe such and such," are absent, it would be impossible to distinguish whether or not something represents the system and belief of a certain author. [694] But if you insist upon actual instances of expressions like, "I believe," "I accept," and "I posit," these are abundant. Nāgārjuna's *Refutation of Objections* states:[517]

> Apart from asserting conventions,
> We offer no explanations.

And also, Nāgārjuna's *Sixty Stanzas of Reasoning* states:[518]

> A thing that arose and was destroyed
> Is labeled as having ceased; likewise,
> Excellent beings accept cessation
> That is like an illusion.

And:

> Everything that arises dependently,
> Like a reflection of the moon in water,
> Is neither real nor unreal.
> Those who accept this are not seduced by dogmatic views.

Also, Nāgārjuna's *Praise of the Transcendent One* states:[519]

> What arises from causes
> Cannot exist without them—
> And so is like a mere reflection.
> How can you not accept something so obvious?

And again from that same text:

> Since it does not exist without what is felt,
> Feeling itself is selfless.
> You [Buddha] also accept that feeling
> Does not exist intrinsically.

And also:

> You have taught action and agent
> In a conventional way.
> You accept that they exist
> In mutual dependence.

And also:

> An effect cannot arise
> From a cause that has been destroyed,
> Nor from a cause that has not been destroyed.
> You assert that effects are produced as in a dream.

And also:

> You hold that whatever arises
> Dependently is empty.

Candrakīrti's *Explanation of the "Middle Way" Commentary* also states:[520]

> Experts are of the opinion that this position has no flaw and is
> highly beneficial. You should accept it without hesitation.

And also:

> Consequently, because we accept that things are dependently imputed, just as we accept dependent-arising—the merely conditional nature of things—our position does not face the absurdity of annihilating all conventions. [695] Others should also accept the same.

These passages state that it is definitely necessary to accept a variety of positions, and there are many more like them. Again, the *Explanation of the "Middle Way" Commentary* explains four theses:[521]

> After stating those four theses, we explain how to establish them through reasoning: "This does not arise from itself, so how could it from something else? Nor does it arise from both itself and something else, and how could it arise without a cause?"

As the *Clear Words* also makes similar statements, the system of Nāgārjuna the Protector and Candrakīrti does have its own beliefs, assertions, and theses.

(4')) Refuting the fourth misinterpretation

This fourth system apparently accepts that intrinsic character exists conventionally, but refutes the conventional existence of intrinsic character that withstands rational analysis. We have already explained that this is wrong.[522] It also maintains that in the system of the master Candrakīrti, when Mādhyamikas use other-centered arguments to prove something to essentialist opponents, they use reasons that meet the three criteria and that are established for both systems. This is incorrect because (1) the *Clear Words* specifically refutes this view, and (2) if you hold such a view, even if you do not call that "a reason based on real fact," it is inevitably an autonomous reason. I have yet to explain these points, so that is all I will say at this point.[523]

20

OUR INTERPRETATION OF THE SVĀTANTRIKA/PRĀSAṄGIKA DISTINCTION

---- ୫୲୫ ----

(2)) Setting forth our own position

Explaining how Prāsaṅgikas set forth their own system via a refutation of Svātantrika brings about an understanding of both systems, so this is how I will proceed. Candrakīrti's *Clear Words* has a great deal to say on this matter, but I am wary of excessive verbiage, so I will teach only the main points here. There are two divisions:

1. The actual refutation of autonomous argument
2. Why the faults we find in autonomous arguments do not apply to us (Chapter 21)

(a')) The actual refutation of autonomous argument

The first of these has two divisions: [696]

1. Demonstrating a fault that pertains to the position—namely, that the basis or subject of an autonomous syllogism is not established
2. Demonstrating that, because of that fault, the reason is also not established

(1')) The subject of an autonomous syllogism is not established

The section has two parts: (1) stating what Bhāvaviveka believes, and (2) refuting it.

(a")) What Bhāvaviveka believes

The passages from Candrakīrti's *Clear Words* on these points appear to be exceedingly difficult to understand, so let me explain by citing and explaining a passage from the *Clear Words*. It says:[524]

> How? In the thesis "sound is impermanent," both the subject and the predicate are construed only in a general sense, not with specific qualifications. If they were taken under specific qualifications, the conventions "inference" and "what is inferred" would cease to exist. For example, if the subject were construed as "sound that evolves from the four great elements," it would not be established for the other party in the debate, the Vaiśeṣikas. And if it were taken as "a quality of space," the subject would not be established for us, the Buddhists. Likewise, when Vaiśeṣikas advance the thesis "sound is impermanent," to Sāṃkhya opponents, if sound is construed as "produced sound," then it would not be established for the Sāṃkhyas. On the other hand, if sound is construed as "something that becomes manifest," then it would not be established for the Vaiśeṣikas themselves. Likewise, however it is placed in an argument, destruction, when qualified as something that requires some other cause than production itself, is not established for us Buddhists; whereas qualified as something that is causeless, it is not established for the other party, the Vaiśeṣikas. Therefore, just as the subject and predicate are taken only in a general sense in the above cases, likewise, in the present case, it is the mere subject, without particular qualification, that is to be understood. This is what Bhāvaviveka says.

This means that when the Buddhists advance the thesis "sound is impermanent" to the Vaiśeṣikas, if "sound that evolves from the elements" is taken as the subject, it will not be established for the

Vaiśeṣikas; if "sound as a quality of space" is taken as the subject, it will not be established for us. Likewise, when the Vaiśeṣikas themselves advance the thesis "sound is impermanent" to those Sāṃkhyas who are manifestationists,[525] if "sound as something produced" were taken as the subject, it would not be established for the manifestationists; if "sound as something that previously exists and comes to be manifested through certain conditions" were taken as the subject, it would not be established for Vaiśeṣika proponents. [697] Therefore, it is impossible to use as a subject something that is incompatible with one's own individual belief system. For, given that the subject is the basis that both parties analyze in order to see whether a specific quality is present, it has to be something established as appearing in common to both.

Just as they must establish a commonly appearing subject, so too both sides must establish the predicate, "impermanent," only in a general sense, without particular qualifications. Also, they must commonly establish any example that they cite, and this must take place before they prove the probandum. The situation is similar when we Mādhyamikas prove to non-Buddhists the nonexistence of something that is produced from itself—whether it is an internal sensory source, such as the visual faculty, or an external sensory source, such as a form—and when we prove to Buddhist essentialists that there is no production from other. If we were to use "a real eye," for instance, as the subject, it would not be established for us, but if we used "an unreal eye" as the subject, it would not be established for the other party. Hence, giving up such specificity, we must use the *mere* eye or *mere* form as the subject. Why? Because it must be established as commonly appearing to both parties, inasmuch as it is the basis that both Mādhyamikas and essentialists analyze in order to see whether there is a specific quality, such as "being produced from itself."

This is what Bhāvaviveka thinks. "To establish as appearing in common" means that the proponent and the opponent use the same kind of valid cognition to establish it.

(b")) Refuting that

This has two parts: (1) showing that the meaning is incorrect, and (2) showing that the example cited is not appropriate.

(1")) The meaning is incorrect

Candrakīrti's *Clear Words* states:[526]

This is not like that, and is instead as follows. Insofar as one accepts the refutation of production as the probandum in this [demonstration that eye, etc. are not ultimately produced], the subject—the basis of that probandum and something found to have its own existence by an inaccurate consciousness—breaks down in reality, and therefore, it will be argued, there would be no commonly appearing subject. He [Bhāvaviveka] himself must accept that this is so. Inaccurate and accurate consciousnesses are different. [698] Therefore, when an inaccurate consciousness takes what is nonexistent as existent, as in the case of someone with eye disease seeing falling hair, it does not perceive even to the slightest degree an object that exists. When an accurate consciousness does not reify what is unreal, as is the case of someone without eye disease looking for the imaginary falling hair, it does not perceive even to the slightest degree objects that are nonexistent insofar as they are merely conventional. That is why the master Nāgārjuna himself states in his *Refutation of Objections*:[527]

> If sensory perception and so forth
> Could actually perceive something
> Then there would be something to prove or to refute.
> But as they do not, I cannot be faulted.

Since inaccurate and accurate consciousnesses are different in this way, inaccurate consciousness cannot exist when accurate consciousness is present. So how could the conventional eye, as the subject of a syllogism, exist for an accurate consciousness? Therefore, since there is for Bhāvaviveka no avoiding the fallacies of a nonexistent position and a nonexistent reason, the response he has given is no answer at all.

I will explain this passage based on the following syllogism, since using this example makes it easier to understand:

> Subject: Visible form
> Predicate: Is not produced from itself
> Reason: Because it exists
> Example: Like the pot that is right in front of you

The passages of the *Clear Words* that reply to Bhāvaviveka show that the subject is not established as appearing in common to the two parties in this debate. How do they show this? Here, in this section, the *Clear Words* states that those to whom it demonstrates how one cannot establish a subject in common with an opponent are those who refute production from self—that is, the Svātantrikas. But in general, the opponents of the *Clear Words* are both (a) the essentialists, who accept that things ultimately have intrinsic nature, and (b) the Svātantrikas, who refute that, but accept that things conventionally have intrinsic character or intrinsic nature. Svātantrika-Mādhyamikas are called "non-essentialists." [699] However, so as to simplify the terminology in this discussion, "opponents of intrinsic existence" will refer to the Prāsaṅgikas, and "advocates of intrinsic existence" will refer to both the essentialists and the Svātantrikas.

According to the advocates of intrinsic existence, visible form, the stated subject of the syllogism, must be established by the valid perceptual cognition of the visual consciousnesses that perceive it. Moreover, if those consciousnesses did not establish visible form in a non-mistaken way, then they could not be perceptions that establish their objects. Hence, they must be non-mistaken. Do nonconceptual perceptions establish their objects in a non-mistaken way? In non-Prāsaṅgika systems, an object's existence by way of its intrinsic character appears to any consciousness that is non-mistaken with respect to that object; moreover, the object must exist just as it appears to that consciousness.

As this is the case, we Prāsaṅgikas say that the kind of valid cognition that establishes the subject for the essentialist opponent will not work for the Mādhyamika proponent. Why? Since no phenomenon can, even conventionally, have a nature that is established by way of its intrinsic character, there is no valid cognition that establishes such a thing. It is with this in mind that the master Candrakīrti refutes the notion of autonomous syllogism. This also explains how to refute the need for an autonomous syllogism as part of the process of initially instilling in others the view that knows that things lack intrinsic nature. I leave aside for the time being the analysis of whether Prāsaṅgikas need to use autonomous syllogisms among themselves as part of the process of developing inferential knowledge of certain objects amongst the diverse conventional objects.

Now let me explain this by tying my analysis to Candrakīrti's text. The meaning of the passage, "Insofar as one accepts the refutation of production... himself must accept that this is so," is as follows. "The basis of the probandum"—a subject such as the eye or form—"breaks down," that is, is not established, "in reality." This is something that Bhāvaviveka himself accepts. What are those subjects [eye and form] like? "Something found to have its own existence by inaccurate consciousnesses" affected by ignorance; this means that conventional consciousnesses, such as the visual consciousness, establish these objects. How is it that "[Bhāvaviveka] himself must accept this?" [700] He must accept it "insofar as," i.e., because the refutation of ultimate production, as the predicate of the probandum, is based upon those subjects; if they did exist in reality, it would contradict that relationship between subject and predicate.

Granted that he accepts things in this way, what does that entail? Those subjects—form, etc.—that neither exist in reality nor are reality itself cannot be considered objects found by non-mistaken consciousnesses. Hence, they are found by conventional consciousnesses, or subjects, that apprehend false objects. And thus those consciousnesses are mistaken; that is, affected by ignorance. Therefore, objects found by non-mistaken consciousnesses do not appear to mistaken consciousnesses, and objects that appear to mistaken consciousnesses are not found by non-mistaken consciousnesses. This is because "the inaccurate" mistaken consciousnesses "and the accurate" non-mistaken consciousnesses "are different," which is to say that each engages its object by excluding the object of the other. This is the meaning of Candrakīrti's statement that "inaccurate and accurate consciousnesses are different."

The explanation of that occurs in the passage, "Therefore, when an inaccurate… are nonexistent insofar as they are merely conventional." There, "inaccurate" refers to a conventional consciousness that is affected by ignorance, such as the visual consciousness. That such consciousness "takes what is nonexistent as existent" refers to the fact that while form, sound, etc. have no essential or intrinsic character, the sensory consciousnesses apprehend them as having such a character. The way that non-conceptual consciousnesses apprehend their objects is in terms of mere appearance, and that is why form and such appear to sensory consciousnesses to exist by way of their intrinsic character. The words, "it does not perceive, even to the slightest degree, an object that exists," mean that because intrinsic character appears, despite its nonexistence, there is no way for those consciousnesses to establish even the slightest object that exists by way of its intrinsic character. The falling hair is an example of an object that does not exist by way of its intrinsic character, yet appears as though it did. [701] These sentences mean that the sensory consciousnesses to which things such as form and sound appear are mistaken, and are therefore not suited to attest that an object exists by virtue of its intrinsic character.

The passage that begins, "When an accurate consciousness…," indicates that non-mistaken consciousness does not at all apprehend form, sound, and such. The word "accurate" refers to non-mistaken consciousness. Noble beings who perceive reality possess such consciousness, and no one else. That non-mistaken consciousness "does not reify what is unreal." This means that it "does not reify," or take as existing, such things as form and sound—which cannot be final reality. For example, it is like the fact that the visual consciousness of someone without eye disease does not see an image of falling hair. In that same sentence, the phrase, "insofar as they are merely conventional," refers to false objects, like form and sound. "Nonexistent" means not existing by way of intrinsic character. Such conventional objects are not established even in part by non-mistaken consciousnesses, that is, by consciousnesses that have final reality as their object. This is because non-mistaken consciousnesses do not see such conventional objects.

On these points, Candrakīrti cites a proof-text by Nāgārjuna the Protector: "If sensory perception and so forth...." This supporting citation states that the four [direct, inferential, scriptural, and analogical] valid cognitions—sensory perception and so forth—do not at all establish an object that exists by way of its intrinsic character.

The sentence that begins, "Since inaccurate and accurate...," summarizes the point Candrakīrti has already explained. The sentence, "So how could the conventional eye, as the subject of a syllogism, exist," is not claiming that subjects such as the conventional eye are nonexistent. Instead, as explained above, it means that a form that exists by way of its intrinsic character, or is established by non-mistaken perception, cannot be the subject of the syllogism even conventionally.

The meaning of "Therefore, since..." is that when both the opponents of essential or intrinsic existence and the essentialists posit visible form as the subject of a syllogism, non-mistaken perception does not establish it as appearing in common to both parties in the debate. [702] Therefore, since there is no valid cognition attesting to a subject that is proven to appear in common for both systems, there will inevitably be a fault in any position that you try to prove to an opponent using an autonomous reason.

Objection: What you say is true in regard to a position that has no essential or intrinsic nature even conventionally. However, since this is not what we [who follow Bhāvaviveka] assert at the conventional level, the subjects and such in autonomous syllogisms do exist. Therefore, the position is free from fallacy.

Reply: The existence of such an intrinsic nature is inadmissible conventionally. Since we have already explained this above, and will explain it again below, your answer is unreasonable.

(2")) The example cited is inappropriate

Candrakīrti's *Clear Words* states:[528]

> The example [i.e., the syllogism proving the impermanence of sound] is also inappropriate. Whereas in this example, neither party wants to qualify the general sense of "sound" or the general sense of "impermanence," here in the case of the syllogism proving that the eye is not ultimately produced, the advocates of emptiness and the advocates of non-emptiness do not both accept that eye, as a generality, exists only conventionally, nor do they both accept that it exists ultimately. That is why the example is inappropriate.

Do not misread this passage to say that the example fails because an eye that is neither true nor false does not exist, but there does exist a sound that is neither evolved from the elements nor a quality of space, as well as a sound that is neither produced nor a causal manifestation of something that already exists; and that there does exist something that is impermanent in a general sense, yet neither relies on causes nor fails to rely on causes. For (1) those [i.e., sound that is neither evolved nor a quality of space, etc.] are things that *neither* of those two parties accept, and (2) if they *were* to accept such things, no one could ever demonstrate that the analogy fails.

Well then, what does this passage mean? In the systems of both of the parties in the example, it is possible to ascertain the existence of sound, unspecified as to whether it is "sound that is evolved from the elements" or "sound that is a quality of space." [703] But in the systems of the advocates of emptiness of intrinsic existence and the opponents of emptiness of intrinsic existence, there is no such thing as an eye or a form as a generality that is established by a valid cognition that is neither a non-mistaken consciousness nor a mistaken consciousness. Its being established by a mistaken consciousness is not established for the opponent, and the Prāsaṅgika-Mādhyamika proponent's valid cognition does not establish its being found by a non-mistaken consciousness. Hence, the analogy fails. This is the meaning of that passage.

The word "non-mistaken" generally refers to the equipoise that directly perceives the ultimate truth. But here, it must refer both to a perceptual valid cognition that is non-mistaken with respect to an intrinsically characterized appearing object and to an inferential valid cognition that is non-mistaken with respect to its intrinsically characterized conceived object. Since there are no such valid cognitions that establish the three criteria,[529] the subject cannot be an object that is found by a non-mistaken consciousness.

Here the term "intrinsic character" is not used, as the logicians use it, simply to mean something that performs a function. Instead, as previously explained,[530] it refers to something's own intrinsic nature, which any functioning thing or non–functioning thing is believed to have. That is why the advocates of intrinsic nature claim that even an inference that comprehends a non-thing is not mistaken regarding a conceived object that has such an intrinsic nature. Every consciousness that is non-mistaken with respect to such an intrinsic nature must also be non-mistaken with respect to its appearing objects and conceived objects; and since this makes such a consciousness non-mistaken with respect to ultimate reality itself, our own system does not hold that such a valid cognition establishes the subject, etc. However, we do not deny that there are, in the mind-streams of both parties, conventional valid cognitions that perceive things like eyes and forms. In fact, even in the mind-stream of the opponent, the forms, etc. that are elicited by sensory consciousnesses that are unimpaired—in the sense previously explained[531]—are ascertained simply as existing, and there is no rational fault in regard to the object of such knowledge.

To explain this in greater detail, we can say that there are three ways of apprehending the existence of, for instance, a seedling: (1) apprehending a seedling as truly existing, which means apprehending it as having an essential or intrinsic nature; [704] (2) apprehending it as existing in a false way, which is the apprehension that the seedling lacks essential existence, but exists like an illusion; and (3) apprehending it as merely existing in general, without specifying whether it is true or false. You might also apprehend the seedling as permanent or impermanent, etc., but since there is no apprehension that does not involve one of these three ways of apprehending, there is no need to explain those other ways here.

Living beings who have not developed within their mind-streams the view that knows the absence of intrinsic nature possess the third and first modes of apprehension, that is, the apprehension of mere existence and the apprehension of true existence, but they lack the apprehension of things as like essenceless illusions. It is completely wrong to claim that before living beings find the view that phenomena are like illusions, any conception they have of something as existing is a conception of true existence. This is something that I have already explained above, in the section that discusses conventional valid cognition and in the section in which I differentiate the four—intrinsic existence, lack of intrinsic existence, existence, and nonexistence.[532]

Suppose that this were not the case—that is, suppose that those who have not yet understood the view that there is no intrinsic nature *did* apprehend everything as truly existent whenever they thought of any conventional thing. There would ensue a complete logical breakdown of the need for Mādhyamikas to accept, conventionally, the objects that are posited by the world's ordinary conventional consciousnesses, insofar as those consciousnesses are not affected by the previously explained circumstances that cause error.[533] Therefore, since there would be no way to distinguish the ontological status of conventional objects from the ontological status of a putative divine creator, this erroneous view would be a great impediment to understanding the meaning of the Madhyamaka.

There are many who show indications of having misunderstood emptiness in this way. They initially engage in many virtuous activities that require conceptual thought. But later, when they systematize the philosophical view that they have found, they see all of their previous activities as grasping at signs and thus as binding them to cyclic existence. They reflect, "Those virtuous activities were taught for those who have not found this definitive view." [705] Developing such an understanding, they repudiate the teaching in many ways with this misconception that regards all conceptual thought as faulty. In this sense they resemble the Chinese abbot Hashang. Before they find the view that things lack intrinsic nature, it is impossible for them to distinguish between mere existence and existence by way of intrinsic character. This is because—as indicated in the passage from Candrakīrti's *Commentary on the "Four Hundred Stanzas"* cited above—they think that anything that exists must exist essentially.[534] As result of this, they take everything that lacks intrinsic nature to be nonexistent, making it impossible for them to posit cause and effect for that which is empty of intrinsic nature. There are many who argue in this way.

Those who have developed in their mind-streams the view that knows the absence of intrinsic nature may apprehend things as existing in all three ways. When that view has been developed, and while its influence has not diminished, the conception of true existence that believes that things essentially exist is temporarily absent. This lasts as long as they are rationally analyzing something so as to determine whether it exists essentially. However, this does not mean that they do not have an innate conception of true existence.

Therefore, even those who have developed the view that knows the absence of essential or intrinsic nature, and who have not let that view degrade, do not always apprehend a seedling as existing like an illusion whenever they apprehend a seedling as existing. Why? If they did, it would lead to the absurdity that they would never again develop a manifest form of the conception of true existence with regard to those seedlings and such.

There are Mādhyamikas—such as the master Bhāvaviveka—who accept that, conventionally, phenomena have essential or intrinsic character. The conventional existence of essential or intrinsic character is their reason for accepting autonomous reasons in their own system. Whether one posits autonomous reasons in one's own system finally depends upon what one posits as the extremely subtle object of refutation. Therefore, in their Svātantrika system, unimpaired sensory perceptions to which essential or intrinsic nature appears are, conventionally, non-mistaken with respect to their appearing objects. [706] The conceptual consciousness that conceives of a subject such as a seedling as having that kind of nature is also non-mistaken with respect to its conceived object. Otherwise, if they accepted that those consciousnesses are mistaken, then what valid cognition would establish the elements of a syllogism as appearing in common for both their system and that of the essentialists? If the sensory perceptions to which essential nature appears establish the elements of a syllogism for the essentialist even though, as Candrakīrti holds, there is no intrinsic nature such as the essential character that appears, then how can one use an autonomous reason? For, one would have already proven the absence of intrinsic nature to the essentialist while establishing the subject.

Opponent: Let the essentialist opponents establish the subject, etc. as they may; it is not necessary for the subject, etc. to be established as appearing in common to both the Mādhyamikas and to them.

Reply: But that is something that Bhāvaviveka himself does not accept, nor is it correct for him to do so, for if he did it would entail that all probative reasons and syllogisms are offered simply in terms of what the other party accepts, and that would make him a follower of the Prāsaṅgikas.

There are [Yogācāra-Svātantrika] masters such as Śāntarakṣita who assert that external objects do not exist conventionally. However, like those Cittamātrins who are Satyākāravādin,[535] they assert that blue and such conventionally exist in the substance of consciousness. Therefore, since the sensory consciousnesses to which blue, etc. appear do have a view of them, apprehending them as

existing by way of their intrinsic character, Śāntarakṣita and others
do not consider the sensory consciousnesses mistaken in their view
of blue itself.

When hidden objects, such as the eye,[536] are posited as the subjects of a syllogism, perception cannot explicitly establish them. Still,
if we work back to the fundamental establishing agent, we must
arrive at a perception. This is a belief of all Buddhist philosophical
schools. Why? Because inference is like a blind person who is
guided by perception. So Śāntarakṣita and his followers accept that,
even in the case of hidden things, the fundamental establishing
agent is, in the end, perception. At that point, they believe that the
fundamental perception is either a non-mistaken cognition of something else or a non-mistaken auto-cognition. Also, as I have already
explained,[537] they believe that an object that exists by way of its
intrinsic character does appear and must objectively exist as it appears. [707] This being the case, there can be no non-mistaken perception that establishes anything as appearing in common both to
them and to Mādhyamikas who maintain that there is no essential
or intrinsic nature.

Even in the case of objects that cannot be traced back to perception, it is still possible to reply. The proponents of intrinsic nature
claim that valid cognitions establish all objects, compounded and
non-compounded. What do they mean by this? Is it necessary for
those valid cognitions to establish objects whose ontological nature
is to exist objectively? If so, then since reason can refute them, they
cannot be valid cognitions that establish their objects.

(2')) Demonstrating that the reason also is not established

Candrakīrti's *Clear Words* indicates this in the passage that states:[538]

> The same method that was used to show that the position is defec-
> tive insofar as its basis is not established should be used to show
> the defect that the reason, "because it exists," is also not established.

Previously, Candrakīrti explained that because there is no valid
cognition that establishes a commonly appearing subject for the
systems of both parties—the proponents and the opponents of
emptiness of essential or intrinsic existence—the thesis, or probandum, which combines the autonomous argument's subject, "visible form," with its predicate, "is not produced from itself," also
does not exist. On this account, the reason, "because it exists," also
is not established, for there is no valid cognition that can attest to

its being established as appearing in common to both parties. You should understand this on the basis of what has been explained above. At this point, the *Clear Words* states:[539]

> This is so, for this logician [Bhāvaviveka] himself accepts implicitly the points we have just made. How so? Another party offers him this proof: "The causes that serve to bring about the internal sensory faculties and such are existent, without qualification; this is the case because the Tathāgata said they are; [708] for whatever the Tathāgata has said is accurate, as in the case of his teaching that 'nirvāṇa is peace.'" [Bhāvaviveka replies,] "What do you believe the import of the reason to be? Is it that such causes exist because the Tathāgata has said so in terms of the conventional? Or is it because he said so in terms of the ultimate? If it is true because he said this in terms of the conventional, the import of the reason would not be established for you. If you take it that the Buddha made this statement in terms of the ultimate, since neither the probandum nor what proves it are established in terms of the ultimate, the reason would not be established and would in fact contradict the thesis." This is how [Bhāvaviveka] states the fault in that proof.
>
> Since it is through such considerations that he asserts that the reason is not established, the reason and so forth are not established for him in any argument that posits a reified thing as the reason, and hence all probative arguments would fall apart.

Some Tibetans who consider themselves followers of Candrakīrti interpret this passage in the following way: Bhāvaviveka's *Blaze of Reasons* and other Svātantrika texts put forward the following syllogism:

Subject: Earth
Predicate: Is not ultimately of the nature of solidity
Reason: Because it is an element
Example: Like wind

They say that Candrakīrti refutes this approach as follows: If you posit "because it is an element ultimately" as the reason, then it is not established for us. If you posit "because it is an element *conventionally*" as the reason, then it is not established for the opponent, the essentialist. If this argument does not induce you to accept that your own reason is not established, then you contradict your belief that a reason that is not established from either of those two points of view [i.e., conventionally and ultimately] must be a reason that is not established.

And there are those who say that [Bhāvaviveka] is refuted because when he states just being an element as the reason, without any specification, reasoned knowledge does not establish it.

But [Candrakīrti's] refutation [of Bhāvaviveka] does not proceed in this way. This is not at all the purport of the *Clear Words*, nor does [Bhāvaviveka] accept any such thing. Hence, these individuals misrepresent both systems.

Well then, how is the passage to be interpreted? [709] In the passage that states, "for this logician himself accepts implicitly the points we have just made,"[540] the phrase "the points we have just made" refers to the previously explained method for showing that the subject is not established and also to the application of that method to the reason, for the text states this in the immediately preceding passage. This being the case, it follows that the valid cognitions such as perceptions that establish the subject and reason are inevitably either mistaken or non-mistaken. If you posit an object found by a mistaken consciousness as the reason or as another part of the syllogism, then it will not be established for the essentialist; if you posit an object found by a non-mistaken consciousness in that role, our own valid cognitions will not establish it. Therefore, autonomous reasons and subjects are not established. This is what we explained above, and it is the meaning of Candrakīrti's phrase, "the points we have just made."

Bhāvaviveka himself asserts that this kind of analysis leads to positing that a syllogism's reason is not established. To show how Bhāvaviveka asserts this, Candrakīrti cites Bhāvaviveka's analysis in terms of the two truths [conventional and ultimate] of his opponent's reason, "because the Tathāgata said so." Contrary to the interpretations proposed above, that analysis is not at all meant as an analysis of whether the stated reason is "because the Tathāgata has said so conventionally" or "because the Tathāgata has said so ultimately." Why? As explained above,[541] it is Bhāvaviveka's position that you must posit the subject without qualifying it either as real or unreal. Just as Bhāvaviveka accepts that subjects with such qualification would not be established for one or the other of the parties, he likewise accepts that such is the case for the reason, the example, and so forth. Therefore, if Bhāvaviveka had faulted the essentialist's reason by applying qualifications such as "conventionally" and "ultimately," his argument would be a gross self-contradiction. How could this consummate scholar make such an error?

Therefore, the correct interpretation of Bhāvaviveka's argument is as follows: Which of the two truths is the referent of the reason, "because the Tathāgata said so"? If it is the conventional one, it is not established for you, the essentialist, since you do not accept that the reason refers to a conventional object; [710] and if it is the ultimate, it is not established for me, since I refute the ultimate production of an effect from a cause that is existent, nonexistent, or both, as well as production that is causeless. Since neither party accepts that there is an object that is neither of the two truths, it is not necessary for Bhāvaviveka to clear that up.

You may interpret Bhāvaviveka's question to his opponent as, "When you say 'because it is an element,' which of the two truths is the element that is posited as the reason?" This interpretation is correct in that it is just like what we have explained above. However, if you claim that Bhāvaviveka is asking, "In terms of which of the two truths [i.e., ultimately or conventionally] is the element stated as the reason?" then you completely misunderstand the position of the opponent [of the *Clear Words*, that is, Bhāvaviveka].[542] If that is what Bhāvaviveka meant, then how could he say to his opponent, "Of the two truths, which is it? If the ultimate, then it is not established for us, and yet, if conventional, it is not established for the other party?" If it *were* possible to claim that Bhāvaviveka's analysis refers to things existing ultimately and conventionally, then since the internal sensory sources that he posits as the subject in his syllogism refuting ultimate production exist conventionally, that subject would not be established for those essentialist opponents.

Well then, how can Candrakīrti claim that Bhāvaviveka accepts "the points we have just made"[543] through his use of the two truths to analyze the reason given by the essentialist? I shall explain. Here Candrakīrti is of the opinion that what is found by a non-mistaken consciousness is the ultimate and what is found by a mistaken consciousness is the conventional. This being the case, the question, "Which of the two truths is it?" is conceived of as a question regarding which of the two consciousnesses it is that finds the reason; it has to be one of these two options. For, if the object stated as a reason is neither the conventional nor the ultimate, then that reason cannot be established; also, if the object stated as a reason is not an object found by either a non-mistaken or a mistaken consciousness, then the object stated as the reason cannot be established. In that the reasons are parallel, Candrakīrti states that Bhāvaviveka himself accepts that his reason,[544] "because of existing," is not established, but he does not say that Bhāvaviveka accepts this explicitly. That is why Candrakīrti, in his *Clear Words*, specifies "reified thing" when he states, "in any argument that posits a reified thing as the reason."[545] [711] The master Bhāvaviveka believes that, of the reasons he posits, some are directly established by non-mistaken perception, while others are not, but are proofs that finally derive from non-mistaken perception. This master [Candrakīrti] refutes this. To prove that it is incorrect to accept objects that exist by way of their intrinsic character, the earlier citation from the *Clear Words*, "Mādhyamikas do not accept others' positions,"—quotes passages such as the *Refutation of Objections* stanza that begins, "If perception and so forth...."[546] By drawing from such citations the conclusion that there are no valid cognitions that perceive intrinsic character, Candrakīrti aims to prove this point to the partisans of master Bhāvaviveka's system.

21

OUR CRITIQUE OF SVĀTANTRIKA DOES NOT HURT OUR OWN ARGUMENTS

(b')) Why the faults we find in autonomous arguments do not apply to us
(b)) Which system to follow so as to develop the view in your mind-stream

———————— ❧ ————————

(b')) Why the faults we find in autonomous arguments do not apply to us

Do our arguments not have the same faults that we find in others' arguments, such as the subjects and reasons not being established? And if they do, should we not refrain from finding contradictions in others' arguments?

The reason others have those faults lies in their acceptance of autonomous arguments. [The *Clear Words*] states that since we do not accept autonomous arguments, we do not have those faults. Here, the term "arguments" refers to syllogisms. If you accept autonomous syllogisms, then you must accept that both parties agree that there are valid cognitions that are valid in regard to intrinsic character. It is therefore necessary to prove the probandum by having both parties establish the three criteria with those non-mistaken valid cognitions. But since such valid cognitions do not exist, the subject and the other parts of the autonomous syllogism cannot be established.

If you do not accept autonomous syllogisms, then you may allow the essentialist to use that kind of valid cognition to establish the subject, etc., but you yourself do not need to establish the subject, etc. with those valid cognitions. Therefore, the arguments found in texts such as the *Clear Words* are "arguments based on what the other party accepts"; their sole purpose is to refute the other party's thesis. They are not autonomous arguments.

For example, the third chapter of Nāgārjuna's *Fundamental Treatise* says:[547]

> Sight does not see
> Its own self. [712]
> How can what does not see itself
> See something else?

This is like the argument that uses an eye's not seeing itself as a reason to prove that an eye does not see other things. In this case, the reason is accepted by the other party while Mādhyamikas also accept the thesis—that the seeing of other things lacks essential existence. Such a syllogism is called "an inference based on what others accept." Candrakīrti's *Clear Words* states:[548]

> We do not use autonomous arguments because the refutation of others' theses is the only effect of our arguments.

This means that the syllogisms he uses are not autonomous syllogisms. He does not say that he does not use syllogisms, for he does accept those that have as their sole purpose the refutation of others' theses. The very next passage of the *Clear Words* states how he uses syllogisms to refute their theses:[549]

> Those who think that the eye sees other things also hold that the eye does not see itself. They also believe that if the eye did not have the quality of seeing other things, it would not see. So we argue: "Anything that does not see itself does not see other things either, as in the case of a pot. The eye also does not see itself; therefore, it too cannot see other things. Therefore, its seeing other things, such as blue, contradicts its not seeing itself. Your position is contradicted by this argument based on what you accept." This is how an argument that is established for them refutes their position.

When "what you accept" is addressed to the opponent, it is the same as saying "what others accept" from the point of view of the Mādhyamika proponent.

This is our procedure for refuting misconceptions by stating a syllogism based on what others accept. As this is very important, I will explain it in detail. The phrase, "that is established for them," at the end of that passage does *not* mean that we do not, in our system, accept (1) the subject—the eye, (2) the example—the pot, (3) the reason—that it does not see itself, and (4) the predicated quality—that it does not see blue, etc. Nor does it mean that the reason, pervasion, and so forth are established only for the opponent since they are simply what others assert. [713]

What does it mean? Even though we do accept these four in our own system, our system does not have, even conventionally, a valid cognition that establishes them and that understands its objects as existing essentially. For proponents of intrinsic existence, the establishment of the subject, etc. definitely depends upon those being established by this kind of valid cognition. Therefore, there is no valid cognition which understands its object as existing essentially that can establish a common appearance of the subject, etc. for both parties. Hence, they are said not to be established for both parties; they are said to be based on what is accepted by, or established for, others.

Query: If such valid cognitions do not exist even conventionally, then reason contradicts the acceptance of what they establish for the opponent, just as it contradicts the superimposition of intrinsic nature. How, then, could you find the Madhyamaka view in reliance upon their testimony? For, if it were possible to find an accurate philosophical view using arguments that valid cognition contradicts, then you could use all sorts of inaccurate tenets to find such a view.

Reply: In this case, even our own system accepts as conventionally existent the objects that the opponent apprehends as existing—namely, (1) the subject—the eye; (2) the reason—that it does not see itself; (3) the example—the pot; and (4) the predicate—that it does not perceive blue and such. So reason does not contradict these. Nonetheless, since the opponent fails to distinguish between their existing and their existing essentially, reason *does* contradict the conceit that valid cognition establishes objects that it understands as essentially existent. Still, reason cannot refute what is established by the unimpaired conventional consciousnesses in the opponent's mind-stream. Therefore, since that essentialist system and our system do not agree as to whether there is valid knowledge which understands objects to be essentially existent, we do not prove things to them with autonomous arguments; rather, we simply expose the contradictions within their own assertions.

How is this done? Let us take the example mentioned above[550] of a syllogism based on what others accept. [714] The reason—i.e., that the subject, the eye, does not see itself—does exist conventionally, but essentially seeing things like blue does not exist even conventionally. Therefore, the former can be used to refute the latter. In the case of the eye, (1) the reason, not seeing itself, and (2) the predicate of the refutation, not seeing other things, are either the same in that both exist or the same in that both do not exist. So how could either contradict the existence of the other? Therefore, in a syllogism based on others' acceptance, the subject, predicate, and reason must be things that exist conventionally; the mere fact that an opponent claims that something exists is not adequate.

The opponents themselves accept the existence of those subjects, such as the eye, as well as the reasons and examples. Therefore, why should the Mādhyamika have to prove them? If they dishonestly disavow what they actually accept, and say, "Since they are not established for us, please establish them," that would mean that there was nothing that they were not prepared to disavow, and it would be pointless to argue with them. Who could ever help them?

Objection: You claim to expose a contradiction between the opponents' assertion that the eye does not see itself and the opponents' assertion that the eye's seeing blue and such has an essential or intrinsic nature. But what kind of cognition understands the contradiction? If it is a valid cognition that establishes the contradiction, it would have to establish it for both parties, so it would not be "based on what others accept." If you posit the contradiction simply by its being asserted, since the opponents accept the eye's not seeing itself and its seeing something else as *non*-contradictory, it is untenable to use *their* assertion to posit a contradiction. If you posit them as contradictory on the basis of your own assertion, this leads to utter absurdity. How can you say to the opponents that it is incorrect for them to accept these two positions as non-contradictory because *you* assert that they are contradictory?

Reply: Our position does not suffer from this fault. That the eye does not see itself contradicts its having an essential or intrinsic nature; valid cognition establishes this contradiction, so it is not posited through simply being asserted.

Query: If it is possible to teach that valid cognition to the opponents and for them to then ascertain the contradiction, why is it necessary to rely on what they accept?

Reply: As the essentialist sees it, for something to be a valid cognition that proves the contradiction, it must understand an essentially existent object. [715] But how can we prove the contradiction by accepting for our own part something that does not exist? Once we have shown them that there is no contradiction in positing something as a valid cognition even though its object lacks essential or intrinsic nature, this type of valid cognition will prove it to them. They will then have found the view that knows that phenomena lack intrinsic nature. So at that point there would be no need to prove to them that if something does not see itself, this contradicts its seeing essentially. Therefore, if you want to understand Candrakīrti's system, you should analyze these points in detail and penetrate their meaning.

Query: But how do you use what they accept to demonstrate the workings of the pervasion—that what does not see itself does not essentially see other things?

Reply: This should be explained as in *Buddhapālita's Commentary on the "Fundamental Treatise"*:[551]

> For example, through association with water, earth is perceived to be wet; through association with fire, water is perceived as hot; and through association with jasmine flowers, a cloth is perceived as fragrant. We see that those perceptions of earth as wet, etc. are contingent upon perceptions of wetness, heat, and fragrance in water, fire, and jasmine flowers respectively. This is something that you yourself accept. Likewise, if things had some essential or intrinsic nature, you would have to perceive that intrinsic nature in regard to the thing itself, and only then could you perceive it in some other associated thing. If you did not first perceive that in the thing itself, then, when it is associated with something else, how could you see it there? For example, if you do not perceive a *bad* smell in jasmine flowers, then you will not perceive a stench in cloth that has been associated with them.

Using examples that are acceptable and familiar to his opponents, he leads them to certainty about the pervasion and counter-pervasion and then applies them to the case at hand. If the eye had some seeing-essence, then its sight of itself should be noticed first, and only then would it be possible to notice that it sees such things as forms, and to notice that it sees the component of form within composite things. [716] But since the eye does not see itself, it does not see other things. This is how we demonstrate the pervasion using what others accept.

Also, Āryadeva's *Four Hundred Stanzas* states:[552]

> If the natures of all things
> First appear within the things themselves,
> Then why should the eye
> Not also apprehend itself?

Objection: Fire burns other things, even though it does not burn itself. Likewise, it is not contradictory for the eye to see other things, even though it does not see itself.

Reply: We do not broadly refute that fire burns fuel or that the eye merely sees forms; instead we refute that the eye essentially sees other things. As this is so, your example will have to be that fire essentially burns fuel. Consequently, your example is wrong, just as what you are trying to prove is wrong. If fire and fuel both had essential or intrinsic nature, then they would have to be either of one nature or of different natures; so which is it? If they are of one nature, then fire would burn itself; also, how could fire be the burning agent and the fuel the object that is burned? Suppose that you insist that they could be. If someone were to argue that fire is the burnt object and fuel is the burning agent, what rebuttal could you give? If they have different natures, fire could be present even without fuel, just as oxen can be present without horses. As Āryadeva's *Four Hundred Stanzas* states:[553]

> Fire burns something that is hot.
> If something is not hot, how can it be burning?
> Therefore, there is nothing called "fuel" apart from fire,
> And except for that fuel, there can be no fire.

So if you claim that burning has essential or intrinsic nature, it follows that what does not burn itself cannot burn other things. Likewise, if you claim that the eye has seeing as its intrinsic nature, you have to accept that if it does not see itself, it cannot see other things. Hence, the above faults do not budge. [717]

When one sees such critiques of the belief in intrinsic nature, one gives up tenets that conceive of the existence of essential or intrinsic nature. One can then understand that objects and agents are tenable in the absence of intrinsic nature; hence, one distinguishes the absence of intrinsic existence from nonexistence. Consequently, one also distinguishes intrinsic existence from existence, so one knows that valid cognitions that have no intrinsic nature comprehend objects that have no intrinsic nature, and so forth.

Query: The valid cognitions that know that fire and fuel lack intrinsic nature cannot be perceptions, and thus you have to believe that they are inferences. If that is so, what reasoning are they based upon?

Reply: If things like fire and fuel have intrinsic nature, they *must* be either the same or different. After you have seen this, you see that a refutation of both intrinsic natures that are the same and intrinsic natures that are different must entail the absence of intrinsic nature. This fulfills the first two criteria of a correct reason. Then, the ascertainment that there is no intrinsic nature that is the same or different fulfills the third criterion, the reason's presence in the subject. Therefore, it is a reason that fulfills the three criteria for being a correct reason capable of inducing inferential knowledge. Based on that reason, one ascertains that fire and fuel lack intrinsic nature; this ascertainment is an inference. In the case of the previously posited syllogism based on what others accept, you should understood that we use this same method to develop the three criteria and the corresponding inference.[554]

In *reductio* form, the argument works as follows: "If fire and fuel had intrinsic nature, they would have to be either the same or different," and "If they are the same, then fire would burn itself," and so forth. This form uses something that the other party accepts as a reason, drawing implications contrary to the other party's beliefs. This example should also allow you to understand how to construct other *reductio* arguments.

So as long as those opponents do not give up their essentialist tenets, they continue to believe that valid cognitions establish the referent objects of the various parts of a syllogism in reliance upon knowledge of things that essentially exist. The moment that they know with valid cognition the essencelessness of any thing, they give up their essentialist tenets. [718] The *Clear Words* states:[555]

> *Query*: Still, does the refutation of the essentialists use an inference in which the subject, etc. are inferentially established for at least one of the two parties, even if not for both?
>
> *Reply*: Yes. It uses a reasoning that is established for the essentialists themselves, and not one that is established for the other party [i.e., the Mādhyamikas], for that is what is seen in the world. In the world, sometimes who wins and who loses a dispute is decided through the testimony of a witness whom both parties accept as reliable. Sometimes, however, this may be decided using only their own testimony, without the need for someone else's testimony to

determine who wins and who loses. This is true as much in the realm of philosophical reasoning as it is in the world, for it is *only* worldly convention that is at stake in philosophical treatises.

This gives an example and an explanation to show that reasons based on what others accept are appropriate.

The logicians claim that the three criteria and the subject, etc. must be established both for the proponent and the opponent, for they say that any valid cognition used to establish the three criteria, etc. for the opponent must also establish these for the proponent. Candrakīrti refutes that. That same text states:[556]

> *Objection*: One can prove or disprove a statement of something that is definite for both parties. But you cannot do this, as you claim that there is doubt as to whether the subject, etc. are established for either or both parties.
>
> *Reply*: Even you who think this way should accept the method that we advocate, namely, that inference is based on the world's view of things. This means that when you use scripture to refute a certain point, you need not use only scriptures that are acceptable to both parties. Why not? Because you can use those that only they accept. What we infer on the opponents' own terms will always be established for the opponents. This method is trustworthy, whereas attempting to establish something for both parties is not. That is why the definitions of the logicians are superfluous, for the buddhas help disciples who do not understand reality by using what those individuals hold or accept. [719]

So, when the reason that is used to prove the probandum is established for both parties with the kind of valid cognition explained previously, this is an autonomous [or "*svatantra*"] reason. When the reason is not established in that way and the probandum is proven using the three criteria that the other party, the opponent, accepts as being present, this constitutes the Prāsaṅgika method. It is quite clear that this is what the master Candrakīrti intended.

(b)) Which system to follow so as to develop the view in your mind-stream

The great Mādhyamikas who follow the noble father Nāgārjuna and his spiritual son Āryadeva split into two different systems: Prāsaṅgika and Svātantrika. Which do we follow? Here, we are followers of the Prāsaṅgika system. Moreover, as explained previously, we refute essential or intrinsic nature even conventionally; yet all that has been taught about cyclic existence and nirvāṇa must be fully compatible with that refutation. Therefore, you should find certain knowledge both of how essential existence is refuted and of how cyclic existence and nirvāṇa are still possible.

The texts of those two masters often say that you should conduct rational analysis that scrutinizes what things would be like if they were accepted as essentially or intrinsically existent. Seeing that the texts of the noble father and his spiritual son are in complete agreement on this, I accept that system. Accordingly, it is apparent that you should accept the Prāsaṅgika position as explained above.

22

ANALYZING A CHARIOT

(3″) How to use that procedure to generate the right philosophical view within your mind-stream
  (a)) How to determine that there is no self in the person
    (1)) Actually determining that the self lacks intrinsic existence
      (a′)) Giving the example
        (1′)) Showing that the chariot exists imputedly, without intrinsic existence
        (2′)) Eliminating objections to that
        (3′)) How to establish the chariot under various names
        (4′)) The advantage that you find the view quickly by using this example

(3″) **How to use that procedure to generate the right philosophical view within your mind-stream**

This third section describes how to develop the right philosophical view in your mind-stream using a Prāsaṅgika procedure. Within this section there are three parts:

1. How to determine that there is no self [i.e., essential self-nature] in the person (Chapters 22-24)
2. How to determine that there is no self in phenomena (Chapter 24)
3. How to eliminate afflictive and cognitive obscurations by becoming accustomed to those views (Chapter 24)

(a)) **How to determine that there is no self in the person**

This section has three parts:

1. Actually determining that the self [i.e., person] lacks intrinsic existence (Chapters 22-23)
2. Teaching that what the self owns is also thereby established as lacking intrinsic existence (Chapter 23)
3. How to apply those lines of reasoning to other phenomena as well (Chapter 24)

(1)) **Actually determining that the self lacks intrinsic existence**

This has two parts:

1. Giving the example [720]
2. Showing what it illustrates (Chapter 23)

(a')) **Giving the example**

A sūtra cited in Candrakīrti's *Explanation of the "Middle Way" Commentary* says:[557]

> "Self" is a demonic mind.
> You have a wrong view.
> These composite aggregates are empty;
> There is no living being in them.
> Just as one speaks of a chariot
> In dependence upon collections of parts,
> So we use the convention "living being"
> In dependence upon the aggregates.

Taking as an example the imputation of a chariot in dependence upon its parts, such as its wheels, the Buddha states that the self or living being is also imputed in dependence upon the aggregates. Therefore, I will first explain the example of the chariot. The explanation of the example has four parts:

1. Showing that the chariot exists imputedly, without intrinsic existence
2. Eliminating objections to that
3. How to establish the chariot under various names
4. The advantage that you find the view quickly by using this example

(1')) **Showing that the chariot exists imputedly, without intrinsic existence**

Candrakīrti's *Commentary on the "Middle Way"* says:[558]

> A chariot is neither asserted to be other than its parts, nor to be non-other. It does not possess them. It does not depend on the parts and the parts do not depend on it. It is neither the mere collection of the parts, nor is it their shape. It is like this.

Thus he says that just as a chariot is a mere imputation since it does not exist in these seven ways—one with its parts, different from its parts, etc.—so it is also for the self and the aggregates. If the chariot had an essential or intrinsic nature, it undoubtedly would be established by reasoned knowledge that analyzes whether it exists intrinsically in any of the seven ways. However, since it is not established by such knowledge in any of the seven ways, it does not intrinsically exist.

The parts of a chariot are the axle, the wheels, the nails, etc. The chariot is not intrinsically one with those parts. [721] If it were one, there would be fallacies such as the following: just as the parts are plural, so the chariot also would be many; just as the chariot is single, so the parts also would be single; agent and the object would be the same.

Nor is a chariot intrinsically separate from its parts because if it were it would be seen separately, apart from them, like pot and cloth, yet it is not. Also, there would be no reason to impute it in relation to those parts.

Two of the positions involve positing a chariot and its parts as basis and dependent. A chariot is not the basis for its parts, like a bowl holding yogurt, nor does it rest in its parts, like Devadatta in a tent, because such relationships could be demonstrated only if a chariot and its parts were essentially separate, but they are not. Here we do not refute mere mutual existence; we refute a basis and dependent that exist by way of intrinsic character. Even the two examples just mentioned refer to situations in which the other party accepts that there are intrinsically characterized bases and dependents. All similar cases should be understood in this way.

The possibility of possession is also untenable. If you hold that a chariot possesses its parts just as Devadatta possesses oxen—i.e., as objects other than himself—then just as the oxen and Devadatta are seen separately, a chariot and its parts should likewise be seen separately, yet they are not. Thus, there is no such possession. It is also unreasonable that a chariot should possess its parts just as Devadatta possesses his ear because we are now refuting intrinsic difference. For things that exist essentially, this type of possession would involve intrinsic oneness, and we already refuted that. Again, we do not refute the conventional existence of Devadatta's merely having an ear, and the same applies to the chariot. [722] Thus we refute intrinsically characterized possession.

As for the two remaining positions, Candrakīrti's *Commentary on the "Middle Way"* says:[559]

> If the mere collection of the parts were a chariot,
> Then a chariot would exist even while its parts lie in pieces.
> Without the whole, the parts do not exist.
> Hence the mere shape also cannot be the chariot.

Some consider the mere collection of the parts or the distinctive shape of the parts to be the chariot. It is not tenable for the chariot to be the mere collection of its parts. There are two points to be made here: (1) It is contrary to reason. A chariot would exist even in a complete collection of separated parts—wheels and such, lying in pieces—since the mere collection of parts is a chariot. (2) It contradicts their assertions. Buddhist essentialists assert that there are no wholes, but only mere groups of parts. If this were so, even parts would not exist because that which has parts, i.e., wholes, would not exist. Therefore, since even mere groups of parts would not exist, the collection of parts could not be a chariot.

The assertions of the master Candrakīrti make it unnecessary to add qualifications to the refutation of the chariot's being the mere collection of its parts. This is because the collection is the basis of imputation of the chariot. For, he says that since the collection of the aggregates is the basis to which the self is imputed, it cannot be the self.[560]

Objection: I do not claim that the mere collection of the parts is the chariot; rather, I posit as the chariot the distinctive shape of the parts when they are arranged.

Reply: In saying this, you contradict your own assertions. As explained above, since you assert that what has parts does not exist, parts also would not exist. Therefore, it is unreasonable to posit the mere shape of the parts as the chariot. The word "also" in the verse just cited means that it is not just the mere collection that cannot be the chariot.

Furthermore, if you say that such a shape is a chariot, then is the chariot the shape of the individual parts or the shape of the collection? [723] If the former, is it a shape no different from the shape of the parts prior to their being assembled? Or is it a shape unlike their shape prior to assembly? Candrakīrti's *Commentary on the "Middle Way"* points out a fallacy in the first position:[561]

> If you say that the shape that each part already had
> Is what we know as a chariot,
> Then just as there is no chariot when the parts are
>   unassembled,
> So it is also when they are assembled.

Also, the shapes of the wheels and such have no features after assembly unlike those they had prior to assembly. Therefore, just as there is no chariot when the parts are separate, there is no chariot when they are assembled.

Suppose that the chariot is some other shape—apart from that of the wheels and such prior to assembly—which appears later when they are assembled, and is unlike the shape of those earlier parts. Candrakīrti's *Commentary on the "Middle Way"* states this fallacy:[562]

> If now while the chariot itself is here,
> There were a different shape in the wheels and such,
> Then it would be evident, but it is not.
> Therefore, the mere shape is not a chariot.

If there were something different, some dissimilar feature, between the shape of the wheels, axle, and such before assembly and their shape after assembly, then this would have to be evident. Yet no matter how you look you do not observe such. Hence it is not reasonable for some shape of the parts after assembly unlike the shape of the parts prior to assembly to be the chariot.

Objection: I do not claim that the individual shapes of the individual parts are a chariot; I consider the general shape of the collection of the parts to be a chariot.

Reply: Candrakīrti's *Commentary on the "Middle Way"* states this fallacy:[563]

> According to you, collections do not exist at all,
> So the shape cannot be that of the collection of parts.
> How could you see a chariot in the shape
> Of something that does not exist at all?

This means that it is unreasonable for the shape of a collection to be a chariot because, inasmuch as collections do not substantially exist, it is untenable to impute shape to a collection. [724] For, you essentialists hold that all imputedly existent phenomena have substantially existent bases of imputation. A collection of parts does not have an essential or intrinsic nature—it lacks substance. If it did intrinsically exist, it would have to be either one with or different from the parts comprising the collection. Whichever you assert, we can refute you as explained above in the case of the chariot.[564]

In our own system, we do not assert that the bases of imputation of imputedly existent phenomena are substantially existent. The shape of the collection of the parts is the basis to which the chariot is imputed. However, since the chariot is an imputedly existent phenomenon which is imputed to that shape, we do not consider the mere shape of the collection to be the chariot. Therefore, in refuting the position that the shape of the collection is the chariot, we do not have to add any qualification like "ultimate" to what we are refuting.

Objection: There is no reason that we cannot impute the chariot to a shape which lacks true existence and which depends upon a collection that lacks true existence.

Reply: In that case, you must agree that there is no reason not to accept the production of all effects lacking true existence—compositional factors, seedlings, and the like—in dependence upon causes that lack true existence—ignorant consciousness, seeds, and so forth. As Candrakīrti's *Commentary on the "Middle Way"* states,[565]

> As this is what you assert,
> You should also understand that all effects
> That have untrue natures are produced
> In dependence upon untrue causes.

This example of the chariot also precludes positing the mere aggregation of the eight particles—form, etc.—to be composites such as pots.[566] It also refutes the imputation of pots and such in dependence upon the eight substantially existent particles; and it refutes the proposition that pots and such are located in the distinctive shapes of substantially existent forms and such. Why? Since form and such are not intrinsically produced, they have no intrinsic nature, and thus it is untenable for them to be substantially existent. [725] Accordingly, Candrakīrti's *Commentary on the "Middle Way"* states:[567]

> It is therefore unreasonable to claim that an awareness of a pot
> Arises in relation to a particular configuration of form.
> Since they are not produced, form and such also do not exist.
> Therefore, it is unreasonable for a pot to be the shape of a
>   collection of forms.

Qualm: If, like a chariot, a pot is not the shape of the aggregation of its parts, this would imply that it is not definitively characteristic of a pot to be round-bellied and so forth, for these qualities constitute a shape.

Reply: We hold that what is round-bellied, long-necked, and so forth is a pot, but we do not accept that the round-bellied shape is a pot; otherwise, we would have to agree that bellies and necks are also pots.

(2')) Eliminating objections to that

Essentialists' objection: When you use reason to analyze the question of intrinsic nature, searching for the chariot in the seven ways just explained, and you do not find it, then the chariot must not exist. Yet if this were so, then conventional designations of chariot would not be made in the world. This is not tenable; witness expressions such as "Fetch a chariot," "Buy a chariot," and "Make a chariot." Therefore, things such as chariots do exist.

Reply: Candrakīrti's *Explanation of the "Middle Way" Commentary* shows that this fallacy befalls only you essentialists, not us.

First, if it were as you say, then worldly conventions such as "Fetch a chariot" could not exist. For, when you posit things as existing, you use reasoned analysis to search so as to see whether they have intrinsic nature; yet when sought by such reasoning, the chariot is not found in any of the seven ways. Since you advance no other method for establishing things, chariots would be nonexistent. [726] It seems that nowadays some who claim to advocate the meaning of Madhyamaka put forward as the Madhyamaka system an argument made by advocates of true existence: "When reasoning searches to see whether a chariot has intrinsic nature and fails to find a chariot, then a chariot does not exist." An undeniable fault of such assertions is that they make it impossible to give any presentation of conventional phenomena.

The following passage from Candrakīrti's *Commentary on the "Middle Way"* shows how our position does not have this problem:[568]

> This chariot is not established in the seven ways,
> Either in reality or for the world.
> Yet without analysis, just for the world,
> It is imputed in dependence upon its parts.

The meaning of this is as follows: When reasoning searches to see whether the chariot intrinsically exists, it is not found in any of the seven ways. This is the case in terms of both of the two truths. But when reason fails to find it in those seven ways, does this refute the chariot? How could it? Reasoning that analyzes whether things intrinsically exist does not establish the assertion of the chariot; rather, leaving reasoned analysis aside, it is established by a mere, unimpaired, ordinary, conventional—i.e., worldly—consciousness. Therefore, the way a chariot is posited is that it is established as existing imputedly; it is imputed in dependence upon its parts.

Objection: When a yogi analyzes in this way, reason does not find a chariot; hence, the chariot does not exist essentially or intrinsically. However, its parts do exist intrinsically.

Reply: You are searching for threads in the ashes of incinerated cloth—it is ridiculous. If the whole does not exist, neither do the parts. As Candrakīrti's *Commentary on the "Middle Way"* says:[569]

> When the chariot itself does not exist,
> Neither the whole nor its parts exist.

Thus, if the whole does not exist, the parts also do not exist.

Qualm: This is untenable because when the chariot is destroyed, the collection of parts—wheels and such—is still evident. [727]

Reply: No, for only those who have seen the chariot before will think, "These wheels and so forth are those of a chariot." Others will not think that. When the chariot is destroyed, the wheels and such are not associated with a chariot and thus they are not parts of a chariot. Therefore, neither the chariot as a whole nor the parts of the chariot exist at that time. At that point, in terms of the chariot, neither the whole nor the parts exist. However, the wheels, etc., are wholes in relation to their own components and these components are their parts. Hence you cannot posit parts without a whole. Moreover, you should use the example of the chariot to understand that parts do not exist without wholes. As Candrakīrti's *Commentary on the "Middle Way"* says:[570]

> When a chariot is burned, its parts do not exist.
> As in this example, when the fire of the analytical mind burns
>   wholes, the parts also do not exist.

(3')) How to establish the chariot under various names

Candrakīrti's *Explanation of the "Middle Way" Commentary* states:[571]

> Our position very clearly establishes the conventional designation of a chariot in terms of what is familiar to the world; what is more, you should also assert any of the chariot's various names in terms of what is familiar to the world, without analysis. It is thus:
>
> > That same chariot is known as a whole, as a composite, and
> >   as an agent.
> > Living beings are established as appropriators of the five
> >   aggregates.

In relation to parts and components such as wheels, a chariot is established as the referent of the conventions "whole" and "composite." Likewise, it is designated with the nominal convention "agent" with reference to its activity of appropriating wheels, etc. and with the nominal convention "appropriator" in relation to the appropriated parts. [728]

Some Buddhists claim that mere groups of components and parts exist, and that since nothing different from that is evident, wholes and composites do not exist.[572] Likewise, they claim that only actions exist, but agents do not, and that since nothing different from appropriation is evident, appropriation exists but the appropriator does not. In terms of the conventions of the world, these positions are inaccurate because, were they accurate, even parts and such would not exist. With that point in mind, Candrakīrti said, "Do not destroy the conventions familiar to the world."[573]

Therefore, what we advocate does not violate the principle of the two truths: Ultimately, just as wholes and so forth do not exist, neither do parts and so forth; conventionally, just as parts and so forth exist, so too do wholes and so forth.

(4')) The advantage that you find the view quickly by using this example

Candrakīrti's *Explanation of the "Middle Way" Commentary* says:[574]

> These worldly conventionalities do not exist when analyzed in that way, but exist only through being taken for granted, without being subject to scrutiny. Therefore, when yogis analyze these worldly conventionalities through this very process, they will very quickly fathom the depths of reality. How?
>
>> "What does not exist in the seven ways—how could it exist?"
>> Thinking thus, yogis do not find the existence of the chariot
>> And thereby easily enter into reality as well.
>> Hence, you should also assert the establishment of the chariot in that way.

This means that it is through such an analysis of the chariot that you quickly fathom the deepest meaning of reality—that there is no intrinsic nature. Thus, it is evident that this is a very crucial point. [729] Yogis who in this way analyze how things exist will develop certainty, thinking: "If this 'chariot' existed intrinsically, then when I search with reasoning that looks to see whether it exists intrinsically in any of the seven ways—same, different, and so forth—I should undoubtedly find it in one of those seven ways. Yet I do not find it in any of those seven ways. It is apparent that—despite its not being found—I cannot repudiate the convention of the chariot; still, 'chariot' is imputed only by way of the mind's eye being corrupted by films of ignorance. It is not intrinsically existent." Such yogis easily enter into reality.

The words "as well" in Candrakīrti's phrase "enter into reality as well" show that this analysis does not harm conventionalities.

As a system for delineating alternatives in the refutation of a chariot's intrinsic existence, the investigation of these seven ways clarifies the possibilities and greatly clarifies the refuting arguments. Thus, it is easy to realize that a chariot lacks intrinsic existence using this analysis.

In brief, there are three advantages to presenting this topic as explained above, beginning with the chariot: (1) the advantage that it is easy to refute the eternalist view that superimposes intrinsic existence on phenomena, (2) the advantage that it is easy to refute the nihilistic view that dependent-arising is invalid in the absence of intrinsic existence, and (3) the yogi's investigative process, which establishes the first two advantages by carrying out analysis in just such a manner. To elaborate on these three:

(1) When you use a highly condensed method of refuting intrinsic existence, refuting just same and different, it is difficult to understand; it again becomes difficult when there are too many alternatives. Thus, the sevenfold analysis is quite appropriate.

(2) In that you refute an object of negation with an added qualification during the initial refutation, you refute intrinsic existence without damaging the conventional existence of actions and agents.

(3) After you have developed certainty that the pervaded—intrinsic existence—does not extend beyond the pervader—the seven ways, such as one and different—you then show that each of those seven is contradicted. When you determine that every one of those seven is contradicted, this negates the pervader, whereby the pervaded is also negated. [730] After you have done this once, you then repeatedly develop decisive certainty that there is no intrinsic existence. After that, when you see that you cannot repudiate the convention of the chariot even though there is no intrinsic existence, you think, "Oh, it is amazing how the magicians of karma and the afflictions conjure up these illusions, such as chariots! Each arises, without even the slightest confusion, from its own causes and conditions; each lacks even the slightest trace of essential or

intrinsic existence." You will be certain that dependent-arising means that things are not intrinsically produced. As Candrakīrti's *Commentary on the "Four Hundred Stanzas"* says:[575]

> Pots and such do not exist under the fivefold analysis as to whether they are the same as their causes or other than their causes. Nevertheless, through dependent imputation, they can do things like hold or scoop honey, or water, or milk. Is this not wonderful?

And:

> What lacks intrinsic existence—and yet is evident—is empty of intrinsic existence, like the circle of a whirling firebrand.

23

THE PERSON LACKS INTRINSIC NATURE

(b')) Showing what the example illustrates

This discussion of what the example of the chariot illustrates has two parts:

1. The example illustrates how the person lacks intrinsic nature
2. The example illustrates how the person is established under various names

(1')) The example illustrates how the person lacks intrinsic nature

This section has four parts:

1. The refutation of the position that the self is one with the aggregates

2. The refutation of the position that the self is different from the aggregates
3. How those arguments also refute each of the remaining positions
4. How the person appears like an illusion based on that refutation

(a")) **The refutation of the position that the self is one with the aggregates**

In the general case, we see in the world that when a phenomenon is mentally classified as accompanied, it is precluded from being unaccompanied, and when it is classified as unaccompanied, it is precluded from being accompanied. In general, therefore, same and different, as well as single and plural, eliminate any further alternative because the unaccompanied and the accompanied are respectively single and plural. **[731]** When you resolve that in general something must be either one or not one, then you will also resolve that for the particular case of what exists essentially, it must be either essentially one or essentially different.

So if a self or a person existed essentially or intrinsically, it could only be one with its aggregates or different from its aggregates. Hence, a yogi analyzes, thinking, "Is this self essentially one with the aggregates? Or is it essentially different?" At first the yogi looks for something that would contradict the position of oneness, thinking, "If self and the aggregates were established as intrinsically one, what could contradict this?" Buddhapālita gives three arguments that contradict that position: (1) It would be pointless to propound a self, (2) there would be many selves, and (3) the self would be subject to production and disintegration. To elaborate:

1. If the self and the aggregates were held to be intrinsically one, then there would be no point in asserting a self because it would be identical to the aggregates, like the moon and the rabbit-bearer.[576] Nāgārjuna's *Fundamental Treatise* also makes this point:[577]

> When there is no self
> Except for the appropriated aggregates,
> The appropriated aggregates are the self.
> In that case, the self that you propose does not exist.

2. If the person and aggregates were intrinsically one, then just as one person has many aggregates, one person would also have many selves. Or, just as there is no more than one self, there would also be one aggregate. These are the fallacies given in Candrakīrti's *Commentary on the "Middle Way"*:[578]

If the aggregates were the self, then since
There are many aggregates, the self would also be many.

3. Nāgārjuna's *Fundamental Treatise* states:[579]

If the aggregates were the self,
Then the self would be subject to production and disintegration.

And:[580] [732]

What is appropriated is not the self;
They arise and disintegrate.

You should understand that "what is appropriated" here refers to the aggregates.

Qualm: What fallacy is there in holding that the self is subject to momentary production and disintegration?

Reply: Candrakīrti's *Commentary on the "Middle Way"* and *Explanation of the "Middle Way" Commentary* give three fallacies in this position: (1) recollection of past lives would be untenable, (2) actions done would perish, and (3) you would encounter the effects of actions that you did not do. To elaborate:

1. If the self arose and disintegrated moment by moment, then, since the self would be essentially arising and disintegrating, former and later selves would be distinct in their intrinsic character. In that case, the Buddha would not have said, "In that life, at the time I was King Māndhātṛ..."[581] because the self of King Māndhātṛ and the self of the Teacher would be distinct in their intrinsic character. For example, it would be like Devadatta trying to recall his past lives and mistakenly remembering, "I became Yajñadatta." Otherwise, if you argue that it is not contradictory for earlier experience to be remembered by a later self despite the former and later selves being different in their intrinsic character, then you have to explain why this situation is different from Yajñadatta's not remembering Devadatta's experience. However, you cannot find a rationale for this.

This is similar to the argument that refutes production from other. To the assertion that seed and seedling exist essentially or intrinsically, yet differ as cause and effect, we reply, "If it were possible for such intrinsically different phenomena to be cause and effect, then even a flame would produce darkness." This does not wipe out the assertion that seed and seedling are merely different.

Did that sūtra teach that the Teacher and Māndhātṛ are one? That passage refutes otherness of *continuum*, but does not teach that they are one. [733] According to Candrakīrti, this is why the sūtra ends by saying, "Do you think that the person in that lifetime was some-one else? Do not look at it that way."

Some who are mistaken about such sūtra statements hold the following position: The Buddha and those living beings from his earlier lives are one. Saying, "I, in a former life, became this being," the sūtra means that those two, the Buddha and the earlier beings, are one and the same. Also, since anything that is compounded dis-integrates moment by moment, and hence cannot be the same, both the Buddha and those earlier beings are permanent.

Of the four wrong views based on theories about the past, this is the first.[582] Nāgārjuna's *Fundamental Treatise* refutes it:[583]

> "I was born in the past"
> Is an untenable claim.
> It is not this very person
> Who was born in those earlier lives.

If it were as such persons claim, then one rebirth would turn into all six rebirths because living beings take up their respective bod-ies in six types and the former and later persons would be perma-nently one.

Nāgārjuna also refutes the assertion that former and later per-sons are essentially distinct. If the self had an intrinsic nature, then former and later selves would either be essentially one, which would entail eternalism; or else they would be essentially differ-ent, which would entail nihilism. Therefore, the learned should not assert that the self has intrinsic nature.

2. Actions done would perish. Some claim that if the self was in each moment arising and disintegrating by way of its own intrin-sic character, then later selves would still enjoy the effects of the actions of earlier selves. I refute this assertion in (3) below, so here I argue that if this were the case, there would be no experience of the effects of previously accumulated karma because the self that is the agent of an action would disintegrate prior to the experience of its effect, and there would be no other self to have such experi-ence. Since earlier and later things are not essentially different, there is no later self that is essentially different from the former. If the effects were not experienced by the earlier self, then the effects must not be experienced. [734] I refute below the reply that such former and later selves are in the same continuum;[584] hence, you cannot escape the fallacy that actions that were performed would perish.

3. You would encounter the effects of actions that you did not do. Some claim that although the earlier self disintegrates, the later

self enjoys the effect; hence, the fallacy of wasting actions that were performed does not arise. If this were the case, then a person could enjoy the effect of karma accumulated by another person, even without accumulating even the slightest karma capable of causing the experienced effect. This is because, according to you, the effects of karma accumulated by an essentially existent person are experienced by another, essentially different person. As Candrakīrti's *Commentary on the "Middle Way"* states:[585]

> Prior to nirvāṇa there would be no karmic effects,
> Because agents that arise and disintegrate in the very moment
>   of an action would not exist to experience its effect.
> Each person would get what others accumulated.

Candrakīrti mentions three other fallacies, but they seem to refute only the assertions of other Buddhists. Since I am advancing a general refutation, I will not give them here.

Nāgārjuna's *Fundamental Treatise* also gives those two arguments:[586]

> If this self were different from that of an earlier life,
> It would arise even without the other having existed.
> Likewise, that earlier self could remain there in that life;
> Without that self dying, this self could be born.

> There would be absurd consequences
> Such as the severing of the continuum, the wasting of actions,
> And each person experiencing the effects
> Of actions performed by others.

This gives the two fallacies that Candrakīrti uses, the wasting of actions and the experiencing of the effects of actions performed by others. The phrase, "If this self were different," means "If the self of an earlier lifetime and the present self were essentially different." If this were the case, then since the present self would not in any way rely upon the self of the earlier life, it would arise without depending upon that former self. [735] Also, just as a cloth does not disintegrate when a pot is created, the former self would remain without disintegrating when the later self was born. We could be born here in this life without dying in our earlier lives. This is what that passage means.

Objection: The selves of former and later lives are essentially distinct, yet these fallacies—that actions would perish and that you would encounter the effects of actions not done—do not arise because there is a single continuum connecting the selves of different lifetimes.

Reply: It is not established that the selves within a continuum are distinct in their intrinsic character, so it seems that you will have to prove it. It is not tenable for things that are essentially different to constitute a single continuum. For example, it is like Maitreya and Upagupta. As Candrakīrti's *Commentary on the "Middle Way"* states:[587]

> If you claim that there is no fallacy in a continuum that exists in
>   reality,
> I already explained the fallacies of such a continuum when I
>   analyzed this above.

As to how it was analyzed, that same text states:[588]

> Because the phenomena [aggregates] associated with Maitreya
>   and Upagupta
> Are different, they are not included in one continuum.
> It is not reasonable that what is distinct in its intrinsic character
> Should be included in a single continuum.

If phenomena are distinct in their intrinsic character, then, like two different continua, they are not to be posited as a single continuum. Also, the twenty-seventh chapter of Nāgārjuna's *Fundamental Treatise* says:[589]

> If a human and a deity were different,
> It would be untenable for them to be a single continuum.

In short, whatever is essentially other must be asserted to withstand analysis by reasoning that analyzes the way that it exists. There is nothing, not even the slightest particle, that withstands analysis when such reasoning analyzes in detail. Hence, if a later self experiences the effects of karma accumulated by an earlier and intrinsically different self in the same continuum, this cannot be distinguished from the completely parallel case of selves that are in different continua. You must realize that this argument applies to all such cases!

Qualm: Since the one who experiences in a past life and the one who remembers in a later life are not the same, the recollection of earlier experiences and the enjoyment of the effects of previously accumulated karma are untenable even in our own system, just as in the case of persons of different continua.

Reply: We do not incur that fallacy. [736] For, in the systems of others who do not assert essential existence it does not work for the experiencer and the rememberer to be in the same continuum, but in our system it is not contradictory for them to be in the same continuum. For example, if a dove has been on the thatched roof of a house in which there is a container of yogurt, one can see its footprints there in the yogurt even though its feet did not enter the container of yogurt.[590] Similarly, the person of this life has not gone back to a former life, yet it is not contradictory that such a person should remember experiences there. Candrakīrti's *Commentary on the "Four Hundred Stanzas"* states:[591]

> We dispense with any notion that causes and effects are the same or different. If there is only an impermanent stream of conditioned factors brought about by their particular causes, then it is reasonable to say that the imputedly existent self that appropriates that stream of factors remembers its lives. Things do not exist by way of intrinsic character; it stands to reason that they encounter various conditions and are changed. Therefore, you should carefully examine the astonishing fact that things have causes that do not exist by way of their intrinsic character. Inside a house, you can see in a container of yogurt—as though it were in wet clay—the footprints of a dove that has been on the heavily thatched roof. Yet the dove's feet have not at all entered the container.

Look in Candrakīrti's *Commentary on the "Middle Way"* for an extensive treatment of this point.

For now, we will explain the implications in ordinary language. The claim that the self is one with the aggregates is completely demolished by Nāgārjuna's challenge, "How could the appropriated become the appropriator?"[592] Since we use the conventional expression, "This person took up this body," the aggregates are the appropriated and the self is the appropriator. [737] If you say that those two are one, then object and agent would be one; hence, cutter and what is cut, pot and potter, fire and fuel, etc. would also be one. Nāgārjuna's *Fundamental Treatise* states:[593]

> If fuel were fire,
> Then agent and object would be one....
>
> The entire process is explained
> For the self and the appropriated aggregates
> Using fire and wood as analogies,
> Along with pot and cloth and so forth.

Also, Candrakīrti's *Commentary on the "Middle Way"* states:[594]

> It is clearly not right for the appropriator to be one with what it
>   appropriates;
> If it were thus, then object and agent would be the same.

Thus, if the self were one with the aggregates, there would be six fallacies: it would be pointless to assert a self; there would be many selves; object and agent would be one; actions that were performed would perish; the effects of actions not done would be encountered; and the statements by the Buddha about remembering past lives would be invalid. So do not assert that the self and the aggregates are one.

(b")) The refutation of the position that the self is different from the aggregates

Question: The self and the aggregates are not intrinsically one, but what fallacy is there in asserting that they are intrinsically different?
Reply: Nāgārjuna's *Fundamental Treatise* states the fallacy in this:[595]

If the self were other than the aggregates,
It would not have the characteristics of the aggregates.

If the self were essentially different from the aggregates, it would not have the aggregates' characteristics of arising, remaining, and disintegrating. For example, a horse is something other than a cow, and so does not have the characteristics of a cow. **[738]** If someone still thinks this, take from Candrakīrti's *Clear Words* this syllogism based on what others accept: "The aggregates cannot be the basis for the conventional imputation of a self and cannot be objects apprehended as a self, because the self is non-composite—like a flower in the sky or nirvāṇa."[596] If the self did not arise and disintegrate, then it would be permanent. Since there is no way to avoid the implication that the self would be permanent, it would be pointless to impute a self because, as Buddhapālita points out, it would be impossible to engage in virtue or turn away from nonvirtue.[597]

Furthermore, if the self had an intrinsic nature different from the defining characteristics of the five aggregates—e.g., being suitable to be form—then this would have to be evident, just as form and mind, for example, are observably different. Since the self is not apprehended in that way, it has no other meaning apart from the characteristics of the aggregates. Nāgārjuna's *Fundamental Treatise* says:[598]

It is just not correct for the self
To be other than the appropriated aggregates.
If it were other, it could be apprehended
Without the appropriated aggregates, yet is not.

And Candrakīrti's *Commentary on the "Middle Way"* says:[599]

Therefore, there is no self other than the aggregates
Because without the aggregates, it is not apprehended.

Non-Buddhist philosophers, not realizing that self is a mere name and yet seeing that it is untenable for it to be one with the aggregates, superimpose a self which is something other than the aggregates as a matter of tenet. However, the ordinary conventional consciousnesses in their mind-streams do not see it that way.

You should repeatedly practice so as to reach solid certainty that arguments such as these contradict the existence of a self that is essentially different from the aggregates. For, if you do not develop genuine certainty about the critique of the positions of one and different, then even though you may decide that the person lacks intrinsic existence, it will be just an unproved proposition; hence, you will not obtain the authentic view.

Seeking to analyze whether the person exists in reality, you should analyze whether the person, if existent in reality, would be one with or different from the aggregates. [739] If the person were one with the aggregates, then there are conclusive criticisms, such as the implication that agent and object—e.g., fire and fuel—would be one. If fire and fuel are held to be one, you must use mundane valid cognition to refute that position; a tenet that is not shared by both parties is not an effective critique. Likewise, there is the argument—to the position that the self and the aggregates are different—that if they were essentially different, then, like form and mind, they would have to be seen as separate, yet they are not. This is presented in terms of the non-apprehension of such a difference by ordinary consciousnesses. Unique tenets are not an effective critique.

Therefore, even when you analyze reality, the final basis for any critique derives from the unimpaired conventional consciousnesses in the mind-streams of both parties. The passage from Candrakīrti's *Commentary on the "Middle Way,"*[600] "The world has no critique in the context of reality," indicates, as explained above, that worldly consciousnesses are not valid cognitions of reality, but this is not to deny that unimpaired conventional consciousnesses can give evidence of contradiction in contexts where reality is under analysis. For, if they could not, then there would be no basis from which to critique the unique claims of others.

There are various positions on the use of scripture in debate—some accept it and some do not; among those who accept it, there is disagreement about what requires interpretation. Hence, you must use reasoning to prove things. And what other kind of reasoning can you use? To the assertions of the other party, you can say, "If you assert this, then you must also assert that," and, "If you do not assert this, then do you also not assert that?" But how can there be certainty without a reason that is derived from shared conventional experience? Therefore, when you trace all the roots of probative and critical arguments back to their source, you arrive at the unimpaired conventional consciousnesses of the two parties. If someone asserts something that contradicts those consciousnesses, then both parties will see that their experience refutes it. As this is so, the system of all Mādhyamikas and Prāmāṇikas is not to go beyond this. [740]

Nevertheless, we avoid the fallacy that conventional consciousnesses would establish the absence of intrinsic existence and such. It is similar to the case of perception establishing that sound is a product, yet not necessarily establishing that sound is impermanent. In brief, the ultimate root of probative and critical argument derives from perception, but it does not follow that perception must establish the root probandum.[601]

(c")) How those arguments also refute each of the remaining positions

If the self and the aggregates were intrinsically different, there would be two ways in which they could be basis and dependent, like yogurt in a bowl. Either the self could exist in dependence upon the aggregates or the aggregates could exist in dependence upon the self. However, as in the explanation of the chariot,[602] since they are not intrinsically different, they do not exist as basis and dependent. Candrakīrti's *Commentary on the "Middle Way"* states:[603]

> The self does not intrinsically depend on the aggregates
> And the aggregates do not intrinsically depend on the self.
> While such conceptions could be correct if they were intrinsi-
>   cally different,
> Since they are not intrinsically different, those are misconceptions.

The position that the self possesses the aggregates is also similar to what was explained with regard to the chariot, so it should be understood accordingly. Candrakīrti's *Commentary on the "Middle Way"* states:[604]

> We do not hold that the self possesses the aggregate of form.
>   Why?
> Since the self does not exist, possession by the self is meaningless.

> If they are different, then it is like having cattle; if not, then it is
> like having form.
> However, the self is neither the same as nor different from
> form.

"Having cattle" is, for example, Devadatta's having oxen. "Having form" is, for example, Devadatta's having form.

Is a mere group of aggregates the self? This is also incorrect because the self is said to be imputed in dependence upon the five aggregates and it is not tenable for the basis of imputation to be the object imputed. The *Commentary on the "Middle Way"*:[605]

> The Buddha's discourses state that the self depends upon the
> aggregates.
> Therefore, a mere group of aggregates is not the self. **[741]**

Furthermore, Candrakirti's *Commentary on the "Middle Way"* and *Explanation of the "Middle Way" Commentary* state the fallacy that if a mere collection of aggregates were the self, agent and object would be one. This is because anyone who claims that the self appropriates the individual aggregates must accept that it appropriates all five aggregates; hence, it would appropriate the collection of the aggregates as well. This passage from the *Commentary on the "Middle Way"* means that the collection is the basis to which the self is imputed, but is not the self; this makes it clear that you must also assert such with regard to the continuum of the aggregates.

Objection: Those are not the self; rather, I posit the self as the particular shape of the collection of form and so forth. For example, when a chariot's wheels, axle, and so forth are assembled, this is considered a chariot if the distinctive shape of a chariot is found.

Reply: Only what has form can have shape, so consciousnesses, etc. could not be posited as the self. The *Commentary on the "Middle Way"*:[606]

> Is it a shape? Since only what has form has shape,
> For you that alone would be called "self."
> Collections of consciousness and so forth
> Would not be the self since they have no shape.

Just as a chariot does not intrinsically exist in any of the seven ways, but is still posited in dependence upon its parts, the self does not intrinsically exist in any of the seven ways—one with the aggregates, different from the aggregates, and so forth—yet is still imputed in dependence upon the aggregates.

This proves what the Buddha stated succinctly, treating chariot and self as example and exemplified.

(d")) How the person appears like an illusion based on that refutation

"Illusion" is said to have two meanings. Statements that the ultimate truth is like an illusion, for instance, mean that although it is established as merely existent, its true existence is negated. Statements that forms and such are illusions mean that what appears as a form, while being empty of intrinsic existence, is like an illusion. [742] It is the latter of these that I am concerned with here. The latter also carries the meaning of "illusion" in the former sense; it is not always certain that the former usage carries the meaning of "illusion" in its latter sense.

How do you establish this latter sense of "illusion"? You use two kinds of awareness—one that apprehends an appearance and one that ascertains emptiness. For example, how can you know that an appearance of a horse or elephant is an illusory or false appearance? You need both a visual consciousness that sees an illusory horse or elephant and a mental consciousness that knows that the horse or elephant does not exist as it appears. Likewise, to be certain that the person, for instance, is an illusory or false appearance, you need both the undeniable appearance of the person to a conventional consciousness and the ascertainment by reasoned knowledge that the person is empty of essential or intrinsic existence. Reasoned knowledge does not establish that the appearance exists, while conventional valid cognition does not establish that it is empty of intrinsic existence. Consequently, you need both reasoned knowledge that searches to see whether things intrinsically exist and conventional awarenesses that apprehend forms and such as existent.

While some say that there are many ways to make form appear like an illusion, it is unnecessary to exert yourself at techniques for generating such, for such appearances spontaneously present themselves to the conventional consciousnesses that apprehend those forms. Analyzing them often with reasoning that examines whether they intrinsically exist, you develop a strong certainty that intrinsic existence is refuted. Then, when you see an appearance arise, it appears like an illusion. There is no separate way to set up an illusion-like emptiness.

Earlier teachers[607] used the term "space-like emptiness" to refer to an emptiness that is the mere elimination, by reasoned knowledge, of intrinsic production, cessation, and so forth in the appearing subject. They used the term "illusion-like emptiness" to refer to the subsequent appearance of forms and such, which appear to be intrinsically existent while being known as actually empty of intrinsic existence. [743] Thus, even when you are engaged in the behavioral aspects of the practice—prostrating, circumambulating, and reciting, etc.—you should first use reason to analyze whether those practices intrinsically exist, and refute their intrinsic existence. By engaging in those practices under the sway of certainty that the practices do not intrinsically exist, you learn to raise illusion-like appearance and to do those practices within that appearance. If you understand this vital point, you will have a solid understanding of how the force of having cultivated space-like emptiness in meditative equipoise gives rise to illusion-like emptiness in the post-equipoise state.

Also, as explained above,[608] if you fail to limit the object of negation when you use reason to investigate whether the self and the aggregates are one, different, and so forth, then when you see the arguments that contradict those positions, you will think, "Persons and such do not exist at all," or, "Things such as persons are non-things, empty of all function, like the horns of a rabbit and such." This is a nihilistic view. Therefore, you should be aware that this is a point where you may slip with regard to the correct view. Āryadeva's *Four Hundred Stanzas* says:

> If this were so, then how could it be said
> That existence is like an illusion?

Candrakīrti's *Commentary on the "Four Hundred Stanzas"* comments:[609]

> When you see dependent-arisings as they are, they are like creations of a magician—not like the son of a barren woman.
> *Qualm*: Because this analysis completely refutes production, it teaches that compounded phenomena are not produced.
> *Reply*: If that were so, then they would not be like illusions. If you could comprehend things with examples such as the son of a barren woman, then it would follow that dependent-arisings do not exist. I am wary of this, so I do not make that comparison; rather, I compare them to illusions and such, examples that do not contradict those dependent-arisings. [744]

Thus, there would be a fallacy if the reasoned knowledge that searches to see whether things intrinsically exist were to apprehend the merely illusory as existent; yet you definitely must develop—in place of the intrinsic existence that is refuted under rational analysis—an apprehension of the existence of things that are merely illusory.[610] So there is no fallacy. For, Candrakīrti's *Commentary on the "Four Hundred Stanzas"* says that an illusory object must be left as a remainder:[611]

> So, when you analyze in this way, things are not established as intrinsically existent; hence, the illusoriness of individual things is left as a remainder.

When you refute the essential or intrinsic existence of a seedling, as long as the effectiveness of the reasoning does not deteriorate, reason analyzes whether intrinsic existence is tenable. You do not develop an apprehension of the seedling as intrinsically existent. However, if you think that the seedling's lack of intrinsic existence is truly existent, or that the illusion-like appearance of that which is empty of intrinsic existence is itself truly existent, this is a misapprehension that you must refute using reasoning. Some think that, beyond this, even the apprehension of the illusory as existent involves clinging to the apprehension of illusoriness, and thus must be eliminated. Pay no heed to this notion, or else you will incur a great fallacy; namely, that any certainty about dependent-arising would be impossible. I have already explained this several times.[612] This is undoubtedly a case of failing to distinguish between the *existence* of the illusory object and the *true existence* of the illusory object.

When your analysis of an object uses reason to obliterate it, you first think, "It is not there." Then, as you also see the analyzer [yourself] in that same way, there is no one even to ascertain that nonexistence. So, with no way to determine what something is or is not, it begins to seem that what appears has become vague and indistinct. This comes about based upon reason refuting everything, without distinguishing intrinsic existence and its absence from *mere* existence and its absence. Thus, this sort of emptiness is an emptiness that destroys dependent-arising. Therefore, illusoriness as we use the term definitely does not refer to the rising of a vague, indistinct appearance brought on by this kind of realization. [745]

Therefore, upon reasoned analysis, you come to think, "This person lacks even the slightest essential or objective existence." On that basis, it is not difficult simply to have these appearances seem vague and indistinct. That sort of experience comes to everyone who aspires to an understanding of Madhyamaka tenets and hears a little of the teaching that shows how things lack intrinsic nature. Still, it is difficult to develop certainty about both (1) the complete refutation of essential or intrinsic nature and (2) the presentation of those very persons who lack intrinsic nature as accumulators of karma, experiencers of the effects of karma, and so forth. It scarcely happens that someone combines the capacities to posit both of these, so it is very difficult to find the Madhyamaka view.

Without that combination, it is undeniable that as certainty about the philosophical view increases, certainty about the behavioral aspects of the practice decreases; insofar as certainty about the behavioral aspects increases, certainty about the view decreases. There is no way to develop equally strong certainty about both. Therefore you will definitely fall either into one extreme—the superimposition conceiving intrinsic existence, the eternalist view, the view of things as existing intrinsically—or else the other extreme—the mistaken denial holding that things are devoid of the capacity to perform functions, the nihilistic view, the view of things as utterly nonexistent. Thus, the *King of Concentrations Sūtra* says:[613]

> Then the Conqueror, who is without sin and endowed with
> The ten powers, explained this supreme concentration:
> The states of cyclic existence are like a dream;
> Herein there is neither birth nor death.

> Living beings, humans, and even life are not found.
> These things are like foam, like a plantain tree,
> Like an illusion, like a flash of lightning,
> Like the reflection of the moon in water, like a mirage.

> There is no one who dies in this world
> And passes or migrates to another.
> Still, actions done are never lost,
> And virtuous and nonvirtuous effects ripen in the world. [746]

> Neither permanent nor falling into annihilation,
> Actions neither accumulate nor endure.
> Yet you cannot do actions without meeting their effects.
> Nor do you experience the effects of others' actions.

Thus, even though reason does not find the person who makes the passage at birth and death, virtuous and nonvirtuous effects do occur among illusion-like phenomena. So you should be certain of what that sūtra says, that those who have done actions will not fail to contact or experience their effects and will not encounter the effects of actions they did not do, those effects being felt or experienced by the other persons who did those actions.

Seek this assurance in the following manner: As previously explained, form a clear concept of the object that reason will be refuting. Then focus on how, if there were such an intrinsically existing person, it could only be one with or different from its aggregates, and how reason contradicts both of those positions. Develop certainty in seeing this critique. Finally, solidify your certainty that the person does not even slightly exist intrinsically. In the phase of meditating on emptiness, practice this often.

Then, bring to mind the conventional person who is undeniably apparent. Turn your mind to dependent-arising, wherein that person is posited as the accumulator of karma and the experiencer of effects, and be certain of how dependent-arising is possible without intrinsic existence. When they seem contradictory, think about how they are not contradictory, taking an example such as a reflection. [747] A reflection of a face is undeniably a conjunction of (1) being empty of the eyes, ears, and such that appear therein and (2) being produced in dependence upon a mirror and a face, while disintegrating when certain of these conditions are gone. Likewise, the person lacks even a particle of intrinsic nature, but is the accumulator of karma and the experiencer of effects, and is produced in dependence upon earlier karma and afflictions. It is not a contradiction. Practice this thought and understand that it is like this in all such cases.

Qualm: Does certainty that reflections and such are empty of what appears constitute knowledge that they lack intrinsic existence? If so, then the perceptions of ordinary beings would constitute knowledge of emptiness; hence, they would be noble beings. If not, then how can reflections work as examples of the lack of intrinsic existence in those persons and such? If you have to use a reason that proves the absence of intrinsic existence even to understand the examples, then there would have to be an endless regression when you examine issues such as what to posit as examples for those examples.

Reply by an earlier scholar: Although ordinary beings have perceptual knowledge that reflections and such lack intrinsic existence, they are not noble beings because they only know the emptiness of a limited subject. In order to become a noble being, one must have perceptual knowledge that all phenomena lack intrinsic existence.

Our position: That reply is not right because Āryadeva's *Four Hundred Stanzas* says that one who knows the emptiness—the lack of intrinsic existence—of one thing can know the emptiness of all phenomena:[614]

> Who sees one thing
> Is said to see everything.

The emptiness of one thing
Is the emptiness of everything.

Therefore, someone who knows that a reflection is empty of being a face does not apprehend it as truly being a face, yet does apprehend it as a truly existent reflection. What contradiction is there in that?

When young, pre-verbal children see reflections of their faces, they play with them and so forth; hence, they do apprehend them as truly being faces. [748] Older, verbal persons are certain that insofar as those reflections are not faces, they are empty of being faces; yet they apprehend as intrinsically existent those very reflections that appear to be faces. That apprehension is a conception of true existence. Experience in our own mind-streams proves that this is how we see reflections.

Nevertheless, reflections and so forth are appropriate examples for the lack of intrinsic existence. Why? We use those examples because perception establishes that they are empty of the entity they appear to be, and thus they are not really what they appear to be. When valid cognition establishes this "emptiness of really being what it appears" in relation to seedlings and such, then it knows the seedlings' lack of intrinsic existence; in this way seedlings and such are different from reflections and such.

Candrakīrti's *Commentary on the "Middle Way"* says:[615]

Just as things such as pots do not exist in reality,
Yet do exist in terms of what is familiar to the world...

As an example of the lack of intrinsic existence, he states "things such as pots" to the advocates of intrinsic existence. Yet, as in the case of reflections and such, he refers to a limited emptiness and not to their lack of intrinsic nature. This is because, as explained previously, many proofs of the lack of intrinsic existence use chariots and such as examples. Similarly, in the case of a magician's illusion, the spectators apprehend it as truly being a horse or an elephant; the magician's knowledge that the horse or elephant is false is knowledge of a limited emptiness.

In a dream, you see an environment and its inhabitants. Upon waking, you understand that they are false in that they are empty of what they appear to be. Even while asleep you may apprehend them in that way. In either case, you understand that what appears to be men and women in a dream is devoid of being other men and women. Nevertheless, this does not constitute knowledge that the dream is empty of intrinsic existence. It is comparable to being certain that there is no face in something such as a reflection.

As cited earlier, Candrakīrti's *Commentary on the "Middle Way"* says, "Things that are ascribed to mirages, magicians' illusions, and so forth do not exist even for the world."[616] **[749]** This means that ordinary conventional valid cognition discredits consciousnesses that apprehend as existent the water, horses, elephants, men, women, and so forth in mirages, illusions, and dreams. Therefore, the knowledge that the objects conceived of by those consciousnesses do not exist is *not* the view that knows the lack of intrinsic existence.

So, you should reflect upon the meaning of illusoriness as explained above, reciting the poetry of the profound sūtra collections. Take this statement from the *King of Concentrations Sūtra*:[617]

> Like a mirage, a phantom city, or an illusion, meditation
>   associated with signs is empty of essence. Know that all
>   phenomena are this way.
> The moon shines in a clear sky and its reflection appears in a
>   clear lake, yet the moon has not moved into the water. Know
>   that the character of all phenomena is like that.
> People in a wooded mountain range hear echoes from song,
>   speech, laughter, and weeping, but what seems to be there is
>   not. Know that all phenomena are this way.
> Although echoes arise from song, music, and even weeping,
>   the tones of those songs and so forth are never in the sound
>   of the echo. Know that all phenomena are this way.
> When people who have something that they want in a dream
>   awake and do not see it, they are fools to desire it and to
>   cling to it. Know that all phenomena are this way.
> When magicians conjure up forms, creating various horses,
>   elephants, or chariots, what appears to be there does not
>   exist at all. Know that all phenomena are this way.
> When a young woman sees the birth and death of son in a
>   dream, she is delighted at the birth but not at the death.
>   Know that all phenomena are this way. **[750]**
> When reflections of the moon appear at night in clear, clean
>   water, they are empty and vain, ungraspable. Know that all
>   phenomena are this way.
> A person tormented by thirst, traveling at midday in summer,
>   sees mirages as pools of water. Know that all phenomena are
>   this way.
> Although water does not exist in a mirage at all, a deluded
>   being wants to drink it. It is false and undrinkable. Know
>   that all phenomena are this way.

Someone may peel away the watery trunk of a plantain tree
looking for a pith, but neither inside nor outside is there any
pith at all. Know that all phenomena are this way.

(2')) The example illustrates how the person is established under various names

When a chariot is imputed in dependence upon things such as
wheels, those parts are the appropriated and the chariot is the appropriator. Likewise, when a self is imputed in dependence upon
the five aggregates, the six constituents, and the six sources, they
are the appropriated and the self is the appropriator. Also, just as a
chariot and its parts are posited as agent and objects, the self is the
agent because it takes up the aggregates and so forth; the aggregates and so forth are the objects because they are what it adopts.
Candrakīrti's *Commentary on the "Middle Way"* says:[618]

> Likewise, in terms of what is familiar in the world,
> The self is held to be the appropriator
> In dependence upon the aggregates, constituents, and six
>   sources.
> The appropriated are the objects and this self is the agent.

Also, as in the case of the chariot, when you analyze reality a self is
not found in any of the seven ways. Thus, while it lacks even the
slightest trace of intrinsic existence, without analysis it does exist
conventionally. [751]

(2)) Teaching that what the self owns is also thereby established as lacking intrinsic existence

When reason searches to see whether the self intrinsically exists, it
does not find it in any of the seven ways. Thus, when it has negated
the intrinsic existence of the self, how could reason find "the eye
that belongs to the self," etc.? Accordingly, what the self owns also
lacks intrinsic existence. When yogis do not see any intrinsic existence in either the self or what the self owns, then they are liberated
from cyclic existence. I will explain this below.[619] Nāgārjuna's *Fundamental Treatise* says:[620]

> If the self does not exist,
> How could there be something owned by the self?

And Candrakīrti's *Commentary on the "Middle Way"* says:[621]

> Since objects do not exist without agents,
> What the self owns does not exist without the self.

Therefore, yogis are liberated through seeing
That the self and what it owns are empty.

On the strength of knowing that the self lacks intrinsic existence, you understand that what the self owns also lacks intrinsic existence. You should be able to understand this point, and how to eliminate qualms about this point, based on what I have said above.

24

OBJECTS LACK INTRINSIC NATURE

(3)) **How to apply those lines of reasoning to other phenomena**

Those arguments also apply to other things. Just as the analysis of the self and the aggregates follows the pattern of the analysis of the chariot, you should realize that this is also the case with things like pots and cloth. When reasoning that searches for intrinsic nature searches in the seven ways by analyzing whether pots and such are one with or different from their forms, etc., they are not found in those seven ways in terms of either of the two truths. Instead, they are posited from the perspective of a non-analytical, conventional consciousness. [752] This is because the Buddha takes up positions without using reason to refute what the world knows, as is demonstrated by his statement in the *Chapter Teaching the Three Vows (Tri-saṃvara-nirdeśa-parivarta-sūtra)*:[622]

> The world debates with me; I do not debate with the world. Whatever is held in the world to exist or not to exist, I also hold as such.

Accordingly, Candrakīrti's *Commentary on the "Middle Way"* says:[623]

> Whatever it is—pot, cloth, tent, army, forest, rosary, tree,
> House, small chariot, guest house, or any such thing—
> You should know the conventions used by these worldly
>   beings.
> Why? Because the Master of Sages does not debate with the
>   world.

> Part, quality, attachment, defining characteristic, fuel, etc.,
> As well as whole, qualified, attached [person], definienda, fire,
>   etc.—
> These objects do not exist in the seven ways under analysis like
>   that applied to the chariot.
> On the other hand, they do exist in terms of what is familiar to
>   the world.

Whatever they may be, the conventions used by these worldly beings should be known only as existent, without analysis. What are these conventions? They are parts and wholes, etc. Take a pot, for example: Pot is the whole, the qualified, and the definiendum; pieces of pot and such are the parts; blue and so forth are the qualities; and bulbous, water-holding, long-necked, etc. are the defining characteristics. Other examples, such as cloth, are handled in the same way.

In that passage, "attachment" refers to intense attachment and clinging; "attached [person]" refers to the basis of that attachment, because Jayānanda's *Explanation of [Candrakīrti's] "Commentary on the "Middle Way""* explains that "attached" refers to a person who has attachment. "Fire" is the agent of burning, and "fuel" is the object burned.

Wholes are imputed in dependence upon parts and parts are imputed in dependence upon wholes, and so it is with each of the other pairs, quality/qualified, etc. up to and including fuel and fire. Fuel is imputed in reliance upon fire, and fire is imputed in reliance upon fuel. Nāgārjuna's *Fundamental Treatise* states:[624]

> Agents arise in dependence upon objects,
> And objects arise in dependence upon those very agents.
> Apart from this, we see no way
> For agents and objects to exist. [753]

And:

> All other things should be understood
> By way of what I explained about agents and objects.

Therefore, produced and producer, path and traveler, viewed and viewer, valid cognition and object of comprehension, etc.—everything should be understood not as existing essentially but only as existing in mutual dependence.

Accordingly, understand how to posit the two truths so that one thing—such as the self—is empty of intrinsic existence under such analysis, yet can act and be acted upon in the absence of intrinsic existence. If you do this, then by extending that understanding to all phenomena, you can easily know their lack of intrinsic existence. Therefore, be certain about the example of the chariot and its meaning as I explained it above.[625] As the *King of Concentrations Sūtra* says:[626]

> As for your perception of the self,
> Extend that sort of understanding to everything.
> The essence of all phenomena is pure, like the sky.
> You can know them all by way of one;
> You can see them all by way of one.
> No matter how many things you can explain,
> Do not be arrogant about it.

(b)) How to determine that there is no self in phenomena

The bases to which the person is imputed include the five aggregates, the six constituents—such as the earth constituent—and the six sources—the eyes and so forth. These are objects. Their emptiness of essential or intrinsic existence is the absence of an objective self. There are many ways to determine that objects lack intrinsic self. However, Candrakīrti's *Commentary on the "Middle Way"* determines that things lack intrinsic existence by refuting four possible types of production. Since the *Explanation of the "Middle Way" Commentary* says that this determination is a determination of the absence of an objective self, I will now give a brief explanation of that refutation of four types of production.

Nāgārjuna's *Fundamental Treatise* says:[627]

> There is no sense in which anything
> Has ever been produced
> Either from itself, from something else,
> From both, or without a cause. [754]

This means, in part: "No internal or external thing is ever in any way produced from itself." Three other theses can be constructed in the same way.

Reductio ad absurdum arguments will refute the claim that something can be produced from itself. Thus, these theses do not offer probative examples or reasons, but offer a critique of the contrary positions.

Here, if something is intrinsically produced, it is limited to two possibilities: either it relies upon a cause or it does not rely upon a cause. Hence, if it relies upon a cause, the cause and the effect are limited to two possibilities: they are either intrinsically one or intrinsically different. Production in which cause and effect are intrinsically one is called production from self; production in which cause and effect are intrinsically different is called production from another. Production that relies upon a cause is certain to be either production from self or production from another—which can be considered individually—or else to be production from both self and other in combination. Individually, there are two cases—production from self and production from other. Therefore, this is how we rule out other possibilities while refuting just four possible types of production.

[(1)) **Refutation of production from self**[628]

If a seedling were produced from itself, its production would be pointless because production means that what is produced has come into being. If it were produced from itself, a seedling would already have come into being—as in the case of a seedling that is clearly manifest. Production also would be endless because if an already-arisen seed were to arise again, the very same seed would have to arise repeatedly. In that case, there is the fallacy that since the seed itself is arising continuously, there is never a chance for the production of seedlings and such. Nāgārjuna's *Fundamental Treatise* says:[629]

> If cause and effect were the same,
> Then the produced and the producer would be the same.

Also, Candrakīrti's *Commentary on the "Middle Way"* says:[630]

> There is no advantage in its arising from itself;
> There is no reason for something which has been produced to
>   be produced again.

> If you suppose that something already produced is produced
>   again,
> Then the production of seedlings and such would not be found
>   in this world. [755]

And:

> Therefore, the imputation that things arise from themselves
> Is reasonable neither in terms of reality nor in terms of the
> world.

[(2)) **Refutation of production from another**]

Opponent: The Buddha said that effects are produced from the four conditions which are other.[631] Therefore, things are produced from another.

Reply: If effects were produced from intrinsically different causes, then thick darkness could arise even from a flame because those two are other.

Furthermore, all things—whether or not they are effects—would be produced from all things—whether or not they are causes—because they are alike in their otherness. This means that if you assert that seed and seedling exist essentially or intrinsically, then it is evident that the way that a rice seedling essentially or intrinsically differs from things that cannot produce it, such as fire, is identical to the way that a rice seedling intrinsically differs from its cause, a grain of rice. That is, when it appears to be intrinsically different from something that cannot produce it, a seedling seems different in the sense of being autonomous and independent, and it would seem different in the same way when it appears to be different from its own seed. If the way they seem different is that they appear to be essentially or intrinsically different, then it is completely impossible to make the distinction that the rice seedling is not produced from fire and such, but is produced from a rice seed.

Objection: We distinguish that which produces a seedling from that which does not. We make this distinction in terms of whether something differs from the seedling in the sense of differing intrinsically.

Reply: This has been shown to be a contradiction. [756] Candrakīrti's *Explanation of the "Middle Way" Commentary* states this clearly:[632]

> Just as a productive rice seed is other than the rice seedling which is its effect, so it is that such things as fire, charcoal, and barley seed—which do not produce it—are also other than that seedling. Yet just as a rice seedling arises from a rice seed which is other, it would also arise from fire, charcoal, barley seed, etc. And just as from a rice seed there arises a rice seedling which is other, so things like pots and cloth would also arise from a rice seed. Yet you never see this. Hence, this is not the case.

Thus, the assertion [by earlier Tibetans] that logical entailments are proven by a multitude of isolated cases [i.e., by induction] is not what Candrakīrti holds. I explained the arguments contradicting that claim above, in the section on the refutation of the position that it is not established that, in a kitchen, the mere presence of smoke entails the mere presence of fire.[633]

Nāgārjuna's *Fundamental Treatise* says:[634]

> If cause and effect were other,
> Then causes and non-causes would be just alike.

Also, Candrakīrti's *Commentary on the "Middle Way"* says:[635]

> If things arose in dependence upon what is other,
> Then thick darkness would arise even from a flame.
> Everything would arise from everything. Why?
> Because, in being other, all of the non-producers of something
>   would be just like its producers.

You cannot answer such *reductio* arguments by distinguishing what produces something from what does not in terms such as whether something is included within the same continuum with the effect. For, as explained above, if things are other in the sense of being intrinsically different, their inclusion within the same continuum cannot be established.[636] Also, it is inadequate to reply that we can see a definite regularity as to what produces a certain effect and what does not. This is because what we are now analyzing is whether such regularity could hold up if the difference between a cause and its effect were essential to objects themselves, rather than being posited by the mind.

[(3)) Refutation of production from both self and another]

Advocates of production from both self and another claim that the production of a clay pot from clay is production from self and the production of a clay pot by a potter, etc. is production from another. [757] Even among Buddhists there are those who advocate production from both as follows: Since Devadatta takes birth in other lifetimes only by way of a life-essence, Devadatta and his life-essence are one. Therefore, he is produced from self. At the same time, Devadatta's being produced from his parents and from his virtuous and nonvirtuous karma constitutes production from other.

Since there is neither production from self alone nor production from another alone, there is no production from the two together. The same arguments given above refute this. Within production from both, the factor of production from self is refuted by the arguments that refute production from self, and the factor of production from another is refuted by the arguments that refute production from another. Candrakīrti's *Commentary on the "Middle Way"* says:[637]

> Production from both is also unreasonable. Why?
> Because the fallacies already explained befall it.
> Production from both together exists neither in terms of the
>   world nor in terms of reality,
> Because, individually, production from self and from another
>   are not established.

[(4)) Refutation of causeless production]

Lokāyata proponents of spontaneous origination argue that the production of things is only a matter of spontaneous origination, for no one is seen working to make lotus roots rough or to make lotus leaves soft, nor is anyone seen catching peacocks and such so as to put on their shapes and colors.[638]

This is incorrect. For if production were causeless, then production such as exists at one place and time would have to exist at all places and times, or else must never exist anywhere. This is because things arise at one place and time, and not at another, due to the presence or absence of their causes—something you do not accept. The "eyes" on the tail feathers of peacocks would also be present on crows and the like.

In brief, if something were produced causelessly, then it would have to be produced from everything, or else it would never be produced. Worldly beings, in order to obtain a desired effect, would not have to work to create the causes of that effect, and everything would be senseless. Candrakīrti's *Commentary on the "Middle Way"* says:[639]

> If it were the case that things are produced without any cause,
> then these worldly beings would not go through hundreds of
> hardships to collect seeds and such for growing crops. [758]

[(5)) How to infer that intrinsic production does not exist]

Thus, by seeing the arguments contradicting the four alternative types of production, you establish that production from these four extremes does not exist. This entails the nonexistence of intrinsic production, as proven above in the section on precluding other possibilities beyond these four.[640] Therefore, you can use these [arguments] to become certain that things do not intrinsically exist.

When you make these *reductio ad absurdum* arguments, inference is thereby generated; at that time there is no syllogistic statement that directly proves the thesis. Candrakīrti's *Commentary on the "Middle Way"* concisely states the point of the arguments contradicting these four possible types of production:[641]

> Because things are not produced from self, another, both,
> Or without relying on causes, they lack intrinsic existence.

This indicates how, as an effect of having stated *reductio ad absurdum* arguments, you can develop an inference based on a syllogistic reason. It is not that you begin by stating to the opponent this sort of syllogism based on what the other party accepts.[642]

By refuting intrinsically existent production in this way, you become certain that things do not intrinsically exist; it is then easy to be certain that non-things [permanent phenomena] also lack intrinsic existence. You thereby find the view of the middle way—that is, the knowledge that all phenomena are empty of intrinsic existence.

Furthermore, Nāgārjuna's *Fundamental Treatise* says:[643]

> That which is dependently arisen
> Is naturally at peace.

Candrakīrti's *Commentary on the "Middle Way"* says:[644]

> Because things arise dependently
> These misconceptions cannot bear scrutiny.
> Therefore, the reasoning of dependent-arising
> Cuts all the entanglements of bad views.

Accordingly, you use dependent-arising as a reason to become certain that seedlings and such are empty of intrinsic existence. When you do this, the eradication of any possible misstep is extremely clear in your mind. Hence, we will say a little about this. [759]

In this case, you use an argument based on what others accept: "A seedling does not intrinsically exist because of arising in dependence upon its causes and conditions, like a reflection." For example, when a reflection of a face appears, young children do not see it and think, "This appearance of eyes, nose, and so forth is like this for the perspective of a mind such as mine, but the way it appears is not the way it exists." Rather, they consider what appears to be the way things actually exist, the way that they are. Similarly, when living beings experience or see a phenomenon, they do not apprehend it as being set up by the power of the mind to which it appears. Rather, they apprehend it as existing just as it appears, i.e., as existing in an essentially objective manner. This is how intrinsic existence is superimposed. The presence of such a nature in the object is what is meant by essence, intrinsic nature, and autonomous existence. Thus, if such a nature were present, this would contradict reliance upon other causes and conditions. If this were not a contradiction, then it would be impossible to hold that an already existing pot does not need to be produced again from causes and conditions. Accordingly, Āryadeva's *Four Hundred Stanzas* says:[645]

> That which arises dependently
> Does not exist autonomously;
> All of these things lack autonomous existence.
> Therefore, they have no self.

And Candrakīrti's *Commentary on the "Four Hundred Stanzas"* comments on that passage:[646]

> That which has its own essence, intrinsic nature, autonomy, or independence from others is self-existent and thus is not a dependent-arising. All compounded phenomena are dependent-arisings. Anything that is a dependent-arising is not autonomous because it is produced in dependence upon causes and conditions. These things all lack autonomy. Therefore, there is no thing which has self, that is, intrinsic nature. [760]

"Autonomous" means something appears to be intrinsically existent, and when it does so (1) it appears to those same consciousnesses as not depending on other phenomena, and (2) it exists as it appears. However, if you take autonomous existence to mean not depending on other causes and conditions, and refute that sort of autonomous existence, then there will be no need to prove the lack of such autonomous existence to our own Buddhist schools. Yet despite refuting that, you will be unable to posit the view of the Madhyamaka middle way. Hence, we take autonomy to mean that something exists in a manner such that it is essentially capable of objectively establishing itself.

Therefore, since emptiness of intrinsic existence refers to the lack of that autonomy just described rather than to the nonexistence of functioning things, you can use dependent-arising as a reason to refute intrinsic existence. The earlier citation of Candrakīrti's *Commentary on the "Four Hundred Stanzas"* continues:[647]

> Therefore, since in this Madhyamaka system to be a dependent-arising is to lack autonomy, lacking autonomy is what emptiness means; emptiness does not mean that nothing exists.

Consequently, the view that functioning things do not exist is a mistaken denial of the existence of illusion-like dependent-arisings, both the pure and the afflicted; hence, it is not accurate. The view that things intrinsically exist is also inaccurate because such intrinsic nature does not exist in anything. Thus, Candrakīrti's *Commentary on the "Four Hundred Stanzas"* continues:[648]

> Therefore, according to this Madhyamaka system, the view that those functioning things do not exist is inaccurate insofar as it mistakenly denies the functioning of dependent-arising and of illusion-like causes, both the pure and the afflicted. Because they do not intrinsically exist, the view that things intrinsically exist is also inaccurate. Therefore, for those who claim that things have intrinsic nature, dependent-arising does not exist and the faults of the views of permanence and annihilation ensue.

Therefore, those who wish to be free from the views of permanence and annihilation should assert both the lack of intrinsic existence and the illusion-like dependent-arising of both pure and afflicted phenomena. [761]

Objection: If you use functional dependent-arisings to refute autonomy, and say that lacking autonomy means being a dependent-arising, then how will you refute us? For, we [other Buddhist schools] also assert functional dependent-arisings. Therefore, there is no difference between you and us.

Reply: Although you assert dependently arisen causes and effects, you are like a small child apprehending a reflection of a face as truly being a face. You reify dependent-arising as intrinsically existent and then call that the essence of things. Thus, you do not accurately know the meaning of dependent-arising and you express its meaning inaccurately. Since we hold that dependent-arisings lack intrinsic existence and say so, that is the difference between you and us. Accordingly, Candrakīrti's *Commentary on the "Four Hundred Stanzas"* continues:[649]

> *Qualm*: If lacking autonomy means to be a dependent-arising, then how will you refute us? What difference is there between you and us?
>
> *Reply*: I will explain this. You do not understand how to know or to express the meaning of dependent-arising accurately. That is the difference. By reifying a reflection as a truth, a young, pre-verbal child obviates its actual nature, emptiness; when the child thinks of the reflection and its nature, those ideas about the reflection are ignorant ones. Similarly, you assert dependent-arising, but while

dependent-arisings, like reflections, are empty of intrinsic nature, you do not understand their nature accurately. This is because you do not apprehend what lacks intrinsic nature as lacking intrinsic nature. [762] You reify an essence that does not exist into an essence that does exist. You also do not understand how to express the meaning of dependent-arising because you do not say that it is the absence of intrinsic existence, and because you call it the essence of things.

While we and they are alike in asserting the dependent-arising of causes and effects, the difference is that we understand, and they do not understand, how to know and to express dependent-arising accurately in terms of intrinsic nature and its absence.

The advocates of intrinsic existence call something "truly existent" if it can be accepted as a functioning thing, and amongst them there are some[650] who conclude that the debate as to whether things truly exist is only a semantic one. Likewise, they say that it is only semantics when we debate with the Svātantrikas—for even the Svātantrikas claim that things exist by way of their intrinsic character—as to whether something that functions conventionally has a nature that conventionally exists by way of its intrinsic character. This teaching by Candrakīrti clearly refutes these ideas. For example, it would be as though someone absurdly claimed that since Sāṃkhyas say that the thing that is known as the object of auditory consciousness is permanent, Buddhists are only quibbling over semantics when they refute the permanence of sound while accepting the thing that is known as the object of auditory consciousness.

When other living beings see something as produced in dependence upon causes and conditions, they see it as essentially or intrinsically existent, and thus they are bound in cyclic existence; but for noble beings, production in dependence upon causes and conditions is reason enough to refute intrinsic existence and develop certainty about the lack of intrinsic existence. Because it cuts the bonds of extreme views, the use of dependent-arising as a reason to prove that there is no intrinsic existence is a marvelous and highly skillful method.

After the Bhagavan saw the force of this point, he said [in the *Question of the Nāga King Anavatapta*]:[651]

Whatever is produced from conditions is not produced;
It is not intrinsically produced.
Whatever depends upon conditions, I consider empty;
One who knows emptiness is diligent. [763]

The first two lines mean that production from conditions entails not being intrinsically produced. The third line states that dependent-arising, which is reliance on conditions, is the meaning of emptiness of intrinsic existence. The fourth line indicates the benefit of knowing emptiness in this way. Similarly, that sūtra says that by knowing dependent-arising, you cut off extreme conceptions:[652]

> The learned will know dependently arisen phenomena,
> And avoid extreme views.

Moreover, if things were essentially or intrinsically existent, the Conqueror and his disciples would have to have seen them in that way, but they did not. And since what intrinsically exists does not in any way work through conditions, it does not cut the net of elaborations, i.e., the conceptions of signs; thus, there would be no liberation. As the *Elephant Ornament Sūtra* (*Hasti-kakṣya-sūtra*) says:[653]

> If phenomena were intrinsically existent,
> Then the Conqueror and his disciples would know it.
> With static phenomena, no one would pass beyond sorrow.
> The learned would never be free from elaborations.

In the third, fourth, and fifth chapters [of Nāgārjuna's *Fundamental Treatise*], there are arguments that refute the intrinsic existence of the sources, aggregates, and constituents. In demonstrating that objects lack self, it is excellent to use those arguments as well. Yet I am wary of becoming long-winded and will not elaborate.

(c)) How to eliminate obscurations by becoming accustomed to those views

After you have seen that the self and that which belongs to the self lack even the slightest particle of intrinsic nature, you can accustom yourself to these facts, thereby stopping the reifying view of the perishing aggregates as the self and that which belongs to the self. When you stop that view, you will stop the four types of grasping—grasping that holds on to what you want, etc.—explained earlier.[654] When you stop these, existence conditioned by attachment will not occur; hence, there will be an end to the rebirth of the aggregates conditioned by existence; you will attain liberation. [764] Nāgārjuna's *Fundamental Treatise* says:[655]

> Because of the pacification of the self and that which the self owns,
> The conception "I" and the conception "mine" will be gone.

And:

> When thoughts of the self and that which belongs to the self
> Are extinguished in regard to internal and external things,
> Grasping will stop;
> Through its extinction, birth will be extinguished.

Accordingly, since grasping is an affliction and potential existence is karma, you are liberated through extinguishing the causes of birth, i.e., karma and afflictions. Nāgārjuna's *Fundamental Treatise* says:

> Through extinguishing karma and afflictions, there is liberation.

As for the extinction through which karma and afflictions are extinguished, that same passage continues:

> Karma and afflictions arise from misconceptions;
> These misconceptions arise from elaborations;
> These elaborations are stopped by emptiness.

That is, the cyclic flow of birth and death arises from karma. Only physical, verbal, and mental compositional activity associated with an afflicted mind constitutes karma that establishes cyclic existence, so karma arises from afflictions. Afflictions that are rooted in the reifying view of the perishing aggregates do not arise without the operation of misconceptions that superimpose upon objects signs such as pleasant and unpleasant. Thus, afflictions such as attachment and hostility—rooted in the reifying view of the perishing aggregates—are produced from such misconceptions. These misconceptions operate mistakenly only by clinging to the notion, "This is real," in regard to the eight worldly concerns,[656] or men and women, or pot, cloth, form, or feeling. Since it is these misconceptions that conceive those objects, they are generated from the elaboration of conceptions of true existence. Candrakīrti's *Clear Words* says:[657]

> Emptiness—viewing all things as emptiness—stops all worldly elaborations. Why? Because when you see something as real, there are going to be elaborations such as those explained. [765] Insofar as the daughter of a barren woman is not seen, the lustful will not engage in elaborations with her as the object. When elaborations are not operating, their object is not going to be misconceived. As misconceptions are not operating, afflictions rooted in the reifying view of the perishing aggregates are not generated through clinging to "I" and "mine." As afflictions rooted in the reifying view of the perishing aggregates are not generated,

actions are not performed. Those who do not perform actions will not experience cyclic existence, which is called "birth, aging, and death."

Candrakīrti's *Clear Words* also states very clearly how knowing emptiness stops those elaborations and misconceptions:[658]

> Why? It is like this: Emptiness is not elaborated insofar as it has the character of thoroughly quelling elaboration. Since it is not elaborated it stops misconceptions; through stopping misconceptions, it stops the afflictions. Stopping karma and afflictions stops birth. Therefore, since only emptiness has the character of stopping all elaborations, it is called "nirvāṇa."

This passage proves that the view of emptiness cuts the root of cyclic existence and is the heart of the path to liberation. Hence, you must gain firm certainty about this.

Accordingly, the treatises of the noble master Nāgārjuna clearly state that even *śrāvakas* and *pratyekabuddhas* can know that all phenomena lack intrinsic existence. For, they state that liberation from cyclic existence is achieved through the view of emptiness of intrinsic existence. *Śrāvakas* and *pratyekabuddhas* meditate on that view for as long as their afflictions remain. [766] When their afflictions are extinguished, they are satisfied and do not persist in meditation; hence they are unable to eliminate cognitive obscurations. Bodhisattvas, not content with mere liberation from cyclic existence through the mere extinction of afflictions, seek buddhahood for the sake of all living beings; hence they meditate so as to utterly extinguish cognitive obscurations. Thus, they meditate for a very long time and are adorned with limitless collections of merit and wisdom.

Accordingly, while the remedy that purges the seeds of both obscurations is the view of emptiness, as explained above, because of the limited duration of their meditation *śrāvakas* and *pratyekabuddhas* can eliminate only afflictive obscurations; they do not eliminate cognitive obscurations. For example, the very same knowledge of the lack of self is the remedy for both the objects which are eliminated on the path of seeing and the objects which are eliminated on the path of meditation. Yet simply directly seeing the lack of self can eliminate the objects that are eliminated on the path of seeing, but cannot eliminate the objects to be eliminated on the path of meditation. Thus, you must meditate for a long time in order to eliminate the objects that are eliminated on the path of meditation. It is similar to this case.

Still, the elimination of the cognitive obscurations cannot be accomplished even by meditating for a long time on that alone; it also involves training in many other sublime activities. Since *śrāvakas* and *pratyekabuddhas* do not cultivate the remedy to cognitive obscurations, but cultivate only the means to eliminate afflictive obscurations, it is said that *śrāvakas* and *pratyekabuddhas* lack full and complete knowledge of the lack of self in phenomena. Candrakīrti's *Explanation of the "Middle Way" Commentary* says: [659]

> Although even *śrāvakas* and *pratyekabuddhas* see this same condition of dependent-arising, they still lack a full and complete cultivation of the lack of self in phenomena; they have only a means to eliminate the behavioral afflictions of the three realms.

Thus what other Mādhyamikas consider a conception of self in phenomena, this master considers afflictive ignorance. Even though *śrāvakas* and *pratyekabuddhas* meditate on the lack of self in phenomena to the point of utterly eliminating afflictive ignorance, they lack a complete meditation on the lack of self in phenomena. [767] These statements should be understood as I have explained them both here and above. [660]

What are cognitive obscurations in this [Prāsaṅgika] system? Certain latent propensities are firmly set in the mind-stream through its being beginninglessly suffused with strong attachment to things regarded as intrinsically existent; these latent propensities give rise to errors of dualistic appearance, so that things appear to be intrinsically existent when they are not. These errors are cognitive obscurations. As Candrakīrti says in his *Explanation of the "Middle Way" Commentary*: [661]

> *Śrāvakas, pratyekabuddhas*, and bodhisattvas who have eliminated afflictive ignorance see composite phenomena as like something that is merely existent, e.g., a reflection. For them, because they lack the inflated sense of true existence, composite phenomena have fabricated natures and are not truths. These fabrications deceive children. For others, they are mere conventions since, like illusions and such, they are just dependent-arisings. Also, because these three types of beings partake of the mere ignorance that has the character of being a cognitive obscuration, these mere conventionalities appear to noble beings whose spheres of activity are associated with appearance, and not to those whose spheres of activity are devoid of appearance.

"Bodhisattvas who have eliminated afflictive ignorance" refers to those who have attained the eighth level, because Candrakīrti's

Commentary on the Four Hundred Stanzas, as cited earlier,[662] states that they are bodhisattvas who have attained forbearance regarding the teaching of non-production. Therefore, bodhisattvas and Hīnayāna arhats who have reached the eighth level have put an end to the creation of new latent propensities for errors of dualistic appearance, but since they have many long-established latent propensities for dualistic appearance that are yet to be cleared away, they still must train for a long time. When they clear away these propensities—stopping all latent propensities for error—they become buddhas. [768]

The noble Nāgārjuna and his successors taught that Hīnayāna and Mahāyāna are alike in their views of the definitive meaning; this implies two marvelous certainties. After you have developed certainty that there is no way to attain even mere freedom from cyclic existence—let alone buddhahood—without the view that knows that all phenomena lack intrinsic existence, you find the stainless view by making great effort at many methods. After you have developed certainty from the very depths of your heart that the features that differentiate Mahāyāna from Hīnayāna are the precious spirit of enlightenment and the sublime bodhisattva activities, you accept the teachings on the behavioral aspects of the practice as the most intimate advice. After you have taken the vows of a conqueror's child [bodhisattva], you train in those activities.

Here I say:

> Going to that most beautiful mountain,
> That lord of mountains called "Vulture Peak,"
> Shaking the universe in six directions,
> And magically filling a hundred pure lands with light,

> The Sage gave forth from his magnificent throat
> The great mother from whom all noble children are born,
> The incomparably eloquent *Perfection of Wisdom,*
> The heart of both sūtra and mantra paths.

> Nāgārjuna, the hero who had been prophesied,
> Gave a precise commentary on it in the best of all treatises,
> That incomparable explanation, as famous as the sun,
> Known as the magnificent *Fundamental Treatise.*

> The treatise by the conqueror's child Buddhapālita
> Explains it well; and what he explained well
> Was well understood by Candrakīrti, whose fine treatise
> Comments on it extensively, clarifying its words and its
>   meaning. [769]

Using words that are easy to understand, I have explained
Their stainless system—how it is that dependently arisen
    objects and agents
Of cyclic existence and nirvāṇa are possible
Among things that, like illusions, lack intrinsic existence.

My friends who study the profound Madhyamaka texts,
Although it is hard for you to posit the dependent-arising
Of cause and effect within the absence of intrinsic existence,
It is better to take the approach of saying,

"Such is the Madhyamaka system."
Otherwise, you will not be able to escape the fallacies
That you have stated to others, and will find yourself drawn
To a non-system. In that case, you must continue to study.

The treatises of the noble Nāgārjuna and his followers
Give good explanations of the way to search out the correct
    view
And are for the sake of the Conqueror's teaching
Remaining for a long time.

25

INSIGHT REQUIRES ANALYSIS

―――――――※―――――――

(b') Classifications of insight

Kamalaśīla's second *Stages of Meditation* sets forth three requisites for insight: (1) reliance on an excellent being, (2) genuinely pursuing extensive study of explanations of reality, and (3) appropriate reflection. By relying upon these three, you will discover the view—the understanding of the two selflessnesses. Then cultivate insight.

What insights should you cultivate? Here, our immediate and primary concern is not the insights of the elevated stages; we are mainly setting forth the insights that you cultivate while you are an ordinary being. For an ordinary being, complete insight is the cultivation of the fourfold, the threefold, and the sixfold insight. The fourfold insight refers to differentiation and so forth, as stated in the *Sūtra Unravelling the Intended Meaning*.⁶⁶³ Differentiation observes the diversity of conventional phenomena. Full differentiation observes the real nature of phenomena. The first [differentiation] is of two types—thorough examination and thorough analysis; and the second [full differentiation] is of two types—examination and analysis. Examination and analysis are distinguished according to whether the object is coarse or subtle. Asaṅga's *Śrāvaka Levels* says:[664]

> What is the fourfold insight? It is thus. [770] Using the serenity within his mind, a monk differentiates, fully differentiates, fully examines, and fully analyzes phenomena. How does he differentiate? He differentiates by way of their diversity the objects of meditation that purify analysis, the objects of meditation of the learned, and the objects of meditation that purify the afflictions. He fully differentiates through analyzing the real nature of those three types of object. Full examination occurs when he uses conceptual attention endowed with those two kinds of wisdom[665] to apprehend the distinguishing signs of those three types of object. When he analyzes them correctly, it is full analysis.

The same four paths of insight are set forth in Asaṅga's *Compendium of Knowledge*. The identification of them in Ratnākaraśānti's *Instructions for the Perfection of Wisdom* also agrees with the *Śrāvaka Levels*.

Regarding the threefold insight, the *Sūtra Unravelling the Intended Meaning* says:[666]

> Bhagavan, how many types of insight are there?
> Maitreya, there are three types: that which arises from signs, that which arises from thorough searching, and that which arises from analytical discrimination. What is insight which arises from signs? It is insight that attends only to a conceptual image within the sphere of concentration. What is insight which arises from thorough searching? It is insight that attends to features which were not well understood by previous wisdom consciousnesses bearing upon the given object, so that those features may be well understood. What is insight which arises from analytical discrimination? It is insight that attends to features that were well understood by earlier wisdom consciousnesses bearing upon the given object, so that you may feel the genuine bliss of liberation. [771]

Regarding this, Asaṅga's *Śrāvaka Levels* says[667] that those at the stage of equipoise may attend to a teaching they have studied and memorized, or to personal instructions. This is attention but it is not contemplation; nor is it consideration, evaluation, or examination. It is involved only in the signs. As you move from contemplation through to examination, you are engaged in thorough searching. To have exact analytical discrimination of what has been thus determined constitutes engaging in analytical discrimination of that for which you have thoroughly searched. Those three are the three doors of insight. To summarize, in the first you might, for example, observe the meaning of selflessness and attend to its signs, but you do not do much to come to a conclusion. In the second, you come to a conclusion in order to determine what you had not previously determined. In the third, you analyze, as before, a meaning that you have already determined.

The sixfold insight refers to the observation of six bases; it is a search procedure for the insight of thorough searching. You thoroughly search for—and, after you have sought, analytically discriminate—meanings, things, characteristics, categories, times, and reasonings. *Searching for meanings* refers to seeking the meaning of a given term. *Searching for things* refers to seeking [to determine] whether something is an internal thing or an external thing. *Searching for characteristics* is of two types: seeking to determine whether something is a general characteristic or a specific characteristic, and seeking to determine whether a characteristic is shared or unique. *Searching for categories* is seeking to determine what is in the negative category based on its faults and defects and seeking to determine what is in the positive category based on its good qualities and benefits. *Searching for times* is seeking to determine how something could have occurred in the past, how it could occur in the future, and how it might be occurring in the present. [772]

Searching for reasoning is of four types: (1) the reasoning of dependence is that effects arise in dependence on causes and conditions. You search from the distinctive perspectives of the conventional, the ultimate, and their bases. (2) The reasoning of performance of function is that phenomena perform their own functions, as in the case of fire performing the function of burning. You search, thinking, "This is the phenomenon, this is the function, this phenomenon performs this function." (3) The reasoning of tenable proof is that something is proven without being contradicted by valid knowledge. You search, thinking, "Is this supported by any of the three forms of valid knowledge—perception, inference, and reliable scripture?" (4) The reasoning of reality gives you confidence in the reality of things as known in the world—e.g., the reality that fire is hot and water is wet—or confidence about inconceivable realities, or confidence about the abiding reality;[668] it does not consider any further reason as to why these things are that way.[669]

A yogi's understanding of the six just presented is of three types: the meaning of the terms expressed, the diversity of objects of knowledge, and the actual nature of objects of knowledge. The first of the six kinds of searching, searching for meanings, falls within the first type, the meaning of the terms expressed. Searching for things and searching for specific characteristics fall within the second type, the diversity of objects of knowledge. Searching for general characteristics and searching for the remaining three of those six fall within the third type, the actual nature of objects of knowledge. Asaṅga's *Śrāvaka Levels* says:[670]

> This is the observation of the three doors of insight and the six categories within the basis. In brief, these fully encompass all types of insight.

This means those that are explained there in the *Śrāvaka Levels* encompass all types of insight.

Furthermore, the doorways to the four insights that we explained first[671] are the three types of insight—that which is arisen from just the signs, etc. It is said that you enter them through searching with the six ways of searching from the point of view of those three doorways, so it seems that the three doorways and the six ways of searching are included within the previous fourfold division. [773] Asaṅga's *Śrāvaka Levels* states that the attention of tight focus, etc.— a set of four explained above[672]—are common to both serenity and insight; hence, insight also has these four attentions. Therefore, Ratnākaraśānti's *Instructions for the Perfection of Wisdom* says:[673]

> Thus, completing the cultivation of the fourfold insight frees you from the bondage of rebirth in the miserable realms. Completing the cultivation of the ninefold serenity frees you from the bondage of signs.

There are a great many texts that say the same thing; hence, insight is cultivated via the four—differentiation and so forth—as they are indicated in the *Sūtra Unravelling the Intended Meaning*.[674] Serenity is cultivated via the nine states of mind which stabilize your attention without any discursive movement from object to object.[675]

(c') How to cultivate insight

This section has two parts: (1) the refutation of other systems and (2) the presentation of our own system (Chapters 25-26).

(1') The refutation of other systems

This section has four parts.

(a″) **The first refutation**

Opponent's position: One does not find any view, any understanding of selflessness; rather, one meditates on the meaning of how things exist by holding the mind in a state that lacks any thought. This is because the way that things exist, emptiness, cannot be identified in terms of what it is or is not. Therefore, setting the mind in that way brings it into accordance with the way that things exist. For, with no object existing at all in the face of emptiness, the mind does not apprehend anything.

Reply: Is it that these meditators for whom no objects exist at all first understand that objects do not exist, and then must set their minds accordingly, in a state of not apprehending anything at all? [774] Or is it that they do not think that objects do not exist, but instead think that the object's ontological status can never be established, and so consider meditation on its ontological status to occur when you go into a state of suspension in which your mind does not apprehend anything at all? If it is the first, it contradicts your assertion that they do not find the view, because you assert that the nonexistence of everything is the definitive view. According to us, such a position fails to restrict the object that reasoning refutes. No matter what might be asserted, you regard it as contradicted by reason, and you then take this to mean that there is nothing whatsoever that can be identified. Since this constitutes a view that mistakenly denies what in fact does exist, stabilizing your mind on such a view is not meditation on genuine emptiness, as I have explained at length above.[676]

If you analyze these phenomena using reasoning that analyzes the way that they exist, that reasoning will not establish the existence of any of these things and non-things. So perhaps, considering the fact that phenomena are ultimately free from all elaborations, you are claiming that a person who is meditating does not know that, but rather stabilizes his or her mind in that way, without identifying anything, and that this way of meditating accords with that lack of elaboration of phenomena. It is most absurd to claim that this is meditation on emptiness. For, none of the sensory consciousnesses think, "This is this, this is not this." Hence they would also all be meditations on the ontological status of phenomena because they would be in accord with the ontological status of their objects. As explained before,[677] there are a great many absurd consequences of such a position, such as the consequence that the meditative serenity of non-Buddhists in which there is no thought whatsoever would be meditation on the emptiness of everything. Furthermore, if you claim that it is enough to have some person other than the meditator recognize the concordance between the ontological status of the object and the way that the meditator's mind is set, then it would be impossible to avoid the consequence that non-Buddhists would meditate on emptiness.

Objection: This is not the case because here the person first recognizes the concordance of the two and then stabilizes the mind.

Reply: Since the recognition of such a concordance is the discovery of the view, this contradicts your assertion that one does not understand the view, but meditates on emptiness by simply stabilizing his or her mind without thinking of anything. [775]

Objection: All conceptual thoughts, no matter what one thinks about, bind one in cyclic existence. Therefore, setting the mind in a nonconceptual state of suspension is the liberating path.

Reply: I refuted this at length earlier.[678] If this is your position, you should not attribute even the slightest fault to the system of Ha-shang. Kamalaśila's third *Stages of Meditation* says:[679]

> Some say that virtuous and nonvirtuous karma are produced by conceptions in your mind, and through this living beings experience results such as high status in cyclic existence and continue to revolve in cyclic existence. Those who think nothing and do nothing will be fully liberated from cyclic existence. Therefore, they do not think about anything when they meditate and they perform no virtuous deeds, such as deeds of generosity. They suppose that practices such as generosity are only taught for foolish beings. But those who say this entirely abandon the Mahāyāna. The root of all vehicles is the Mahāyāna, so if you abandon it, you abandon all vehicles. If you say that you should not think about anything, you abandon the wisdom which has the nature of correct analytical discrimination. The root of the sublime wisdom that knows reality is correct analytical discrimination; if you abandon it, you sever the root, and thus abandon the wisdom which passes beyond the world. By saying that one should not practice generosity and such, you utterly abandon methods such as generosity. In brief, wisdom and method are the Mahāyāna. As the *Foremost of Gayā Sūtra* (*Gayā-śīrṣa-sūtra*) says:[680]
>
> > The path of bodhisattvas, in brief, is twofold. What are the two? Method and wisdom.
>
> The *Sūtra of Showing the Tathāgata's Inconceivable Secret* (*Tathāgatācintya-guhya-nirdeśa-sūtra*) says:[681]

All the paths of bodhisattvas are included in these two:
method and wisdom. [776]

Because of this, abandoning the Mahāyāna creates a great obstacle
on the path. Therefore, they abandon the Mahāyāna, they do minimal study, they consider their own view to be supreme, they do
not respect the learned, they do not know the way taught in the
Tathāgata's scriptures. After they have ruined themselves, they
ruin others. Their words are contaminated by the poison of contradicting scripture and reason. The learned who seek what is
good should leave them at a great distance, like poisoned food.

This refers to the position of Ha-shang. This passage clearly sets
forth how it completely abandons the Mahāyāna, and while it may
be that this is what Ha-shang asserts, you yourself should recognize this position.

Objection: We are not like that because we practice generosity.

Reply: If it is the case that Ha-shang and you must be distinguished only in terms of practices such as deeds of generosity, then
this indicates that you and Ha-shang are alike in meditating on the
definitive view. Otherwise, it would be fitting that you also distinguish yourself from him on the issue of the concentration that does
not think about anything at all.

Furthermore, if all conceptual thoughts whatsoever bind one in
cyclic existence, then do you seek liberation from cyclic existence?
If so, then inasmuch as giving gifts and maintaining ethics must
involve conceptual thought, what purpose is there in performing
them? I have already explained this point at length.[682] Therefore, if
you assert that all thoughts whatsoever serve to bind one in cyclic existence, then you might as well adopt the position of Ha-
shang; one who takes your position will be saddled with a load
of contradictions.

Also, some who follow this line of thought entertain the following
view: If one does much analysis of an object that has been conceived
to have signs of the two selves and thereby stops the grasping by the
subject that apprehends such an object, this is to eliminate elaborations
from the outside, like a dog chasing after a ball.[683] [777] But to hold the
mind without distraction from the outset is to eliminate all elaborations from within. By this very act, one prevents the mind from scattering to those objects in which signs would be apprehended, like a
dog grabbing the ball right from the hand that is about to throw it.
Hence, those who train in scriptures and reasonings that determine
the view are devotees of mere conventional words.

This vile misconception dispenses with the scriptures of the Buddha and with all of the texts of scholars such as the Six Ornaments,[684] for it is they who strive only to determine the import of scripture and reason. Furthermore, after you carefully analyze how your mind conceives of signs of the two selves and what the object of ignorance is like, genuine scripture and reasoning must pulverize the deep falsehood of error by bringing about certainty that things do not exist as they are conceived by that ignorant mind. It may be that when you merely hold your mind without finding any such certainty, it does not scatter to objects such as the two selves, but this does not constitute an understanding of the meaning of the two selflessnesses. If it did, then it would most absurdly follow that even those who are falling asleep or passing out would understand selflessness because their minds do not scatter to those objects. For example, if you are frightened, wondering whether there is a demon in a strange cave at night, your fear is not dispelled until you light a lamp and carefully investigate whether it is there. Their position is something like saying, "Hold the mind and do not allow it to move to the thought of a demon." Kamalaśila's third *Stages of Meditation* says that what they say is like the cowardice of those who in battle shut their eyes when they see a powerful enemy, instead of behaving as heroic warriors who open their eyes and look well to see where the enemy is. [778] As the *Play of Mañjuśri Sūtra* (*Mañjuśrī-vikrīḍita-sūtra*) says:[685]

> Daughter, how are bodhisattvas victorious in battle?
> Mañjuśri, when they analyze, they do not observe any phenomena.

Thus, yogis open the eye of wisdom and defeat the enemy of the afflictions with the weapon of wisdom. They are fearless; they do not shut their eyes like cowards.

Therefore, when you are frightened upon mistaking a rope for a snake, you have to stop the suffering of fear and error by developing certain knowledge that the coiled thing is a rope rather than a snake. Likewise, you are mistaken in thinking that the two selves exist, and this mistake creates the sufferings of cyclic existence. But decisive scripture and reasoning bring certainty that the object of the conception of the self does not exist, and you understand that the conception of self is a mistake. Through then growing accustomed to this fact, you overcome that misconception. When you stop that misconception, you overcome all the sufferings of cyclic existence which it created. Therefore, this is the reason that the collections of Madhyamaka arguments[686] and other such works refute objects by analyzing them. Āryadeva's *Four Hundred Stanzas* says:[687]

> When you see that objects have no self,
> The seeds of cyclic existence will cease.

Candrakīrti's *Commentary on the "Middle Way"* says:[688]

> There will be conceptions if you accept the existence of real
>   things;
> We have already fully analyzed how it is that real things do not
>   exist.

He says that conceptions which are extreme views arise when such misconceptions hold that real things exist. So he gives many ways of analyzing how the objects of those misconceptions do not exist. Candrakīrti's *Commentary on the "Middle Way"* also says:[689]

> Having understood that the self is the object of this ignorance,
> Yogis put an end to the self.

The Lord of Reasoning [Dharmakīrti, in his *Commentary on the "Compendium of Valid Cognition"* (*Pramāṇa-varttika*)] says:[690]

> Without negating the object of this conception of self,
> It is impossible to eliminate it. [779]
> In reaction to good qualities and faults
> There is attachment, hostility, and so forth.
> You eliminate them by not seeing their objects as real,
> Rather than by purifying the external object of attachment.

There are many such statements.

Some say that all conceptual thought of any sort binds you to cyclic existence, and thus all thoughts cease when you meditate on emptiness. This has to be analyzed. For ordinary beings who meditate on emptiness, is emptiness—the meaning of selflessness—manifest or hidden? If it is the former, then those persons would be noble beings because they perceive the meaning of selflessness. If you say that it is not contradictory for someone to be an ordinary being and yet to perceive the meaning of selflessness, then we would say that it is not contradictory for a person for whom the meaning of selflessness is hidden to be a noble being, for the two cases are completely similar.

Also, if such ordinary persons perceived reality, they would not understand that their object was reality. Therefore, someone else would have to identify their object for them by using scriptural evidence to prove that it was reality. To scholars, this is ridiculous because you are claiming that the teacher uses inference to prove something that the student has established with perception. You should not talk like this in the presence of those who understand philosophical reasoning. You cannot argue that even though perception establishes the meaning of reality, reason establishes its conventional name. For, Dharmakirti, the Lord of Reasoning, says:[691]

> That is a point for someone who is extremely ignorant
> Because it is taken for granted by women who herd cattle.

He is referring to the case of arguing with someone who is ignorant of something which even herders take for granted, that is, that when a meaning is established, one knows to use the term. So if you claim that this sort of profoundly ignorant person perceives reality, you must tell us what kind of fool does not know reality. [780]

Even if we did allow that reality is something an ordinary person can perceive, perception alone is not tenable as the defining characteristic in terms of which reality is posited—just as a *dkar-zal* [a Holstein-like cow] is a cow but is not appropriate as the defining characteristic of a cow. Since to argue that this is tenable would contradict even your own assertions, it is obvious that there is nothing left to say about your claim that perception establishes the meaning of reality, but reason is still needed to establish its conventional name. I will not elaborate.

If the meaning of emptiness—the selflessness which is the object of meditation—is hidden from the meditator, then it is ridiculous to claim that this hidden object is apprehended by a consciousness which is free from conceptual thought.

In brief, if the minds of ordinary beings who are meditating on emptiness are not directed toward selflessness as their object, then it is contradictory to claim that they are meditating on emptiness. If they are directed at that object, then it is certain that the object is either manifest or hidden. If it were manifest to them, then they would be noble beings. Therefore, it must be held that for ordinary beings the meaning of selflessness is hidden. As this is so, they know the meaning of selflessness by way of a concept, so it is contradictory to claim that this knowledge is free from conceptual thought.

Furthermore, as it is asserted that even someone on the great level of the supreme mundane quality stage of the path of preparation[692] knows the meaning of emptiness by way of a concept, it is most contradictory to claim that a beginner meditates on emptiness with a mind that is free from conceptual thought. If an ordinary being's consciousness could know the meaning of selflessness without conceptual thought, this would readily prove that this consciousness is non-mistaken. It would therefore be a yogic perception because it would be a non-mistaken, nonconceptual awareness of the meaning of selflessness.

There are those who claim that one meditates on the meaning of selflessness by merely holding the mind in check and not allowing it to scatter to the two selves, yet without discovering the correct view which uses reason to refute the object of the conception of self. And there are those who claim that ordinary beings meditate on selflessness with a consciousness that is free from conceptual thought. For the reasons given, those who make these claims go far astray from the path of scripture and reason. [781]

(b″) **The second refutation**

Opponent's position: We agree that it is not correct for meditation on emptiness to be the mere setting of the mind in a state that lacks any thought, without finding the view of emptiness which is selflessness. Therefore, the position given above is not correct. However, once someone finds the view which is the definitive meaning of selflessness, all cases of that person placing the mind in a nonconceptual state are meditations on emptiness.

Reply: This is not correct. Your claim implies that because a person has found the view of the definitive meaning, all of his or her nonconceptual meditations are meditations on the meaning determined by the definitive view. If that is the case, then please tell us why that person's meditation on the spirit of enlightenment would not be a meditation on the view of the definitive meaning.

Opponent: The meditation on the spirit of enlightenment is the meditation of a person who has found the view of the definitive meaning. Yet it is not a meditation during which one is mindful of the view and stabilizes the mind upon it.

Reply: Indeed, I agree that when a person who has found the definitive view meditates, it may be considered meditation on emptiness if it is a meditation in which he or she is mindful of the view and then stabilizes the mind on the view. But how could this entail that all instances of that person placing the mind in a nonconceptual state are meditations sustaining the view?

Therefore, although you have found the view, when sustaining the view you must meditate on emptiness by remembering the meaning which the view previously determined. Simply placing your mind in a state of nonconceptual suspension does not constitute meditation on emptiness. Our own system's understanding of the meaning of the phrase "without any discursive thought" has already come up several times in the sections on serenity and insight. It means to keep holding the mind on the object of meditation without engaging in a great deal of analysis which thinks, "This is that and this is not that." We do not accept the claim that it means being free from conceptual thought.

(c") **The third refutation**

Opponent's position: We also do not agree with the first position which says that meditation on emptiness means setting the mind in a nonconceptual state, without finding the view. Nor do we agree with the second position which says that after one has found the view, any placement of the mind in a nonconceptual state is a meditation on emptiness. [782] However, one should meditate without any discursive thought in alternating periods, beginning with a period devoted to analysis using discriminating wisdom. Following that, any placement of the mind in a nonconceptual state is a meditation on the meaning of emptiness.

Reply: This also is not correct because, if this were the case, it would most absurdly follow that when someone analyzes the view while falling asleep, that person's subsequent nonconceptual condition during sleep would be a meditation on emptiness. This is because the two situations are alike in that they are preceded by analysis of the view, and because apparently your position is that meditation on emptiness does not require placement of your mind on the view at that same time.

Therefore, after you have analyzed the view, you stabilize your mind on the conclusion that phenomena do not intrinsically exist. If it then moves slightly, its placement on the view is lost. At that point, keeping your mind in a generalized condition of thoughtlessness does not constitute meditation on emptiness. Therefore, you must train in conceptual analysis. You have to monitor whether your attention is remaining on the view, and then sustain the view in meditation.

(d") **The fourth refutation**

Opponent's position: We do not agree with the previous three. When one meditates on emptiness, one brings about certain knowledge of the view. Then, holding the mind on that point, one stabilizes the mind without analyzing anything else. This is genuine meditation on emptiness because unlike the first system, it is not the case that the mind is not even turned toward emptiness; unlike the second system, it is not the case that one is not mindful of the view of emptiness while sustaining a nonconceptual state; unlike the third system, it is not the case that one first analyzes the view and then stabilizes the mind in a nonconceptual condition in which the mind does not remain on the view.

Reply: What you call "analysis of the view" is simply remembering the view and then performing only stabilizing meditation on the view. To claim that this is meditation on emptiness is not correct because, if it were, there would be only serenity which performs stabilizing meditation on emptiness; there would be no analytical meditation, which is the method for sustaining insight. [783] Therefore, this is a one-sided practice that cannot sustain the union of serenity and insight.

(2') The presentation of our own system

If you do not find the definitive view of selflessness, your mind will not be directed toward selflessness in any of your meditations. Therefore, you must find the view of selflessness. Furthermore, mere understanding is not enough; when sustaining the view, you must remember it and analyze it, and you must meditate on what you have analyzed. In order to do that, you must have both forms of meditation: non-analytical stabilization on the meaning and analysis with discriminating wisdom. Each by itself is insufficient.

This section has three parts:

1. Why both stabilizing meditation and analytical meditation are necessary
2. Overcoming objections to that
3. A summary of the key points for sustaining insight and serenity (Chapter 26)

(a") Why both stabilizing meditation and analytical meditation are necessary

If you are not certain about the view—i.e., you have not reached firm conclusions about the meaning of selflessness—then the knowledge which is insight will not develop. This is because the Buddha said that certainty about the view is the cause of insight and that failing to study instructions that explain the view is a hindrance to insight. The *Sūtra Unravelling the Intended Meaning* says:[693]

Bhagavan, from what causes do serenity and insight arise?

Maitreya, they arise from the cause of pure ethics and from the cause of an authentic view based on study and reflection.

And:

Failure to willingly study the instructions of noble beings is a hindrance to insight.

Also, the *Questions of Nārāyaṇa* (*Nārāyaṇa-paripṛcchā*) says:[694]

Study gives rise to wisdom and it is wisdom that eliminates the afflictions.

I cited many such statements earlier.

How does the view create insight? When you set out to determine the view, you determine it through analysis using many lines of reasoning and scriptural citations. [784] When you have determined it, you repeatedly analyze it using discriminating wisdom. Stabilizing meditation alone, without sustaining the view, will not create insight. Therefore, when you meditate after having attained serenity, you must sustain the view through continued analysis.

Opponent: We do not claim that there is no analysis at the beginning. However, once study and reflection have determined the view, if you then practice analytical meditation during a session of meditation, these thoughts are conceptions of signs.

Reply: It is not tenable to fail to sustain the view in this way, for we have given abundant refutation of the claim that any conceptual thoughts are conceptions of signs and of the claim that ordinary beings meditate on selflessness with a wisdom that is free from conceptual thought.[695] Furthermore, because you claim that all of those conceptual thoughts are conceptions of true existence, if they had to be stopped during meditation on the view, then they would also have to be stopped when determining the view inasmuch as conceptual thought is needed to make those determinations. And since you must use conceptual thought for everything, such as teaching students, debating, composing, and thinking about the view, you would also have to stop it at those times because you cannot make even the slightest distinction which allows for a conception of true existence that must be stopped during meditation, but which does not need to be stopped at other times.

Opponent: We do not agree with that. One conducts analysis using many lines of reasoning and scriptural citations in order to know something that one does not yet know—the meaning of selflessness.

During meditation, such analysis is unnecessary because the view has already been found.

Reply: If this were so, then since noble beings have perceptual knowledge of selflessness on the path of seeing, it would be pointless for them to meditate on the selflessness that they have already seen.

Opponent: They must meditate on the emptiness already perceived on the path of seeing; by becoming accustomed to it, they eliminate the afflictions to be eliminated on the path of meditation. The path of seeing alone cannot eliminate those afflictions.

Reply: Yes, and this case is similar because here, even though previous study and reflection have already determined the view with certainty, you must become accustomed to what you have determined. This is because ascertainment of the view becomes strong, long-lasting, clear, and steady to the extent that one becomes accustomed to what one has determined. [785] Therefore, as Dharmakīrti's *Commentary on the "Compendium of Valid Cognition"* says:[696]

> Ascertainment and the reifying mind
> Are of the nature of the canceled and that which cancels.

Because those two are the canceled and that which cancels, reification is canceled as your ascertainment takes on qualities such as steadiness and strength. Therefore, here again you must maximize your ascertainment of the absence of intrinsic existence; you must reflect on many lines of refutations and proof.

Suppose that this were not the case. Someone could arrive at an understanding of something such as impermanence, karma and its effects, the faults of cyclic existence, the spirit of enlightenment, love, or compassion. Then, without analyzing them further, that person would need simply to hold the single thought, "I am going to die," and then sustain it in order to have full knowledge of impermanence. The reasons why you must continue analysis of the view are entirely similar. In order to bring about genuine ascertainment, it is not enough to have just a pronouncement such as, "I am going to die," or "I will attain buddhahood for the sake of living beings," or "I feel compassion for living beings." You must reflect on those things using many lines of reasoning. Likewise, for a steady and strong ascertainment of the absence of intrinsic existence, it is not enough to hold onto some pronouncement. You have to reflect on it using many lines of refutation and proof. I have already explained this at length in the section on the person of small capacity.[697]

Accordingly, all three of Kamalaśila's *Stages of Meditation* say that when you meditate after you have achieved serenity, you must do much analysis in meditation. And Candrakīrti's *Commentary on the "Middle Way"* says things like, "Yogis refute the self,"[698] meaning that when they meditate they carry out those analyses. This is because yogis do this analysis in order to find either serenity or insight; and because it is not the case that there is no search for understanding of the view prior to achieving serenity. Also, analyses of the view are set forth in the context of the perfection of wisdom, after the perfection of meditative stabilization; the critical point implied by this order is that you still analyze the two selflessnesses after achieving meditative stabilization. [786] Bhāvaviveka's *Heart of the Middle Way* says:[699]

> After your mind is set in equipoise,
> This is how wisdom investigates
> These things, these phenomena
> Which are conceived of in conventional terms.

Bhāvaviveka's own commentary on this says that analyses of the view are done after achieving concentration.[700] Also, in *Engaging in the Bodhisattva Deeds*, Śāntideva says that you achieve serenity in accordance with what appears in the chapter on meditative stabilization. Then, when you cultivate wisdom, you cultivate it via rational analysis. Therefore, the sequence of the last two perfections and the sequence of the last two trainings are in all cases sequences in which wisdom is cultivated after you have previously achieved concentration. In discussions of how to cultivate that wisdom, every statement about analysis of the real nature and the diversity gives this same sequence of meditation, so do not imagine that it is the other way around. Beyond just these sources, there are many great texts that say this, so there is no doubt that you must analyze during meditation.

While this is so, if you perform *only* analytical meditation when cultivating insight after you have achieved serenity, your earlier serenity will be destroyed. Since it was not refreshed, serenity will be gone; thus, as explained earlier, insight also will not develop. Therefore, you must sustain the serenity that previously set up a condition of mental stability. Since you must also practice analytical meditation, both are necessary. Furthermore, in the practice of insight, at the conclusion of analytical meditation, you practice stabilizing meditation on that meaning. By doing this, you will achieve a union of serenity and insight focused upon selflessness. The second of Kamalaśila's *Stages of Meditation* says:[701]

The *Cloud of Jewels Sūtra* says:

> Thus, those who are skilled in eliminating faults take up the practice of meditation on emptiness in order to be free from all elaborations. [787] Through much meditation on emptiness, their minds spread everywhere. When they search for the nature of the places where the mind is happy, they realize that it is empty. When they search for what the mind is, they realize that it is empty. When they search everywhere for the nature of the mind that knows that emptiness, they realize that it is empty. By realizing this, they enter signless contemplation.

> This shows that only those who have previously carried out a full examination will enter into signlessness. It very clearly shows that it is impossible simply to eliminate mental activity altogether, and that it is impossible for wisdom to enter the nonconceptual state without having analyzed the nature of things.

This passage states that when you investigate the places where your mind spreads and the mind which spreads there, you realize that they are empty; that when you search for or analyze the knowledge that they are empty, you realize that it is empty; and that those analyses are done during meditation on emptiness. It also says that the person who analyzes and realizes that they are empty will enter the yoga of signlessness. Therefore, it clearly shows the impossibility of what Ha-shang claimed—that by merely withdrawing your mind and eliminating bringing anything to mind, you can enter into a signless or nonconceptual state without first using rational analysis to search analytically.

Therefore, as I explained before, the sword of reasoning cuts through phenomena, revealing that they lack even a shred of the two selves, and brings forth certainty about selflessness. So if a thing possessed of the two selves does not exist, then how could the nonexistence which is its negation be established in reality? The conception that the nonexistence that is the absence of the son of a barren woman really exists must be based on the observation of a barren woman and her son. If those two are never observed, then no one thinks to construct the expression, "The nonexistence of the son of a barren woman truly exists." In the same way, when you see no truly existent thing anywhere at all, you also do not give rise to the conception that the nonexistence of that truly existent thing is something truly existent. [788] Therefore, you stop *all* thoughts conceiving of signs, because if a thought conceives of true existence, it must be a thought that conceives of the true existence of either an existent or a nonexistent. So if the larger category is negated, then the subcategory is negated. This is what Kamalaśila's *Stages of Meditation* says.

Thus, to achieve the nonconceptual sublime wisdom, you alternate (1) developing certainty, profound certainty, that there is not even a particle of true existence in any thing or non-thing whatsoever, and (2) stabilizing your mind on the conclusion thereby reached. You cannot achieve such wisdom by simply constricting mental activity without any analysis of an object, because this approach does not make it possible to eliminate the conception of true existence. This is because it is merely not thinking of true existence; it is not knowledge of the absence of true existence. In the same way, it is merely not thinking of a self, but is not knowledge of the lack of self, so cultivating it does not stop the conception of self. Therefore, you must distinguish between (1) not thinking about true existence or the existence of the two selves, and (2) knowing the lack of true existence or the nonexistence of the two selves. Remember this critical point.

(b") Overcoming objections to that

Objection: Since analytical discrimination of the meaning of selflessness is conceptual, it is contradictory that it should produce the nonconceptual sublime wisdom. This is because there must be harmony between an effect and its cause.

Reply: The Bhagavan himself spoke about this using an example. The *Kāśyapa Chapter Sūtra* (*Kāśyapa-parivarta-sūtra*) says:[702]

> Kāśyapa, it is thus. For example, two trees are dragged against each other by the wind and from that a fire starts, burning the two trees. In the same way, Kāśyapa, if you have correct analytical discrimination, the power of a noble being's wisdom will emerge. With its emergence, correct analytical discrimination will itself be burned up. [789]

This means that the wisdom of a noble being emerges from analytical discrimination. Kamalaśila's second *Stages of Meditation* says:[703]

> Thus, yogis analyze with wisdom and when they definitely do not apprehend the essence of any thing ultimately, they enter into the nonconceptual concentration. They know that all phenomena lack essence. There are some whose meditation does not involve the use of wisdom to investigate the essence of things; they only cultivate the sheer and complete elimination of mental activity.

Their conceptions never end and they never know the absence of essence because they lack the light of wisdom. Thus, when the fire which is a precise understanding of reality arises from correct analytical discrimination, then—as in the case of the fire from the friction of two sticks rubbed together—the wood of conceptual thought is burned up. This is what the Bhagavan said.

Otherwise, since it would be impossible for an uncontaminated path to arise from a contaminated path, an ordinary being could not attain the state of a noble being because of the dissimilarity between the cause and the effect. In the same way, it is evident that there are limitless cases of dissimilar causes and effects, such as the production of a green seedling from a gray seed, the production of smoke from fire, and the production of a male child from a woman. A noble being's nonconceptual sublime wisdom is perceptual knowledge of the meaning of selflessness—the emptiness of the object of the conception of the two selves. In order to develop that sort of wisdom at a higher stage, your meditation must now precisely analyze the object of the conception of self and realize that it does not exist. Therefore, although this is conceptual, it is a cause which is very conducive to the nonconceptual sublime wisdom. As previously cited, the *King of Concentrations Sūtra* says:[704]

> If you analytically discriminate the lack of self in phenomena
> And if you cultivate that precise analysis in meditation,
> This will cause you to reach the goal, the attainment of nirvāṇa.
> There is no peace through any other cause.

Therefore, Kamalaśila's third *Stages of Meditation* says,[705]

> Even though it has a conceptual nature, its nature is one of proper mental activity. [790] Therefore, because it engenders the nonconceptual sublime wisdom, those who seek the sublime wisdom should rely upon it.

Objection: The Perfection of Wisdom sūtras say that if one is involved in the idea that things such as forms are empty and selfless, then one is involved in signs. Therefore, analytical discrimination of emptiness is not tenable.

Reply: Such statements in sūtras refer to holding emptiness to be truly existent; as I have explained frequently above, they do not refer to holding simply, "This is empty." Otherwise, those sūtras would not speak of analysis when cultivating the perfection of wisdom:[706]

> A bodhisattva, a great being, who practices the perfection of wisdom and cultivates the perfection of wisdom should carefully

investigate and definitely consider the following: What is this perfection of wisdom? Whose is this perfection of wisdom? Is the nonexistence and non-observation of any phenomenon the perfection of wisdom? When one carefully investigates and definitely considers this....

And in answer to the question of how to practice the profound perfection of wisdom, the *Heart Sūtra* says,[707] "Correctly regard even those five aggregates as empty of intrinsic nature." Also, the *Verse Summary of the Perfection of Wisdom in Eight Thousand Lines* says:[708]

> When wisdom destroys the conditioned and the uncondi-
> tioned,
> And the positive and negative, and not even a particle is
> observed,
> Then this counts in the world as the perfection of wisdom.

This means that you reach the perfection of wisdom when, having analyzed phenomena with wisdom, you see without regarding even a particle as ultimately real. How can your assertion that conceptual analysis is a hindrance to insight not contradict these many statements about the need for precise investigation of such reasonings?

Objection: I disagree with this approach. There are scriptural statements that one should not investigate phenomena. How do you account for this? [791]

Reply: If you, like Ha-shang, claim that all thoughts whatsoever bind you in cyclic existence, then you must accept that you are bound in cyclic existence by all thoughts such as, "I have received personal instructions on the nonconceptual; I will meditate on this." I refuted this at length earlier.

Thus, the meaning of scriptural passages which seem to say that you should not investigate is that you should not conceive of those things as truly existent. Stopping the thought which conceives of true existence is like this illustration: If suffering arises through mistaking a rope for a snake, you overcome this error when you are certain that the snake does not exist as you had imagined. There is no other way. Likewise, you must use a correct reason to be certain that the object that you had thought of as truly existent does not truly exist, and you must make yourself intimately familiar with this conclusion. You cannot stop the thought which conceives of true existence by simply withdrawing the mind that conceives of true existence.

Furthermore, you must agree that the conception of true existence is mistaken; if it were not mistaken, there would be no point in stopping it. If you agree that this awareness is mistaken, then how are you to recognize that it is mistaken unless you recognize that the object held by it does not exist? For one can determine whether an awareness is mistaken only by whether an object exists as it is apprehended by that awareness. A mere proclamation will not prove that the object does not exist as it is conceived to exist by the conception of true existence. So you rely on defect-free combinations of scripture and reason to prove it. After you have done that, you arrive at a conclusion about the absence of true existence. You then stabilize your mind without conceiving of true existence; this is our position. Therefore, this meditation must be the kind of nonconceptual state that is preceded by the analysis of discriminating wisdom; simply being a nonconceptual state is not enough. You should understand this in accordance with what is said in Kamalaśila's third *Stages of Meditation*:[709]

> Thus, see that in the scriptures of the excellent teaching, correct analytical discrimination precedes the absence of mindfulness and the absence of mental activity because it is only correct analytical discrimination that can create the absence of mindfulness and the absence of mental activity. [792] There is no other way.

And:[710]

> Scriptures such as the *Cloud of Jewels Sūtra* and the *Sūtra Unraveling the Intended Meaning* state that insight has the nature of correct analytical discrimination. The *Cloud of Jewels Sūtra* says:
>
> > After you have investigated with insight, you know the absence of essence. This is entry into signlessness.
>
> The *Descent into Laṅka Sūtra* says:
>
> > Mahāmati, because specific and general characteristics are not known when mentally investigated, it is said that all phenomena lack essence.
>
> Failing to perform correct analytical discrimination would contradict the many pronouncements about correct analytical discrimination which the Bhagavan made in these sūtras. Thus, it is acceptable to say, "I have little wisdom, little effort, and I am not capable of pursuing extensive study." But since the Bhagavan praised extensive study, it is not right to abandon it forever.

Similarly, the statements that the mind should not remain on anything, from form to omniscience, mean that it is not appropriate to hold that those phenomena truly exist as places for the mind to remain. Otherwise, since even things like the six perfections are spoken of in that way, it would mean that the mind must not remain even on them. As explained earlier, it is not appropriate to remain within the conception of things as truly existent. There are statements in sūtras that by relying on the knowledge that phenomena do not truly exist, you will not remain with and not conceive of such phenomena. Know that all such statements refer only to the preceding correct analytical discrimination which refutes that objects intrinsically or truly exist. [793] Therefore, scriptural references to things such as the inconceivable, or to what is beyond awareness, are made to prevent the conceit that the profound can be known by mere study or reflection; those are objects of a noble being's individual self-knowledge. Therefore, those statements mean that it is inconceivable, etc. to the minds of others who are not noble beings, and their purpose is to stop the incorrect idea that the profound truly exists. Recognize that they do not refute proper analysis by discriminating wisdom. Kamalaśīla's third *Stages of Meditation* says:[711]

> So wherever you hear words such as "inconceivable," they are for the purpose of stopping the inflated sense of pride of those who think that reality is known only by mere study and reflection. Such expressions indicate that phenomena are to be understood with the individual self-knowledge of a noble being. Understand this as a correct refutation of an incorrect idea; these statements are not refuting correct analytical discrimination. Otherwise, it would contradict a great many reasonings and scriptures.

How would it contradict many scriptures? It would contradict such statements as this from the *Kāśyapa Chapter Sūtra*:[712]

> Kāśyapa, what is correct analytical discrimination of phenomena on the middle way? Kāśyapa, where there is analytical discrimination of the nonexistence of a self and analytical discrimination of the nonexistence of a sentient being, a living being, a nourished being, a creature, a person, a human being, a human—Kāśyapa, this is called the correct analytical discrimination of phenomena on the middle way.

Kamalaśīla's first *Stages of Meditation* says [794]:[713]

> The *Formula for Entering the Nonconceptual* (*Avikalpa-praveśa-dhāraṇī*) says, "You get rid of the signs of form and such by not applying the mind." What about this? Again, the intended meaning is that when using wisdom to investigate, you do not apply

your mind to that which is unobservable. It is not that you strictly have no mental activity. In the meditative absorption of non-discrimination you do simply eliminate mental activity, but this does not get rid of the beginningless attachment to things such as form.

This is also clear in this master's commentary on that formula.

In brief, in the Mahāyāna there is no view other than the two kinds of view explained extensively in the texts of the noble Nāgārjuna and the noble Asaṅga. It is evident that the excellent scholars and adepts of India and Tibet definitely rely on one or the other of the two views as explained by those two masters. So there is no doubt that you must seek the view of one or the other of these two masters, as presented by their respective texts. I previously explained the procedure for seeking the view based on the texts of the noble father and his spiritual son [Nāgārjuna and Āryadeva].

According to the noble Asaṅga, objects and subjects are, in reality, completely devoid of being different substantial entities, yet appear as different substantial entities to childish beings. Such appearances are the imaginary objects which childish beings conceive to truly exist just as they appear. Through scripture and reasoning, you find a firm ascertainment of the perfectly real, the nonduality which is the total negation of the imaginary in relation to the contingent. It is then necessary to perform both stabilizing meditation on that view and meditation that analyzes it with discrimination. Even with such an understanding of the view, if during meditation you merely enter a nonconceptual state, and do not stabilize your mind on that view, then this does not constitute meditation on emptiness. [795] You should look at Ratnākaraśānti's *Instructions for the Perfection of Wisdom*, as it is the clearest on this system's methods for determining the view, its methods for separately sustaining serenity and insight with regard to what you have determined, and its methods for entering the union of serenity and insight. It is wonderful to know this system well and to meditate in accordance with what is found in its scriptures.

Each Mahāyāna scripture—from summaries to the most extensive texts—gives a great many teachings on the profound meaning, but also leaves many things out. So you must draw points that are not taught in certain texts from other texts that do teach them, and you must draw points that are not taught extensively in certain texts from other texts where they are taught extensively. You should understand that this is true for the category of the vast bodhisattva deeds as well. A partial path, in which either the profound or the vast is missing, cannot be considered complete. This is why it is often said that you must be skilled in all vehicles in order to be a guru who is fully qualified to teach the path.

26

UNITING INSIGHT AND SERENITY

(c") A summary of the key points for sustaining insight and serenity

As I have explained, when you have found the view of what has definitive meaning, you will have determined that the self and that which belongs to the self do not intrinsically exist in the basis in relation to which the conceptions of "I" and "mine" arise. And just as when you initially made this determination, you continue to use extensive analysis with discriminating wisdom to bring the force of certainty to bear upon that conclusion. You alternate between stabilizing meditation—which stays with that conclusion without scattering—and analysis with discriminating wisdom. At that time, if stability decreases due to excessive analytical meditation, do more stabilizing meditation and restore stability. As stability increases under the influence of extensive stabilizing meditation, if you lose interest in analysis and thus fail to analyze, then your ascertainment of reality will not become firm and powerful. In the absence of a firm and powerful ascertainment of reality, you will not do even the slightest damage to the countervailing superimpositions which conceive of the existence of the two selves. Therefore, cultivate a balance of serenity and insight by doing extensive analytical meditation. Kamalaśīla's third *Stages of Meditation* says:[714]

> When, through cultivating insight, wisdom becomes extremely strong, serenity decreases. [796] Therefore, like a flame placed in the wind, the mind wavers so that it does not see reality very clearly. For that reason, you should then cultivate serenity. Also, when serenity becomes very strong, you will not see reality very clearly, like a person who is asleep. Therefore, you should then cultivate wisdom.

Understand that the way to prepare for a session, the way to conclude a session, and the way to conduct yourself between sessions are just as I explained them in the section on persons of small capacity.[715] In the section on serenity, I explained how to identify laxity and excitement, how to use mindfulness and vigilance to eliminate them, and how to relax your efforts after you have attained an equanimity which operates naturally, without being unbalanced by laxity or excitement.[716] Realize that all of this is the same when meditating on selflessness.

Ratnākaraśānti's *Instructions for the Perfection of Wisdom* says that sustaining serenity with respect to the object of meditation produces pliancy, and that the analytical meditation of insight into that object also produces pliancy. After you have established those two separately, you then unite them. According to this text, it is not required that you do analysis and stabilization within one continuous session. Hence, Ratnākaraśānti explains that it is acceptable to do them in separate sessions. Here the important point is that by eradicating the cognitive process in which ignorance reifies things, you produce a powerful certainty about emptiness—the absence of intrinsic existence, the opposite of this reification—and that you must then meditate on emptiness. If you fail to refute the conceptions of self and the cognitive processes of ignorance, and you put emptiness off to one corner, then your meditation will do nothing to hinder the two conceptions of self. Earlier teachers often said, "It is like sending an effigy to the western door to ward off a demon at the eastern door."[717] It is evident that this is quite true.

The things that I have said here are only a rough explanation. [797] To understand the fine points of what is advantageous and disadvantageous when meditating, you must rely on wise teachers, and you have to use your own meditative experience. Therefore, I will not elaborate.

Regarding these meditations, I have taken the earlier instructions on the stages of the path as a foundation and then enlarged upon them. One of those early instructions, Bo-do-wa's (Po-to-ba) *Little Digest of Instructions (Be'u bum)*, says:[718]

> Some say that you determine the absence of intrinsic existence
> Using reason during study and reflection,
> But meditate strictly without conceptual thought at the time of
>   meditation.
> If this were so, then this would be an emptiness disconnected
>   from that of study and reflection.
> And, because of being meditated upon in a separate way, it
>   would not be a remedy.
> Therefore, even at the time of meditation
> Analytically discriminate by using whatever you are accus-
>   tomed to—
> Such as the lack of being single or plural, or dependent-
>   arising—
> And then stabilize your mind without even the slightest
>   discursive thought.
> If you meditate in that way, it will remedy the afflictions.
> For those who wish to follow the Sole Deity [Atisha]
> And for those who wish to practice the system of the perfec-
>   tions,
> This is the way to cultivate wisdom.
> By first becoming accustomed to the selflessness of the person,
> You can then proceed in this way.

Also, Atisha [in his *Introduction to the Two Truths (Satya-dvayāvatāra)*] said:[719]

> Who understood emptiness?
> Candrakīrti, the disciple of Nāgārjuna—
> Who was prophesied by the Tathāgata
> And who saw the true reality.
> One will learn the true reality
> From instructions which derive from him.

This teaching is like what Atisha says in his *Madhyamaka Instructions (Madhyamakopadeśa)*; he says that you alternate between analytical meditation and meditation which stabilizes on the conclusions of such analysis. There is no difference between this and the system of the master Kamalaśila. As explained before, the intended meanings of Candrakīrti's *Commentary on the "Middle Way,"* Bhāvaviveka's *Heart of the Middle Way*, and the writings of master

Śāntideva are also the same. This is also explained many times in the teachings of Maitreya and in the texts of the noble Asaṅga, and it is clearly explained in the *Instructions for the Perfection of Wisdom* by the scholar Ratnākaraśānti, who considers Asaṅga's system to be accurate. [798] Therefore, it is evident that the texts and instructions deriving from Nāgārjuna and Asaṅga agree about the way to sustain insight.

(d') The measure of achieving insight through meditation

When you meditate using discriminating wisdom to analyze in this way, you have an approximation of insight until you develop such pliancy as I explained above; once you develop pliancy, it is genuine insight. The nature of pliancy and the way to produce it are as I explained them above.[720] Pliancy is also induced by a previously attained and continuing serenity, so insight is not simply a matter of having pliancy. What is it? Insight is when the power of analytical meditation itself is able to induce pliancy. In this regard, insight observing the diversity and insight observing the real nature are alike. Thus, the *Sūtra Unravelling the Intended Meaning* says:[721]

> Bhagavan, when bodhisattvas who have not attained mental and physical pliancy attend internally to an object of concentration which is an image based on how they have understood those conventional phenomena in deep reflection, what is that attention called?
>
> Maitreya, it is not insight; you can say that they have a conviction that is an approximation of insight.

Also, Ratnākaraśānti's *Instructions for the Perfection of Wisdom* says:[722]

> Thus, the attainment of insight lies in the attainment of physical and mental pliancy. As you have a strong interest in the object of internal concentration, which is an image based upon this same object as you have reflected upon it, you will carry out analytical discrimination. Until you develop physical and mental pliancy, this attention is an approximation of insight; when pliancy does develop, this attention is insight. [799]

This means that in meditation on the diversity of conventional phenomena, serenity, insight, and the way they are united are comparable to what is done in meditation on the real nature. When analysis itself can induce pliancy, it can also induce one-pointed focus. Therefore, the advantage of having already attained serenity is that the analytical meditation of discrimination can itself induce this one-pointed focus. So for those who have well-established serenity, even analytical meditation helps serenity. Thus, do not think, "If I carry out the analytical meditation of discrimination, my stability will diminish."

Your meditation will constitute an insight that combines stabilizing meditation and analytical meditation on the real nature only when you meet the standard of having found an authentic, accurate understanding of the philosophical view of either of the two selflessnesses and after having focused and meditated upon this. This is what distinguishes genuine insight; it cannot be distinguished by any other means.

What kinds of things do *not* distinguish it? Meditation on any object may stop the coarse perception of the dualistic appearance of object and subject, leaving your mind like a stainless sky; your mind may be endowed with qualities of knowledge, clarity, and limpidity. Like a flame undisturbed by wind, the mind may remain steady for a long time; external and internal objects may appear to your mind like rainbows or wispy smoke, and may continue to appear that way for a long time. When you focus attention on any object that appears before the mental consciousness, it may not be able to stand even the slightest attention, and then your serenity is restored. At first, coarse external objects such at forms and sounds do appear, but as you grow accustomed to this meditative state, eventually it seems that understandings and experiences of the sort which you formerly possessed have been expelled; when you focus your mind on them, they disappear without bearing the slightest attention. [800] Such experiences occur, but cannot be considered cases of finding the view which knows the reality beyond the two extremes; nor can these hazy, indistinct appearances be at all considered as "illusion-like" in the Madhyamaka sense. This is because many such things appear when you sustain stability for a long time, even when your mind is not directed toward the view. As I explained before,[723] the sense of "illusion-like" requires that an appearance be based on two factors: (1) the certainty of a reasoning consciousness which has concluded that phenomena lack essence, and (2) conventional valid cognition's undeniable establishment of appearances.

Things such as forms may appear to your mind under a sheer and diaphanous aspect, like a rainbow; this is simply the combination of the absence of any tangible object and a glimmering appearance which occurs despite the absence of anything tangible. Thus, since this sort of ascertainment lacks even the slightest certainty about the absence of intrinsic existence, it is not right to consider this an illusion-like appearance, because to do so is to call the tangible "intrinsic existence," treating two objects of negation—intrinsic existence and the tangible—as though they were the same. Otherwise, if you did claim that the Madhyamaka sense of illusion and falsity is something of this sort, then when a rainbow and wispy smoke are taken as the substrata, the idea that they intrinsically exist would never occur, because according to your approach the very ascertainment of the substrata would be an ascertainment that they appear but lack intrinsic existence. Also, when the tangible is itself taken as the substratum, this approach would not lead to the ascertainment that the tangible lacks intrinsic existence, because according to your approach the ascertainment of the substratum is a conception of intrinsic existence. Therefore, when form and such appear in that way, this is not what it means to appear like an illusion, because there is not even the slightest refutation of the object of the misconception which thinks that this sheer and diaphanous appearance is the mode of being, or ontological status, of those objects. As I explained, illusion-like appearance refers to what appears to someone who has previously found, and who has not forgotten, the authentic view.[724] [801]

The stages of the path tradition deriving from Geshe Gön-ba-wa (dGe-bshes dGon-pa-ba)[725] describes how to generate that understanding of emptiness as follows: First, you meditate on the selflessness of the person. You then meditate on the meaning of the selflessness of objects, bringing mindfulness and vigilance to bear. In a long session, failure to use mindfulness will cause you to fluctuate between laxity and excitement, and thus there will be little benefit. Therefore, doing four sessions in each of the four periods—morning, evening, dusk, and dawn—you meditate in sixteen sessions per day. When you think that the object is becoming clear or that you are having some experience, you should stop. When you meditate in this way, and then, supposing that you have not been meditating long, check the time and see that the night or day have been foreshortened, this means that the mind has linked to its object. If you check the time supposing that you have been meditating a very long time and see that no time has passed, this means that your mind is not linked to its object. When the mind is linked to its object, afflictions diminish in your mind, and you wonder whether you will ever need to sleep again.

When you are successful in each session of the day and night, your concentration will develop four characteristics: (1) non-discursiveness—when you are in equipoise, you will not feel the movement of inhalation and exhalation, and your breath and thought will become very subtle; (2) brightness—it will be just like the brightness of the sky at noontime in autumn; (3) limpidity—it will be like the clarity you see when you pour water into a clear metal cup and put it in the sun; and (4) subtlety—watching from within the condition that has the former three characteristics, you see what happens to a fraction of a split hair-tip. This approximates the creation of nonconceptual wisdom. As compared to actual nonconceptual wisdom, its nature is conceptual; it is therefore said to be mistaken. This explains what is stated in Maitreya's *Separation of the Middle from the Extremes*,[726] "The approximation is mistaken." According to what is said in the *Separation of the Middle from the Extremes*, even the most auspicious meditation on emptiness by an ordinary being is an approximation and must be considered mistaken. [802]

When you meditate on the meaning of the accurate view as explained above, then even though the other characteristics have not arisen, this is meditation on the meaning of selflessness. If you do not meditate on the meaning of the view, accurately determined, then even if the four characteristics arise, it cannot be considered meditation on the definitive meaning. Therefore, whether something is a meditation on the meaning of the real nature is determined as I explained above. The way that things appear as illusions after meditation on that real nature should be understood in accordance with what I explained above.[727]

(iii) How to unite serenity and insight

As I explained in the sections on the standards for achieving serenity and insight,[728] if you do not achieve them, then there will not be anything to unite. Therefore, in order to unite them, you must definitely attain the two. Also, from the time that you first attain insight, you will have that union. So it is said that the way to attain that union is to perform analytical meditation based upon earlier serenity, sequentially developing the four attentions—such as tight focus—here at the time of insight. Thus, when you have developed the fourth attention [spontaneous focus] as explained above,[729] this constitutes union. Also, at the end of analytical meditation, you practice and sustain stabilizing meditation; it is union when the serenity thus attained becomes stabilizing meditation of this kind. Thus, Asaṅga's *Śrāvaka Levels* says:[730]

How do you combine and balance serenity and insight? And why is it called a path of union? It is said that it is reached through the nine mental states. Based on having attained the ninth, equipoise, and having fully achieved concentration, you apply yourself to the higher wisdom—the differentiation of phenomena. At that time, you naturally and effortlessly enter the path of differentiating phenomena. [803] Because the path of serenity is unencumbered by striving, insight is pure, clean, comes after serenity, and is fully suffused with delight. Therefore, your serenity and insight combine and are balanced; this is called the path of the union of serenity and insight.

Kamalaśila's third *Stages of Meditation* says:[731]

Through being isolated from laxity and excitement, your mind becomes balanced and operates naturally. When this makes your mind extremely clear about reality, you achieve equanimity by easing your effort. Understand that you have then achieved the path of the union of serenity and insight.

Why is this called "union"? Prior to attaining it, the analytical meditation of discrimination cannot by itself bring about the stability of non-discursiveness. Therefore, you must work at cultivating analytical meditation and stabilizing meditation separately. Upon attaining both, the activity of the analytical meditation of discrimination can itself bring about serenity. Therefore, it is called union. Also, analysis at this point is insight. The stability at the end of analysis is a special serenity observing emptiness. Ratnākaraśānti's *Instructions for the Perfection of Wisdom* says:[732]

Thereafter, the mind observes that discursive image. When that mind experiences both serenity and insight in a continuous and uninterrupted stream of attention, then this is called the path of union (*zung 'brel*) of serenity and insight. Serenity and insight are a pair (*zung*); connection (*'brel ba*) means possessing each other; they operate bound to each other. [804]

"Uninterrupted" means that after you finish the analytical meditation itself, you do not have to stabilize your mind in a non-discursive state, but your analytical meditation itself brings about non-discursiveness. "Experiences both" means that you experience both serenity which observes a non-discursive image and insight which observes a discursive image. They are not simultaneous, but you experience them within a continuous process, without interruption of your meditative attention.

Question: Is it not contradictory to explain that, after previously achieving serenity, you use the analytical meditation of discrimination to establish stability?

Reply: If, prior to achieving serenity, you repeatedly alternate between analysis and post-analytical stabilization, then it will be impossible to achieve serenity. Doing such meditation *after* reaching serenity indicates that you are achieving an enhanced serenity. Therefore, there is no contradiction.

Moreover, there is one special case to consider: The analytical meditation immediately preceding the achievement of insight *can* induce one-pointed focus. I did explain above that it is impossible to establish serenity if, prior to achieving insight, you repeatedly alternate between analysis and post-analytical stabilization, and I explained that after you reach serenity, analytical meditation cannot induce non-discursiveness. I made these explanations in terms of the situation prior to the attaining of insight, leaving aside the exceptional case of analysis at the inception of insight. In brief, prior to achieving serenity, it is impossible to reach serenity by doing stabilizing meditation in alternation, stabilizing your mind at the conclusion of analysis. Once serenity is established, but prior to achieving insight, analytical meditation cannot itself induce a solid, one-pointed stability. Therefore, reaching solid stability through analysis—extensive analysis by discriminating wisdom—comes about when insight is achieved; thus the union of insight and serenity is also posited at that point. [805]

So do not mistake the union of serenity and insight for a composite in which wisdom can analytically discriminate the meaning of selflessness from within an essentially unchanging non-discursive state of solid stability, like a small fish moving beneath still water without disturbing it.

Know how to unite serenity and insight according to what appears in the original texts. Do not put confidence in explanations derived from anything else. From the viewpoint of these Indian texts, it would seem that I must distinguish the many features of how you sustain serenity and insight in meditation. But I am wary of being long-winded, so I will write no more.

27

SUMMARY AND CONCLUSION

b' How to train specifically in the Vajrayāna

———— ✠ ————

Now I will give a brief summation of the general meaning of the path. At the outset, the root of the path derives from your reliance upon a teacher, so consider this seriously. Then, once you have developed an uncontrived desire to take advantage of your leisure, this desire will spur you to practice continually. Therefore, in order to develop this, meditate on the topics connected with leisure and opportunity. Unless you then stop the various sentiments which seek the aims of this life, you will not diligently seek the aims of future lives. So work at meditating on how the body you have is impermanent in the sense that it will not last for long, and on how after death you will wander in the miserable realms. At that time, by creating a genuine awareness which is mindful of the frights of the miserable realms, build certainty from the depths of your heart about the qualities of the three refuges. Be constant in the common vow of going for refuge and train in its precepts. Then, from a range of perspectives develop faith, in the sense of conviction, in karma and its effects—this being the great foundation of all positive qualities. Make this faith firm. Strive to cultivate the ten virtues and to turn away from the ten nonvirtues, and always stay within the path of the four powers.[733]

When you have thus trained well in the teachings associated with a person of small capacity and have made this practice firm, you should contemplate often the general and specific faults of cyclic existence, and in general turn your mind away from cyclic existence as much as you can. Then, having identified the nature of karma and the afflictions—the causes from which cyclic existence arises—create an authentic desire to eliminate them. Develop broad certainty about the path that liberates you from cyclic existence, i.e., the three trainings, and particularly make effort at whichever of the vows of individual liberation you have taken. [806]

When you have thus trained well in the teachings associated with a person of medium capacity and have made this practice firm,[734] consider the fact that just as you yourself have fallen into the ocean of cyclic existence, so have all beings, your mothers. Train in the spirit of enlightenment which is rooted in love and compassion, and strive to develop this as much as you can. Without it, the practices of the six perfections and the two stages[735] are like stories built on a house with no foundation. When you develop a little experience of this spirit of enlightenment, confirm it with the rite. By making effort in this training, make the aspiration as solid as you can. Then study the great waves of the bodhisattva deeds, learning the boundaries of what to discard and what to adopt, and make a strong wish to train in those bodhisattva deeds. After you have developed these attitudes, take the vow of the engaged spirit of enlightenment through its rite. Train in the six perfections that mature your own mind and the four ways of gathering disciples which mature the minds of others. In particular, risk your life in making a great effort to avoid the root infractions. Strive not to be tainted by the small and intermediate contaminants and faults, and even if you are tainted, work to repair it.[736] Then, because you must train specifically in the final two perfections, become knowledgeable in the way to sustain meditative stabilization and then achieve concentration. As much as you can, develop the view of the two selflessnesses, a purity free from permanence and annihilation. After you have found the view and stabilized your the mind upon it, understand the proper way to sustain the view in meditation, and then do so. Such stabilization and wisdom are called serenity and insight, but they are not something separate from the last two perfections.[737] Therefore, after you have taken the bodhisattva vows, they come about in the context of the training in its precepts.

You have reached a critical point when, while meditating on the lower levels, you increasingly wish to attain the higher levels, and when studying the higher levels, your wish to practice the lower levels becomes stronger and stronger. [807] Some say to expend your energy only to stabilize your mind and to understand the view, ignoring all earlier topics, but this makes it very difficult to get the vital points. Therefore, you must develop certainty about the whole course of the path. When you meditate on these topics, train your understanding and then go back to balance your mind. So if it seems that your faith in the teacher who instructs you on the path is decreasing, since this will cut the root of everything good that has come together, work on the methods for relying on the teacher. Similarly, if your joy in your practice loses strength, make meditation on the topics connected with leisure and opportunity your primary focus; if your attachment to this life increases, make meditation on impermanence and the faults of the miserable realms your primary focus. If you seem to be lazy about the proscriptions you have accepted, consider that your certainty about karmic cause and effect is meager and make meditation on karma and its effects your primary focus. If your sense of disenchantment with all of cyclic existence decreases, your desire to seek liberation will become just words. Therefore, contemplate the faults of cyclic existence. If your intention to benefit living beings in whatever you do is not strong, then you will sever the root of the Mahāyāna. Therefore, frequently cultivate the aspirational spirit of enlightenment together with its causes. Once you have taken the vows of a conqueror's child and are training in the practices, if the bondage of the reifying conception of signs seems strong, use reasoning consciousnesses to destroy all objects which are apprehended by the mind which conceives of signs, and train your mind in the space-like and illusion-like emptiness. If your mind is enslaved to distraction and does not remain on a virtuous object, you should primarily sustain one-pointed stability, as former teachers have said. From these illustrations, you should understand the cases I have not explained. In brief, without being partial, you have to be able to use the whole spectrum of virtues.

Among the stages of the path of a person of great capacity, I have explained how one who trains in the bodhisattva path practices insight, which is wisdom. [808]

b' How to train specifically in the Vajrayāna[738]

After you have trained in this way in the paths common to both sūtra and mantra, you must undoubtedly enter the mantra path because it is very much more precious than any other practice and it quickly brings the two collections to completion. If you are to enter it, then as Atisha's *Lamp for the Path to Enlightenment* says, you must first please the guru—even to a greater extent than explained earlier—with deeds such as respect and service and with practice that is in accordance with the guru's words.[739] And you must do this for a guru who meets at least the minimum qualifications of a teacher explained there.[740]

Then, at the outset, your mind should be matured through the ripening initiation as explained in a source tantra. You should then listen to the pledges and vows to be taken, understand them, and maintain them. If you are stricken by root infractions, you may make these commitments again. However, this greatly delays the development of the good qualities of the path in your mind. Make a fierce effort not to be tainted by those root infractions. Strive not to be tainted by the gross infractions, but in the event that you are tainted, use the methods for restoring your vows. Since these are the basis of the practice of the path, without them you will become like a dilapidated house whose foundation has collapsed. The *Root Tantra of Mañjuśrī* (*Mañjuśrī-mūla-tantra*) says,[741] "The Master of the Sages does not say that faulty ethical discipline achieves the tantric path," meaning that those with faulty ethical discipline have none of the great, intermediate, or low attainments. And it says in the highest yoga tantra texts that those who do not maintain their vows, those who have inferior initiation, and those who do not understand reality do not achieve anything despite their practice. Therefore someone who talks about practicing the path without maintaining the pledges and vows has completely strayed from the tantric path. [809]

In order to cultivate the mantra path someone who keeps the pledges and vows should at the outset meditate on the stage of generation, the complete divine wheel as explained from a source tantra. The unique object to be eliminated on the tantric path is the conception of ordinariness which regards the aggregates, constituents, and sensory sources as common. It is the stage of generation itself that eliminates this and transforms the abodes, bodies, and resources so that they appear as special. The conquerors and their children continually bless the person who clears away the conception of ordinariness in this way; such a person easily brings to completion the limitless collections of merit, thereby becoming a suitable vessel for the stage of completion.

This person should then meditate on what appears in the source tantras on the stage of completion. Neither the tantras nor the scholars who explain their intended meanings hold that you should discard the first stage and merely classify it within the latter stage, training only in individual portions of the path. Therefore, you must bear in mind the vital points of the two stages of the complete corpus of the path of highest yoga tantra.

Considering only the terms, I have described a mere fraction of what is involved in entering into the mantra path. Therefore, understand this in detail by using works on the stages of the mantra path. If you train in this way, you will train in the entirely complete corpus of the path, which includes all the vital points of sūtra and mantra. As a result, your attainment of leisure in this lifetime will have been worthwhile, and you will be able to extend the Conqueror's precious teaching within both your own and others' minds. [810]

DEDICATION

To know precisely all scriptural systems with a single eye that
    sees the Sage's boundless scriptures
Is a way that delights the wise; I rely on a spiritual teacher well-
    trained in such a way,
And as my refuge, I take the Adibuddha Mañjughoṣa, through
    whom I discern reality.
May this greatest of all scholars, a master, always protect me.

The stages of the enlightenment path have been carefully
    transmitted
Through the generations from Nāgārjuna and Asaṅga,
The crown-ornaments of the scholars of Jambudvīpa,
Banners resplendent among beings.

Because they fulfill the wishes of humankind,
These instructions are a wish-granting jewel;
Because they gather the rivers of a thousand textual systems,
They are an ocean of glorious eloquence.

It was the great scholar Dipaṃkara [Atisha]
Who revealed them in the snowy mountain range,
So that in this region, the eye that sees the Conqueror's good
    path
Did not close for a long time.

Then, when there were no more scholars
With accurate knowledge of all the teaching's vital points,
This auspicious path declined for a long time. [811]
After I saw this situation, in order to spread these teachings,

I organized everything the Conqueror said
In all his variety of teachings
Into stages of a path for a single fortunate person
Who is riding on the supreme vehicle.

Through a process of proper analysis using scripture and
    reasoning,
I drew from those teachings a method of practice—
Not too extensive, yet with all the crucial points intact—
That even someone of little intelligence could easily under-
    stand.

The gateway of the conquerors' children is very difficult to
    discern.
I am a fool even among fools.
Thus, whatever faults there are here
I confess before those who see things as they are.

By accumulating through long effort
The two collections as vast as the sky
May I become the chief of the conquerors,
Guide of all beings whose minds are blinded by ignorance.

Also, in all lives until I reach that point
May Mañjughoṣa look after me with loving-kindness.
After I find the supreme path, complete in the stages of the
    teaching,
By accomplishing it may I please the conquerors.

By skill in means inspired by strong loving-kindness,
May the vital points of the path that I precisely know
Clear away the mental darkness of beings.
May I then uphold the Conqueror's teachings for a long time.

In regions where the supreme, precious teaching has not spread
Or where it has spread but then declined,
May I illumine that treasure of happiness and benefit
With a mind deeply moved by great compassion.

May this treatise on the stages of the path to enlightenment,
Well-founded on the wondrous deeds of the conquerors and
    their children,
Bring glory to the minds of those who want to be free,
And long preserve the Conqueror's achievements.

As for all who provide conditions that support integration of
    the good path
And clear away conditions that inhibit that integration—

Whether they are human or not, may they never be separated
    in all their lifetimes
From the pure path praised by the Conquerors.

When I strive to properly achieve the supreme vehicle
Through the ten deeds of the teaching, [812]
May I be accompanied always by those who have power,
And may an ocean of good fortune pervade all directions.

COLOPHON

This is *The Stages of the Path to Enlightenment*, a presentation that fully sets forth all the stages practiced by the persons of the three capacities. It is a compendium of all of the vital points in all of the Conqueror's scriptures, the religious system of the supreme person who proceeds to the state of omniscience, and the path blazed by the two great trailblazers, Nāgārjuna and Asaṅga.

I have sincerely accepted words of exhortation from the following excellent beings:

Kön-chok-tsül-trim (dKon-mchog-tshul-khrims)—the great regent of the great conquerors' child Ngok Lo-den-shay-rap (rNgog-blo-ldan-shes-rab)—skillfully studied the scriptural collections of Buddhist learning and took them to heart by practicing their meaning. In leading many beings, he served as an excellent friend of the precious teaching.

The great abbot of Zul-pu (Zul-phu), Kön-chok-bal-sang-bo (dKon-mchog-dpal-bzang-po)—regent of Cha-dul-wa-dzin (Bya-'dul-ba-'dzin), the excellent one—was unanimously praised by the ascetics of former times. Adorned with wisdom and compassion, and many other precious qualities of knowledge and scripture, he was a great ascetic who rose above the crowd of ascetics in the Snowy Land of Tibet, like the top of a banner.

Kyap-chok-bal-sang-bo (sKyabs-mchog-dpal-bzang-po) was exhorted by many seekers from earlier times and was well trained in the boundless sūtras and tantras of later times. He thereby became the chief of those who uphold the textual systems, greatly cherishing the three precious trainings in a variety of ways. He was the consummate teacher and great being, a speaker of two languages, and without any rival in bearing the burden of teaching alone.

From the excellent and venerable person named Nam-ka-gyel-tsen (Nam-mkha'-rgyal-mtshan) I received the lineage descended from Kön-ba-wa (dKon-pa-ba) to Neu-sur-ba (sNe'u-zur-pa) and the stages of the path of the lineage descended from Jen-nga-wa (sPyan-snga-ba).

From the excellent and venerable person whose name ends in Sang-bo (bZang-po),[742] I received the stages of the path lineage descended from Bo-do-wa to Sha-ra-wa (Sha-ra-ba), and the lineage descended from Bo-do-wa to Döl-wa (Dol-ba).

As for Atisha's *Lamp for the Path to Enlightenment*, the basic text on these instructions whose meaning I have studied, I have not cited anything apart from merely indicating the general definitions of the three types of persons, thinking that the rest of the words are easy. Instead, taking as my basis the arrangement of the stages of the path by the father and son, the great translator [Ngok (rNgog)] and Dro-lung (Gro-lung),[743] I have compiled the vital points from many [texts] on the stages of the path. [813] It is complete in all aspects of the path, easily put into practice, and arranges the path without confusing the order. The great trailblazer of the Snowy Range, the superior and venerable Ren-da-wa (Red-mda'-ba), is a marvelous *mahāsattva* [bodhisattva] who pleases the conquerors and their children because he properly practices the meaning of the great textual systems with virtuous confidence, unintimidated by the boundless scriptures. I, the one who puts my head in the dust at his feet and at the feet of my other excellent gurus, the easterner Tsong-kha-pa Lo-sang-drak-pay-bal (Blo-bzang-grags-pa'i-dpal), the very learned monk and renunciate, composed this treatise at the monastery of the Conqueror's Hermitage of northern Ra-dreng (Rva-sgreng) in the mountain range of Lion's Foot Crag. The scribe was Sö-nam-bal-sang-bo (bSod-nams-dpal-bzang-po). May this make it possible for the precious teaching to spread in every way in all directions.

APPENDIX 1
OUTLINE OF THE TEXT

[Part One *Mediatative Serenity* 11]

[Chapter One *Serenity and Insight* 13]

2" In particular, how to train in the last two perfections 13

    (a) The benefits of cultivating serenity and insight 13

    (b) How serenity and insight include all states of meditative concentration 15

    (c) The nature of serenity and insight 15

    (d) Why it is necessary to cultivate both 19

    (e) How to be certain about their order 23

[Chapter Two *Preparing for Meditative Serenity* 27]

    (f) How to train in each 28

        (i) How to train in meditative serenity 28

            (a') Relying on the preconditions for meditative serenity 28

                (1') Dwelling in an appropriate area 28

                (2') Having little desire 29

                (3') Being content 29

                (4') Completely giving up many activities 29

                (5') Pure ethical discipline 29

                (6') Completely getting rid of thoughts of desire, etc. 29

            (b') How to cultivate serenity on that basis 30

                (1') Preparation 30

                (2') Actual practice 31

                    (a") Meditative posture 31

                    (b") The meditative process 31

                        (1") How to develop flawless concentration 33

                            (a)) What to do prior to focusing the attention on an object of meditation 33

[Chapter Three *Focusing Your Mind* 47]

APPENDIX 2
GLOSSARY

accurate	*phyin ci ma log pa*
accustom	*goms pa*
acquired	*kun brtags*
actions and their effects	*las 'bras*
actualize	*mngon sum du byed pa*
affliction	*nyon mongs*
afflictive obscurations	*nyon sgrib*
aggregate	*phung po*
aggregation	*tshogs pa*
analysis	*dpyad pa*
analytical meditation	*dpyad sgom*
annihilationist	*chad lta ba*
appropriation	*nyer len*
arhat	*dgra bcom pa*
aspiration	*smon pa*
attachment	*sred pa, 'dod chags*
attention	*yid la byed pa*
attractive	*sdug*
attribute	*khyad chos*
authority	*tshad ma*
autonomous	*rang dbang*
autonomous argument	*rang rgyud*
basis of imputation	*gdags gzhi*
beginner	*dang po ba*
beginningless	*thog ma med pa*
beings	*skye bo*
benefit	*phan yon*

Bhagavan	*bcom ldan 'das*
bliss	*bde ba*
bodhisattva	*byang chub sems dpa'*
bondage	*bcings*
buddha	*sangs rgyas*
Buddhist	*nang pa*
cause	*rgyu*
certain knowledge	*nges shes*
certainty	*nges pa*
cessation	*'gog pa*
Cittamātrin	*sems tsam pa*
clarity	*gsal ba*
clinging	*zhen pa*
cognition	*rig pa*
cognitive obscurations	*shes sgrib*
cognitive processes	*'dzin stangs*
collection of merit	*bsod nams kyi tshogs*
collection of wisdom	*shes rab kyi tshogs*
commonly appearing subject	*chos can mthun snang ba*
compassion	*snying rje*
composite	*'tshogs pa*
compounded phenomena	*'dus byas*
concealer	*kun rdzob*
concentration	*ting nge 'dzin*
conceptual image	*don spyi*
conceptual thought	*rtog pa*
condition	*rkyen*
conditioned	*'du byed*
confusion	*rmongs pa*
conqueror	*rgyal ba*
conqueror's child	*rgyal sras*
constituent	*khams*
contaminated	*zag bcas*
contingent entities	*gzhan dbang*
contingently posited	*ltos nas bzhag pa*
continuum	*rgyun, rgyud*
contradiction	*'gal ba*
contradictory equivalent	*'gal zla*
conventional consciousness	*tha snyad pa'i blo*
conventional truth	*kun rdzob bden pa*
conventionality	*tha snyad pa*
conventionally	*kun rdzob tu*

correct view	*yang dag pa'i lta ba*
counterfeit reasoning	*gtan tshigs ltar snang*
counter-pervasion	*ldog khyab*
cyclic existence	*srid pa, 'khor ba*
datura	*thang phrom*
deceptive	*slu ba*
defilement	*dri ma*
definiendum	*mtshon bya*
defining characteristic	*mtshan nyid*
definite knowledge	*nges shes*
definitive	*nges don*
definitive view	*nges don gyi lta ba*
delight	*dga' ba*
delusion	*gti mug*
dependent arising	*rten 'byung*
dependent designation/ imputation	*brten nas gdags pa/ bdags pa*
determine	*nges pa*
differentiation	*rnam par 'byed pa*
diligence	*bag yod*
direct	*mngon sum*
discouragement	*zhum pa*
discriminating/discerning wisdom	*so sor rtog pa'i shes rab*
discursive thought	*rtogs pa*
disenchantment	*skyo shas*
disintegration	*'jig pa*
distraction	*g.yeng ba*
diversity of phenomena	*ji snyed pa*
divine creator	*dbang phyug*
divine wheel	*lha'i 'khor lo*
dualistic appearance	*gnyis snang*
effect	*'bras, 'bras bu*
elaboration	*spros pa*
element	*dbyings*
emanation	*sprul pa*
embodiment of form	*gzugs sku*
embodiment of truth	*chos sku*
emptiness	*stong pa nyid*
entity	*ngo bo*
environment and inhabitants	*snod bcud*
equanimity	*btang snyoms*

essence	*ngo bo nyid, ngo bo*
essentialist	*dngos por smra ba*
essentially exist	*ngo bo nyid kyis yod*
ethical discipline, commitments	*tshul khrims*
examination	*rtog pa*
excellent being	*dam pa*
excitement	*rgod pa*
exertion	*brtson pa*
expert	*mkhas pa*
expression	*brjod pa*
external object	*phyi rol, phyi don*
fabricated	*bcos ma*
faculties	*dbang po*
faith	*dad pa*
fallacy	*skyon*
false certainty	*nges pa phyin ci log*
false inference	*rjes su dpag pa ltar snang ba*
falsity	*brdzun pa*
familiarize	*goms pa*
focus	*gtad*
forgetfulness	*brjed ngas*
four alternatives, possibilities	*mu bzhi*
four attentions	*yid la byed pa bzhi*
four ways of gathering disciples	*'du ba'i dngos po bzhi*
four wrong views based on theories of the past	*sngon pa'i mtha' la brten pa'i lta ba ngan pa bzhi*
freedom	*grol ba*
full differentiation	*rab tu rnam par 'byed pa*
functionality	*don byed*
generosity	*gtong pa'i sems*
good qualities	*yon tan*
grasping at signs	*mtshan mar 'dzin pa*
guru	*bla ma*
habituate	*goms pa*
hidden objects	*lkog gyur*
highest yoga tantra	*rnal 'byor bla med kyi rgyud*
Hinayāna	*theg dman*
hostility	*sdang ba, zhe sdang*
ignorance	*ma rig pa, mi shes pa*
illusion-like	*sgyu ma lta bu*
imaginary construct	*kun brtags*
immutable	*gzhan du mi 'gyur pa*

impaired	*skyon ldan*
impermanent	*mi rtag pa*
in conventional terms	*tha snyad du*
inaccurate	*phyin ci log pa*
inappropriate denial or negation	*skur 'debs*
inference	*rjes dpag*
initiation	*dbang*
innate	*lhan skyes*
insight	*lhag mthong*
instruction	*gdams ngag*
intended meaning	*dgongs pa*
intense	*ngar*
intrinsic character	*rang mtshan*
intrinsic nature	*rang bzhin*
karma	*las*
know	*rtogs*
latent propensity	*bag chags*
laxity	*bying ba*
lazy	*le lo, g.yel ba*
leisure	*dal ba*
levels and paths	*sa lam*
liberation	*thar pa*
life-essence	*srog, srog gi bdag nyid*
limpidity	*dwangs cha, dwangs ba*
lineage	*rigs*
line of reasoning	*rigs pa*
living being	*sems can*
logician	*tog ge ba*
Lokāyata	*'jig rten rgyang pan pa*
love	*byams pa*
loving-kindness	*brtse ba*
Mādhyamika/Madhyamaka	*dbu ma pa*
Mādhyamikas of the fundamental texts	*gzhung phyi mo'i dbu ma*
mahātma	*che ba'i bdag nyid can*
Mahāyāna	*theg chen*
manifestationist	*gsal byed pa*
mantra	*sngags*
Master of Sages	*thub dbang*
meditate, cultivate	*sgom*
meditative equipoise	*mnyam bzhag*
meditative serenity	*zhi gnas*

meditative stabilization	*bsam gtan*
memory consciousness	*dran pa*
method	*thabs*
middle way	*dbu ma*
mindfulness	*dran pa*
mind-stream	*rgyud*
mine	*nga'i*
miserable realm	*ngan 'gro*
mistaken	*'khrul ba*
mundane	*'jig rten gyi*
mutable	*gzhan du 'gyur pa*
nature	*rang bzhin*
naturelessness	*ngo bo nyid med pa*
negation	*dgag pa*
nihilist	*chad lta ba, med pa ba*
nihilistic extreme	*chad lta*
nine mental states	*sems gnas dgu*
nirvāṇa	*myang 'das*
noble being, noble	*'phags pa*
noble father and spiritual son	*yab sras*
non-Buddhist	*phyi, phyi rol pa*
non-Buddhist philosophers	*mu stegs pa*
non-conceptual	*cir yang mi rtog pa*
non-deceptive	*mi slu ba*
non-discursiveness	*mi rtog pa*
non-inquisitive	*ma brtags pa*
non-mistaken	*ma 'khrul ba*
nonvirtue	*mi dge ba*
object	*yul*
object negated	*dgag bya*
object of comprehension	*gzhal bya*
object of knowledge	*shes bya*
objectively	*yul gyi steng tu*
objective self	*chos kyi bdag*
objects and agents	*bya byed*
obscurations	*sgrib pa*
observation	*dmigs pa*
omniscient consciousness	*rnam mkhyen, kun mkhyen*
one-pointed	*rtse gcig*
ontological status	*sdod lugs, gnas tshul*
opportunity	*'byor ba*
ordinariness	*tha mal ba, rang dga' ba*

ordinary being	*so so skye bu*
ordinary consciousness	*rang dga' ba'i shes pa*
origin	*kun 'byung*
overly negative view	*skur 'debs kyi lta ba*
part	*cha shas, yan lag*
particle	*rdul*
partisan Mādhyamikas	*phyogs 'dzin pa'i dbu ma*
partless	*cha med*
path	*lam*
path of preparation	*sbyor lam*
perception	*mngon sum*
perfection	*phar phyin, pha rol tu phyin pa*
permanence, permanent	*rtag pa*
personal instruction	*man ngag*
personal self	*gang zag gi bdag*
pervasion	*khyab pa*
phenomena	*chos*
philosophical determinations	*lta bas gtan la 'bebs*
pledges	*dam tshigs*
pliancy	*shin sbyangs*
position	*phyogs*
post-equipoise state	*rjes thob*
power	*stobs*
Prāsaṅgika	*thal 'gyur pa*
pratyekabuddha	*rang sangs rgyas*
precepts	*bslab bya*
predicate of the probandum	*sgrub bya'i chos*
pre-verbal	*brda la ma byang ba*
pride	*nga rgyal*
primal essence	*gtso bo*
probandum	*bsgrub bya*
probative	*sgrub byed kyi*
proof	*sgrub pa*
proscription	*bcas pa*
protector	*mgon po*
provisional	*drang don*
pure phenomena	*rnam par byang pa'i chos*
real nature	*chos nyid*
reality	*de kho na nyid, de nyid, de bzhin nyid, yang dag pa*
reason	*rigs pa, gtan tshig, rtags*
reasoning	*rigs, gtan tshigs*

reasoning, reason	*rigs pa*
reasoning consciousness	*rigs shes*
reductio, reductio ad absurdum	*thal 'gyur*
referent object	*zhen yul*
reflection	*bsam pa*
refuge	*skyabs*
refutation	*dgag pa*
reifying view of the perishing aggregates	*'jig tshogs la lta ba*
reify	*sgro btags*
relaxed, loose	*lhod*
release	*grol*
requiring interpretation	*drang don*
resources	*longs spyod*
rite	*cho ga*
root infractions	*rtsa ba'i ltung ba*
Sāṃkhya	*grangs can pa*
sage	*thub pa, drang srong*
Saṃmitīya	*bkur ba'i ste ba*
Satyākāravādin	*rnam bden pa*
Sautrāntika	*mdo sde pa*
scattering	*'phro ba*
seed	*sa bon*
self	*bdag*
selflessness	*bdag med pa*
selflessness of objects	*chos kyi bdag med*
selflessness of persons	*gang zag gi bdag med*
sensory consciousness	*dbang shes*
serenity	*zhi gnas*
sign	*mtshan ma*
signlessness	*mtshan ma med pa*
sin	*sdig pa*
skill in means	*thabs mkhas*
sources	*skye mched*
source tantra	*rgyud sde khungs*
spirit of enlightenment	*sems bskyed, byang chub kyi sems*
śrāvaka	*nyan thos*
stability	*gnas cha*
stabilizing meditation	*'jog sgom*
stage of completion	*rdzogs rim*
stage of generation	*bskyed rim*
stream	*rgyun*

study	*thos pa*
subject	*chos can, yul can*
sublime wisdom	*ye shes*
substantially existent	*rdzas yod*
substrata	*khyad gzhi*
suffering	*sdug bsngal*
superimpose	*sgro btags*
supramundane	*'jig rten las 'das pa'i*
supreme mundane quality stage	*chos mchog*
sustain	*skyong*
sūtra	*mdo*
Svātantrika	*rang rgyud pa*
syllogism	*sbyor ba*
system	*lugs*
tathāgata	*de bzhin shegs pa*
taut	*grims*
tenet	*grub mtha'*
tetralemma	*mtha' bzhi*
that which belongs to the self	*bdag gi ba*
thesis	*dam bca'*
thing	*dngos po*
thoroughly non-abiding	*rab tu mi gnas*
three criteria	*tshul gsum*
tight	*bsgrims*
trailblazer	*shing rta chen po*
training	*bslab pa*
truly existent	*bden par yod*
truth	*bden pa*
truth-for-a-concealer	*kun rdzob bden pa*
ulterior meaning	*dgongs pa*
ultimate	*don dam*
ultimately	*don dam tu*
ultimate truth	*don dam bden pa*
unattractive	*mi sdug*
uncontaminated	*zag med*
unfabricated	*ma bcos pa*
unimpaired	*gnod pa med pa*
union	*zung 'brel*
union of serenity and insight	*zhi lhag zung 'brel*
unreal	*dngos min*
Vaibhāṣika	*bye brag smra ba*
Vaiśeṣika	*bye brag pa*

Vajrayāna	*rdo rje'i theg pa*
valid cognition	*tshad ma*
validity	*tshad ma*
Vatsiputriya	*ma bu ba*
verbal (person)	*brda la byang ba*
view	*lta ba*
view of annihilation	*chad lta*
vigilance	*shes bzhin*
virtue	*dge ba*
vow	*sdom pa*
vows of individual liberation	*so so thar pa'i sdom pa*
whole	*yan lag can*
wisdom	*shes rab*
wishlessness	*smon pa med pa*
worldly convention	*'jig rten gyi tha snyad*
wrong view	*lta ngan, log lta*
Yogācāra	*rnal 'byor spyod pa*
yogi	*rnal 'byor pa*

APPENDIX 3
EMENDATIONS TO THE TIBETAN TEXT

511.19: *sa ba'i*—*sa pa'i*, Ganden Bar Nying: 255b.1.

530.14: *brjed nges kyi*—*brjed nges kyis*, Ganden Bar Nying: 264b.3.

549.6: *la sog sa*—*la sogs pa*, Ganden Bar Nying: 274b.2.

549.15: *zhig nas*—*zhi gnas*, Ganden Bar Nying: 274b.5.

558.8: *'jig rten ni*—*'di la rten ni*, Ganden Bar Nying: 279a.5.

576.20: *gzhi bdag*—*bzhi phung po lnga bdag*, PPs: 345.13-346.3.

586.1: *phyir*—*de*, Lindtner 1982: 64; see note 278 to translation.

594.16: *yin pa de*—*yin pa de ltar de*, Toh 3865: 175b.2.

597.7-12: Cf. Nar-thang edition cited by Bhattacharya 1931: 226.

598.2: *nges na* (also in Ganden Bar Nying 300b.1)—*des na*, Cśṭ, D3865: 183a.1, 182b.4.

601.13: *na*—*nas*, P5658: 176.1.3.

605.13: *de ltar na yang*—*de lta na*, D3865: 224b.2.

606.1: *med pa bar smra ba* (*med pa par smra ba*, Ganden Bar Nying: 304a.4)—*med par smra ba*, D3842: 255b.4.

609.6: *skye 'gag med pa rnyed pa*—*skye 'gag med par rnyed pa*, mChan: 283.04.

609.15: *ltos*—*bltos*, Ganden Bar Nying: 305b.6; La Vallée Poussin 1970b: 180.16.

617.11: *'jig rten gyi*—*'jig rten gyis*, Ganden Bar Nying: 309b.3.

620.1-3: Cf. P5259: 293.2.2, *tshig tu brjod pa tha snyad 'dogs pa'i kun brtags pa'i ngo bo nyid hang yin pa de*, and 620.04, *gzhan dbang gi ngo bo la*.

699.1: *bskyang*—*bskyung*, Ganden Bar Nying: 348a.2.

709.16: *rags pa—rigs pa, mChan*: 566.6.

713.15: *'gal ba'i—'jal ba'i*, Ganden Bar Nying: 355b.5, cf. 713.3.

751.14: *shing rta nyid byed pa—shing rta'i dpyad pa*, Ganden Bar Nying: 375a.5.

765.1: *chags pa can dang—chags pa can dag*, Ganden Bar Nying: 381b.6.

790.4: *dpyod—spyod*, Ganden Bar Nying: 394a.5.

800.7: *drangs—dwangs*, Ganden Bar Nying: 399a.6.

NOTES

The citation reference in the notes first supplies the Sanskrit reference if extant, giving first the chapter and then the verse, or simply the page number(s). This is followed by the Suzuki (1955-61) reference (identified by the abbreviation P), giving the page, folio, and line numbers. Where the translators did not locate a citation in Suzuki, its location in the Tohoku catalogue has been given. This has been made possible by the recent appearance of Tsultrim Kelsang Khangkar's extremely helpful critical edition of the Tibetan text (Khangkar 2001), which covers the section on the person of great capacity.

Chapter One *Serenity and Insight*

1. The outline heading 2" *In particular, how to train in the last two perfections* is the second of a two-part subheading in the section of the LRCM entitled 3) *Training the mind in the stages of the path of the person of great capacity* (LRCM: 283). The two-part subheading (LRCM: 364) c" *The process of learning the six perfections* includes both 1" *How to train in bodhisattva deeds in general* and 2" *In particular, how to train in the last two perfections.*

2. *Ārya-saṃdhi-nirmocana-nāma-mahāyāna-sūtra* (Sn), Lamotte 1935: 111; P774: 17.3.3-4.

3. *Ārya-mahāyāna-prasāda-prabhāvanā-nāma-mahāyāna-sūtra*, P812: 239.4.4-5.

4. Sn, Lamotte 1935: 111; P774: 6.2.6-7.

5. *Prajñāpāramitopadeśa*, P5579: 246.2.8-3.1.

6. Sn, Lamotte 1935: 110; P774: 17.2.8-3.1.

7. Third *Bhāvanā-krama* (Bk3), Tucci 1971: 1; D3917: Ki 55b6-56a1.

8. Second *Bhāvanā-krama* (Bk2), P5311: 31.3.8.

9. Sn, Lamotte 1935: 89; P774: 13.4.5-7.

10. The twelve branches are given in Sn, Lamotte 1935: 89. Conze (1990: 52) lists discourses, discourses in prose and verse mingled, predictions, verses, summaries, origins, thus-was-said, introduction, expanded texts, life stories, tales, and marvels. They are discussed at length in Pagel 1995: 7ff.

11. Sn, Lamotte 1935: 89; P774: 13.4.7-13.5.2.

12. See the exhaustive bibliography in Ruegg 1989 for information about putative followers of the Chinese master Ha-shang (Hva-shang) who participated in the bSam-yas debate (c. 792-794).

13. *Ārya-ratna-megha-nāma-mahāyāna-sūtra*, D231: Wa 92b1.

14. *Mahāyāna-sūtrālaṃkāra-kārikā* (MSA): 14.8; P5521: 10.1.6-7.

15. Ba-so-chos-kyi-rgyal-mtshan (*mChan*: 10.6) says that "Abbreviating the name of a phenomenon" would be, for example, condensing "All composite phenomena are impermanent" to "impermanent" and stabilizing your attention on that.

16. MSA: 18.66; P5521: 10.5.1.

17. *Bodhisattva-bhūmi* (Bbh), Wogihara 1936: 1.109; Dutt 1966: 77.5-12; P5538: 150.4.1-5.

18. Bk2, P5311: 32.4.8-33.1.2.

19. *Prajñāpāramitopadeśa*, P5579: 246.2.8-246.3.1.

20. Sn, Lamotte 1935: 88; P774: 13.3.7-13.4.1.

21. For clarification of "the limits of existence" and "achievement of your purpose," see below (LRCM: 491), where the four types of objects mentioned here are discussed in greater detail.

22. The Regent is Maitreya/Maitreyanātha. The five texts attributed to him by Tibetan tradition are the MSA; *Dharma-dharmatā-vibhāga* (*Separation of the Dharmas from the True Nature of Dharmas*); *Madhyānta-vibhāga* (*Separation of the Middle from the Extremes*); *Abhisamayālaṃkāra-prajñā-pāramitopadeśa-śāstra* (*Ornament for Clear Knowledge*) (AA); and *Ratna-gotra-vibhāga-mahāyānottara-tantra-śāstra* (*Sublime Continuum*) (RGV).

23. For more on "limpid" (*dwangs cha*) and vivid intensity (*gsal cha'i ngar*), see below, LRCM: 516.

24. The two selflessnesses are the lack of an intrinsically existent self of persons and the lack of an intrinsically existent self in phenomena (LRCM: 577-579, 661-664).

25. Bk2, P5311: 31.5.7-32.1.4. The *Great Final Nirvāṇa Sūtra* (*'Phags pa yongs su mya ngan las 'das pa chen po'i mdo*) (D119: Ta 148a6-b1) is translated from the Chinese. The *Candra-pradīpa-sūtra* is another name for the *Samādhi-rāja-sūtra* (*Sarva-dharma-svabhāva-samatā-vipañcita-samādhi-rāja-sūtra*) (SR). SR: 7.10ab, Vaidya 1961: 36.21-22; P795: 281.2.1.

26. *Ārya-dharma-saṃgīti-nāma-mahāyāna-sūtra*, D238: Zha 52a6, cited in the first *Bhāvanā-krama* (Bk1), Tucci 1986: 181.11.

27. Bk1, Tucci 1986: 205; P5310: 25.1.8-25.2.1.

28. *Bodhisattva-caryāvatāra* (BCA), P5272: 254.4.5.

29. Ibid., P5272: 248.5.4.

30. Bk2, P5311: 31.4.2-31.5.5.

31. Sn, Lamotte 1935: 132; P774: 21.1.3.

32. SR, Vaidya 1961: 49; D127: Da 27a7-b1; cited at Bk3, Tucci 1971: 18. The phrase "worldly persons" is taken from the slightly different version of this verse cited at LRCM: 564-565.

33. Udraka (*Lhag dpyod*) is probably Udraka Rāmaputra, one of two teachers who instructed Siddhārtha Gautama after the future Buddha's renunciation of the householder's life. Udraka taught a yoga system that led to the Peak of Cyclic Existence, the fourth absorption of the formless realm, which is a state capable of suppressing but not uprooting the causes of cyclic existence.

34. The *Ārya-bodhisattva-piṭaka-nāma-mahāyāna-sūtra*, chapter 12 of the *Ratna-kūṭa*, Pagel 1995: 344; D56: Ga 161b3-5.

35. The full name of the collection of forty-nine works (Pagel 1995: appendix III) is *Ārya-mahā-ratna-kūṭa-dharma-paryāya-śata-sāhasrika-grantha*, P760, vols. 22-24.

36. *Ārya-mahāyāna-prasāda-prabhāvanā-nāma-mahāyāna-sūtra*, P812: 239.4.2.

37. BCA: 8.4; P5272: 254.4.7-8.

38. Bk1, Tucci 1986: 207; P5310: 25.4.2.

39. This is a paraphrase of Sn, Lamotte 1935: 90; P774: 13.5.2-5, cited below at LRCM: 537, 798.

40. Sn, P774: 13.4.5-13.5.2, cited at LRCM: 471, 537.

41. LRCM: 473.

42. Ye-shes-grags-pa (Jñānakīrti) is the author of the *Pha rol tu phyin pa'i theg pa'i bsgom pa'i rim pa'i man ngag (Perfection Vehicle Stages of Meditation)*. The Sanskrit title is reconstructed as *Prajñāpāramitā-bhāvanā-kramopadeśa*.

43. *Abhidharma-samuccaya* (AS), Pradhan 1975: 75.21, according to Wayman 1978; P5550: 263.3.3.

44. Meditative stabilization is divided into access (*nyer bsdogs, sāmantaka*) and actual (*dngos gzhi, maula*) attainment; only the latter is counted as a full attainment.

45. *Yoga-caryā-bhūmi (Sa'i dngos gzhi)*, P5536: 283.4.2-3. The title *Sa'i dngos gzhi* is rendered here loosely as *Levels of Yogic Deeds (Yoga-caryā-bhūmi)* to accord with Suzuki 1955-61 usage. lCang-skya-rol-ba'i-do-rje's *Grub pa'i mtha'i rnam par bzhag pa gsal bar bshad pa thub bstan lhun po'i mdzes rgyan* (Varanasi: Pleasure of Elegant Sayings Press, 1970), p. 155, identifies *Sa'i dngos gzhi* as a collection of four titles: (1) *The Many Levels (Bahu-bhūmikā, Sa mang po pa)*; (2) *Śrāvaka Levels (Śrāvaka-bhūmi [Śbh], Nyan sa)*; (3) Bbh; and (4) *The Sequence of the Levels (Bhūmi-krama, Sa'i go rim)*. This is supported by pp. 226-316 of the catalogue *bsTan 'gyur rin po che srid zhi'i rgyan gcig gi dkar chag rin chen mdzes pa'i phra tshom* for the *gSer bris bstan 'gyur* (Sichuan: Krung go'i mtho rim nang bstan slob gling gi bod brgyud nang bstan zhib 'jug khang, 1989). *The Many Levels* is the same treatise as Suzuki's (1955-61) *Levels of Yogic Deeds* (P5536). *The Sequence of the Levels* can be found at the end of Bbh (P5538: 230.2.4-231.1.7). Tsong-kha-pa refers to numbers 2 and 3 by their own names, and is therefore using the name *Sa'i dngos gzhi* to refer to numbers 1 and 4, presumably because numbers 2 (Śbh) and 3 (Bbh) are well-known titles. Tsong-kha-pa also uses the terms *sa sde* ("texts on the levels") (LRCM: 523.6, etc.) and *sa sde lnga* ("five texts on the levels") (LRCM: 488.5, etc.), which include the *Sa'i dngos gzhi*. See note 58 below to LRCM: 488.5.

46. LRCM: 529-532.

47. The types of analysis characteristic of insight are mentioned above (LRCM: 471-475) and discussed in detail below (LRCM: 769ff).

Chapter Two *Preparing for Meditative Serenity*

48. MSA: 8.7; P5521: 10.2.2.

49. Bk1, Tucci 1986: 205; P5310: 25.2.1-3; Sn, P774: 21.2.5-7.

50. *Bodhi-patha-pradīpa*, P5343: 21.2.7-8.

51. The entire section from the Śbh, P5537: 43.3.3-43.4.1, is translated by Wayman (1978: 31-43). The thirteen are: (1) the chief prerequisites, i.e., familiarity with the teaching and inner discipline; and, additionally, (2) excellence of one's own aims; (3) excellence of others' aims; (4) desire for the teaching; (5) renunciation; (6) vows of ethical discipline; (7) restraint of the senses; (8) moderation in eating; (9) the practice of wakefulness; (10) dwelling vigilantly; (11) solitude; (12) cleansing of obscurations; and (13) proper basis of concentration.

52. LRCM: 33-280 (*Great Treatise* 2000: 69-353).

53. Bk2, P5311: 32.4.5-8. Bk3, Tucci 1971: 3; D3917: Ki 57a1-3.

54. Śbh, P5537: 100.1.2-6.

55. *Madhyānta-vibhāga*, P5522: 20.4.8-20.5.1. Tsong-kha-pa discusses the five faults and and eight antidotes below, LRCM: 528-529.

56. Ruegg (*Great Treatise* 2000: 26) mentions Sha-ra-ba/Shar-ba-pa Yon-tan-grags (1070-1141) as the author of the *Be'u bum dmar po*. As at LRCM: 528.8, there are six faults when laxity and excitement are counted separately.

57. On the use of *sa sde* ("texts on the levels") see note 45 above (at LRCM: 483.13) and note 58 below (at LRCM: 488.5).

58. The five texts on the levels (*sa sde lnga*) are (1) *Levels of Yogic Deeds* (*Bhūmi-vastu, Sa'i dngos gzhi*); (2) *Compendium of Bases* (*Vastu-saṃgraha, gZhi bsdu ba*); (3) *Compendium of the Enumerations* (*Paryāya-saṃgraha, rNam grang bsdu ba*); (4) *Compendium of Explanations* (*Vivaraṇa-saṃgraha, rNam par bshad pa'i sgo bsdu ba*); and (5) *Compendium of Determinations* (*Viniścaya-saṃgrahaṇi, rNam par gtan la dbab pa bsdu ba*). The collective title *rNal 'byor spyod pa'i sa* (*Yoga-caryā-bhūmi*) is used in the *bstan 'gyur* for all these five treatises. Tsong-kha-pa occasionally uses this title (see *Great Treatise* 2000, note 379). Regarding *Levels of Yogic Deeds*, see note 45 above to LRCM: 483.13.

59. *Madhyānta-vibhāga*: 4.5ab, D4021: Phi 43a4.

60. The five aggregates are form, feeling, discrimination, compositional factors, and consciousness. The eighteen constituents are the six sensory faculties—those of the eye, ear, nose, tongue, and body, as well as the mental sensory faculty; the six consciousnesses—those of the eye, ear, nose, tongue, and body, as well as the mental consciousness; and the six objects of these consciousnesses—forms, sounds, odors, tastes, tangible objects, and phenomena. The twelve sources are the same six sensory faculties and their objects. The four truths are the noble truths of suffering, origin, cessation, and path.

61. The thirty-six (Wayman 1978: 443 n. 33; Zahler, et al. 1983: 83) are: hair, nails, teeth, sweat and body odor, skin, flesh, liver, lungs, small intestines, large intestines, stomach, esophagus, urinary bladder, spleen, rectum, saliva, snot, oily connective tissue, lymph, marrow, fat, bile, phlegm, pus, blood, brain, the membrane covering the brain, urine, and old-age spots.

62. There are nine external uglinesses (Zahler, et al. 1983: 83-84): the blue, black, pus color, and red color of a corpse; a face chewed on or torn apart by animals; a corpse partly or more thoroughly consumed by worms, etc.; and a rigid corpse.

63. The twelve factors of dependent-arising are (1) ignorance, (2) compositional activity, (3) consciousness, (4) name-and-form, (5) six sources, (6) contact, (7) feeling, (8) craving, (9) grasping, (10) potential existence, (11) birth, (12) aging-and-death. See LRCM: 249-252 (*Great Treatise* 2000: 315-19).

64. Diverse causes are specific kinds of karma leading to specific kinds of effects, as distinct from the general teaching, in the context of dependent-arising, that effects arise based on past karma. See Ngag-dbang-rab-brtan, *mChan*: 42.4.

65. Cyclic existence includes three realms: the desire, form, and formless realms. The form realm includes four progressively higher levels of meditative stabilization, and the formless realm includes four meditative absorptions, of which the third is called "Nothingness"(*ci yang med; ākiṃchanya*). For a more detailed account, see Zahler, et al. 1983: 129-33.

66. The sixteen aspects are set out in detail at LRCM: 269 (*Great Treatise* 2000: 341-42).

67. Bk2, P5311: 33.1.4-7. On the sources for the three progressive levels, see Wayman 1978: 444 n. 40. For the twelve branches of scripture, see note 10 above.

68. That is, the list of universal objects of meditation is another way of talking about objects of meditation generally; it is not a set of special objects distinct from the three types just listed.

69. LRCM: 340-355, 564ff.

70. Bk1, Tucci 1986: 206; P5310: 25.4.2, cited at LRCM: 481.

71. *Bodhi-patha-pradīpa*, P5343: 21.2.8.

72. Śbh, D4036: Dzi 77a4-6; Dzi 77a7. No title of the work is given. Shukla (1973: 197 n. 1) says the dialogue, not found elsewhere, is probably part of a lost Sanskrit canon of an Indian Buddhist school, probably the Mahāsaṃghika. The citations from the Śbh here and below are from a slightly different version than found in Shukla 1973: 198-99.

73. As at LRCM: 496, this involves differentiating things into the six constituents: earth, water, fire, air, space, and consciousness.

74. Śbh, Wayman 1978: 445 n. 47; P5537: 96.1.2-4.

75. Ibid., Wayman 1978: 445 n. 48; P5537: 96.1.4-5.

76. Ibid., P5537: 73.3.7-73.4.3.

77. Here "confusion" renders *mongs pa*; compare the use of *gti mug*, "ignorance," at LRCM: 496.1.

78. Śbh, Wayman 1978: 445 n. 50; P5537: 73.4.3-6.

79. Ibid., Shukla 1973: 195; cf. Wayman 1978: 445 n. 52; P5537: 72.5.1-3.

80. LRCM: 497.

81. In his *Samādhi-sambhāra-parivarta* (*Chapter on the Collections of Concentration*), according to Wayman 1978: 445 n. 53; D3924: Ki 90a3-6. *Great Treatise* 2000: 139 incorrectly says the author of this work is Atisha.

82. A khaṭvāṅga (as the Tibetan transliterates the Sanskrit) is a tantric staff carried by deities and yogis. It is crowned by a trident and decorated with skulls.

83. SR: 4.20-21, cited at LRCM: 139 (Great Treatise 2000: 186).

84. Bk3, Tucci 1971: 4.12-14; D3917: Ki 57a3-5.

85. SR: 4.13, Vaidya 1961: 21.7-10; D130: Da 13b5.

86. LRCM: 491.

87. Pāramitā-samāsa-nāma (PS): 5.12; P5340: 6.1.8-6.2.1.

88. Bodhi-patha-pradīpa, D3947: Khi 240a1.

89. Bk1, Tucci 1986: 206; P5310: 25.2.7-8.

90. Sn, P774: 16.5.3-17.2.1. The full list of emptinesses is given in Conze 1990: 144-48 and Hopkins 1983: 204-05.

Chapter Three Focusing Your Mind

91. MSA: 19.28-29; P5021: 10.5.3.

92. Those on the eighth bodhisattva level and above.

93. Mahāyāna-sūtrālaṃkāra-bhāṣya on MSA: 18.53; Lévi 1907: 143.2-3; D4026: Phi 227a2.

94. AS, Pradhan 1975: 6.6, according to Wayman 1978; P5550: 238.3.8.

95. Madhyamaka-hṛdaya-kārikā, D3855: Dza 4a6.

96. Bk2 P5311: 33.2.5-6.

97. LRCM: 505.

98. LRCM: 504.8.

99. LRCM: 515-516.

100. Deśanā-stava (the Tibetan title here is bShags bstod), D1159: Ka 205b5.

101. Deśanā-stava-vṛtti, D1160: Ka 219b5.

102. Ibid., Ka 220a1.

103. Deśanā-stava, D1159: Ka 205b6-7.

104. Deśanā-stava-vṛtti, D1160: Ka 220b3-4.

105. On the nine mental states, see LRCM: 529-532; on the attention of tight focus used during first two of these, see LRCM: 535-536.

106. Śbh, P5537: 101.1.3.

107. Bk1, Tucci 1986: 207; P5310: 25.3.6.

108. Bk2, P5311: 33.2.2.

109. Ibid., P5311: 33.2.2-3.

110. Śbh, P5537: 100.2.6-100.3.1.

111. Madhyānta-vibhāga-ṭikā, Yamaguchi 1934: 175.7-8; P5528: 128.2.4.

112. Bk3, Tucci 1971: 11.18-20; D3917: Ki 51a3.

113. LRCM: 506.

Chapter Four *Dealing with Laxity and Excitement*

114. AS, Pradhan 1950: 9.9-10, P5550: 239.5.3-4.

115. *Deśanā-stava*, D1159: Ka 205b4-5.

116. For a description of the twenty secondary afflictions, see Hopkins 1983: 261-66 and Rabten 1988: 61-67.

117. Bk2, P5311: 33.2.1.

118. Sn, Lamotte 1935: 112; P774: 17.4.7-8.

119. AS, Pradhan 1975: 9.8; P5550: 240.1.4.

120. *Abhidharma-kośa-bhāṣya*, Shastri 1972: 191; P5591: 145.4.6.

121. Bk2, P5311: 33.2.3-4.

122. Ibid., P5311: 33.2.4-5. Bk3, Tucci 1971: 9; D3917: Ki 59a5-6.

123. *Madhyānta-vibhāga*: 4.5b, D4021: Phi 43a4-5.

124. LRCM: 506-08.

125. BCA: 5.33a-c; P5272: 249.1.9.

126. *Madhyānta-vibhāga-ṭīkā*, Yamaguchi 1934: 175.9-11; P5528: 128.2.4.

127. BCA: 5.108; P5272: 250.3.6.

128. PS: 1.15ab; P5340: 17.4.8-17.5.1.

129. AS, Pradhan 1975: 5-6; P5550: 238.3.4-5.

130. Bk1, Tucci 1986: 206; P5310: 25.3.5-6.

131. PS: 5.13ab; P5340: 16.2.1-2.

132. *Madhyamaka-hṛdaya-kārikā*, D3855: Dza 4a7.

133. *Śikṣā-samuccaya*, Vaidya 1960: 112.24; D3940: Khi 114a6.

134. For the Three Jewels, see LRCM: 131-158 (*Great Treatise* 2000: 177-207); leisure, LRCM: 77-86 (*Great Treatise* 2000: 117-28); spirit of enlightenment, LRCM: 283-340.

135. For a description of these six recollections, see Conze 1990: 551-53.

136. Śbh, Wayman 1978: 448 n. 100; cf. Shukla 1973: 421-22; P5537: 111.3.3-6.

137. Ibid., Wayman 1978: 448 n. 101; P5537: 100.1.8. For further discussions of the technical term "sign" (*mtshan ma, nimitta*) that refers to the key characteristic of a phenomenon by which it is conceptually grasped, see Vajirañāṇa 1975: 31-34 and Conze 1990: 11-12.

138. Bk1, Tucci 1986: 206-07; P5310: 25.3.6-7.

139. *Madhyamaka-hṛdaya-kārikā*, D3855: Dza 4a6-7.

140. Ibid., D3855: Dza 4a7.

141. Śikṣā-samuccaya, Vaidya 1960: 112.24; D3940: Khi 114a6-7.

142. PS: 5.13cd; P5340: 16.2.2.

143. Śbh, P5537: 92.5.3-6.

144. Yoga-caryā-bhūmi (Sa'i dngos gzhi), P5536: 273.2.4-7.

145. Ibid., P5536: 273.2.7-273.3.2.

146. LRCM: 61-69 (Great Treatise 2000: 101-08). The four are restraining the sensory faculties, acting with vigilance, appropriate diet, and lastly how to practice diligently without
sleeping and how to act properly at the time of sleep.

147. Bk2, P5311: 33.2.6-7.

148. Ibid., P5311: 34.3.3. Bk3, Tucci 1971: 11; D3917: Ki 60a2-3.

149. In the context of serenity the term btang snyoms is rendered "equanimity," but in the
context of feeling and the four immeasurables it is translated as "impartiality." The four
immeasurables are immeasurable love, compassion, sympathetic joy, and impartiality. For
a detailed discussion, see Vajirañāṇa 1975: 263-313 and Ñāṇamoli 1991: 288-319.

150. Śbh, Wayman 1961: 117-118; P5537: 105.5.3-6.

151. Ibid., Wayman 1961: 118; P5537: 105.5.6-7.

152. Ibid., Wayman 1961: 118; P5537: 105.5.7.

153. Madhyānta-vibhāga, D4021: Phi 43a3-5.

154. The first four faults are explained at LRCM: 489-504; mindfulness and vigilance at
LRCM: 505-512; application, LRCM: 515-525; non-application, LRCM: 525-529.

155. "Vehicle of dialectics" (mtshan nyid kyi theg pa) refers to the Perfection Vehicle.

156. Saṃpuṭi-nāma-mahā-tantra, D381: Ga 76b3-77a1.

Chapter Five Attaining Serenity

157. This and the following citations are from MSA: 14.11-14; P5521: 10.5.3-5.

158. Bk1, Tucci 1986: 207; P5310: 25.4.4-5.

159. Prajñāpāramitopadeśa, P5579: 246.4.4-5.

160. This and the following citations are from Śbh, P5537: 100.3.8-100.5.5.

161. Prajñāpāramitopadeśa, P5579: 246.4.7.

162. Śbh, Wayman 1978: 450 n. 127; D4036: Dzi 133a7-b1.

163. Bk1, Tucci 1986: 207; P5310: 25.4.4-5.

164. LRCM: 537-543.

165. Śbh, P5537: 101.1.2-6.

166. LRCM: 484-487.

167. PS: 5.10cd-11; P5340: 18.1.7-8.

168. LRCM: 484-536.

169. Sn, Lamotte 1935: 90; P774: 13.5.2-3; paraphrased at LRCM: 481.

170. MSA: 14.15a-c; P5521: 10.5.5-6.

171. LRCM: 543.15.

172. Bk2, P5311: 33.2.7-8.

173. Bk1, Tucci 1986: 207; P5310: 25.4.2.

174. *Prajñāpāramitopadeśa*, P5579: 247.2.2-247.3.4.

175. LRCM: 537; also cf. LRCM: 471, 557.

176. The nine levels include the level of the desire realm, four levels in the form realm, and four in the formless realm.

177. *Yoga-caryā-bhūmi* (*Sa'i dngos gzhi*), P5536: 267.3.6-8.

178. AS, Pradhan 1975: 6; P5550: 238.4.8.

179. *Triṃśikā-bhāṣya*, Lévi 1925: 27.16-19; D4064: Shi 156b5-6.

180. Śbh, Wayman 1978: 450 n. 138; P5537: 114.4.5-6.

181. Ibid., Wayman 1978: 451 n. 139; P5537: 114.4.7-5.1.

182. The sensation has been compared to the feeling of a warm hand placed upon a bald head.

183. Śbh, Wayman 1978: 451 n. 140; P5537: 114.6.1-3.

184. Ibid., Wayman 1978: 451 n. 141; P5537: 114.5.3-5.

185. The single Tibetan term *rlung* renders both Sanskrit *vāyu* (air) and *prāṇa* (energy). In the context of the four elements it is rendered "wind" and in other contexts, "energy."

186. *Triṃśikā-bhāṣya*, Lévi 1925: 27.19-21; D4064: Shi 156b6.

187. Śbh, Wayman 1978: 451 n. 143; P5537: 114.5.5-8.

188. This is a line from the MSA, cited at LRCM: 537.15.

189. See the discussion of serenity and its relation to the seven types of attention below, at LRCM: 555-561.

190. Śbh, Wayman 1978: 451 n. 145; P5537: 114.5.8.-115.1.1.

191. The five obstructions are (1) sensual desire, (2) malice, (3) lethargy and sleepiness, (4) excitement and regret, and (5) doubt. For a detailed account, see Gunaratana 1985: 28-48.

192. Śbh, Wayman 1978: 451 n. 148; P5537: 115.1.1-3.

193. Ibid., Wayman 1978: 452 n. 150; P5537: 115.1.6-7.

194. Ibid., Wayman 1978: 452 n. 151; P5537: 115.1.7-8.

195. Ibid., Wayman 1978: 452 n. 152; P5537: 115.2.4-7.

196. LRCM: 537-542.

197. LRCM: 543-544.

198. The five paths are the paths of accumulation, preparation, seeing, meditation, and no more learning.

199. The Madhyamaka *Stages of Meditation* are primarily Kamalaśila's three *Stages of Meditation*. In the same Madhyamaka section of the bsTan-'gyur are listed other *Stages of Meditation* by Jñānakīrti (cf. LRCM: 483), Klu-grub, Nag-po, and dGe-ba'i-go-cha.

200. On the three realms and meditative stabilizations and meditative absorptions, see note 65 above to LRCM: 493.12.

201. This refers to the passages from the *Śravaka Levels* that describe some of the nine mental states. LRCM: 530-532.

202. Sn, cited at LRCM: 474.

203. Śbh, Wayman 1978: 452 n. 155; P5537: 72.4.7-72.5.1.

204. Ibid., Wayman 1978: 452 n. 156; P5537: 110.3.2-4.

205. Bk1, Tucci 1986: 207; P5310: 25.4.1-2.

206. *Prajñāpāramitopadeśa*, P5579: 247.3.3.

207. LRCM: 472.

Chapter Six *Serenity as Part of the Path*

208. Śbh, Wayman 1961: 125; P5537: 115.2.2-3.

209. Ibid., Wayman 1961: 125; P5537: 115.2.3-7.

210. LRCM: 269 (*Great Treatise* 2000: 341-42).

211. Śbh, Wayman 1961: 125-26; P5537: 115.2.7-115.3.1.

212. *Abhidharma-kośa-kārikā* (AK): 4.24; P5590: 124.3.8. "The path of accumulation" renders *mthar pa cha mthun* (literally "aids to liberation").

213. Sn, Lamotte 1935: 111; P774: 17.6.2-6; cited at LRCM: 470.

214. The Peak of Cyclic Existence (*srid rtse, bhavāgra*) is the highest of the four meditative absorptions in the formless realm, also called "neither discrimination nor non-discrimination." See note 65 above.

215. *Varṇāha-varṇe-bhagavato-buddhasya-stotre-śakya-stava*, D1138: Ka 96a3-4.

216. The four Māras are: (1) the psycho-physical aggregates, (2) afflictions, (3) death, and (4) Māra the Devaputra, the embodiment of evil, often appearing, at times with his hosts, as a tempter in Buddhist narrations.

217. LRCM: 802.

218. By means of discernment of characteristics that distinguish one meditative stabilization or meditative absorption from another, there is progress from the relatively coarse attributes of the lower meditative states to the relative calm of the higher states.

219. MSA: 14.15d-16ab; P5521: 10.5.6-7.

220. Śbh, P5537: 88.1.4-6.

221. The higher and lower texts on knowledge (*chos mngon pa*): the Mahāyāna *Compendium of Knowledge* (*Abhidharma-samuccaya*) and the Hīnayāna *Treasury of Knowledge* (*Abhidharma-kośa*).

222. LRCM: 539.

223. Sn, MSA, Bk1 cited at LRCM: 537.

224. Sn and Bk2 cited at LRCM: 479.

225. This translation follows the reading *'di la rten ni* found in the Ganden Bar Nying: 279a5.

226. Śbh, P5537: 115.3.5-7.

227. Śbh, P5537: 116.4.1.

228. The six elements are meaning (*don*), entity (*dngos*), characteristic (*mtshan nyid*), direction (*phyogs*), time (*dus*), and search for the reason (*rigs pa yongs su 'tshol ba*).

229. The five superknowledges are divine eye, divine ear, knowledge of others' minds, memory of former lives, and knowledge of the extinction of contaminations. For more detailed accounts, see Vajirañāṇa 1975: 443-53 and Conze 1990: 79-82.

230. Śbh, P5537: 120.2.3-8. For a detailed account of the above seven types of attention, see Zahler, et al. 1983: 92-115.

231. *Yoga-caryā-bhūmau-vastu-saṃgraha*, P5540: 152.1.1-2.

Chapter Seven *Why Insight Is Needed*

232. LRCM: 504, 549.

The section from here to Chapter Twelve (LRCM: 564-606.9) was translated and published previously by Elizabeth S. Napper as *Dependent-Arising and Emptiness* (Boston: Wisdom Publications, 1989). The original Tibetan text has been completely retranslated here. In *Dependent-Arising*, Napper provides very useful and detailed analyses, annotations, and appendices, to which the reader is referred.

233. "Non-Buddhist" here is a loose translation of the Tibetan term *mu stegs pa* ("those holding up the edges") that renders the Sanskrit *tīrthika* ("forder").

234. Bk1, Tucci 1986: 209-10; P5310: 26.1.5-7.

235. SR: 9.36, Vaidya 1961: 49; D130: Da 27a7.

236. See note 33 above on Udraka.

237. Tsong-kha-pa gives only the first line of this verse, cited in full at LRCM: 479-480. See note 32.

238. Bk2, P5311: 31.4.5; cf. LRCM: 479-480.

239. Tsong-kha-pa is paraphrasing his earlier citation of the *Bodhisattva-piṭaka* (LRCM: 480.3-9, note 34), included within the citation from Kamalaśīla (Bk2, P5311: 31.4.7-31.5.2).

240. Bk2, P5311: 33.2.8-33.3.4.

241. Sn, Lamotte 1935: 9.26; P774: 22.5.4-5. Cited by Kamalaśīla, Bk2, P5311: 33.3.4-6.

242. This paraphrases the *Ārya-mahāyāna-prasāda-prabhāvanā-nāma-mahāyāna-sūtra,* cited above at LRCM: 479-480 (see note 36). Tsong-kha-pa seems to be using Kamalaśīla as his source in this section, rather than the sūtras themselves.

Chapter Eight *Relying on Definitive Sources*

243. *How to train in insight* is the second part of the three-part heading given at the beginning of Chapter 2 (LRCM: 484).

244. *Akṣayamati-nirdeśa-sūtra*, P842: 64.3.6-64.4.1.

245. Ibid., P842: 64.4.4-7. This differs in many small points from Tsong-kha-pa's citation, which accords almost exactly with the version in Kamalaśila's *Madhyamakāloka* (*Illumination of the Middle Way*), P5287: 46.3.1-4.

246. SR: 8.5, Vaidya 1961: 36.1-4; P795: 281.1.5-6.

247. *Madhyamakāloka*, P5287: 46.3.5-8.

248. The "collections of Madhyamaka arguments" is a list of texts, usually by Nāgārjuna, that includes *Mūla-madhyamaka-kārikā* (MMK); *Ratnāvalī* (Rā); *Vigraha-vyāvartanī* (VV); *Śūnyatā-saptati; Yukti-ṣaṣṭikā* (YS); and *Vaidalya-prakaraṇa*. Here Tsong-kha-pa includes with them at least the *Catuḥ-śataka* (Cś) of Āryadeva (LRCM: 650, 653-654, 778).

249. *Madhyamakāloka*, P5287: 46.1.5-6; with minor variation from the text as it appears there.

250. 'Jam-dbyangs-bzhad-pa (*mChan*: 170.3-4) says that the object arrived at upon the elimination of elaborations is a composite of appearance and emptiness. The phenomenon under analysis continues to appear along with its emptiness. Thus, this is a negation with a remainder, and therefore a conventional truth.

251. In other words, even though the actual terms "Svātantrika" and "Prāsaṅgika" as names of the two Mādhyamika schools are not found in Candrakīrti's *Prasanna-padā* (*Clear Words*), to separate these two terms out as names for the two schools is quite in accordance with the intent of the *Prasanna-padā* in that a large portion of that text focuses on a defense of Buddhapālita's use of consequences (*prasaṅga*) and a rejection of Bhāvaviveka's use of autonomous (*svatantra*) syllogisms as means for generating in a person a correct understanding of emptiness, and these are concerned with a primary difference in tenet between the two systems.

252. The full title is *Prajñā-nāma-mūla-madhyamaka-kārikā* (MMK) (*Fundamental Treatise on the Middle Way, Called "Wisdom"*). Both Tibetan abbreviations of the title (*rTsa ba shes rab* and *dBu ma'i bstan bcos*) are here rendered *Fundamental Treatise*.

Chapter Nine *The Stages of Entry into Reality*

253. *Prasanna-padā*, La Vallée Poussin 1970 (PPs): 340.3-13; de Jong 1978: 224; P5260: 52.5.5-8. *Madhyamakāvatāra* (MAV): 6.120, La Vallée Poussin 1970b: 233. Note that Tsong-kha-pa reads *gzhi* in place of *gyu* in the phrases referring to the aggregates as the basis of designation of the self.

254. PPs: 340.13-15, P5260: 53.1.1-4.

255. The qualm is that all that has been described is a state of removing the obstructions to liberation, or afflictive obscuration—karma and afflictions—which is achieved even by Hīnayānists, and no mention has been made of removing the obstructions to omniscience, or cognitive obscurations, which must be eliminated if one is to achieve Buddhahood. The second part of the qualm concerns the fact that all that is explicitly mentioned is realization of the selflessness of the person, whereas Mahāyānists must realize the selflessness of both persons and all other phenomena.

256. PPs: 345.13-346.3; D3796: Ha 112a4-7. MMK: 18.2ab (verse numbering follows de Jong 1977).

257. *Madhyamakāvatāra-bhāṣya* (MAVbh), La Vallée Poussin 1970b: 20.5-9; P5263: 111.2.3-4.

258. *Ratnāvalī* (Rā): 1.35ab, Hahn 1982: 14-15; Dunne and McClintock 1998: 14; P5658: 174.3.6-7.

259. *Buddhapālita-mūla-madhyamaka-vṛtti* (Bpālita) on MMK: 18.2, Lindtner 1981: 201; D3842: Tsa 240b2.

260. A *dngos po yod par smra ba*, "proponent of true existence," is usually abbreviated in Tibetan to *dngos smra ba*, and is rendered here throughout as "essentialist."

261. *Abhisamayālaṃkāra-vivṛtti*, P5191: 291.4.3-4.

Chapter Ten *Misidentifying the Object to Be Negated*

262. BCA: 9.140ab; P5272: 260.4.5. The word "entity" renders *dngos po, bhāva*.

263. SR: 9.23, Vaidya 1961: 47; P795: 283.5.1-2.

264. MAV: 6.31a, La Vallée Poussin 1970b: 112.18. Cited with an explanation at LRCM: 613.

265. MAV: 6.36, La Vallée Poussin 1970b: 122.14-17.

266. Referring to the so-called diamond slivers argument derived from the first chapter of Nāgārjuna's *Fundamental Treatise*.

267. MAV: 6.32d, La Vallée Poussin 1970b: 114.4.

268. *Yukti-ṣaṣṭikā* (YS): 60, Lindtner, 1982: 160; P5225: 12.2.5-6.

269. LRCM: 340-356.

270. LRCM: 579-582.

271. MMK: 24.1; D3824: Tsa 14b4.

272. *Vigraha-vyāvartanī* (VV): 1, Johnston and Kunst, 1990: 3; P5228: 14.3.5.

273. MMK: 24.13-14, de Jong 1977: 35; D3824: Tsa 15a3-4. Note that in 24.14 Nāgārjuna switches from using the terms *śūnya* ("empty") and *śūnyatā* ("emptiness") determined only by meter. Both are rendered in Tibetan as *stong pa nyid*.

274. PPs: 500.1-3; D3796: Ha 116a2-2. This is the transition passage between MMK: 24.13 and 24.14.

275. The twelve factors of dependent-arising are explained at LRCM: 257 (*Great Treatise* 2000: 324-25) and above at note 63.

276. MMK: 24.18-19, D3824: Tsa 15a6-7.

277. VV: 70 and concluding homage; P5228: 15.4.7-8. Johnston and Kunst 1990: 52-53. The concluding homage is also in *Vigraha-vyavārtinī-vṛtti* (VVv), P5232: 64.3.8-64.4.1. Tsong-kha-pa's reading *gang zhig stong dang rten 'byung dang* in place of *gang zhig stong dang rten 'byung dag* is supported by the Sanskrit and PPs: 504.15-16, where it says that emptiness, dependent designation, and middle path are different names for dependent-arising.

278. *Śūnyatā-saptati*: 68; P5227: 14.2.5-6; Lindtner 1982: 64. P5227 differs in wording from Nāgārjuna's *Śūnyatā-saptati-vṛtti* (*Commentary on the "Seventy Stanzas on Emptiness"*), P5231: 57.2.5. Tsong-kha-pa here cites the latter translation. Tsong-kha-pa apparently reads the text amending *kyis* to *kyi* in the second line and *de* to *phyir* in line three.

279. YS: 43-45; P5225: 12.1.1-2; Lindtner 1982: 114. In place of *de dag gis ni*, Tsong-kha-pa reads *gang dag gis ni*.

280. *Lokātīta-stava*: 21-22, Lindtner 1982: 134, 136; D1120: Ka 69a7-b1. The last two lines of verse 21 read *rgyu med rtog ge pa yis 'dod / khyod kyis rten cing 'brel bar gsungs* in place of Lindtner's *rgyu med par ni rtog ge 'dod/ khyod kyis brten nas 'byung bar gsungs*. In verse 22 the Tibetan translation of the Sanskrit that would literally be rendered *stong pa nyid* ("emptiness") is instead *stong pa* ("empty"; see note 273 above). Also in verse 22 *mnyam med* ("unequalled") is rendered following the Sanskrit, where it agrees in gender and number with "lion's roar" rather than following the Tibetan where it would modify "you."

281. MMK: 24.14, cited at LRCM: 584.

Chapter Eleven   *Dependent-Arising and Emptiness*

282. PPs: 500.5-501.8; PPd: 422.7-423.10; D3796: Ha 166a3-b3.

283. MMK: 24.14ab, de Jong 1977: 35. The Sanskrit adds a sentence: "This means that for that [system] in which an emptiness of intrinsic existence of all things is suitable, all these things mentioned above are suitable and agreeable."

284. LRCM: 583-584.

285. VV: 22; P5228: 14.5.4-5. Also, Johnston and Kunst 1990: 55.

286. VVv, Johnston and Kunst 1990: 55-56; P5232: 59.5.7-60.1.6.

287 The Tibetan omits a third example found in the Sanskrit—that a cart is able to carry wood, straw, and earth. The Tibetan *'o thug* ("soup") renders the Sanskrit *payas*.

288. MMK: 24.12, de Jong 1977: 35; D3824: Tsa 15a3.

289. Rā: 2.16-18, Hahn 1982: 46-47; Dunne and McClintock 1998: 27; P5658: 176.1.1-3.

290. MMK: 24.1, cited at LRCM: 583.

291. VV: 1; P5228: 14.3.5; cited above at LRCM: 583.

292. This is a paraphrase of PPs on MMK: 24.13-14, cited at LRCM: 587-588.

293. MAV: 6.37-38ab, La Vallée Poussin 1970b: 123.11-16.

294. MMK: 24.15-16, de Jong 1977: 35; D3824: Tsa 15a4-5.

295. MMK: 24.20, de Jong 1977: 35; D3824: Tsa 15a7. Cf. 24.1 cited at LRCM: 583.

296. *Bodhisattva-yoga-caryā-catuḥ-śataka-ṭīkā* (Cśṭ) on *Catuḥ-śataka* (Cś) 11.10, P5266: 249.1.6-8.

297. PPs: 329.10-17, on MMK: 17.30; D3796: Ha 109a5-b2.

298. Cśṭ leading into Cś 14.23, P5266: 270.3.3-6.

299. "Thing," *dngos po, bhāva*; "intrinsic existence," *rang bzhin, svabhāva*; "the capacity to perform a function," *don byed nus pa, artha-kriyā-śakti*.

300. Cśṭ on Cś 11.25, P5266: 252.3.6-4.3.

301. VV: 26cd; P5228: 14.5.7-8. Also, Johnston and Kunst 1990: 59; Lindtner 1982: 79.

302. The Tibetan verb "to be" takes two forms, one ontological—"exists" (*yod pa*) and "does not exist" (*med pa*)—and one linking—"is" (*yin*) and "is not" (*min*). Some might try to claim

that the rule of two negatives making a positive and the equivalency of "not is" (*ma yin*) and "is not" (*min*) is true of the linking form but not of the ontological. Tsong-kha-pa rejects this, saying that the same rules apply to both.

303. MMK: 15.10, de Jong 1977: 20; D3824: Tsa 9a2-3.

304. PPs: 273.4-9; D3796: Ha 92b2-4. The passage begins immediately following Candrakīrti's citation of the last two lines of MMK: 15.10. The stanza cited within the passage is MMK: 15.11.

305. Bpālita, D3842: Tsa 226a6: "To explain the way in which the fallacy of having views of permanence and annihilation is entailed if one views existence and nonexistence...."

306. MMK: 24.11ab, de Jong 1977: 35; D3824: Tsa 15a2.

307. PPs: 495.12-496.9; D3796: Ha 164b4-7. Rā: 2.19, Hahn 1982: 46-47; Dunne and McClintock 1998: 19-20; P5658: 176.1.3. The Sanskrit differs in part from the Tibetan translation.

308. Rā: 2.20, Hahn 1982: 47; Dunne and McClintock 1998: 20; P5658: 176.1.3-4.

309. MMK: 15.11cd, de Jong 1977: 20; D3824: Tsa 9a3.

310. PPs: 495.3-5; PPd: 418.2-6; D3796: Ha 164a6-7.

311. Tib. *rgyang pan pa*. On Lokāyata/Cārvāka materialists, or nihilists, see Hopkins 1983: 149-150, 327-333.

312. PPs: 368.4-12, on MMK: 18.7-8; D3796: Ha 117b4-118a1.

313. 'Jam-dbyangs-bzhad-pa (*mChan*: 267.2) suggests that the phrase "regard... as naturally existent" (*rang bzhin gyis dmigs*) means "causelessly" (*rgyu med par*), alluding to the Lokāyata position that phenomena arise from their own natures.

314. PPs: 368.13-15; PPd: 302.17-303.1; D3796: Ha 118a1.

315. Cf. LRCM: 598-599.

316. PPs: 368.16-369.4; D3796: Ha 118a2-6.

317. Cṣṭ on Cś: 15.10ab; P5266: 272.2.7-272.3.1.

318. Bpālita, D3842: Tsa 255b.3-4.

Chapter Twelve *Rational Analysis*

319. Cṣṭ on Cś: 13.11, P5266: 261.3.3-4; cited more fully at LRCM: 611.18. This passage from Candrakīrti is the dGe-lugs-pa tradition's primary Indian source for the fact that ultimate analysis is not seeking mere objects but intrinsically existent ones.

320. Geshe Palden Drakpa explains that another way of expressing this is that this reasoning is analyzing whether or not phenomena are established as they appear (*snang ba ltar tu grub ma grub*).

321. Cṣṭ on Cś: 13.21, P5266: 263.2.4-6.

322. 'Jam-dbyangs-bzhad-pa (*mChan*: 283.5) identifies the "earlier scholars" as the great translator Blo-ldan-shes-rab and Phya-ba. Zhwa-dmar: 76.1-3 mentions rNgog, i.e., Blo-ldan-shes-rab; Phya-ba-chos-kyi-seng-ge; and Gro-lung-pa-chen-po.

323. MAV: 6.83; La Vallée Poussin 1970b: 180.15.

324. MAVbh, La Vallée Poussin 1970b: 180.20-181.3; P5263: 133.5.3-4.

325. Tsong-kha-pa is arguing that you cannot reduce the meaning of "in conventional terms" to "for the uneducated." Zhwa-dmar: 77.2-6.

326. Cśṭ on Cś: 15.10, P5266: 272.3.8-272.4.2.

327. Cśṭ on Cś: 13.11, P5266: 261.3.2-5. Partially cited at LRCM: 607.

328. That is, you should distinguish the mere object, which is not refuted, from the object's intrinsic existence, which is refuted.

329. PPs: 69.1-5; PPd: 54.8-14; D3796: Ha 23b1-3.

Chapter Thirteen *Valid Establishment*

330. MAV: 6.31a, cited at LRCM: 581.

331. MAVbh on MAV: 6.30, La Vallée Poussin 1970b: 111.18-112.7; P5263: 124.4.4-6.

332. MAVbh on MAV: 6.31b, La Vallée Poussin 1970b: 112.13-19; P5263: 124.4.8-124.5.2.

333. *Yukti-ṣaṣṭikā-vṛtti* (YSv): 3; P5265: 172.4.5-7. The sūtra passage is SR: 9.23, cited at LRCM: 581.3.

334. Cśṭ on Cś: 13.1, P5266: 259.4.1-4.

335. Cśṭ on Cś: 13.1, P5266: 259.1.2-5.

336. LRCM: 619-621.

337. Cśṭ on Cś: 13.12, P5266: 261.5.7-262.1.1.

338. Quotation from *Commentary on the "Four Hundred Stanzas,"* cited at LRCM: 614-615.

339. PPs: 75.9; P5260: 13.4.7-8.

340. PPs: 75.10-11; P5260: 13.5.1.

341. MAV: 6.24-25, La Vallée Poussin 1970b: 103-104; P5262: 101.5.5-7.

342. MAVbh on MAV: 6.25, La Vallée Poussin 1970b: 104.8-10; P5263: 123.3.8-123.4.1.

343. Tsong-kha-pa, in *dGongs-pa-rab-gsal* (Dharamsala ed., 200.4), glosses *da du ra* as *thang phrom/thang khrom*. Das (1985: 568) says this is *dhūstūra*, or thorn-apple (*Datura stramonium*). Hubert Decleer reports that *dadhura* is a tall plant with white flowers that grows wild in Nepal. In small amounts it is a potent hallucinogen; in larger amounts it is poisonous.

344. MAVbh on MAV 6.25, La Vallée Poussin 1970b: 104.10-19; P5263: 123.4.1-4.

345. P5253: 253.4.6-7.

346. P5259: 292.2.8-292.3.2.

347. Sn: 7.3, Lamotte 1935: 67-70; P774: 9.3.7-9.4.4; also 11.2.5-11.3.3.

348. *Madhyamakāloka*, D388: Sa 146a1-155a4. The three naturelessnesses are naturelessness in terms of character, naturelessness in terms of production, and ultimate naturelessness.

349. Tsong-kha-pa is paraphrasing MAVbh, La Vallée Poussin 1970b: 201.7-202.2; P5263: 136.4.7-136.5.4.

350. MAV: 6.97bc, La Vallée Poussin 1970b: 199.14-15; P5262: 103.3.4-5.

351. Tsong-kha-pa is paraphrasing the *Madhyamaka-hṛdaya-vṛtti-tarka-jvālā*, P5256: 94.5.1-2.

352. Ibid.; paraphrase of P5256: 94.5.3-7.

353. LRCM: 617-619.

354. MAVbh, La Vallée Poussin 1970b: 406.14-407.3; P5263: 166.2.3-6.

355. Cṣṭ on Cś: 14.18; P5266: 268.3.1.

356. Cṣṭ, P5266: 259.2.1-8.

357. Cited at LRCM: 615.

358. MAVbh on MAV: 6.28, La Vallée Poussin 1970b: 107.11-17; P5263: 124.1.2-3.

359. MAV: 6.25, cited at LRCM: 618.

360. MAV: 6.28.

361. MAVbh, cited at LRCM: 624.

Chapter Fourteen *Conventional Existence*

362. According to theistic Sāṃkhyas, the supreme god initiates and oversees the creation of the world out of "fundamental nature" (*rang bzhin, prakṛti*), otherwise known as "primal essence" (*spyi gtso bo, pradhāna*).

363. MAV 6.26, La Vallée Poussin 1970b: 105.9-12; P5262: 101.5.7-8.

364. From Bhāvaviveka. See note 352 at LRCM: 621-622.

365. YSv on YS: 7b; P5265: 173.4.2-3.

366. "Eight" refers to the four errors—seeing cyclic existence as permanent, blissful, pure, and having self—and the four proper conceptions of these things as impermanent, suffering, impure, and devoid of self. See LRCM: 98 (*Great Treatise* 2000: 145); Hopkins 1983: 292-96.

367. MAV: 6.28, La Vallée Poussin 1970b: 107.1-3; D3796: Ha 205b2.

368. This paragraph is mainly a paraphrase of MAVbh on MAV: 6.28, La Vallée Poussin 1970b: 108.2-6. The phrase in quotation marks is a direct quote.

369. Cṣṭ on Cś: 4.10; P5266: 220.1.6-7.

370. The "performance class" (*spyod phyogs*) refers to method—compassion and skillful means—as distinct from the "emptiness/view class" (*stong phyogs, lta phyogs*).

Chapter Fifteen *Production Is Not Refuted*

371. MAV: 6.115, La Vallée Poussin 1970b: 228.1-4; P5262: 103.5.7.

372. MAV: 6.114, La Vallée Poussin 1970b: 226.6-9; P5262: 103.5.6-7.

373. MAV: 6.36a-c, La Vallée Poussin 1970b: 122.14-16; P5262: 102.1.8, cited at LRCM: 581.

374. MAVbh on MAV: 6.36, La Vallée Poussin 1970b: 122.9-13; P5263: 126.1.1-2.

375. MAVbh on MAV: 6.36c, La Vallée Poussin 1970b: 123.1-3; P5263: 126.1.4.

376. MAV: 6.111, La Vallée Poussin 1970b: 221.20-222.3; P5262: 103.5.3-4.

377. YS: 48cd, Lindtner 1982: 114; P5225: 12.1.5.

378. YSv, D3864: Ya 26b6-27a2.

379. *Anavatapta-nāga-rāja-paripṛcchā-sūtra*, P823: 139.3.6. Wayman 1978 gives the title as *Anavatapta-hradāpasaṃkramaṇa-sūtra*. 'Jam-dbyangs-bzhad-pa (*mChan*: 368.4) glosses "diligent" (*bag yod*) as "abiding in a path of liberation" (*thar lam la gnas pa*).

380. *Laṅkāvatāra-sūtra*, D107: Ca 107a2, cited at PPs: 504.5-6; P5260: 42.4.8.

381. LRCM: 666-672.

382. LRCM: 675, 680-681.

383. Cf. LRCM: 597.16.

384. MMK: 13.7, de Jong 1977: 13; D3824: Tsa 8a6.

385. If the mind of ultimate analysis that finds that there is no essence in the seedling were also to think, "Now here is something that does exist, the absence of intrinsic existence," then the absence of intrinsic existence would itself be withstanding ultimate analysis. In that case, emptiness would itself be intrinsically existent.

386. Cṣṭ on Cṣ: 16.7; P5266: 276.3.2-4.

387. VV: 26; P5228: 14.5.7-8. Also, Johnston and Kunst 1990: 59; Lindtner 1982: 79; cited in part above at LRCM: 599.

388. VVv on VV: 26; P5232: 60.3.5-8. Also, Johnston and Kunst 1990: 59. The objector supposes that only things that have intrinsic nature can function. Nāgārjuna has argued that all things, even his own words, lack intrinsic nature. The objector argues that without intrinsic nature Nāgārjuna's words would be unable to function as a refutation of intrinsic nature, and thus intrinsic nature would remain.

389. MMK: 13.7, cited at LRCM: 638.

390. MMK: 13.8, de Jong 1977: 13; D3824: Tsa 8a6.

391. Bpālita on MMK: 13.8; P5242: 101.4.7-101.5.2.

392. PPs: 247.4, on MMK: 13.8.

393. *Prajñāpāramitā-ratna-guṇa-sañcaya-gāthā*, Conze 1973: 10; P735: 187.1.7.

394. Rā: 2.3, Hahn 1982: 41; Dunne and McClintock 1998: 25; P5658: 175.4.7-8; cited at PPs: 369.2-6.

395. *Prajñāpāramitā-hṛdaya-sūtra*, D21: Ka 145a4-5.

396. *Prajñāpāramitā-ratna-guṇa-sañcaya-gāthā*, Conze 1973: 12; P735: 187.4.1.

397. MAV: 6.165cd, La Vallée Poussin 1970b: 287.18-19; P5262: 105.1.2-3.

398. Cṣṭ on Cṣ: 12.13a; P5266: 256.2.5-256.3.3.

399. Wayman 1978: 463 n. 178—following Gadjin Nagao, *A Study of Tibetan Buddhism* [in Japanese] (Tokyo, 1954), note 141—says this text is not available in Sanskrit or Tibetan, but exists in Chinese as *gāthā* set attributed to Nāgārjuna.

Chapter Sixteen *Not Negating Enough*

400. MMK: 15.1-2, de Jong 1977: 19; P5224: 6.3.1-2.

401. The "two selves" are the self of persons and the self of phenomena.

402. MAV: 6.140, La Vallée Poussin 1970b: 264.2-5; P5262: 104.3.4-5.

403. MAVbh on MAV: 6.141, La Vallée Poussin 1970b: 264.9-14; P5263: 145.3.8-145.4.1. MAV: 6.141 is found in the *Subhāṣita-saṃgraha ("Compendium of Eloquent Sayings")* edited by Cecil Bendall (1903 and 1904) and cited by Wayman (1978: 464 n. 183).

404. LRCM: 643.

405. 'Jam-dbyangs-bzhad-pa (*mChan*: 394.4) states that this is found in a Perfection of Wisdom sūtra. It is found in the *Daśa-bhūmika-sūtra (Sūtra on the Ten Levels)* (Wayman 1978: 464 n. 186).

406. MAVbh, La Vallée Poussin 1970b: 305.19-306.12; P5263: 151.2.3-7.

407. Wayman 1978: 464 n. 185 says this is in the *Daśa-bhūmika-sūtra.*

408. PPs: 263.5-264.4, on MMK: 15.2; P5260: 42.5.6-43.1.1.

409. MAVbh on MAV: 182, La Vallée Poussin 1970b: 308.6-9; P5263: 151.4.1-2.

410. 'Jam-dbyangs-bzhad-pa (*mChan*: 400.1) glosses *glo bur* ("incidental") with *tha snyad du* ("conventionally").

411. MAVbh, La Vallée Poussin 1970b: 307.9-308.5; P5263: 151.3.4-151.4.1.

412. LRCM: 594-596.

413. PPs: 265.3-4, on MMK: 15.2; P5260: 43.1.6-7.

414. P5260: 43.1.8-43.2.1.

415. On the Madhyamaka "collections of arguments" (*dbu ma rigs tshogs*) see note 248 above to LRCM: 570.

Chapter Seventeen *The Actual Object to Be Negated*

416. *Madhyānta-vibhāga* 2.17, Lindtner 1982: 85; P5522: 20.2.6-7.

417. VV: 27; P5228: 14.5.8. Also, Johnston and Kunst 1990: 59-60.

418. VVv, P5232: 60.4.1-4. Also, Johnston and Kunst 1990: 59-60.

419. VV: 64; P5228: 15.4.3.

420. VVv, P5232: 63.4.8-63.5.7. Also, Johnston and Kunst 1990: 132.

421. P5260: 91.5.3-6. On the Sanskrit for this passage, which is not in La Vallée Poussin's edition of the *Prasanna-padā*, see Wayman 1978: 465 n. 201.

422. Cṣṭ on Cś: 14.25, P5266: 270.5.7-271.1.3.

423. Cṣṭ on Cś: 6.10, P5266: 220.1.5-6.

424. Cf. LRCM: 235 (*Great Treatise* 2000: 300-01), where Tsong-kha-pa gives a Cittamātra explanation of ignorance as distinct from and prior to the view of the perishing aggregates.

425. LRCM: 655 on Cś: 14.25.

426. MAVbh on MAV: 6.28, La Vallée Poussin 1970b: 107.5-8; P5263: 123.5.8-124.1.1.

427. MAVbh, La Vallée Poussin 1970b: 107.17-19; P5263: 124.1.3-4.

428. LRCM: 766-767. For the twelve factors, see LRCM: 249-257 (*Great Treatise* 2000: 315-25).

429. Rā: 35b, cited at LRCM: 577.

430. *Śūnyatā-saptati*: 64-65; Lindtner, 1982: 62-65; P5227: 14.2.2-4.

431. MMK: 26.11-12, de Jong 1977: 41; P5224: 10.3.5-6.

432. Cited at LRCM: 577, 656.

433. Cited at LRCM: 655. Here the wording of the second citation differs.

434. Bpālita, P5242: 73.5.6-74.1.2.

435. Bpālita on MMK: 26.1, P5242: 126.5.6-7.

436. Bpālita on MMK: 27.1, P5242: 127.3.3-4.

437. Cś: 26.23cd, Lang 1986: 150; P5246: 140.2.3.

438. Cśṭ on Cś: 26.23cd; P5266: 279.1.3.

439. Cś: 8.7, Lang 1986: 80; P5246: 136.2.4-5.

440. Cś: 14.23cd, Lang 1986: 134; P5246: 139.2.7-8.

441. Cśṭ, P5266: 270.3.6-7.

442. Ibid., P5266: 229.5.5-6.

443. Ibid., P5266: 256.1.7-256.2.1.

444. MAV, P5262: 104.1.3 and MAVbh, P5263: 141.2.7.

445. MAVbh on MAV: 6.120, P5263: 141.2.3.

446. Ibid., P5263: 141.2.7-8.

447. LRCM: 613ff, 626.

448. Cśṭ, P5266: 265.1.3-5.

449. MAVbh on MAV: 6.173; Conze 1990: 196; La Vallée Poussin 1970b: 295.8-16; P5263: 149.5.1-4.

450. *Śūnyatā-saptati*: 1, Lindtner 1982: 34; P5227: 13.1.5-6.

451. Rā: 1.28ab and 1.29cd, Hahn 12-13; Dunne and McClintock 1998: 13; P5658: 174.3.1-3.

452. Rā: 2.11, Hahn 1982: 44-45; Dunne and McClintock 1998: 26; P5658: 175.5.5.

453. Bpālita on MMK: 24.8, P5242: 122.5.4-8.

454. YSv: P5265: 182.1.7-182.2.1. In this and the following citations Tsong-kha-pa is either giving a gloss of the text, or, more likely, using a different translation.

455. Ibid., P5265: 182.2.1.

456. Ibid., P5265: 182.1.4.

457. MAV: 6.93cd; P5262: 103.3.1-2.

458. MAV: 6.113; P5262: 103.5.5-6.

459. MAVbh on MAV: 6.12, La Vallée Poussin 1970b: 86.11-15; P5263: 121.1.6-7.

460. *Madhyamaka-hṛdaya*: 3.26, P5255: 4.2.5-6.

461. *Tarka-jvālā*, P5256: 27.3.1-4.

462. Ibid., P5256: 27.5.6-28.1.1.

463. *Madhyamakāloka*, cf. P5287: 83.5.1-4.

464. *Madhyamakālaṃkāra-pañjikā*, P5286: 16.5.5-8.

465. *Prajñā-pradīpa-mūla-madhyamaka-vṛtti*, P5253: 210.2.3-4.

466. Ibid., P5253: 210.2.4-5. Tsong-kha-pa has omitted an intervening line from 210.2.5-6 and pulled up from 210.2.6 the concluding phrase "we have no fault."

467. Ibid., P5253: 211.1.1-2.

468. 'Jam-dbyangs-bzhad-pa (*mChan*: 465.1-2) says that being produced indicates that things depend on causes and conditions.

Chapter Eighteen *Misinterpretations of the Svātantrika/Prāsaṅgika Distinction*

469. MMK: 1.1, de Jong 1977: 1.

470. The editors have added subheadings for each of the four misinterpretations in this section.

471. *Madhyamakāvatara-ṭīkā*, P5271: 121.5.3.

472. Ibid., P5271: 121.5.8-122.1.5.

473. The three criteria (*tshul gsum*) of a correct sign. In Buddhist logic, a correct reason must meet three criteria: (1) the presence of the reason in the subject, or its bearing on the subject. This is the "minor premise" of a syllogism. Of the two types of pervasion, the forward pervasion is the major premise and the counter-pervasion is its contrapositive, which corresponds to the minor premise; (2) the forward pervasion, which corresponds to the major premise; and (3) the reverse pervasion, which corresponds to the contrapositive of the major premise.

474. As an example of a follower of Jayānanda who advocates this view, 'Jam-dbyangs-bzhad-pa (*mChan*: 473.4) mentions the translator Khu mDo-sde-'bar (Do-day-bar), a teacher of Madhyamaka who flourished in the latter half of the eleventh century.

475. 'Jam-dbyangs-bzhad-pa (*mChan*: 477.3) says it is asserted by certain Tibetans.

476. VV: 29-30; P5228: 15.1.1-2. Also, Johnston and Kunst 1990: 113-15.

477. YS: 50, P5225: 12.1.6.

478. Cś: 16.25, Lang 1986: 150-51; P5246: 140.2.4-5.

479. PPs: 16; D3796: Ha 6a1-2.

480. Ibid.; D3796: Ha 6a2.

481. MAV: 6.173, La Vallée Poussin 1970b: 294; D3861: Ha 212b7-213a1.

482. MAV: 6.81, La Vallée Poussin 1970b: 179; D3861: Ha 208a3.

483. VV: 64; P5228: 15.4.2-3.

484. While Tsong-kha-pa does not list this as a separate system, 'Jam-dbyangs-bzhad-pa (*mChan*: 480.5) identifies this as the view of rMa-bya Byang-chub-brtson-'grus (Map-cha Chang-chub-tsön-dru) and other followers of Pa-tshab Nyi-ma-grags (Ba-tsap Nyi-ma-drag).

485. This renders *dngos po'i stobs zhugs kyi tshad ma.*

Chapter Nineteen *Refuting Misinterpretations of the Svātantrika/ Prāsaṅgika Distinction*

486. LRCM: 652-653.

487. PPs: 501-502; D3796: Ḥa 166b4-5.

488. MAV: 6.147cd, La Vallée Poussin 1970b: 259; D3861: Ḥa 211b2.

489. MAV: 6.81, La Vallée Poussin 1970b:179; D3861: Ḥa 208a3. The first two lines are:
     Real dependent phenomena such as you accept,
     I will not assert even as conventional entities.
     I say they exist for the effect....

490. This is a paraphrase of MAVbh on MAV: 80-81, La Vallée Poussin 1970b: 178.17-179.1; D3861: Ḥa 275b4-6.

491. VV: 29, cited at LRCM: 677.

492. For the three criteria of a correct reason, see note 473.

493. Below, at LRCM: 695ff

494. LRCM: 583, 588-589.

495. VV: 30; P5228: 15.1.1-2; cited at LRCM: 677.

496. PPs: 75.10-11; P5260: 13.5.1, cited at LRCM: 617.

497. VV: 6; P5228: 14.3.6-7. Also, Johnston and Kunst 1990: 99-100.

498. VVv, D3832: Ḥa 122b5-7; Johnston and Kunst 1990: 99-100.

499. Cś: 16.25, cited at LRCM: 677, 689.

500. MAVbh, La Vallée Poussin 1970b: 297.11; P5263: 150.1.4-5.

501. LRCM: 637ff.

502. YSv (D3864: Ya 27b7-28a1) on YS as cited at LRCM: 677.

503. YSv (D3864: Ya 26a5-6) on YS: 47; P5225: 12.1.3-4.

504. PPs: 16, on MMK: 1; D3796: Ḥa 6a2-4.

505. VV, cited at LRCM: 678.

506. VVv on VV: 30; Johnston and Kunst 1990: 114-15; P5232: 63.4.5-6.

507. VV: 23; P5228: 14.5.5-6; Johnston and Kunst 1990: 108.

508. VV: 66-67, D3828: Tsa 29a4; Johnston and Kunst 1990: 133.

509. PPs, cited at LRCM: 677, note 480.

510. MAV: 6.173, cited at LRCM: 677, note 481.

511. MAVbh on MAV: 6.173, La Vallée Poussin 1970b: 295.8ff; P5263: 149.5.4-6.

512. *Pañca-viṃsati-sāhasrikā-prajñāpāramitā*, Conze 1990: 196, cited at LRCM: 666.

513. MAVbh, P5263: 149.5.4-6.

514. Ibid., P5263: 149.5.7ff.

515. 'Jam-dbyangs-bzhad-pa (*mChan*: 516.1-2) explains that from an essentialist perspective,

an argument refuting intrinsic nature is improper (*'thad pa dang bral*) because it does not prove the existence of an intrinsically existent object.

516. MAVbh, P5263: 149.2.6-3.2.

517. VV: 28; P5228: 15.1.1. Also, Johnston and Kunst 1990: 111.

518. YS: 8, P5225: 11.2.8-11.3.1.

519. *Lokātīta-stava*, D1120: Ka 68b6-69a7. The last stanza is cited in full at LRCM: 586.

520. MAVbh, P5263: 147.4.5-6, 147.2.8-147.3.1.

521. Ibid., P5263: 120.3.2-3.

522. LRCM: 619-626.

523. For the three criteria see note 473. Other-centered (*gzhan don*) argument (*rjes dpag*)—Tsong-kha-pa uses the word loosely to refer to reasoning—and reasons based on fact are explained at length at LRCM: 696ff.

Chapter Twenty *Our Interpretation of the Svātantrika/Prāsaṅgika Distinction*

524. PPs: 28.4-29; D3796: Ha 9a7-b3.

525. Sāṃkhyas believe that since effects already exist in their causes, effects become manifest rather than produced anew. See Hopkins 1983: 442.

526. PPs: 29.7-30; D3796: Ha 9b3-10a1.

527. VV: 30; P5228: 15.1.1-2; cited above at LRCM: 677 and explained at LRCM: 687ff.

528. PPs: 30.12-14; D3796: Ha 10a1-2.

529. See note 473.

530. LRCM: 594-596.

531. LRCM: 617-619.

532. LRCM: 596-604.

533. LRCM: 617-619.

534. Cśṭ, cited at LRCM: 659.

535. Cittamātrins are divided into Satyākāravādin and Alīkākāravādin. Unlike the latter, the former assert that the form (*rnam pa*) of the blue in the eye-consciousness perceiving blue is real.

536. The eye itself is not a hidden phenomenon. Tsong-kha-pa is referring to the visual sensory faculty (*skye mched*, *āyatana*) of the eye, the subject that Bhāvaviveka uses in his example of what a correct syllogism should be; cf. Hopkins 1983: 456.

537. LRCM: 619.

538. PPs: 30.15-16; D3796: Ha 10a2-3.

539. PPs: 31.1-5; D3796: Ha 10a3-5.

540. The word "logician" has been supplied from the citation at LRCM: 707.

541. LRCM: 696-697.

542. In this difficult passage (LRCM: 710.2-7), lines 2-4 restate a version of Bhāvaviveka's analysis that Tsong-kha-pa *is* comfortable with (cf. *mChan*: 568.1, where 'Jam-dbyangs-bzhad-pa inserts the word '*thad pa*); *gyi* (second syllable in line 710.4) is *disjunctive*, indicating the shift from wording Tsong-kha-pa will accept to what he will not accept; and *bden gnyis kyis* (710.4) means "*in terms of the two truths*" which here, as often, means "conventionally or ultimately." It does *not* mean "which of the two truths."

543. LRCM: 707.

544. Cited at LRCM: 698. In fact (see 'Jam-dbyangs-bzhad-pa, *mChan*: 569.3-4), Bhāvaviveka does not accept this explicitly; instead he thinks that his reasons refer to objects posited by non-mistaken perceptions.

545. Cited at LRCM: 708.

546. VV, cited at LRCM: 677; PPs, cited in notes 340 and 496.

Chapter Twenty-one *Our Critique of Svātantrika Does Not Hurt Our Own Arguments*

547. MMK: 3.2, de Jong 1977: 5.

548. PPs: 34.6-10; D3796: Ha 11a4.

549. PPs: 34.10ff; D3796: Ha 11a4-7.

550. LRCM: 711-712.

551. Bpālita, D3842: Tsa 175a2-b3.

552. Cś: 13.15, Lang 1986: 122-23; D3846: Tsha 14a7.

553. Cś: 14.16, Lang 1986: 130-31; D3846: Tsha 15b7.

554. The previously posited syllogism (LRCM: 714) is: The eye does not essentially see other things because it does not see itself.

555. PPs: 34.13-35; D3796: Ha 11b1-3.

556. PPs: 35.5-36; D3796: Ha 11b3-6.

Chapter Twenty-two *Analyzing a Chariot*

557. MAVbh on MAV: 6.135, La Vallée Poussin 1970b: 257-58; P5263: 144.4.4-5. 'Jam-dbyangs-bzhad-pa (*mChan*: 594.6) adds that Bhāvaviveka also cites this non-Mahāyāna sūtra.

558. MAV: 6.151, La Vallée Poussin 1970b: 271-72; D3861: Ha 211b4-5.

559. MAV: 6.152, La Vallée Poussin 1970b: 272; D3861: Ha 211b5.

560. Cf. MAV: 6.135cd (La Vallée Poussin 1970b: 258), "It says that the self is imputed in dependence upon the aggregates. Therefore, the mere collection of the aggregates is not the self," and MAV: 6.138-139 (La Vallée Poussin 1970b: 262), "Since the Sage taught that the self depends upon the six elements... and six bases... the self is none of these either individually or collectively...."

561. MAV: 6.153, La Vallée Poussin1970b: 273; D3861: Ha 211b6.

562. MAV: 6.154, La Vallée Poussin 1970b: 274; D3861: Ha 211b6-7.

563. MAV: 6.155, La Vallée Poussin 1970b: 274; D3861: Ha 211b7.

564. LRCM: 720.

565. MAV: 6.156, La Vallée Poussin 1970b: 275; D3861: Ha 211b7-212a1.

566. Vaibhāṣikas say that the gross objects of the material world are ultimately constituted of extremely subtle particles that are "directionally partless" inasmuch as they lack an east side and a west side, a top and a bottom, and so forth. However, these particles are only *directionally* partless, and not utterly partless, because each is an aggregate particle including at least eight substance particles: earth, water, fire, air, form, smell, taste, and touch.

567. MAV: 6.157, La Vallée Poussin 1970b: 275-76; D3861: Ha 212a1-2.

568. MAV: 6.158, La Vallée Poussin 1970b: 277; D3861: Ha 212a2-3.

569. MAV: 6.161ab, La Vallée Poussin 1970b: 280; D3861: Ha 212a4.

570. MAV: 6.161cd, La Vallée Poussin 1970b: 280; D3861: Ha 212a4-5.

571. MAVbh on MAV: 6.159a-c, La Vallée Poussin 1970b: 278; P5263: 147.3.1-2.

572. LRCM: 722.

573. MAV: 6.159d, La Vallée Poussin 1970b: 278; D3861: Ha 212a3.

574. MAVbh on MAV: 6.160, La Vallée Poussin 1970b: 279; P5263: 147.3.8-147.4.2.

575. Cṣṭ, P5266: 264.1.3-5, 265.3.2.

Chapter Twenty-three *The Person Lacks Intrinsic Nature*

576. The "man-in-the-moon" looks like a rabbit in silhouette to Indians and Tibetans.

577. MMK: 27.5, de Jong 1977: 41; D3824: Tsa 18a1.

578. MAV: 6.127ab, La Vallée Poussin 1970b: 245; D3861: Ha 210b1-2.

579. MMK: 18.1ab, de Jong 1977: 24; D3824: Tsa 10b6.

580. MMK: 27.6ab, de Jong 1977: 41; D3824: Tsa 18a1-2.

581. *Laṅkāvatāra-sūtra*, Suzuki 1932: 122.

582. In the *Brahma-jāla-sūtra* (the first section of the *Dīgha Nikāya*), sixty-two wrong views are explained. Of these, the first eighteen are based on theories about the past and the first four of these are eternalist views. In the first of these, an ascetic concludes that the self and world are eternal, based on memories of many past existences.

583. MMK: 27.3, de Jong 1977: 41, D3824: Tsa 17b7.

584. LRCM: 735ff.

585. MAV: 6.128b-d, La Vallée Poussin 1970b: 247; D3861: Ha 210b2.

586. MMK: 27.10-11, de Jong 1977: 42; D3824: Tsa 18a3-4.

587. MAV: 6.129ab, La Vallée Poussin 1970b: 249; D3861: Ha 210b3.

588. MAV: 6.61, La Vallée Poussin 1970b: 154; D3861: Ha 207a3-4.

589. MMK: 27.16cd, de Jong 1977: 42; D3824: Tsa 18a6-7. Yet humans can be reborn as deities and *vice versa*.

590. Geshe Yeshay Tapkay (oral communication) and Geshe Thupten Jinpa (private correspondence) explain that it was a common belief in India that this happens. It was not regarded as a paranormal phenomenon.

591. Cṣṭ on Cś: 10.7, Lang 1986: 96-97; P5266: 242.5.8-243.1.4.

592. MMK: 27.6cd, de Jong 1977: 41; D3824: Tsa 18a2.

593. MMK: 10.1ab, 10.15, de Jong 1977: 14-15; D3824: Tsa 6b6; 7a6.

594. MAV: 6.137ab, La Vallée Poussin 1970b: 259; D3861: Ha 211a1-2.

595. MMK: 18.1cd, de Jong 1977: 24; D3824: Tsa 10a6.

596. A paraphrase of PPs: 343.5-6; D3796: Ha 111a7-b3.

597. Bpālita on MMK: 18.1; D3824: Tsa 240a6-7.

598. MMK: 27.7, de Jong 1977: 41; D3824: Tsa 18a2.

599. MAV: 6.124ab, La Vallée Poussin 1970b: 242; D3861: Ha 210a6-7.

600. MAV: 6.31b, explained at LRCM: 614ff.

601. That is, ordinary direct perception does not get at emptiness, but emptiness can be logically deduced from what is observable to the ordinary person.
On the Pramāṇa school that begins with Dignaga and Dharmakirti, see Dreyfus 1997.

602. LRCM: 721.

603. MAV: 6.142, La Vallée Poussin 1970b: 265; D3861: Ha 211a5.

604. MAV: 6.143, La Vallée Poussin 1970b: 266; D3861: Ha 211a5-6.

605. MAV: 6.135cd, La Vallée Poussin 1970b: 258; D3861: Ha 210a7; MAVbh, P5263: 144.5.3-4.

606. MAV: 6.136, La Vallée Poussin 1970b: 259; D3861: Ha 211a1.

607. 'Jam-dbyangs-bzhad-pa (*mChan*: 657.2) glosses this as "pandits and translators during the time of kings and ministers."

608. LRCM: 579-580.

609. Cṣṭ on Cś: 15.10, P5266: 272.3.7-272.4.2.

610. It would be an error to claim that a pot, for example, is found under ultimate analysis. The pot is not found at all by such a reasoning consciousness. However, this does not mean that the pot does not exist. When the pot later appears to a person who has realized its emptiness, that person will come to an understanding of the pot's illusoriness.

611. Cṣṭ on Cś: 15.25, P5266: 274.4.3-4.

612. LRCM: 587-606, etc.

613. SR, D127: Da 96a2-5. 'Jam-dbyangs-bzhad-pa (*mChan*: 665.3-6) says living beings and so forth are like foam (i.e., water bubbles), because they appear by happenstance and are destroyed by very slight conditions; they are like plantain trees, because when analyzed they lack pith; like illusions, because they appear in a variety of ways but are empty of whatever appears; like lightning, because they appear and vanish in an instant; like a moon

in water, because they appear to go from one life to another, but do not really do so; and like a mirage, because they seem to exist intrinsically as resources, but do not.

614. Cś: 8.16, Lang 1986: 82-83; D3846: Tsha 9b6.

615. MAV: 6.113ab, La Vallée Poussin 1970b: 223; D3861: Ḥa 209a6.

616. MAV: 6.26cd; cited at LRCM: 627.

617. SR: 9.11-17 and 9.19-22, D127: Da 26a6-b4.

618. MAV: 6.162, La Vallée Poussin 1970b: 281; D3861: Ḥa 212a5

619. LRCM: 763-768.

620. MMK: 18.2ab, de Jong 1977: 24; D3824: Tsa 10b6.

621. MAV: 6.165, La Vallée Poussin 1970b: 287; D3861: Ḥa 212a7.

Chapter Twenty-four *Objects Lack Intrinsic Nature*

622. The *Trisaṃvara-nirdeśa-parivarta-sūtra* is section 1 of the *Ratna-kūṭa*, D45: Ka 9b5.

623. MAV: 6.166-167, La Vallée Poussin 1970b: 288-89; D3861: Ḥa 212a7-b2.

624. MMK: 8.12, 8.13cd, de Jong 1977: 12; D3824: Tsa 6a6.

625. LRCM: 719-751.

626. SR, D127: Da 44a2-3.

627. MMK: 1.1, cited at LRCM: 672.

628. This and the following bracketed headings have been added by the editors and do not occur in the text.

629. MMK: 20.20ab, de Jong 1977: 28; D3824: Tsa 12a4.

630. MAV: 6.8cd-6.9ab, 6.12cd, La Vallée Poussin 1970b: 82-83; D3861: Ḥa 204a6-7.

631. The four conditions are causal condition, observed object condition, immediately preceding condition, and dominant condition. "Other" means they are other than the result they cause.

632. MAVbh on MAV: 6.14, La Vallée Poussin 1970b: 89; P5263: 121.3.8-121.4.3.

633. LRCM: 673, 679-680; Hopkins 1983: 145-47.

634. MMK: 20.20cd, de Jong 1977: 28; D3824: Tsa 12a4-5.

635. MAV: 6.14, La Vallée Poussin 1970b: 89; D3861: Ḥa 204b4-5.

636. LRCM: 735-736.

637. MAV: 6.98, La Vallée Poussin 1970b: 202-05; D3861: Ḥa 209a1-2.

638. See LRCM: 602, note 311. Cārvākas acknowledge causation in the case of artificially created objects such as a pot. However, they argue that natural objects such as thorns arise spontaneously.

639. MAV: 6.99, La Vallée Poussin 1970b: 206; D3861: Ḥa 209a2.

640. Cf. LRCM: 754, where intrinsic production is limited to four possibilities.

641. MAV: 6.104ab, La Vallée Poussin 1970b: 215; D3861: Ḥa 209a6.

642. 'Jam-dbyangs-bzhad-pa (*mChan*: 700.6-702.2) comments that persons with sharp faculties will generate inference based on the initial *reductios* alone, while the syllogism is then added to assist persons of dull faculties.

643. MMK: 7.16ab, de Jong 1977: 9; D3824: Tsa 5a5.

644. MAV: 6.115, La Vallée Poussin 1970b: 228; D3861: Ha 209b7-210a1. MAV: 6.114 restates the refutation of the four extreme types of production and links this to dependent-arising: "Because things are not produced causelessly, nor from causes such as Iśvara, nor from self, other, or both, they are dependently produced."

645. Cś: 14.23, Lang 1986: 134-135.

646. Cśṭ, P5266: 270.3.6-4.1.

647. Cśṭ, P5266: 270.4.1-2.

648. Cśṭ, P5266: 270.4.2-4.

649. Cśṭ, P5266: 270.4.4-7.

650. According to 'Jam-dbyangs-bzhad-pa (*mChan*: 710.6), "earlier Tibetans and others."

651. *Anavatapta-nāga-rāja-paripṛcchā-sūtra*, cited above at LRCM: 636, note 379.

652. Ibid., P823: 139.3.5-6. The P words are different but the meaning is the same.

653. *Hasti-kakṣya-sūtra*, cited at PPs: 388.1 (Wayman 1978: 477 n. 386); D3796: Ha 171a4-5.

654. LRCM: 251 (*Great Treatise* 2000: 318) The other three are grasping that holds on to views, to ethical discipline and conduct, and to the assertion that there is a self.

655. MMK: 18.2cd, 18.4-5, de Jong 1977: 24; D3824: Tsa 10b6, 10b7. For a detailed explanation of the process of dependent-arising and cessation, see LRCM: 248-257 (*Great Treatise* 2000: 315-25).

656. The eight worldly concerns are liking (1) rewards, (2) happiness, (3) praise, and (4) a good reputation, and disliking (5) not receiving rewards, (6) unhappiness, (7) criticism, and (8) anything which damages our reputation (Rinchen 2001: 47).

657. PPs: 350.10-351.4, on MMK: 18.5; D3796: Ha 113b7-114a3.

658. PPs: 351.8-10, on MMK: 18.5; D3796: Ha 114a3-5.

659. MAVbh on MAV: 6.179, La Vallée Poussin 1970b: 302; P5263: 150.5.2-3.

660. LRCM: 576-579.

661. MAVbh on MAV: 6.28, La Vallée Poussin 1970b: 107-08; P5263: 124.1.4-7.

662. LRCM: 655, note 422.

Chapter Twenty-five *Insight Requires Analysis*

663. Sn, Lamotte 1935: 89, cited at LRCM: 471. The four are given as part of a list of nine items. P774: 13.4.8-13.5.1.

664. Śbh, P5537: 101.1.6-7; cf. LRCM: 472.

665. The "two kinds of wisdom" are knowing (1) the diversity and (2) the real nature.

666. Sn, Lamotte 1935: 92; P744: 14.2.3-5.

667. Śbh, P5537: 101.2.3-6.

668. 'Jam-dbyangs-bzhad-pa (*mChan*: 738.5-6) says that inconceivable realities are, for example, the fact that Buddha can place all universes within a single pore, or the fact that a pigeon walking on the roof of a house can leave its tracks in some yogurt inside the house. The abiding reality is phenomena's lack of essential existence.

669. 'Jam-dbyangs-bzhad-pa (*mChan*: 739.1-2) explains: If something bulbous, etc. is called a pot, then something's being bulbous, etc. is reason enough to call it a pot; it is pointless to look for some other reason for something's being a pot.

670. Śbh, P5537: 101.4.2-3.

671. LRCM: 769-770.

672. LRCM: 535-536, citing Śbh, P5537: 101.1.2-6.

673. *Prajñāpāramitopadeśa*, P5579: 247.1.4-5.

674. Sn, P774: 13.4.8-13.5.1. See LRCM: 769.

675. LRCM: 529ff.

676. LRCM: 579ff.

677. LRCM: 547-550.

678. LRCM: 594-595.

679. Bk3, Tucci 1971: 13-14, D3917: Ki 61b1-62a1.

680. *Gayā-śīrṣa-sūtra*, D109: Ca288b7-289a1.

681. The *Tathāgatācintya-guhya-nirdeśa-sūtra* is section 3 of the *Ratna-kūṭa*, P760.

682. LRCM: 332ff.

683. Literally, "chasing a rock." The phrase "external elimination" (*phyi chad*) is intended to imply a superficial and thus inadequate remedy. These followers of Ha-shang argue that if every time you misapprehend something, you have to run out like a dog chasing a ball to analyze the misapprehended object, then there will never be an end to the cycle of elaborating and then analyzing so as to eliminate elaborations on a case-by-case basis.

684. The Six Ornaments of the World are Nāgārjuna, Āryadeva, Asaṅga, Vasubandhu, Dignāga, and Dharmakīrti.

685. Bk3, Tucci 1971: 17-18, D3917: Ki 63a3-5. The *Mañjuśrī-vikrīḍita-sūtra* is cited as *Mañjuśrī-vikurvita-sūtra* in Bk3.

686. See note 248 to LRCM: 570; also LRCM: 653-654.

687. Cś: 14.25, Lang 1986: 134-35; D3846: Tsha 16a5.

688. MAV: 6.116ab, La Vallée Poussin 1970b: 229; D3861: Ha 210a1.

689. MAV: 6.120cd, La Vallée Poussin 1970b: 233; D3861: Ha 210a5.

690. *Pramāṇa-varttika-kārikā*, Miyasaka 1971-72: 32-33; P5709: 87.2.7-8.

691. Ibid., Miyasaka 1971-72: 54-55; P5709: 90.1.5.

692. Emptiness is first known directly on the path of seeing, at which point one is no longer an ordinary being but becomes a noble being. Prior to attaining the path of seeing,

a bodhisattva is on the path of preparation, which has four stages: heat, peak, forbearance, and supreme mundane quality. Each stage is divided into three levels—the lesser, the intermediate, and the great. Consequently, the great level of the supreme mundane quality stage of the path of preparation is the highest level that an ordinary being can attain. Tsong-kha-pa's point is that even the most advanced type of meditation on emptiness found on the path of preparation is conceptual.

693. Sn, Lamotte 1935: 110-11; P774: 17.3.1-2.

694. *Nārāyaṇa-paripṛcchā*, cited in *Śikṣā-sammucaya*, Vaidya 1960: 105; P5336: 232.1.1-2. Also cited at LRCM: 456. A citation with similar meaning is at LRCM: 21 (*Great Treatise* 2000: 56).

695. LRCM: 69-77 (*Great Treatise* 2000: 109-116), LRCM: 342ff, 547ff, 596-604, 614ff.

696. P5709: 79.1.4.

697. LRCM: 86-205 (*Great Treatise* 2000: 129-263).

698. MAV: 6.120d, La Vallée Poussin 1970b: 233; D3861: Ha 210a4.

699. *Madhyamaka-hṛdaya-kārikā*, D3855: Dza 4b1-2.

700. *Madhyamaka-hṛdaya-vṛtti-tarka-jvālā*, D3856: Dza 58a7-b2.

701. Bk2, P5311: 34.1.5-34.2.2. The passage from the *Ratna-megha-sūtra*, D231: Wa 92a4-5, is cited in Bk3, Tucci 1971: 7-8, D3917: Ki 64a4-5.

702. *Kāśyapa-parivarta-sūtra* is section 43 of the *Ratna-kūṭa*; Staël-Holstein 1977: 102-03; D87: Cha 133a7-b1.

703. Bk2, P5311: 34.1.2-5.

704. SR, cited at LRCM: 479-480.

705. Bk3, Tucci 1971: 20; D3917: Ki 64a3-4.

706. Conze 1990: 102-03.

707. *Prajñāpāramitā-hṛdaya-sūtra*, D21: Ka 145a4-5.

708. *Prajñāpāramitā-ratna-guṇa-sañcaya-gathā*, Conze 1973: 22; D13: Ka 6a6-7.

709. Bk3, Tucci 1971: 17; D3917: Ki 62b6-7.

710. Bk3, Tucci 1971: 18-19, D3917: Ki 63a6-b3. *Ratna-megha-sūtra*, P897: 211.3.2-3. The Bk3 citation is a paraphrase of the sūtra passage. *Laṅkāvatāra-sūtra*, D107: Ca 101a5-6.

711. Bk3, Tucci 1971: 19, D3917: Ki 63b7-64a2.

712. *Kāśyapa-parivarta-sūtra*, Staël-Holstein: 82-83; D87: Cha 130b2-3.

713. Bk1, Tucci 1986: 212; P5310: 26.4.2-3. *Arya-avikalpa-praveśa-dhāraṇī*, P810: 231.3.4-5.

Chapter Twenty-six *Uniting Insight and Serenity*

714. Bk3, Tucci 1971: 10-11, D3917: Ki 59b2-3.

715. LRCM: 55-69 (*Great Treatise* 2000: 93-108).

716. LRCM: 514-536.

717. Thurman 1984: 246, n. 86, says: "This proverb arises from popular exorcistic rites,

wherein a scapegoat made of barley flour and ritually set up to receive all the negative force to be exorcised is subsequently flung out of the house in which the rite is performed—obviously it has to be flung in the direction from which the disturbance is coming."

718. This is the *Be'u bum sngon po*, a bKa'-gdams-pa explanation of the path taught by Po-to-ba Rin-chen-gsal and arranged by Dol-pa Shes-rab-rgya-mtsho.

719. *Satya-dvayāvatāra*, D3902: A 7b4-5.

720. LRCM: 537-543.

721. Sn, Lamotte 1935: 90; P774: 13.5.4-5; cf. LRCM: 537.

722. *Prajñāpāramitopadeśa*, P5579: 248.3.1-3.

723. LRCM: 741-750.

724. LRCM: 442-450. For an explanation of illusion-like appearances associated with the Kālacakra Tantra that Tsong-kha-pa is objecting to here, see Stearns 2000.

725. Gön-ba-wa is dGon-pa-ba-dbang-phyug-rgyal-mtshan (Gön-ba-wa Wang-chuk-gyel-tsen) (1016-1082). The bKa'-gdams-pa (Kadampa) teachings descended from Atisha to dGe-bshes 'Brom-ston-pa-rgyal-ba'i-'byung-gnas (Geshe Drom-dön-ba). 'Brom-ston-pa's disciples then passed them on in three lineages, the "Textual" (*gzhung pa ba*), "Instructional" (*man ngag ba*), and "Stages of the Path" (*lam rim ba*), which were transmitted to Po-to-ba (Bo-do-wa) (1027/31-1105), sPyan-snga-tshul-khrims-'bar (Jen-nga-tsul-trim-bar) (1038-1103), and Geshe dGon-pa-ba respectively. The followers of the Stages of the Path lineage relied on texts called "Stages of the Teaching" (*bstan rim*), which were explanations of the stages of the path, some of which texts Tsong-kha-pa based his *Great Treatise* upon. See note 743 below; see also Tharchin and Engle 1990.

726. *Madhyānta-vibhāga*: 4.12a, D4021: Phi 43a4.

727. LRCM: 741-750.

728. This refers to the immediately preceding section on the measure of having achieved insight and to the section on the measure for successful cultivation of serenity, LRCM: 536ff.

729. LRCM: 535-537.

730. Śbh, P5537: 107.5.2-6.

731. Bk3, Tucci 1971: 9; D3917: Ki 59b1-2.

732. *Prajñāpāramitopadeśa*, P5579: 246.3.5-6.

Chapter Twenty-seven *Summary and Conclusion*

733. The meditations given so far are covered in LRCM: 32-205 (*Great Treatise* 2000: 68-263). The four powers are explained at LRCM: 196-199 (*Great Treatise* 2000: 251-59).

734. LRCM: 203-280 (*Great Treatise* 2000: 264-353).

735. The two stages are the tantric stages of generation and of completion, outlined at LRCM: 808-809.

736. This is the general explanation of Mahāyāna (LRCM: 281-468).

737. LRCM: 468-805.

738.   The outline heading *b' How to train specifically in the Vajrayāna* is the second of a two-part subheading in the section of the LRCM entitled *3) Training the mind in the stages of the path of the person of great capacity* (LRCM: 283). The two-part subheading (LRCM: 356) *iii) Explanation of the process of learning the precepts* includes both *a' How to train in the Mahāyāna in general* and *b' How to train specifically in the Vajrayāna*.

739.   P5343: 21.4.7-21.5.1

740.   LRCM: 39 (*Great Treatise* 2000: 75).

741.   *Mañjuśrii-mūla-tantra,* cited in *Mahāyāna-sūtra-saṃgraha,* Vaidya 1964: 86ab; D543: Na 157a4. Cf. LRCM: 274 (*Great Treatise* 2000: 34) and note 582).

Colophon

742.   Chos-skyabs-bzang-po (Chö-kyap-sang-bo).

743.   This refers to the *bstan rim* ("stages of the teaching") texts composed by rNgog Blo-ldan-shes-rab (1059-1109) and his disciple Gro-lung-pa Blo-gros-'byung-gnas. The latter wrote the text entitled *A Presentation of the Stages of the Path for Entering the Precious Teaching of the Tathāgata (bDe bar gshegs pa'i bstan pa rin po che la 'jug pa'i lam gyi rim pa rnam par bshad pa),* for which the Lhasa-printed manuscript is currently extant. For more information, see *Great Treatise* 2000: 25 and note 11.

ABBREVIATIONS

AA	*Abhisamayālaṃkāra*
AK	*Abhidharma-kośa-kārikā*
A-kya	A-kya-yongs-'dzin, *Lam rim brda bkrol*
AS	*Abhidharma-samuccaya*
Bbh	*Yoga-caryā-bhūmau Bodhisattva-bhūmi*
BCA	*Bodhisattva-caryāvatāra*
Bk1	First *Bhāvanā-krama*
Bk2	Second *Bhāvanā-krama*
Bk3	Third *Bhāvanā-krama*
Bpālita	*Buddhapālita-mūla-madhyamaka-vṛtti*
Cś	*Catuḥ-śataka-śāstra-kārikā-nāma*
Cśṭ	*Bodhisattva-yoga-caryā-catuḥ-śataka-ṭīkā*
D	*sDe dge* edition of the Tibetan Tripiṭaka as found in Kanakura 1934 and 1953
Great Treatise	Cutler, et al., 2000
LRCM	Tsong-kha-pa 1985, *sKyes bu gsum gyi rnyams su blang ba'i rim pa thams cad tshang bar ston pa'i byang chub lam gyi rim pa*
MAV	*Madhyamakāvatāra*
MAVbh	*Madhyamakāvatāra-bhāṣya*
mChan	'Jam-dbyangs-bzhad-pa, et al., *Lam rim mchan bzhi sbrags ma*
MMK	*Prajñā-nāma-mūla-madhyamaka-kārikā*
MSA	*Mahāyāna-sūtrālaṃkāra-kārikā*
P	Suzuki 1955-61
PPd	*Prasanna-padā*, Dharamsala 1968

PPs	*Prasanna-padā*, La Vallée Poussin 1970
PS	*Pāramitā-samāsa-nāma*
RGV	*Ratna-gotra-vibhāga (Mahāyānottara-tantra-śāstra)*
Rā	*Rāja-parikathā-ratnāvali*
Śbh	*Yoga-caryā-bhūmau Śrāvaka-bhūmi*
Skt.	Sanskrit
Sn	*Saṃdhi-nirmocana-sūtra*
SR	*Samādhi-rāja-sūtra*
VV	*Vigraha-vyāvartanī*
VVv	*Vigraha-vyavārtinī-vṛtti*
YS	*Yukti-ṣaṣṭikā*
YSv	*Yukti-ṣaṣṭikā-vṛtti*

BIBLIOGRAPHY

Indian sūtras and tantras are listed alphabetically by title in the first section; Indian śāstras are listed alphabetically by title in the second section; Tibetan commentaries are listed alphabetically by author in the third section; works by modern writers are listed alphabetically by author in the fourth section.

For the first two sections, the Suzuki (1955-61) reference has been provided, except for where it is not found, in which case the Kanakura (1934 and 1953) reference has been supplied.

Information on available translations into English and other languages, as well as other relevant information about the works cited, is available in Tulku (1982). Other bibliographic information is available in Pfandt (1983), de Jong (1987), Nakamura (1989), and Hirakawa (1990).

A. Sūtras and Tantras

Ārya-akṣayamati-nirdeśa-nāma-mahāyāna-sūtra, 'Phags pa blo gros mi zad pas bstan pa zhes bya ba theg pa chen po'i mdo. P842, vol. 34. According to Lamotte (1949: 342) it is also called the *Catuḥ-pratisaraṇa-sūtra*.

Ārya-anavatapta-nāga-rāja-paripṛcchā-nāma-mahāyāna-sūtra, 'Phags pa lu'i rgyal po ma dros pas zhus pa zhes bya ba theg pa chen po'i mdo. P823, vol. 33.

Ārya-avikalpa-praveśa-dhāraṇī, 'Phags pa rnam par mi rtog par 'jug pa gzungs. P810, vol. 32.

Ārya-kāśyapa-parivarta-nāma-mahāyāna-sūtra, 'Phags pa 'od srung gi le'u zhes bya ba theg pa chen po'i mdo. Section 43 of the *Ratna-kūṭa*. P760, vol.22.

Ārya-gayā-śīrṣa-nāma-mahāyāna-sūtra, 'Phags pa gayā mgo'i ri zhes bya ba theg pa chen po'i mdo. P777, vol. 29.

Ārya-mañjuśrī-vikrīḍita-nāma-mahāyāna-sūtra, 'Phags pa 'jam dpal rnam par rol pa zhes bya ba theg pa chen po'i mdo. P764, vol. 27.

Ārya-prajñāpāramitā-ratna-guṇa-sañcaya-gāthā, 'Phags pa shes rab kyi pha rol tu phyin pa sdud pa tshigs su bcad pa. P735, vol. 21.

Ārya-mahāyāna-prasāda-prabhāvanā-nāma-mahāyāna-sūtra, 'Phags pa theg pa chen po la dad pa rab tu sgom pa shes bya ba theg pa chen po'i mdo. P812, vol. 32.

Ārya-mahā-ratna-kūṭa-dharma-paryāya-śata-sāhasrika-grantha, 'Phags pa dkon mchog brtsegs pa chen po'i chos kyi rnam grangs le'u stong phrag brgya pa. P760, vols. 22-24.

Ārya-ratna-megha-nāma-mahāyāna-sūtra, 'Phags pa dkon mchog sprin ces bya ba theg pa chen po'i mdo. P897, vol. 35.

Ārya-laṅkāvatāra-mahāyāna-sūtra, 'Phags pa lang kar gshegs pa'i mdo. P775, vol. 29.

Ārya-saṃdhi-nirmocana-sūtra, 'Phags pa dgongs pa nges par 'grel pa zhes bya ba theg pa chen po'i mdo. P774, vol. 29.

Ārya-sarva-buddha-viṣayāvatāra-jñānālokālaṃkāra-nāma-mahāyāna-sūtra, 'Phags pa sangs rgyas thams cad kyi yul la 'jug pa'i ye shes snang ba'i rgyan zhes bya ba theg pa chen po'i mdo. P768, vol. 28.

Candra-pradīpa-sūtra: see *Samādhi-rāja-sūtra*.

Tathāgatācintya-guhya-nirdeśa-sūtra: *Ārya-tathāgatācintya-guhya-nirdeśa-nāma-mahāyāna-sūtra*, 'Phags pa de bzhin gshegs pa'i gsang ba bsam gyis mi khyab pa bstan pa shes bya ba theg pa chen po'i mdo. Section 3 of the *Ratna-kūṭa*. P760.

Tri-saṃvara-nirdeśa-parivarta-nāma-mahāyāna-sūtra, sDom pa gsum bstan pa'i le'u zhes bya ba theg pa chen po'i mdo. Section 1 of the *Ratna-kūṭa*. P760, vol. 22.

Daśa-bhūmika-sūtra, Sa bcu pa'i mdo. Section 31 of the *Avataṃsaka*. P761, vols. 25-26.

Dharma-saṃgīti: *Ārya-dharma-saṃgīti-nāma-mahāyāna-sūtra*, 'Phags pa chos yang dag par sdud pa shes bya ba theg pa chen po'i mdo. P904, vol. 36.

Nārāyaṇa-paripṛcchā-ārya-mahāmayā-vijaya-vāhinī-dhāraṇī, Sred med kyi bus zhus pa 'phags pa sgyu ma chen mo rnam par rgyal ba thob par byed pa zhes bya ba'i gzungs. This work is not found in P. D684.

Pañca-viṃśatisāhasrikā-prajñāpāramitā, 'Phags pa shes rab kyi pha rol tu phyin pa stong phrag nyi shu lnga pa. P731, vol.18.

Pratyutpanna-buddha-saṃmukhāvasthita-samādhi-sūtra: *Ārya-pratyutpanna-buddha-saṃmukhāvasthita-samādhi-nāma-mahāyāna-sūtra*, 'Phags pa da ltar gyi sangs rgyas mngon sum du gshugs pa'i ting nge 'dzin ces bya ba theg pa chen po'i mdo. P801, vol. 32.

Bodhisattva-piṭaka: *Ārya-bodhisattva-piṭaka-nāma-mahāyāna-sūtra*, 'Phags pa byang chub sems dpa'i sde snod ces bya ba theg pa chen po'i mdo. Section 12 of the *Ratna-kūṭa*. P760, vol. 22.

Brahma-jāla-sūtra, Tshangs pa'i dra ba'i mdo. This is the first section of the *Dīgha Nikāya*. P1021, vol. 40.

Bhagavatī-prajñāpāramitā-hṛdaya, bCom ldan 'das ma shes rab kyi pha rol tu phyin pa'i snying po. P160, vol. 6.

Mañjuśrī-mūla-tantra: *Ārya-manjuśrī-mūla-tantra*, 'Phags pa 'jam dpal gyi rtsa ba'i rgyud. P162, vol. 6.

Mahā-parinirvāṇa-sūtra: *Ārya-mahā-parinirvāṇa-sūtra*, 'Phags pa yongs su mya ngan las 'das pa chen po'i mdo. P787, vol. 30.

Saṃpuṭi/a-nāma-mahā-tantra, Yang dag par sbyor ba zhes bya ba'i rgyud chen po. P26, vol. 2.

Samādhi-rāja-sūtra: *Sarva-dharma-svabhāva-samatā-vipañcita-samādhi-rāja-sūtra*, Chos thams cad kyi rang bzhin mnyam pa nyid rnam par spros pa ting nge 'dzin gyi rgyal po'i mdo. P795, vol. 31.

Hasti-kakṣya-nāma-mahāyāna-sūtra, Glang po'i rtsal zhes bya ba theg pa chen po'i mdo. P873, vol. 34.

B. Śāstras:

Abhidharma-kośa: Abhidharma-kośa-kārikā, Chos mngon pa'i mdzod kyi tshig le'ur byas pa. Vasubandhu. P5590, vol. 115.

Abhidharma-kośa-bhāṣya, Chos mngon pa'i mdzod kyi bshad pa. Vasubandhu. P5591, vol. 115.

Abhidharma-samuccaya, Chos mngon pa kun las btus pa. Asaṅga. P5550, vol. 112.

Abhisamayālaṃkāra: Abhisamayālaṃkāra-nāma-prajñāpāramitopadeśa-śāstra-kārikā. Maitreyanātha. P5184, vol. 88.

Abhisamayālaṃkāra-nāma-prajñāpāramitopadeśa-śāstra-[vi]vṛtti, 'Phags pa shes rab kyi pha rol tu phyin pa'i man ngag gi bstan bcos mngon par rtogs pa'i rgyan gyi zhes bya ba'i grel pa. Haribhadra. P5191, vol. 90.

Catuḥ-śataka: Catuḥ-śataka-śāstra-kārikā-nāma, bsTan bcos bzhi brgya pa zhes bya ba'i tshig le'ur byas pa. Āryadeva. P5246, vol. 95.

Tarka-jvālā: Madhyamaka-hṛdaya-vṛtti-tarka-jvālā, dBu ma'i snying po'i 'grel pa rtog ge 'bar ba. Bhāvaviveka. P5256, vol. 96.

Triṃśikā-bhāṣya, Sum cu pa'i bshad pa. Sthiramati. P5565, vol. 113.

Deśanā-stava, bShags pa'i bstod pa. Candragomin. P2048, vol. 46.

Deśanā-stava-vṛtti, bShags pa'i bstod pa'i 'grel pa. Buddhaśānti. P2049, vol. 46.

Pāramitā-samāsa-nāma, Pha rol tu phyin pa bsdus pa shes bya ba. Āryaśūra. P5340, vol. 103.

Prajñā-nāma-mūla-madhyamaka-kārikā. See *Mūla-madhyamaka-kārika.*

Prajñā-pradīpa-ṭīkā, Shes rab sgron ma'i rgya cher 'grel pa. Avalokitavrata. P5259, vols. 96-97.

Prajñā-pradīpa-mūla-madhyamaka-vṛtti, dBu ma'i rtsa ba'i 'grel pa shes rab sgron ma. Bhāvaviveka. P5253, vol. 95.

*Prajñāpāramitā-bhāvanā-kramopadeśa.*The Sanskrit title is reconstructed. *Pha rol tu phyin pa'i theg pa'i bsgom pa'i rim pa'i man ngag.* Ye shes grags pa (Jñānakīrti). P5317, vol. 102.

Prajñāpāramitopadeśa, Shes rab kyi pha rol tu phyin pa'i man ngag. Ratnākaraśānti. P5579, vol. 114.

Pramāṇa-vārttika-kārikā, Tshad ma rnam 'grel gyi tshig le'ur byas pa. Dharmakīrti. P5709, vol. 130.

Prasanna-padā: Mūla-madhyamaka-vṛtti-prasanna-padā, dBu ma rtsa ba'i 'grel pa tshig gsal ba zhes bya ba. Candrakīrti. P5260, vol. 98. Also: Dharamsala: Tibetan Publishing House, 1968.

Buddhapālita-mūla-madhyamaka-vṛtti, dBu ma'i rtsa ba'i 'grel pa. Buddhapālita. P5242, vol. 95.

Bodhi-patha-pradīpa, Byang chub lam gyi sgron ma. Atisha. P5343, vol. 103.

Bodhi-mārga-pradīpa-pañjikā-nāma, Byang chub lam gyi sgron ma'i dka' 'grel. Atisha. P5344, vol. 103.

Bodhisattva-caryāvatāra, Byang chub sems dpa'i spyod la 'jug pa. Śāntideva. P5272, vol. 99.

Bodhisattva-yoga-caryā-catuḥ-śataka-ṭīkā, Byang chub sems dpa'i rnal 'byor spyod pa bzhi brgya pa'i rgya cher 'grel pa. Candrakīrti. P5266, vol. 98.

Bhāvanā-krama, sGom pa'i rim pa. Kamalaśīla. P5310-5312, vol. 102.

Madhyamakālaṃkāra-pañjikā, dBu ma'i rgyan gyi dka' 'grel. Kamalaśīla. P5286, vol. 101.

Madhyamakālaṁkāra-kārikā, dBu ma'i rgyan gyi tshig le'ur byas pa. Śāntarakṣita. P5284, vol. 101.

Madhyamakāloka-nāmā, dBu ma snang ba zhes bya ba. Kamalaśīla. P5287, vol. 101.

Madhyamaka-hṛdaya-kārikā, dBu ma'i snying po'i tshig le'ur byas pa. Bhāvaviveka. P5255, vol. 96.

Madhyamakāvatāra-nāma, dBu ma la 'jug pa shes bya ba. Candrakīrti. P5262, vol. 98.

Madhyamakāvatāra-bhāṣya, dBu ma la 'jug pa bshad pa zhes bya ba. Candrakīrti. P5263, vol. 98.

Madhyamakāvatara-ṭīkā, dBu ma la 'jug pa'i 'grel bshad ces bya ba. Jayānanda. P5271, vol. 99.

Madhyamakopadeśa-nāma, dBu ma'i man ngag ces bya ba. Atisha. P5324, vol. 102.

Madhyānta-vibhāga-kārikā, dBus dang mtha' rnam par 'byed pa'i tshig le'ur byas pa. Maitreya. P5522, vol. 108.

Madhyānta-vibhāga-ṭīkā, dBus dang mtha' rnam par 'byed pa'i 'grel bshad. Sthiramati. P5528, vol. 108.

Mahāyānottaratantra-śāstra, Theg pa chen po rgyud bla ma'i bstan bcos. Also called *Ratna-gotra-vibhāga, dKon mchog gi rigs rnam par dbye ba.* Maitreyanātha. P5525, vol. 108.

Mahāyāna-sūtrālaṃkāra-kārikā, Theg pa chen po'i mdo sde'i rgyan gyi tshig le'ur byas pa. Maitreyanātha. P5521, vol. 108.

Mahāyāna-sūtrālaṃkāra-bhāṣya/vyākhyā, Theg pa chen po'i mdo sde'i rgyan gyi bshad pa. Vasubandhu. P5527, vol. 108.

Mūla-madhyamaka-kārikā: Prajñā-nāma-mūla-madhyamaka-kārikā, dBu ma rtsa ba'i tshig le'ur byas pa shes rab ces bya ba. Nāgārjuna. P5224, vol. 95.

Yukti-ṣaṣṭikā-kārikā-nāma, Rigs pa drug cu pa'i tshig le'ur byas pa zhes bya ba. Nāgārjuna. P5225, vol. 95.

Yukti-ṣaṣṭikā-vṛtti, Rigs pa drug cu pa'i 'grel pa. Candrakīrti. P5265, vol. 98.

Yoga-caryā-bhūmi, rNal 'byor spyod pa'i sa. See note 45 to the translation. Asaṅga. P5536, vols. 109-110.

Yoga-caryā-bhūmi-nirṇaya-saṃgraha, rNal 'byor spyod pa'i sa rnam par gtan la dbab pa bsdu ba. This is the *Viniścaya-samgrahaṇi.* The Skt. title here suggests *rNal 'byor spyod pa'i sa rnam par nges pa bsdu pa.* Asaṅga. P5539, vols. 110-111.

Yoga-caryā-bhūmau-bodhisattva-bhūmi, rNal 'byor spyod pa'i sa las byang chub sems dpa'i sa. Asaṅga. P5538, vol. 110.

Yoga-caryā-bhūmau-vastu-saṃgraha, rNal 'byor spyod pa'i sa las gzhi bsdu ba. Asaṅga. P5540, vol. 111.

Yoga-caryā-bhūmau-śrāvaka-bhūmi, rNal 'byor spyod pa'i sa las nyan thos kyi sa. Asaṅga. P5537, vol. 110.

Ratnāvalī: Rāja-parikathā-ratnāvalī, rGyal po la gtam bya ba rin po che'i phreng ba. Nāgārjuna. P5658, vol. 129.

Lokātīta-stava, 'Jig rten las 'das par bstod pa. Nāgārjuna. P2012, vol. 46.

Varṇāha-varṇe-bhagavato-buddhasya-stotre-śakya-stava, Sangs rgyas bcom ldan 'das la bstod pa bsngags par 'os pa bsngags pa las bstod par mi nus par bstod pa. Āryaśūra/ Matricita/Mātṛceṭa. P2029, vol. 46.

Vigraha-vyāvartanī-kārikā-nāma, rTsod pa bzlog pa'i tshig le'ur byas pa zhes bya ba. Nāgārjuna. P5228, vol. 95.

Vigraha-vyavārtinī-vṛtti, rTsod pa bzlog pa'i 'grel pa. Nāgārjuna. P5232, vol. 95.

Viniścaya-saṃgrahaṇī. See *Yoga-caryā-bhūmi-nirṇaya-saṃgraha*.

Śikṣā-samuccaya, bSlab pa kun las btus pa. Śāntideva. P5336, vol. 102.

Śūnyatā-saptati-kārikā-nāma, sTong pa nyid bdun bcu pa'i tshig le'ur byas pa zhes bya ba. Nāgārjuna. P5227, vol. 95.

Satya-dvayāvatāra, bDen pa gnyis la 'jug pa. Atisha. P5298, vol. 101.

Samādhi-sambhāra-parivarta. Ting nge 'dzin gyi tshogs kyi le'u. Bodhibhadra. P3288, vol. 69 and P5398, vol. 103.

C. Tibetan Works

Anonymous. 1964. *Byang chub lam rim chen mo'i sa bcad*. Dharamsala: Shering Parkhang.

Ngag-dbang-rab-brtan (sDe-drug-mkhan-chen-ngag-dbang-rab-brtan). See 'Jam-dbyangs-bzhad-pa, et al.

'Jam-dbyangs-bzhad-pa. 1962. *Grub mtha' chen mo*. Mussoorie: Dalama.

———. 1967. *dBu ma chen mo*. Buxaduor: Gomang.

'Jam-dbyangs-bzhad-pa, et al. 1972. *mNyam med rje btsun tsong kha pa chen pos mdzad pa'i byang chub lam rim chen mo'i dka' ba'i gnad rnams mchan bu bzhi'i sgo nas legs par bshad pa theg chen lam gyi gsal sgron* (abbreviated title *Lam rim mchan bzhi sbrags ma*). New Delhi: Chophel Lekden.

Pha-bong-kha (Pha-bong-kha-pa-byams-pa-bstan-'dzin-'phrin-las-rgya-mtsho). 1973. *Byang chub lam rim chen mo mchan bu bzhi sbrags kyi skor dran gso'i bsnyel byang mgo smos tsam du mdzad pa*. In *The Collected Works of Pha-boṅ-kha-pa Byams-pa-bstan-'dzin-phrin-las-rgya-mtsho*. Vol. 5. New Delhi: Chophel Legdan.

Ba-so-chos-kyi-rgyal-mtshan. See 'Jam-dbyangs-bzhad-pa, et al.

Bra-sti (Bra-sti-dge-bshes-rin-chen-don-grub). See 'Jam-dbyangs-bzhad-pa, et al.

Tsong-kha-pa. 1985. *sKyes bu gsum gyi rnyams su blang ba'i rim pa thams cad tshang bar ston pa'i byang chub lam gyi rim pa/ Byang chub lam rim che ba*. Zi-ling (Xining): Tso Ngön (mTsho sngon) People's Press.

    Also: Ganden Bar Nying, early fifteenth century, and Dharamsala, 1991.

———. 1973. *dGongs pa rab gsal*. Sarnath: Pleasure of Elegant Sayings Press.

    Also: Dharamsala: Tibetan Cultural Printing Press, n.d.

———. *dBu ma la 'jug pa'i rnam bshad dgongs pa rab gsal*. In *The Complete Works of Tsong-kha-pa*, vol. Ma: 1-267. dGa' ldan phun tshogs gling wood blocks, gTsang, Tibet, n.d.

————. *dBu ma rtsa ba'i tshig le'ur byas pa'i rnam bshad rig pa'i rgya mtsho*. Also called *rTsa she ṭik chen*. In *The Complete Works of Tsong-kha-pa*, vol. Ba: 1-282. dGa' ldan phun tshogs gling wood blocks, gTsang, Tibet, n.d.

————. *Byang chub lam gyi rim pa chung ba*. Also called *Lam rim 'bring*. In *The Complete Works of Tsong-kha-pa*, vol. Pha: 1-201. dGa' ldan phun tshogs gling wood blocks, gTsang, Tibet, n.d.

————. n.d. *rTsa shes ṭik chen*. Sarnath: Pleasure of Elegant Sayings Press.

Also: rJe Tsong kha pa'i gsung dbu ma'i lta ba'i skor edition, Sarnath: Pleasure of Elegant Sayings Press, 1975.

————. 1973. *Legs bshad snying po*. Sarnath: Pleasure of Elegant Sayings Press.

Zhwa-dmar-bstan-'dzin. 1972. *Lhag mthong chen mo'i dka' gnad rnams brjed byang du bkod pa dgongs zab snang ba'i sgron me*. Delhi: Mongolian Lama Guru Deva.

A-kya-yongs-'dzin, dByangs-can-dga'-ba'i-blo-gros. 1971. *Byang chub lam gyi rim pa chen mo las byung ba'i brda bkrol nyer mkho bsdus pa* (abbreviated title *Lam rim brda bkrol*). In *The Collected Works of A-kya Yoṅs-ḥdzin*, vol. l. New Delhi: Lama Guru Deva.

D. Modern Works

Bagchi, S., ed. 1967. *Suvarṇaprabhāsottamasūtra*. Darbhanga: Mithila Institute.

————, ed. 1970. *Mahāyāna-Sūtrālaṅkāra of Asaṅga*. Darbhanga: Mithila Institute.

Bareau, André. 1955. *Les Sectes bouddhiques du Petit Véhicule*. Saigon: École française d'Extrême-Orient.

Bendall , C., ed. 1903, 1904. "*Subhāṣita-saṃgraha*: An anthology of extracts...." *Le Muséon* 4, no. 4 (1903): 375-402 and 5, no. 1 (1904): 5-46.

Bendall, C. and W.H.D. Rouse. 1971 [1922]. *Śikṣā Samuccaya*. Reprint, Delhi: Motilal Banarsidass.

Bhattacharya, Vidhushekhara. 1931. *The Catuḥśataka of Āryadeva*. Calcutta: Visva-Bharati Bookshop.

————, ed. 1960. *Bodhicaryāvatāra*. Calcutta: The Asiatic Society.

Buescher, John. 1982. "The Buddhist Doctrine of Two Truths in the Vaibhāṣika and Theravada Schools." Ph.D. diss., University of Virginia.

Chandra, Lokesh. 1982 [1959-1961]. *Tibetan-Sanskrit Dictionary*. Indo-Asian Literature 3. New Delhi: International Academy of Indian Culture. Reprint, Kyoto: Rinsen.

Conze, Edward. 1954. *Abhisamayālaṅkāra*. Serie Orientale Roma 6. Rome: Istituto italiano per il Medio ed Estremo Oriente.

————. 1973. *The Perfection of Wisdom in 8,000 Lines and Its Verse Summary*. Bolinas, CA: Four Seasons Foundation.

————, ed. and trans. 1990 [1975]. *The Large Sūtra on Perfect Wisdom*. Reprint, Delhi: Motilal Banarsidass.

Cozort, Daniel. 1986. *Highest Yoga Tantra*. Ithaca, NY: Snow Lion Publications.

Crosby, Kate and Andrew Skilton. 1995. *The Bodhicaryāvatāra*. Oxford and New York: Oxford University Press.

Cutler, Joshua W.C., et al. 2000. *The Great Treatise on the Stages of the Path to Enlightenment*. Vol. 1. Ithaca, NY: Snow Lion Publications.

Das, Sarat Chandra. 1985 [1902]. *Tibetan-English Dictionary*. Reprint, New Delhi: Motilal Banarsidass.

Dreyfus, Georges. 1997. *Recognizing Reality: Dharmakīrti's Philosophy and Its Tibetan Interpretations*. Albany: State University of New York Press.

Driessens, Georges, trans. 1990 and 1992. *Le grand livre de la progression vers l'éveil*. 2 vols. Jujurieux and Saint-Jean-le-Vieux: Editions Dharma.

Dunne, John and Sara McClintock. 1998. *Precious Garland*. Boston: Wisdom Publications.

Dutt, Nalinaksha, ed. 1966. *Bodhisattva-bhūmi*. Tibetan Sanskrit Works Series, 7. Patna: K.P. Jayaswal Research Institute.

Eckel, Malcolm David. 1987. *Jñānagarbha's Commentary on the Distinction Between the Two Truths*. Albany: State University of New York Press.

Edgerton, F. 1972 [1953]. *Buddhist Hybrid Sanskrit Grammar and Dictionary*. Reprint, Delhi: Motilal Banarsidass.

Ferrari, A., ed. 1946. "Il 'Compendio delle Perfezioni' di Āryaśūra." *Annali Lateranensi* 10: 9-101. Rome: Pubblicazione del Pontificio Museo Missionario Etnologico.

Garfield, Jay. 1995. *The Fundamental Wisdom of the Middle Way*. New York: Oxford University Press.

Gokhale, V.V. 1946. "The Text of the *Abhidharmakośa* of Vasubandhu." *Journal of the Bombay Branch, Royal Asiatic Society* 22: 73-102.

———. 1947. "Fragment of the *Abhidharma-samuccaya* of Asaṅga." *Journal of the Bombay Branch, Royal Asiatic Society* 23: 13-38.

Gunaratana, Henepola. 1985. *The Path of Serenity and Insight: An Explanation of the Buddhist Jhānas*. Columbia, Missouri: South Asia Books.

Hahn, Michael. 1982. *Nāgārjuna's* Ratnāvalī. Vol. 1. Bonn: Indica et Tibetica Verlag.

Hirakawa, A. 1990. *A History of Indian Buddhism*. Asian Studies at Hawaii, no. 36. Honolulu: University of Hawaii Press.

Hopkins, Jeffrey. 1980. *Compassion in Tibetan Buddhism*. London: Ryder and Co.

———. 1983. *Meditation on Emptiness*. Boston: Wisdom Publications.

Horner, I.B. 1938-1966. *The Book of Discipline*. Vols. 1-3. London: Humphrey Milford. Vols. 4-6. London: Luzac and Company, Ltd.

Hurvitz, Leon. 1976. *Scripture of the Lotus Blossom of the Fine Dharma*. New York: Columbia University Press.

Johnston, E.H., ed. 1950. *Ratna-gotra-vibhāga-mahāyānottara-tantra-śāstra*. Patna: Bihar Research Society.

Johnston, E.H. and Kunst, A. 1990. "The *Vigrahavyāvartanī* with the author's commentary." *Mélanges chinois et bouddhiques* 9 (1951): 99-152. In *The Dialectical Method of Nāgārjuna*. Third edition. Delhi: Motilal Banarsidass.

de Jong, J.W., ed. 1977. *Madhyamaka-kārikā*. Madras: Adyar Library and Research Centre.

―――. 1978. "Textcritical Notes on the Prasannapadā." *Indo-Iranian Journal* 20: 25-59 and 217-52.

―――. 1987. *A Brief History of Buddhist Studies in Europe and America*. 2nd rev. ed. Bibliotheca Indo-Buddhica, no. 33. Delhi: Sri Satguru Publications.

Kanakura, Yensho, ed. 1934 and 1953. *A Complete Catalogue of the Tohoku University Collection of Tibetan Works on Buddhism*. Sendai: Tohoku Imperial University.

Khangkar, Tsultrim Kelsang, ed. 2001. *rJe tsong kha pa'i lam rim chen mo'i lung khungs gsal byed nyi ma*. Japanese and Tibetan Culture Series 6. Kyoto: Tibetan Buddhist Culture Association.

Krang-dbyi-sun, et al., eds. 1985. *Bod rgya tshig mdzod chen mo*. Beijing: Mi-rigs-dpe-skrun-khang.

van der Kuijp, Leonard W.J. 1983. *Contributions to the Development of Tibetan Buddhist Epistemology from the Eleventh to the Thirteenth Century*. Alt- und Neu-indische Studien 26. Wiesbaden: Franz Steiner Verlag.

La Vallée Poussin, Louis de, ed. 1970 [1903-13]. *Mūla-madhyamaka-kārikā de Nāgārjuna avec la Prasannapadā Commentaire de Candrakīrti*. Bibliotheca Buddhica 4. Reprint, Osnabrück: Biblio Verlag.

―――. 1970b [1907]. *Madhyamakāvatāra par Candrakīrti*. Bibliotheca Buddhica 9. Reprint, Osnabrück: Biblio Verlag.

―――. 1971. *L'Abhidharmakośa de Vasubandhu*. Vol. 3. Brussels: Institut belge des hautes études chinoises.

Lamotte, Étienne, ed. and trans. 1935. *Saṃdhinirmocana Sūtra: L'Explication des mystères*. Louvain: Bureaux du recueil, Bibliothèque de l'Université.

―――. 1949. "La critique d'interprétation dans le bouddhisme." *Annuaire de l'Institut de philologie et d'histoire orientales et slaves* 9: 341-61.

Lang, Karen. 1986. *Āryadeva's Catuḥśataka*. Indiske Studier 7. Copenhagen: Akademisk Forlag.

―――. 1990. "sPa tshab Nyi ma grags and the Introduction of Prāsaṅgika Madhyamaka into Tibet." In *Reflections on Tibetan Culture*, edited by Lawrence Epstein and Richard Sherburne. Lewiston, NY: Edwin Mellen Press.

Lévi, Sylvain, ed. and trans. 1907. *Mahāyāna-Sūtrālaṃkāra, exposé de la doctrine du Grand Véhicule selon le système Yogācāra*. Tome 1. Paris: H. Champion.

―――. 1925. *Vijñaptimātratāsiddhi. Deux traités de Vasubandhu*. Paris: H. Champion.

Lindtner, Christian. 1981. "Buddha Pālita on Emptiness." *Indo-Iranian Journal* 23: 187-217.

―――. 1982. *Nagarjuniana*. Indiske Studier 4. Copenhagen: Akademisk Forlag.

Lopez, Donald S., Jr. 1988. *The Heart Sūtra Explained: Indian and Tibetan Commentaries*. Albany: State University of New York Press.

Meadows, Carol. 1986. *Āryaśūra's Compendium of the Perfections: Text, Translation and Analysis of the Pāramitāsamāsa*. Ed. by Michael Hahn. Indica et Tibetica 8. Bonn: Indica et Tibetica Verlag.

Mimaki, K. 1982. *Blo Gsal Grub Mtha'*. Kyoto: University of Kyoto.

————. 1983. "The *Blo Gsal Grub Mtha'* and the Mādhyamika Classification in Tibetan *grub mtha'* Literature." In *Contributions on Tibetan Buddhist Religion and Philosophy*, edited by E. Steinkellner and H. Tauscher. Pp. 161-67. Vienna: Universität Wien.

Miyasaka, Y., ed. 1971/72. *Pramāṇavārttika-kārikā (Sanskrit-Tibetan)*. Acta Indologica 2. Tokyo.

Monier-Williams, M. 1984 [1899]. *A Sanskrit-English Dictionary*. Reprint, Delhi: Motilal Banarsidass.

Mookerjee, S. and H. Nagasaki. 1964. *The Pramāṇa-vārttikam of Dharmakīrti*. Nava Nālānda Mahāvihā Research Publication 4. Patna.

Nakamura, Hajime. 1989 [1980]. *Indian Buddhism: A Survey with Bibliographical Notes*. Reprint, Delhi: Motilal Banarsidass.

Namdol, Gyaltsen. 1985. *Bhāvanā-krama*. Varanasi: Institute of Higher Tibetan Studies.

Ñāṇamoli, Bhikkhu, trans. 1991. *The Path of Purification*. Fifth edition. Kandy: Buddhist Publication Society.

Napper, Elizabeth. 1989. *Dependent-Arising and Emptiness*. London and Boston: Wisdom Publications.

Obermiller, E. 1931 "Sublime Science of the Great Vehicle to Salvation." *Acta Orientalia* 9: 81-306.

————. 1935. "A Sanskrit Ms. from Tibet—Kamalaśila's *Bhāvanā-krama*." *The Journal of the Greater India Society* 2: 1-11.

Pagel, Ulrich. 1995. *The Bodhisattvapiṭaka: Its Doctrines, Practices and Their Position in Mahāyāna Literature*. Buddhica Britannica Series Continua 5. Tring, U.K.: Institute of Buddhist Studies.

Pandeya, J.S., ed. 1994. *Bauddhastotrasaṃgraha*. Varanasi: Motilal Banarsidass.

Pfandt, Peter. 1983. *Mahāyāna Texts Translated into Western Languages: A Bibliographical Guide*. Köln: E.J. Brill.

Powers, John. 1995. *Introduction to Tibetan Buddhism*. Ithaca, N.Y.: Snow Lion Publications.

————. 1995b. *Wisdom of Buddha: The Saṃdhinirmocana Mahāyāna Sūtra*. Berkeley: Dharma Publishing.

Pradhan, P., ed. 1975 [1950]. *Abhidharmasamuccaya of Asaṅga*. Reprint, Shantiniketan: Visva-Bharati.

Pruden, Leo M., trans. 1988. *Abhidharmakośabhāṣyam/ by Louis de La Vallée Poussin*. Berkeley: Asian Humanities Press.

Rabten, Geshe. 1988. *Treasury of Dharma*. London: Tharpa Publications.

Rahula, Walpola. 1971. *Le compendium de la super-doctrine (philosophie) (Abhidharma-samuccaya) d'Asaṅga*. Publications de l'École française d'Extrême-Orient, 78. Paris: École française d'Extrême-Orient.

Rinchen, Geshe Sonam, and Ruth Sonam. 1994. *Yogic Deeds of Bodhisattvas*. Ithaca, NY: Snow Lion Publications.

———. 2001. *Eight Verses for Training the Mind*. Ithaca, NY: Snow Lion Publications.

Roerich, George N. 1979 [1949-53]. *The Blue Annals*. Reprint, Delhi: Motilal Banarsidass. [This is a translation of 'Gos-lo-tsā-ba-gzhon-nu-dpal's *Bod kyi yul du chos dang chos smra ba ji ltar byung ba'i rim pa deb ther sngon po*.]

Ruegg, David Seyfort. 1963. "The Jo naṅ pas: A School of Buddhist Ontologists according to the *Grub mtha' shel gyi me loṅ*." *Journal of the American Oriental Society* 83: 73-91.

———. 1969. *La Théorie du Tathāgathagarbha et du Gotra*. Paris: École française d'Extrême-Orient.

———. 1981. *The Literature of the Madhyamaka School of Philosophy in India*. Wiesbaden: Otto Harrassowitz.

———. 1983. "On the Thesis and Assertion in the Madhyamaka/dBu ma." In *Contributions on Tibetan and Buddhist Religion and Philosophy*, edited by E. Steinkellner and H. Tauscher. Vienna: Universität Wien.

———. 1989. *Buddha-nature, Mind and the Problem of Gradualism in a Comparative Perspective: On the Transmission and Reception of Buddhism in India and Tibet*. London: School of Oriental and African Studies.

Sakaki, Ryōzaburō, ed. 1962. *Mahāvyutpatti*. Tokyo: Kokusho Kankōkai.

Shastri, Swami Dwarikadas, ed. 1968. *Pramāṇavārttika of Āchārya Dharmakīrti*. Varanasi: Bauddha Bharati.

———. 1972. *Abhidharma-kośa and Bhāṣya of Ācārya Vasubandhu with Sphuṭārthā Commentary of Ācārya Yaśomitra*. Varanasi: Bauddha Bharati.

Shukla, Karunesha, ed. 1973. *Śrāvakabhūmi of Ārya Asaṅga*. Patna: K.P. Jayaswal Research Institute.

Sopa, Geshe Lhundrup and Jeffrey Hopkins. 1989. *Cutting Through Appearances*. Ithaca, NY: Snow Lion Publications.

Staël-Holstein, A. von, ed. 1977 [1926]. *Kāśyapaparivarta, A Mahāyānasūtra of the Ratnakūṭa Class Edited in the Original Sanskrit, in Tibetan, and in Chinese*. Reprint, Tokyo.

Stcherbatsky, Th. and E. Obermiller, eds. 1970 [1929]. *Abhisamayālaṃkāra-prajñāpāramitā-upadeśa-śāstra: The Work of the Bodhisattva Maitreya*. Fasc. I, Introduction, Skt. Text and Tib. Trans. Bibliotheca Indica 23. Reprint, Osnabrück: Biblio Verlag.

Stearns, Cyrus. 2000. *The Buddha from Dolpo*. Albany: State University of New York Press.

Suzuki, D.T. 1932. *The Lankavatara Sutra*. London: G. Routledge and Sons.

———, ed. 1955-61. *The Tibetan Tripiṭaka, Peking Edition*. Reprinted under the supervision of the Otani University, Kyoto. 168 volumes. Tokyo and Kyoto: Tibetan Tripiṭaka Research Institute.

Tharchin, L. and A.B. Engle. 1990. *Liberation in Our Hands*. Howell, NJ: Mahayana Sutra and Tantra Press.

Thurman, Robert A.F., ed. 1982. *Life and Teachings of Tsong Khapa*. Dharamsala: Library of Tibetan Works and Archives.

———. 1984. *Tsong Khapa's Speech of Gold in the Essence of True Eloquence*. Princeton: Princeton University Press.

Tucci, Giuseppe. 1971. *Minor Buddhist Texts Part III*. Rome: Istituto per il Medio ed Estremo Oriente.

———. 1986. *Minor Buddhist Texts Parts I and II*. Rome: Istituto per il Medio ed Estremo Oriente, 1956-1958. Reprint, Delhi: Motilal Banarsidass.

Tulku, Tarthang. 1982. *The Nyingma Edition of the sDe-dge bKa'-'gyur and bsTan-'gyur: Research Catalogue and Bibliography*. Oakland, CA: Dharma Publications.

Vaidya, P.L., ed. 1960. *Śikṣāsamuccaya*. Darbhanga: Mithila Institute.

———. 1961. *Samādhirājasūtra*. Darbhanga: Mithila Institute.

———. 1963. *Laṅkāvatārasūtra*. Darbhanga: Mithila Institute.

———. 1964. *Mahāyānasūtrasaṃgraha*. 2 vols. Darbhanga: Mithila Institute.

Vajirañāṇa, Paravahera. 1975. *Buddhist Meditation in Theory and Practice*. Kuala Lumpur, Malaysia: Buddhist Missionary Society.

Wayman, Alex. 1961. *Analysis of the* Śrāvakabhūmi *Manuscript*. Berkeley: University of California Press.

———. 1978. *Calming the Mind and Discerning the Real*. New York: Columbia University Press.

———. 1980. "The Sixteen Aspects of the Four Noble Truths and Their Opposites." *Journal of the International Association of Buddhist Studies* 3, no. 2: 67-76.

Wogihara, Unrai. 1936. Ed. *Bodhisattvabhūmi*. Tokyo: The Tōyō Bunko.

———. 1973 [1932-35]. *Abhisamayālaṃkārālokā Prajñā-pāramitā-vyākhyā: The Work of Haribhadra*. Reprint, Tokyo: Sankibo Buddhist Book Store.

Wylie, T. 1959. "A Standard System of Tibetan Transcription." *Harvard Journal of Asiatic Studies* 22: 261-67.

Yamaguchi, S., ed. 1934. *Madhyāntavibhāgaṭīkā de Sthiramati, exposition systématique du Yogācāravijñaptivāda*. Nagoya: Librairie Hajinkaku.

Yuyama, A., ed. 1976. *Prajñā-pāramitā-ratna-guṇa-sañcaya-gāthā: Sanskrit Recension A*. Cambridge: Cambridge University Press.

Zahler, Leah, et al. 1983. *Meditative States in Tibetan Buddhism*. London and Boston: Wisdom Publications.

INDEX